THE DISAPPEARED

Remnants of a Dirty War

SAM FERGUSON

POTOMAC BOOKS
AN IMPRINT OF THE UNIVERSITY OF NEBRASKA PRESS

Potomac Books is an imprint of the University of Nebraska Press.
Manufactured in the United States of America.

♾

Library of Congress Control Number: 2022045782

Set in Arno Pro by Scribe Inc.

To Vasudha,
for her unending patience, love,
encouragement, and support

CONTENTS

ILLUSTRATIONS

ACKNOWLEDGMENTS

Writing a book about events decades removed in a foreign country is, in ordinary circumstances, a fool's errand. It is doubly difficult when the topic lies beyond ordinary experience. I have approached this book with a healthy dose of humility and an acknowledged skepticism about my qualifications to embark on this project. It would not have been possible without the help of dozens of colleagues to whom I am forever indebted.

The genesis of this project stemmed from a happenstance encounter with José Sebastián Elias at Yale Law School during orientation week. He was starting his studies as an LLM, and I was beginning my studies for a JD. After striking up a conversation, I quickly became friends with Seba and his wife, Naty Carrillo. Sebastián soon introduced me to the *Simón* decision, which cemented Argentina's decision to repeal its amnesty laws, and asked me to help him edit a paper on the topic.[1] I was drawn into the challenging issues surrounding a decision to repeal an amnesty law—the conflict between liberal norms against ex post facto and retroactive laws and the acute need to confront the perpetrators of one of the worst massacres in Latin American history.

That encounter led me to participate in the Linkages Program during the 2006–7 academic year, a legal exchange founded by Prof. Owen Fiss as a way to foster connections between legal academics from the United States and Latin America. Through that program I explored the topic for three months in Argentina in the summer of 2007 and met some of Argentina's leading legal practitioners and academics, many of whom have since become good friends. Lucas Arrimada, María Laura Roteta, and Lisandro Pellegrini deserve special mention.

Lucas was a generous host and a skillful guide who spent days and nights with me (months, in fact) discussing all things profound and mundane. Whenever I had a question about Argentina, the law, or the dictatorship, he was always my first point of contact. His knowledge of Argentina is matched—even exceeded—by his knowledge of U.S. law and popular culture. I discovered as many things from Lucas about my home country as I did about his.

Laura introduced me to Comodoro Py and walked me through the minutiae of Argentine criminal procedure. She helped me acclimate to Argentina and made sure I remembered to have fun while researching this anxiety-producing topic. Her accomplishments and intelligence are often overshadowed by her outsized generosity and sunny disposition, which makes her an interesting and fun colleague to have met.

Lisandro had already spent nearly a decade working in human rights in Argentina by the time I met him and seemed to know everyone I needed to talk to for this project. He also welcomed me into his home, where I spent many Sundays with his family enjoying an *asado*.

After a summer in Argentina in 2007, with the assistance of Professor Fiss, I published an article in the *Boston Review*—"The Unending War: Argentina's Quest for Justice"—about the trial of Father Christian von Wernich, accused of perverting the confession into a torture tactic for the Buenos Aires Provincial Police.[2] With Professor Fiss's encouragement, I used my research for the article as a springboard into this book and returned to Buenos Aires in 2008, 2009, and 2010 to follow the ESMA trial, supported successively by grants from the Oscar M. Ruebhausen Fund and the Robina Foundation Human Rights Initiative at Yale Law School and the Fulbright program. Professor Fiss read numerous drafts of both the *Boston Review* article and this book, helped sharpen my thinking, and provided context and contacts that were invaluable. This book would not have been possible without his significant mentorship and encouragement; indeed, I never would have dreamed of writing it without his inspiration.

At Yale Law School, I was also greatly assisted by Profs. Paul Kahn and James Silk, both of whom encouraged me to present portions of this manuscript at the human rights workshop and made Argentina's post-transition human rights history a focus of the 2008 Bernstein Symposium, titled "Justice Delayed? The Impact of Time on the Trials of Gross Atrocities." We were privileged to include the late Argentina Supreme Court minister Carmen Argibay; the current vice president of the Argentine Supreme Court, Carlos Rosenkrantz; Horacio Verbitsky, and Catalina Smulovitz as participants.

In Argentina, a number of professors provided invaluable feedback and encouragement. Roberto Saba met with me whenever I needed and graciously hosted several classes and talks at the Universidad de Palermo. Jaime Malamud Goti spent countless hours with me discussing Argentina's transition and the philosophical implications of prosecuting mass atrocity. Jaime was also one of a few friends I came to count on as a host during some of my stays in Buenos Aires between 2011 and 2013. Supreme Court vice president Carlos Rosenkrantz graciously invited me to the Universidad de San Andrés, where I gave several talks in preparation for this book, and warmly hosted me to break the fast at his home after Yom Kippur in 2009. Marcelo Alegre and Paola Bergallo (and Ivan!) provided intellectual and spiritual nourishment in both Buenos Aires and New Haven. Robert Barros provided insights for me on the differences between Argentina and Chile, which helped focus my thinking. Roberto Gargarella, Leonardo Filippini, Lucas Grosman, and Celeste Braga all likewise assisted with this project and my research.

Uki Goñi, who is one of the most informed writers about the ESMA, provided generous advice and guidance. I am forever indebted to Uki for sharing his knowledge and helping me navigate the complex history of the ESMA. A lucid observer and a sharp writer, I will always be playing catch-up to his example.

My late nights at the Bangalore pub with Darío Schvarzstein proved illuminating, humorous, and educational; I often felt he should be writing this book in my place as the superior onlooker and storyteller.

Peter and Amy Bernstein took a chance on taking me as a client, and I am grateful for their help in getting this book published. I am likewise grateful to Tom Swanson and Taylor Rothgeb at Potomac Books and the University of Nebraska Press as well as Brianna Blackburn at

Scribe Inc. for their enthusiasm for this project and their patience as I worked through several drafts.

I was supported by many others, some of whom have asked not to be identified and some of whom I am undoubtedly forgetting. In no particular order, I must also thank Bob Cox and F. A. "Tex" Harris for their reflections on Argentina's darkest years, which they lived firsthand; Tina Rosenberg for her pioneering reporting in the 1980s and her assistance with my writing; Marguerite Feitlowitz for her insightful reporting in the 1990s and her continued encouragement; Graciela Fernández Meijide for speaking with me for dozens of hours; Horacio Verbitsky, an unrivaled reference point for everyone who writes about Argentina, the dictatorship, and the Argentine Catholic Church; Joshua Cohen and Simon Waxman at the *Boston Review*; Maya Schenwar at *Truthout*; Matt Clark at the *Christian Science Monitor*; Ruti Teitel, who pioneered (and continues to lead) the field of transitional justice and invited me to give talks at New York Law School and Hebrew University; Leora Bilsky for hosting me at the University of Tel Aviv; Mirna Goransky for her insight, patience, and support and for her mastery of the sprawling ESMA casefile; María Luisa Piqué for her time explaining the intricacies of Argentine criminal procedure and for her friendship; Marco Gallo, Claudia Touris, José María Poirier, Loris Zanatta, Santiago del Carril, and Gabriel Seisdedos, who assisted my research of Pope Francis's role during the Dirty War; Ram Natarajan, my fellow traveler at months of hearings at the ESMA trial; Ryan Dodge, Mark Ferguson, Alex Woodson, and Zach Marco for their help through the writing project; Jay Caspian Kang for reviewing excerpts of the Pope Francis chapter and discussing the project over long lunches in Flushing; Alison Burke and Teresa Miguel at Yale Law School Library, who never balked at any of my research requests for the most obscure materials; Manuel Garrido for his insight into the politics of Argentina's courts; Miriam Lewin, Marta Álvarez, Miguel Lauletta, Carlos Lordkipanidse, Graciela García, Carlos García, Ricardo Coquet, Lisandro Cubas, Nilda Noemí Actis Gorretta, Víctor Basterra, María Eva Bernst, Enrique Fukman, Juan Gaspari (a.k.a. Gasparaini), Carlos Loza, Osvaldo Barros, and many others who will go unnamed—all survivors of the ESMA—who spent long interview sessions with me recounting painful experiences; Carolina Varsky, Rodolfo Yanzón, Pablo Parenti, Carlos "Maco" Somigliana, Federico Delgado, Horacio Méndez Carreras, Alan Iud, Lucas Tassara, and Luis Zamora for patiently assisting with my research of the case and keeping me abreast of fast-moving developments; Stratos Pahis, Yahonnes Cleary, and Jeff Sandberg for their companionship on the Linkages Program (special thanks to Stratos for reviewing several drafts of portions of the manuscript); the late Jonathan Schell for his example; Elizabeth Gómez Alcorta for her moral compass; Naomi Roht-Arriaza for serving as my official reviewer; and Greil Marcus and Cecily Marcus for their encouragement, patience, and perspective.

None of this would have been possible without the support of my parents, Lori and Michael Ferguson. Throughout my life they have encouraged me to pursue my passions. Though the project required moving five thousand miles from home, they were never far away.

Finally, to my wife, Vasudha Talla, who endured this project with me: we developed a lifelong bond as coparticipants in the Linkages Program. She has played the unenviable roles of editor, copyreader, sounding board, cheerleader, instructor, taskmaster, mentor, therapist, coach, and teacher. I never would have completed this project without her reassurance, her unwavering belief in its importance, and her faith in me.

INTRODUCTION

Just outside Buenos Aires, Argentina, in the depths of the brown and murky waters of the Río de la Plata and the frigid expanses of the South Atlantic lie the remains of an unknown number of missing souls. Certainly hundreds, and probably thousands, it was into these waters that the military regime that ruled Argentina from 1976 to 1983 disposed of its political opponents during its self-styled "War against Subversion." More commonly known as the Dirty War, the seven-year period of repression was nominally a fight against guerrilla organizations that formed during the tumultuous 1960s. But the military's dragnet targeted union members, human rights activists, leftist sympathizers, high school and college students, journalists, psychiatrists, and all others thought to pose an existential threat to the military's idea of the Argentine way of life.

Throughout the country, the military used various techniques to implement what former dictator Gen. Jorge Rafael Videla described shortly before his death in 2013 as the "final disposition."[1] In the interior province of Córdoba, army officers at the La Perla base are rumored to have shot their captives, burned the bodies, and disposed of them in mass graves dug among the expansive grasslands surrounding the secret prison.[2] In Buenos Aires, the army and federal police often staged shoot-outs in the streets and whisked the victims away to be buried in anonymous paupers' graves.[3] But of all the inventive methods, it was the navy that came up with the most ruthless yet elegantly efficient means of administrative massacre—the death flights.

Perhaps it was inevitable that the navy looked not to the land but to the sea to carry out its share of the extermination, unconsciously drawn to River Plate, a forty-mile expanse of murky waters at the northeast border of Buenos Aires. On a visit to Buenos Aires in 1929, Le Corbusier famously commented that the city turned its back to the river.[4] Just the right place for the dirty work of the Dirty War.

Survivors from the Naval Mechanics School (Escuela de Mécanica de la Armada, or ESMA), the dictatorship's largest and longest-lasting secret torture center, recall that prisoners were taken out on Wednesdays in weekly "transfers." Groups of shackled prisoners were covered with white hoods and taken from the attic of the officer's hall at the ESMA, where many of them had spent weeks or months in captivity on dirty mattresses on the floor in total sensory deprivation, into the basement. The "gentlemen" of the ESMA—the commissioned officers who kidnapped prisoners, tortured new inductees, and ran the "intelligence" unit to fish for future victims—did not escort their captives during their final moments. Instead, this work was left to junior noncommissioned officers who ushered the prisoners away. Rumors abounded inside the camp as to the destination. Would they be legalized and presented in front of a judge and sent to prison? Sent to a "recuperation" camp in Patagonia, as the dictatorship had publicly advertised? Quietly released to concerned family members and friends under threat that any mention of their captivity would result in immediate death to their loved ones and those still trapped on the inside? The officers in charge of these transfers kept the destination purposefully vague.[5]

In time the prisoners who miraculously survived these weekly transfers learned the truth. In the basement the transferees were injected with a sedative, escorted out a side entrance, boarded onto trucks, and taken to the local airport, where they were prepped for the death flights.[6] A confession in 1995 by a former naval officer, Adolfo Scilingo, filled in the details. At the airport, the prisoners were loaded onto military transport planes and then put to sleep. The planes—small Skyvans as well as Lockheed Electras—were flown over the open ocean, far enough from shore that cargo dumps would be swept out to sea. One by one the dormant but live prisoners were thrown out of the planes.[7] Their limp bodies crashed violently on the water. Their deaths were likely instantaneous; the blunt force trauma from impact at high speeds fragmented their bones and pounded their bodies. Years later, forensic anthropologists who unearthed several of these bodies noted perimortem trauma consistent with injuries one would expect from a high fall.[8] Though secret, small bureaucratic fingerprints of these excursions remain, such as trip logs with a single origin and destination noting a flight path close to the limit of the plane's range.[9]

Scilingo recalled that naval chaplains and high-ranking officers blessed the procedure as a "Christian death," a humane way to painlessly dispose of their enemies.[10] A tragic and necessary burden for the officers charged with the awful task of saving the *patria*.

The object of the Dirty War's campaign of kidnapping, torture, and forced disappearances was as much to execute and kill as it was to terrorize and disorient. Both were resourcefully achieved by secretly disposing of enemies in the sea. The missing, the military cynically suggested, maybe never died at all.

The victims of these death flights and the thousands of others who went missing are known as *los desaparecidos* (the disappeared)—legions of young men and women who were secretly executed and never acknowledged by the regime. The tactic of forced disappearance was a calculated response to social upheaval: employ maximum terror to discipline society and impose order in line with the military's notion of a properly ordered Argentina. It proved disorienting and excruciating for those who sought information on the disappeared's whereabouts. Requests for information were systematically denied. In the courts, habeas corpus petitions were ignored; in government offices, formal requests on official letterhead were answered with polite rebukes; and in other spheres—union halls, churches—informal entreaties were met with apologetic replies that nothing could be done.[11] Even the Mothers of the Plaza de Mayo, older women who donned white headscarves and protested every Thursday afternoon for information on their children, could not break through the military's obfuscation. (Three of these women were "disappeared" for trying to break through the regime's barricade of silence.) The information vacuum kept those who were searching in a traumatic limbo, trapped between the hope that the missing might be alive and the nagging and uncomfortable suspicion that the disappeared were probably dead.

"The horror of this all," recalls Graciela Fernández Meijide, whose son Pablo was disappeared when he was just seventeen, "is that they made me kill my own son. I've never been told where he went or when and how he died. I've never seen his remains. I myself had to decide to give up hope, to stop looking, and to accept that he was dead."[12] Not everyone has made the same choice. For years, some relatives even blocked efforts to unearth the remains of the disappeared, fearing that exhumations would relieve the military of having to explain what happened.

In 1984 Meijide was hired by the National Commission on the Status of the Disappeared (in Spanish, Comisión Nacional sobre la Desaparición de Personas, or CONADEP), a blue-ribbon truth commission convened shortly after the transition to civilian rule in December 1983, to look into the fate of the disappeared. After Pablo's disappearance, Meijide spent years working with the Permanent Assembly for Human Rights cataloging disappearances in real time, work that proved invaluable when the government ultimately called upon her to assist with an official count of the missing. With Meijide's help, the CONADEP documented 8,960 missing people in a report, *Nunca más* (Never again), published shortly after the return of civilian rule.[13] The commissioners, however, admitted that owing to the tight time constraints of their mandate, they undoubtedly undercounted. Human rights groups maintain that the true number is 30,000.

Whatever the figure, the existential question that has confronted and confounded modern Argentina has been what to do in the wake of this catastrophe. How does one make sense of a society in which compatriots are convinced of the moral urgency of shoving their brethren out of airplanes? How can one confront the Dirty War?

Meijide's tragic decision to symbolically "kill" her own son illustrates the difficulty of personally confronting the Dirty War. But her response is unique; she is just one of thousands struggling to deal with the aftereffects of a missing relative, friend, coworker, or acquaintance. Add to this the social dimension of apportioning responsibility for the violence—judicially, politically, culturally, and morally—and the problem seems almost overwhelming. The enigma of responsibility is demarcated within a vast moral gray area between those who killed and those who resisted.

Tragically, Argentina is not the first society to wrestle with what to do in the wake of mass atrocity. For most of history, perpetrators of systematic state crimes such as torture, forced disappearances, arbitrary detention, summary executions, and genocide have been spared punishment and accountability—the official denial of the Armenian genocide in the Ottoman Empire by the Turks or the "Pact of Forgetting" forged in the wake of Francisco Franco's fascist rule in Spain are the most recent examples of a historical trend dating back millennia.

But since the Allied trials of Nazi war criminals at Nuremberg after World War II, humanity has awakened to the call for justice: that grave violations of human rights warrant a meaningful, organized, and legal response. The Nuremberg trials, as well as the military tribunals and Nazi purges throughout Germany during the Allied occupation, embodied the idea that atrocity demands accountability and that if future atrocities are to be prevented, justice and punishment are essential. In South Africa in the wake of the collapse of apartheid, Nelson Mandela and Desmond Tutu pushed for truth and reconciliation by offering perpetrators of racist violence the chance to admit to their crimes in exchange for amnesty from prosecution, all as part of a broader social experiment that would allow former perpetrators and victims to live together and construct society anew. In Rwanda and the former Yugoslavia, international courts sponsored by the United Nations have investigated and indicted state officials responsible for genocide in an effort to bolster humanity's role in preventing gross violations of human rights. All these initiatives have had their drawbacks. Nuremberg has been followed by decades of atrocities in its wake, calling into question the preventive efficacy of punishment; South Africa is still plagued by poverty and racial inequality; the Rwanda and Yugoslavia trials have arguably harmed local efforts for accountability by shipping judicial justice overseas.

This is a book about Argentina's pathbreaking and novel response: a decision in 2003 to repeal a series of amnesty laws passed in the 1980s that shielded the Dirty Warriors for a generation. Prosecutors have since set their sight on as many aging military officers implicated in human rights abuses as they can identify. This is a virtually untested experiment. Unlike the Allied trials of Nazi war criminals, it is not a decision that has been imposed by the force of an occupying army; unlike the truth and reconciliation process in South Africa, the trials reflect Argentina's decision to reject reconciliation and coexistence as a political goal; and unlike the fairly contemporaneous prosecutions of perpetrators by the Yugoslav and Rwandan tribunals, the Argentine prosecutions are proceeding more than thirty years after the crimes were committed in domestic courts. As of September 15, 2022, 1,088 aging military officers have been convicted for their involvement in the Dirty War, and nearly thirty-five hundred have been or are being investigated. Over 286 cases have gone to verdict.[14]

The overwhelming majority of those sent to trial (nearly 90 percent) have been found guilty. But the central question about these belated and widespread trials is not the easy and by now well-settled issue of the individual officers' guilt—the country has long moved past the dictatorship's cynical attempts to deny the scope and scale of its violence. It is whether the law is capable of doing justice at all.

The answer is not obvious. That Argentina has reopened the Dirty War prosecutions so many years after the fact is a testament to Argentina's own struggle to define the proper place of criminal prosecution as a means of responding to mass atrocity. Ever since December 10, 1983, when the country first returned to civilian rule, the question has been at the center of Argentine life. It was then that Raúl Alfonsín, the country's first democratically elected president after the 1983 transition, announced the prosecutions of the highest-ranking military officers responsible for the Dirty War as well as a handful of the leading guerrilla commanders who were responsible for approximately five hundred deaths in the years preceding the 1976 coup. As Alfonsín conceived it, the law had a central but circumscribed role to play in confronting the Dirty War. Alfonsín saw prosecution as a tool to construct respect for the rule of law and democracy following a period of authoritarian rule, to delineate certain behavior that would not be tolerated in a decent society, to clarify what happened to the missing, and to insist that political conflict be channeled through the ballot box, Congress, and the courts—not the barrel of a gun. Nevertheless, Alfonsín also saw that there were limits to the law. He believed that a full-scale legal assault on the military would lay too much blame at the feet of junior officers, not to mention risk a backlash from the military and threaten democratic consolidation.[15] Indeed, as was stated in the prologue to the *Nunca más* truth report,

> The tragedy which began with the military dictatorship in March 1976, the most terrible our nation has ever suffered, will undoubtedly serve to help us understand that it is only democracy which can save a people from horror on this scale, only democracy which can keep and safeguard the sacred, essential rights of man. Only with democracy will we be certain that *never again* will events such as these, which have made Argentina so sadly infamous throughout the world, be repeated in our nation.[16]

It was a legalistic response meant not only to confront the Dirty War but to correct a decades-long history of weak democratic institutions and military coups. Alfonsín had tremendous successes, most notably the 1985 Juicio a las Juntas (Trial of the Juntas), in which nine commanders from the army, navy, and air force were put on trial for 711 cases of kidnapping, torture, and murder as representative of the systematic atrocities committed under their rule. It was hailed worldwide as a first-of-its-kind moment—never before had a country successfully put the perpetrators of mass atrocity on trial in a domestic court shortly after a political transition. It gave birth to an entire field of study called "transitional justice" that spawned hope for a generation that the early Argentine experiment foreshadowed a new era—that investigating crimes against humanity would no longer be an aspiration but a reality.[17] If Nuremberg was the birth of human rights, the Trial of the Juntas was its maturity.

But Alfonsín's initiative proved both too bold for the still powerful military and too timid for those who had been directly victimized. By 1987—less than four years after the transition—Alfonsín's human rights initiative collapsed, with just six officers serving time for human rights crimes. Alfonsín tried to limit the time frame of the trials in December 1986 by successfully urging passage of the *punto final* (full stop) law, which imposed a sixty-day statute of limitations on prosecutions, meaning that all Dirty Warriors would be indicted or definitively let free by February 1987. But in April 1987, a group of rebellious army officers staged a revolt against Alfonsín's human rights agenda, forcing the government to pass an amnesty law called the due obedience law, which effectively ended the Dirty War trials except for a handful of the highest-ranking officers. The law gave junior-ranking officers a conclusive legal presumption that they had followed orders and hence were legally justified in whatever actions they had taken while following superior command.[18]

Alfonsín was forced from office six months before the end of his term with his human rights agenda shattered. In 1989 and 1990, amid runaway inflation and a series of additional military rebellions, Pres. Carlos Saúl Menem, Alfonsín's successor, stopped the few remaining trials still underway by pardoning both those who had been convicted and those who were still facing trial.[19] Among those freed from jail were Gen. Jorge Rafael Videla, the military regime's first dictator and former commander in chief of the army, and Adm. Emilio Eduardo Massera, the navy's representative on the dictatorship's first junta and the former commander in chief of the navy. Both had been sentenced to life in prison for their roles in dozens of deaths and hundreds of disappearances.

In Menem's analysis, the traumatic conclusion of Alfonsín's human rights agenda signified that the law was essentially powerless. Law and prosecution could not serve as substitutes for self-reflection and mutual understanding. The Dirty War, so Menem believed, was not the result of a lack of respect for the rule of law or constitutional values; the response to the past, therefore, could not be legalistic. The problem, Menem thought, was primarily religious and cultural—a divine tragedy that had disturbed Argentina's communal harmony. So when he signed pardons in 1989 and 1990, he explained that they were necessary to "overcome the consequences of the confrontations that have happened between Argentines, which are a result of the constant disturbance in our social spirit." Prosecutions, Menem argued, had failed to "overcome the profound disagreements in our society." It was his objective to end "the feeling of hatred—understandable as it may be—and replace it with magnanimity, without which we will never achieve interior peace and national unity." Quoting the Argentine Episcopal Conference, which had long opposed trials and had never supported the human rights movement, Menem said that national reconciliation would only be possible if "each individual extinguishes their spirit of hatred." He decreed that each Argentine had "the valor to perform a sincere self-criticism acknowledging their own errors."[20]

Whereas Alfonsín had articulated a classically liberal response to the Dirty War—conceived, in large part, by a group of legal philosophers he convened as architects for his transitional strategy—Menem reached for nationalist ideas of magnanimity and greatness. The roots of the Dirty War were to be found in personal vice, which had undermined Argentina's Christian social harmony. Menem's antidote, consistent with his background as a populist Peronist leader, was to call for national unity.

But Menem's call for unity suppressed deep and legitimate grievances. Pardon-by-fiat could not compel true interpersonal forgiveness, the exercise of which rests with the individual who is victimized and asked to pardon. Menem's "pardons," therefore, did more to cover up the Dirty War than they did to heal social divisions. During the years of Menem's impunity, torturers walked the streets, and countless survivors recall crossing paths with their former tormentors at coffee shops or local grocery stores. In one way or another, Menem's justification for the pardons—unity and social harmony—cast those who insisted on memory and justice as the ideological enemies of progress, a paradox too strong to succeed. To be sure, it worked for nearly a decade, in large measure due to Menem's fanciful economic policies that inflated the value of the peso by pegging its value to the dollar, known as *plata dulce* (sweet cash), which effectively bribed Argentines and kept them distracted from the problem. Indeed, when Menem left office in 1999, his policy of impunity was intact, though beginning to show cracks. After a devastating economic collapse in 2001, when the peso lost nearly two-thirds of its value overnight and five presidents passed through the Casa Rosada within weeks, the ensuing social convulsion provided the perfect context for a reexamination of the country's past. When Néstor Kirchner was elected to the presidency in 2003, he pushed to reopen the Dirty War trials, part of a larger political agenda to break with all the policies of his predecessors and chart a new course for his country. Within months of Kirchner's surprising and astonishing election, Argentina's Congress repealed Alfonsín's amnesty laws and opted to prosecute the authors of the Dirty War a generation after the collapse of the dictatorship.[21]

Kirchner once again placed the law front and center as a means of confronting the past. But unlike Alfonsín, Kirchner did not frame the trials as a tool of liberal democratic consolidation. Indeed, so many years after the transition, there was no threat that the military might once again intervene in democratic life. Rather, Kirchner cast the trials as a tool of historical reckoning that would cure the wounds of the Dirty War and re-create Argentina. "I have dreamed all of my life that this—our country—could change for the better," Kirchner proclaimed during his inaugural address to the country in 2003. "We arrive here without hate but with memory," he continued, evoking his place in the generation of young Argentines who committed themselves to a social revolution in the 1960s and found their project eviscerated by state-sanctioned terror in the 1970s.[22]

Kirchner's confrontation with the past was decidedly political—and partisan. In presenting a romantic image of the revolutionary struggles of the 1960s and 1970s, Kirchner forged a connection between the need for prosecution and the need for greater social inclusion, casting the legacy of the Dirty War as the evisceration of a revolutionary social project that was replaced by neoliberal economic policies and the loss of national sovereignty. By extension human rights trials were part of a contemporary political agenda to reverse the political consequences of the repression. Confronting the past required confronting the politics of the past and—in Kirchner's calculus—carrying on the project of the lost generation. When the prologue to the *Nunca más* truth report was updated in 2006, Kirchner's secretary of human rights, Eduardo Luis Duhalde, made the connection explicit: "We have before us the immense task of changing the status quo of impunity and social injustice, which requires defeating the hostility of powerful sectors who through their complicity with State Terrorism both yesterday and today made neoliberal policies possible."[23]

How to prosecute has always been nearly as controversial as whether. The rallying cry for the recent wave of trials has been for memory, truth, and justice—a slogan oft repeated by Néstor and his wife, Cristina Fernández, who succeeded him as president from 2007 until 2015. (Néstor died in 2010.) As the slogan suggests, the trials are conceived not so much as a tool of democratic stability as they are a tool of social and historical reckoning. The architects of the trials—both the politicians who support them as well as many of the human rights activists who have insisted on justice for decades—see prosecution as a means to confront the dictatorship, change the character of Argentine democracy, and shape public memory. Justice is conceived not just as punishment but as a political project to confront and live with the country's tragic past. The object of memory in this recent wave of prosecutions is as much to remember what the dictatorship did as it is to challenge the once-thought-settled consensus that emerged after the transition in the 1980s. It is a shift from an idea that the Dirty War was a consequence of the violent confrontation between two extremes—the revolutionary left and the reactionary military—to a reckoning with the singularity of state terrorism. For them, the violence committed by the state is qualitatively different than that committed by civilian groups and must be faced accordingly.

This project has not been universally embraced, and indeed, by 2015—as Cristina Fernández de Kirchner presided over runaway inflation and a stagnant economy—an ascendant right took hold. Mauricio Macri, the former neoliberal mayor of Buenos Aires, won the presidency in 2015. As a candidate he had promised to end the "con job of human rights."[24] At the time he made the statement, he was referring to the worst kind of Kirchnerist corruption—a bloated federal program where the Mothers of the Plaza de Mayo had been given an enormous contract to build thousands of units of public housing, despite the group's complete lack of expertise. Their general counsel, Sergio Schoklender, who had killed his parents in 1981 before he befriended the Mothers' controversial leader, Hebe de Bonafini, in prison, allegedly siphoned as many as two hundred million pesos from the project—equivalent to tens of millions of dollars.[25] But Macri's statement was clearly an assault not just on the housing scandal but on the human rights movement more broadly. His actions followed his words: under his administration, public expenditures for human rights prosecutors plummeted, and his secretary of human rights never met with any of the leading figures in

Argentina's human rights movement. After Macri appointed two new Supreme Court justices early in his administration, the Supreme Court in 2017 confirmed what many feared was Macri's plan—the court ruled that the two-for-one law in effect from 1994 to 2001 applied retroactively to human rights convicts, granting them double credit for time served while in pretrial detention.[26] (The court reasoned that the rule of leniency, a bedrock principle of criminal law, required that the most beneficial law be applied in any case.)

The effect was to potentially release from prison hundreds of military officers. But after massive protests in swift opposition to the ruling, Congress overturned the decision in just two days.[27] Macri's administration even found it prudent to settle into a begrudging acquiescence with the forward progress of the trials. On March 24, 2016, Pres. Barack Obama visited Argentina and announced, together with Macri, that the United States would declassify thousands of documents from the CIA and other intelligence divisions regarding the United States' role in the Dirty War. (Leaders of the human rights movement did not attend the ceremony.)[28] And after Congress overturned the two-for-one law, Macri announced that he was "against any type of instrument that facilitates impunity," though it took him three days to release his statement.[29]

Since Alberto Fernández won the presidency in 2019, after four years of ruinous economic policies under Macri, human rights have once again settled into a slow march forward. Fernández was Néstor and Cristina Fernández de Kirchner's chief of staff before resigning over the Kirchners' confrontation with farmers in 2008. But as with many things in Argentine politics, nothing lasts forever, and Cristina Fernández de Kirchner became his vice president.

The disagreements over human rights, however, are as political as they are conceptual. The demands that prosecutions satisfy the objectives of memory and truth are political demands in the broadest sense of the term. Precedent and legal practices are expected to yield to the greater interest of justice, conceived more broadly as social and historical reckoning. The architects of the trials expect them not just to convict individual defendants but to encounter truth, foster memory, and do justice for the past.

These objectives are not necessarily compatible. Fostering memory through trials does not sit comfortably with classic notions of criminal procedure, for memory has as its object a lesson, not a judgment. Viewing the object of the trials as spawning memory threatens to reduce the defendants to mere ciphers intended to teach larger lessons about the past rather than focus on their individual responsibility. Paradoxically, though, the goal of memory through law is fundamental, for an adequate reckoning with the past requires the official acknowledgment of past wrongs and social repudiation. What better way to do so than through the cold, dispassionate vernacular of the law?[30]

The challenge of memory, too, is determining what is to be remembered and whether trials are adequate mechanisms for doing so. The narrative of the trials tends to focus on discreet episodes of pain and trauma—kidnappings, torture sessions, sexual assaults, assassinations. While it is critical to hear these stories, it can also be paralyzing, as a trial's fixation on suffering obscures larger political questions and themes about the past. Who was responsible for the violence? What was the role of various civilian actors in provoking and executing the violence? How does society remember the victims? How does society engage with (or banish) the victimizers? And how do these moral intuitions map onto long-established principles of criminal liability?

The goal of finding truth is also not easily satisfied by prosecution. A trial typically has as its focus the laser-like question of guilt or innocence. Finding truth in this context is a specific and ritualized inquiry, a process far from the broad-ranging examination of the historian. Finally, the demand for justice resists easy classification. On the one hand, individual criminal sanction generally requires strict adherence to formal legal procedures, but prosecuting state violence in the wake of a political transition necessitates casting aside the old legal regime. Likewise, confronting a history of mass atrocity is bound to be ad hoc, for state violence is perpetrated under a cloak of legality and procedure; the official sanctioning of the conduct under the positive law of the old regime creates intractable problems of both substantive and procedural law for liberal reformers who want to repudiate the past. The ambition for justice tends to outpace the capacity of the law, for the activists who push for trials often insist on their transformative dimensions, but law is typically expected to be ordinary and predictable.[31] This problem has been compounded in the recent wave of trials, as the defendants accumulated decades of favorable court decisions before the country's 180-degree reversal on the need for prosecution in 2003.

To explore these tensions, this book focuses on one of the most high-profile trials to proceed through Argentina's courts since the repeal of its amnesty laws: a nearly two-year-long trial against eighteen officers from the ESMA, charged with eighty-six crimes but collectively responsible for as many as five thousand disappearances. From its operating base in the officers' club of the ESMA, the task force called the Grupo de Tareas (GT) 3.3/2 became the dictatorship's most fearsome repressive spy group. The crimes committed at the ESMA embody all the ferocity, callousness, savagery, and horror of the Dirty War: prisoners stripped naked, pinned to metal bedframes, and subjected to electrical shock; captives kept in total sensory deprivation for months without reprieve; human rights activists disappeared for seeking information on their loved ones; mothers who were executed in captivity after giving birth, their children stolen away and given over for secret adoption to military sympathizers; and women taken as sexual slaves by their captors, to name but a few of the litany of abuses. Despite the fact that more than thirty years have passed since the commission of the crimes, the terror and pain still felt by the ESMA's victims speaks to the moral urgency of accountability. When a state violently strips its citizens of all their rights and legal status, the only response that approximates reparation is for the state to restore the rule of law by punishing the perpetrators and giving voice to their victims.

Yet as recounted in the pages of this book, the trial also revealed the limits of using criminal law to respond to mass atrocity. At times, the demand for social reckoning was so overwhelming that the trial became unmoored from the task of adjudicating the defendants in the dock charged with individual crimes. At no point was this clearer than when Jorge Mario Bergoglio—now known as Pope Francis—was called to testify and answer questions about his suspected involvement in the disappearances of two Jesuit priests under his supervision in 1976. While Bergoglio was not on trial, activists used the opportunity to question Bergoglio not just about his role in the incident but about the broader role of the church in supporting the military regime. The urge to settle accounts with the past—not just with the defendants—compelled examination beyond the scope of the acts committed by the individual defendants.

Argentina's human rights trials are extraordinary. In thinking about criminal justice, *extraordinary* is often anathema. But the response to mass atrocity—when the state assaults its own citizens, when the guarantor of rights becomes an instrument of repression—begs for inventiveness and creativity. It is not enough for the response to limit itself to the dry procedures of the courtroom; the social impact must be transformative.

Though my conclusions here are only tentative—we will undoubtedly need another generation before we can fully appreciate the impact of the recent wave of trials in Argentina and on the world more generally—my hope is that illuminating the issues will ultimately prove more valuable than any conclusion I reach.

THE DISAPPEARED

1

A Beginning of Sorts

Buenos Aires, Argentina, December 11, 2009

It has been a generation since the collapse of Argentina's last dictatorship. Twenty-six years and one day to be exact. Too long, one might imagine, for the legacy of the military government's "Dirty War" to be anything other than a matter of private sorrow or academic concern, for societies have a way of relegating their traumatic histories to the fringes of public life. But this morning Buenos Aires's Retiro courthouse is stirring with nervous excitement. Eighteen retired and aging officers from Argentina's security forces, accused of operating a "clandestine center of detention, torture, and extermination"[1] in the officers' club of the Naval Mechanics School (ESMA), are about to stand trial for crimes against humanity committed during the 1970s.

The prosecution has charged the defendants—fourteen naval officers, two police officers, one army officer, and one coast guard officer—with kidnapping, robbery, torture, and murder in eighty-six cases. But the trial is as much about the "symbols of the dictatorship" who created an "Argentine Auschwitz" as it is about the individual crimes enumerated in the charging papers, as *Clarín* reports the next day.[2] The ESMA was the dictatorship's largest and longest-running secret torture center. The ESMA's notorious task force, Grupo de Tareas (GT) 3.3/2, was nominally charged with pursuing the Montonero guerrillas, the most significant of several armed political groups in Argentina in the 1960s and 1970s, but union activists, students, journalists, clergy, lay activists, other "subversives," and family members who were thought to have information about their relatives' political activities were also its victims. Thousands were disappeared by the GT 3.3/2 between 1976 and 1983, a large percentage of the 8,960 people who officially went missing during this period. Some survived to tell horrifying tales of torture, beatings, sensory deprivation, and sexual humiliation. But most were not so lucky. Those who remain missing—*los desaparecidos,* "the disappeared"—were drugged, loaded onto military transport planes, stripped naked, and pushed out into the South Atlantic.

Spectators gather at the courthouse beginning at 6 a.m. to secure seats for the opening hearing, and by midmorning there are dozens of people anxiously lurking around the lobby, the hallways, and the perimeter of the imposing nine-story building. All of Argentina's major newspapers are on hand—*Clarín, La Nación, Página/12,* and *Perfíl*—in addition to international outlets such as the Associated Press, *El País, Le Monde, La Croix,* and *Figaro*. News vans park in front of the courthouse, and a small rally of human rights activists and union members banging drums blocks the street.

Publicly, the mood is exuberant. "We have had to wait a long time," Rodolfo Yanzón, a human rights lawyer in the case, tells the television cameras, "but today is an important day in the fight against impunity in Argentina. We are finally starting the trial of the most emblematic crimes committed by the last civil-military dictatorship." Julio Alak, Argentina's minister of justice, tells the press that the trial is *trancendente* (transcendent). Thirty years after most of the crimes were committed, "the *genocidios* responsible for the worst tragedy in the history of Argentina will finally have the judicial punishment that they denied to thousands of victims."[3] The government of France, through its foreign minister Bernard Kouchner, releases a statement to "salute the new political will which has sparked Argentine authorities to continue ahead with [prosecutions] against the dictatorship," alluding to then president Néstor Kirchner's 2003 push to repeal the country's amnesty laws, which eventually opened hundreds of new Dirty War prosecutions. Graciela Daleo, a former revolutionary who spent more than a year as one of the ESMA's secret prisoners, tells *Página/12,* "Not even in my deepest dreams in *Capucha*"—the nickname for the attic where prisoners were detained while hooded and shackled—"did I begin to imagine that one day, we would be judging them in a court of bourgeois society."[4]

As the soaring quotes suggest, the proceeding is much more than a trial; it is a great legal experiment, an initiative to see if the law is capable of doing justice for a history of mass atrocity. The case is not just about the pedestrian task of sorting through legally admissible evidence to sustain a set of charges beyond a reasonable doubt. It is about the loftier ambitions of memory, truth, and justice—demands that have been at the heart of human rights activists' campaign for prosecutions for nearly thirty years. If justice is to be done, so the architects of this extraordinary proceeding believe, procedural fidelity and proof beyond a reasonable doubt will not be enough; the trial must show the ESMA in all of its destructive dimensions. The eighty-six victims in the case are stand-ins for the thousands of people who passed, hooded and shackled, through the iron gates surrounding the ESMA compound and were never seen again. "State terrorism" and the ESMA itself are on trial as much as the eighteen men in the dock, a proceeding to confront and comprehend the legacy of what happened. The *genocidios* in the dock are the objects of the trial as much as they are symbols of the human suffering, terror, destruction, and catastrophe wrought by the dictatorship—years of military rule that destroyed the country's institutions and obliterated its economy.

But some activists close to the case suspect that these ambitions are too large given the time that has elapsed since the commission of the crimes and Argentina's two decades of democracy. Human rights lawyer Horacio Méndez Carreras, who has pursued the ESMA officers since 1984 in search of justice for the disappearance of two French missionary nuns, tells me, "This should have happened thirty years ago. Society was more interested; they claimed it more. After thirty years people tire, including myself." In a whisper, a police officer working a metal detector at the entrance to the courthouse provides a more direct assessment of his country's interest: "The common people don't care about this."

Indeed, to many, the trial feels like déjà vu, a worrying sign given that it was derailed in the 1980s after a military rebellion and political fatigue. Even though the trial is set to begin in a matter of hours, there is as much anxiety and skepticism about the future of the case as there is hope and relief. The Kirchners—Néstor and his wife, Cristina, who succeeded him as president in 2007—have made human rights a centerpiece of their administrations, but their popularity has recently plunged. Creeping inflation and fights with the country's farmers, media, and the church have dampened the couple's purported ambition to rule for decades through alternating tenures, a parlor trick to circumvent the constitutional limit of two consecutive terms. Former president Eduardo Duhalde, a 2011 presidential contender, suggested recently that a general amnesty should be submitted to the voters. For now, his idea is repudiated by most of Argentina's political class, but it skulks in the background as a reminder of the fleeting quality of apparent victories in Argentina, where presidents tend to dismantle the legacies of their predecessors. "It's just another stage; we'll see what happens," the daughter of one of the victims in the case says to me before she quickly walks away.

This paranoia is justified. Since the repeal of the amnesty laws in 2003, setbacks have been the norm rather than the exception. Only fifty-three people have been convicted of human rights abuses in six years, roughly one conviction for every two hundred or six hundred people who are missing, depending on who is counting. *Página/12* notes that at the current pace, it will take twenty-three years—another generation—to prosecute all 860 officers currently under investigation, completely leaving aside whether to seek additional targets.[5] The last case before this court, which is handling most of the human rights cases in Buenos Aires (which is to say, most of the trials in the country), ended with the acquittal of three of five local army chiefs.[6] Before that, the first ESMA case ended in mystery and tragedy when the defendant, coast guard officer Héctor Febres, was found dead in his prison cell, poisoned by cyanide.[7] The talk here is that Febres was "suicided," killed by fellow military officers who were scared that he was prepared to talk if convicted. Febres was an assistant to several births inside of the ESMA and therefore a guardian of some of the navy's darkest secrets, including its connections to the Argentine church, which facilitated many of these births with secret baptisms and covert adoptions.[8] It is a reminder that even if the military does not wield enough power to stage a military coup, the aging officers still command allegiances to perpetrate real harm. "Governments change, but the intelligence community stays the same," the ESMA officers ominously warned survivor Víctor Basterra as he was freed from captivity in 1983.[9]

I meet one of the defendants' former comrades, a retired naval officer, in the lobby, though he discreetly declines to give me his name as we shake hands. I can't help but think that only the macabre methodology of the Dirty War has spared him from being in the dock with his friends. "Where are you from?" he asks me, though he does not wait for a response. He tells me that the trial is a "circus" and a "judicial farce." He slaps his open palm with his fist clenched by his thumb, a gesture meaning "money." He continues, "It's all business, the *human rights* groups get the money," saying "human rights" in English. I ask him about the charges: Could he really deny that people were secretly held prisoner at the ESMA and later disappeared? "The *desaparecidos*?" he asks. "There is no such thing as a 'disappeared.' This was a war." The propaganda persists.

At 10:30 a.m. we are ushered into the courtroom, a two-story repurposed movie theater embellished with fading pink drapes. (The courthouse building used to be a union hall.) I am directed to the upper balcony of the vaulted room, where I take my seat beside the press and the defendants' supporters; human rights activists and the victims' family members sit below in an unadorned room segregated from the courtroom floor by a wall of bulletproof glass. The floor is crammed with dozens of lawyers. The prosecutors, Drs. Mirna Goransky and Pablo Ouviña, sit with five assistants in the front two rows to the left of the center aisle. Their associates are young—just children during the dictatorship—but their median age speaks to the multigenerational demand that has propelled these trials forward.

Behind the prosecution sit nearly two dozen lawyers from Argentina's leading human rights organizations as well as renowned private lawyers representing the victims. Their presence is fitting. Technically, the Argentine code of criminal procedure allows private attorneys to represent victims alongside the state's representation of the people, but their appearance in this case is more a nod to the movement's responsibility for reopening the trials. Since 1987, when Raúl Alfonsín's amnesty laws appeared to close all avenues for further trials, the human rights movement found openings to keep the issue alive for two decades—pushing cases before the Inter-American Commission on Human Rights, testing the limits of and exceptions to the amnesty laws, bringing nonpunitive "truth trials" in the 1990s, and working with activists abroad to indict Argentine military officers under the theory of universal jurisdiction. Carolina Varsky, the lead attorney for Argentina's most well-respected human rights group, the Centro de Estudios Legales y Sociales (CELS), was the lead attorney on the *Simón* appeal challenging the constitutionality of the amnesty laws in Argentina's Supreme Court.[10] After a victory in 2005, the Supreme Court cemented the legality of these delayed proceedings. There are five separate private victims' groups permitted a place at the counsel's table, representing dozens of organizations and individuals. (A combination of personal rivalries and philosophical differences prevented the groups from being unified under one lead attorney.)

Representing the defendants, attorneys sit in four rows on the right side of the courtroom's center aisle. At their helm, Alfredo Solari, an aging private defense attorney, is the most ideologically aligned with his clients; he represents a nucleus of five navy line officers (at the time, all lieutenants) who were responsible for the day-to-day administration of the GT 3.3/2. He has publicly chastised the supposed illegality of the proceedings and has defended his clients' conduct during the Dirty War, saying that his clients helped defend Argentina from the worldwide advance of Cuban-style communism. The trials are designed, in Solari's estimation, "to first delegitimize, and later annihilate, the Nation's armed forces, and to replace them with *Chavista* popular militias and bring to Argentina a Castroist-Chavista regime with a Marxist stamp."[11] To his side sits Guillermo Coronel, who represents his father, Julio César Coronel, the lone army officer on trial for crimes committed at the ESMA. Like Solari, Coronel is absolutely aligned with his father's political defense of the military regime, though he typically takes his legal cues from the more technically able Solari.

In the rows behind them sit several groups of public defense attorneys. Víctor Valle, a lead defense attorney, has been involved in human rights cases for decades, having previously served as dictator Jorge Rafael Videla's public defender in the Trial of the Juntas in 1985. The rest of the public defenders, representing various groups of officers, have all been specially convened for these cases.

The oldest and highest-ranking of the defendants, retired Adm. Oscar Montes—who eventually rose to become the dictatorship's foreign minister—is already seated when we enter the courtroom, confined to a wheelchair to the right of the defense attorneys. Half an hour later, around 11 a.m., fifteen defendants are escorted in, handcuffed together in pairs. (Two defendants are excused from the first day's proceeding for health reasons.) Dressed in blazers and with an affinity for conservative English style, the defendants, in the late stages of middle age, receive glowing smiles and kisses from their supporters seated in the upper gallery. "¡Vamos muchachos!" one supporter yells. Juan Carlos Rolón, a former navy captain and one of the alleged torturers, responds in kind with a triumphant wave.

The star of this parade is Alfredo Astiz, who everyone immediately recognizes. He is known euphemistically as the "Blond Angel of Death," the most enigmatic of the Dirty War's criminals. As a young lieutenant, aged twenty-five, Astiz infiltrated the Mothers of the Plaza de Mayo, a group of women who courageously protested against the dictatorship in public, seeking information on the whereabouts of their disappeared children. Astiz, who introduced himself to the mothers as Gustavo Niño, claimed that he too was seeking information on a missing sibling. In December 1977 three of the mothers, along with two French missionary nuns and seven other human rights activists, were kidnapped outside of the Holy Cross Church in Buenos Aires as they were preparing to publish an advertisement in the newspaper demanding information about the missing. ("Where are they?" the advertisement was to read.) Astiz is said to have marked his targets with a kiss on the cheek—the traditional Argentine salutation—as they congregated to collect signatures and gather funds for the advertisement. From there, the activists were detained by a mob of plainclothes officers in a caravan of unmarked cars, taken to the ESMA, tortured, and held incommunicado for a week.[12] Five of these victims' bodies washed up on shore two weeks later and were buried anonymously in paupers' graves, only identified in 2005 after exhumation and DNA testing.[13] The seven other victims remain missing, most likely resting or decomposed in the far reaches of the

South Atlantic, Argentina's largest mass grave. Astiz, like his codefendants, has never said a word about their whereabouts.

They call him a "Judas," but his sister, Lucrecia, tells me as we wait for the trial to begin that this is not fair—not because the charges against him are false but merely because "he didn't betray them; he was never one of them. He was just collecting information. Did you know those nuns weren't even nuns? They carried weapons."

Astiz was recognized as the infiltrator when he surrendered the South Georgia Island to the British in the Falklands War in 1982 and his image was printed in newspapers around the world. Activists recognized the dashing officer captured aboard the HMS *Plymouth* as Gustavo, the young man who circled the Plaza de Mayo in protest and stood between the old ladies and the police. While he was Britain's prisoner of war, France and Sweden requested his extradition for his suspected involvement in the disappearances of their citizens, but the request was denied, and Astiz returned home. (The Geneva Conventions make no provisions for the extradition of prisoners of war suspected of human rights violations, so Astiz was repatriated to Argentina—saved by a treaty that he studiously ignored in his own holy war.) Though criminal complaints were filed against him in the 1980s, and he spent some time in a navy prison, Astiz never went to trial. He was definitively spared from prosecution in 1987, after the due obedience law granted Astiz and other low-ranking officers an irrefutable presumption that they had simply followed orders. For years, he was seen tanning on the Atlantic coast or socializing in Buenos Aires's upscale nightclubs after he was freed by Alfonsín's amnesty; reviled by human rights activists as the callous face of the Dirty War, he was equally revered by his friends and female admirers.[14] But his fortunes eventually shifted. Over time, he faced a number of random assaults on the streets during the years of impunity as the most famous Dirty Warrior and was publicly shamed through protests (known as *escraches*) organized by Hijos por la Identidad y la Justicia contra el Olvido y el Silencio (HIJOS), an organization made up of the children of the disappeared.[15]

Today, he is the only one among his colleagues not in jacket and slacks, a slight to the tribunal he believes has no authority to pass judgment on his actions. He has opted for a ragged white polo shirt, a blue house cardigan, jeans, and loafers. His face has fattened and sagged and is now a distant imitation of the image of him as a vigorous young lieutenant in his pressed white officer's suit.

The other recognizable defendant marching to his seat is Capt. Jorge Eduardo Acosta, the former intelligence chief of the GT 3.3/2. His supporters yell "Tigre!" (Tiger!) from the balcony above, one of the aliases he used during the Dirty War to shield his identity from his prisoners. In pretrial filings, Acosta repeatedly denied using this moniker, but he immediately responds when he hears it from his supporters upstairs. If most officers like Astiz participated in the Dirty War out of a profound but perversely misguided sense of duty, survivors describe Acosta as one of the few who seemed to take pleasure in the repression. A man of reportedly enormous ambition and a sophomoric but active intellect, he more than any of the other defendants found inside the ESMA a chance for social mobility. The War against Subversion, for Acosta, was a project that shaped his life, provided an opportunity for his upward advance, and ultimately lead to his unraveling. In court statements, he would later say that he was just a *militarcito* (little soldier), but survivors recall that Acosta was at the heart of the GT 3.3/2. It was Acosta who lived in the ESMA twenty-four hours a day, supervising raids, torturing new detainees, and speaking with prisoners. It was Acosta who took charge just months after the military coup when his immediate superior, Capt. Salvio Menéndez, was injured in a firefight during a raid. (One version of events is that Menéndez was shot by his own troops in an incident of friendly fire as a way to make room for Acosta.) It was Acosta who conceived of the "process of recuperation," a macabre initiative in which officers chose a small group of prisoners to live and work inside the ESMA for years before earning their freedom. It was Acosta who enjoyed escorting female prisoners to nice meals and dance clubs, an endeavor, he used to say, to help them turn away from political activism and "recover their feminine side."[16] It was Acosta who would take male prisoners from their ramshackle mattresses on the floor outside into the ordinary world for a whiskey at a local bar. It was Acosta who commissioned his prisoners to write political reports on nearly every aspect of Argentine public life, including union politics, education, and the Falkland Islands—memorandums that were eventually used by Adm. Emilio Eduardo Massera to launch his own operation to become president. It was Acosta who received "exceptional" marks in his yearly performance review in 1979 from the commander in chief of the navy, Adm. Massera, who cited Acosta's "dedication" and "decisiveness" in giving him such high praise for his contributions to the War against Subversion.[17] And it was Acosta who was so efficacious, so creative, and so steadfast that when the dictatorship finally collapsed, the navy forced him into an undignified early retirement in 1984. Whereas the navy circled its wagons around Astiz during the transition as he became a publicly recognized supervillain, Acosta was too toxic for the navy to protect as it tried to negotiate its future under civilian rule.

The other defendants are only recognizable to the most informed observers, and the reporters in the courtroom struggle to identify who is who. Some of the defendants enjoyed brief moments of fame, such as Ricardo Cavallo, who was arrested in Mexico in 2000 and subsequently extradited to Spain, where the pioneering Judge Baltasar Garzón indicted Cavallo and other Argentine Dirty Warriors in 1999 pursuant to the concept of "universal jurisdiction"—that is, any court may invoke jurisdiction to prosecute violations of international human rights norms, even if their home country has shielded them with an amnesty. Juan Antonio Azic, the only coast guard officer in the group, put a bullet through the back of his throat in a failed suicide attempt after investigators discovered that his "daughter" is the stolen child of a woman who gave birth inside the ESMA and was killed shortly after. As if the saga of Azic raising a stolen baby was not enough, it was his codefendant Adolfo Donda who is rumored to have turned over his own brother and sister-in-law, José and María Hilda, after they joined the Montoneros. After José and María Hilda were killed, Donda gave his niece, Victoria, to Azic to raise as his own. She was known as Claudia Azic until her true identity was discovered in 2004 when she was twenty-seven years old.

Most of the defendants are indignant. "I am not being judged in military court!" "This is revenge!" "Where are my bosses?" "The so-called victims are all collaborators, double traitors!" and "I followed orders!" are defenses soon to be lodged in court. But the defendants must also be thinking privately that their great mistake—at least the mistake of their superiors—was choosing to let a group of prisoners survive. For in contrast to the other 339 secret prisons run during the Dirty War, the automatic rule at the ESMA was not extermination. "The ESMA prioritized life," Captain Acosta has unsettlingly repeated over the years to anyone willing to listen, explaining what he sees as his righteous decision to select a small group of prisoners for "recuperation." At first, prisoners survived because they became part of the repressive machinery—individuals who, owing to extraordinary pressure or simple ideological reorientation, began to collaborate with the GT 3.3/2 by marking their former comrades and feeding the camp with new detainees. Over time, a larger group survived, for any number of reasons or no reason at all. In "prioritizing life," Acosta and the ESMA task force created a problem they did not adequately appreciate, for their "recuperated" prisoners became their accusers and virtually the only source of evidence against them. One of these survivors, Víctor Basterra, managed to smuggle dozens of documents out of the ESMA, including photos of officers and copies of false identification papers he forged for them, after they put him to work performing counterintelligence activities.

In the dozens of cases moving through the courts alongside the ESMA case, investigators have struggled to compile evidence against the ESMA's colleagues from the army and the police. Investigators suspect that just as many people were disappeared at the Campo de Mayo military base as the ESMA, but only a handful of officers have been implicated in the repression there, benefactors of their macabre modus operandi that left no one to testify about their crimes.

At 11:13 a.m. the clerk unceremoniously announces, "De pie, por favor," and we rise to our feet. Four judges, without robes, ascend to their seats behind the dais. A small wooden cross adorns the wall behind them. "Good morning again to everyone," says presiding judge Daniel Obligado with an aloof demeanor, a career bureaucrat from the *familia judicial* seemingly unprepared for a case of this magnitude and profile. He is flanked by Judges Oscar Hergott, Ricardo Farías, and Germán Castelli. The judges take their seats, and the trial postponed for a generation finally gets underway.

Or so we think. It turns out that Montes and Astiz have fired their lawyer in a last-ditch effort to delay the trial, the latest in a series of motions and appeals that have already helped delay this trial for six years. (Their attorney, Juan Maria Aberg Cobo, tells me later that day that he had no idea he would be fired and that his clients decided it would be futile for him to defend them in court. But Montes and Astiz's motion to substitute counsel was written with Aberg Cobo's signature formatting—bold lettering, underlined points, and italicized phrases—indicating it was all planned in advance with Aberg Cobo's participation.) After a long pause, the court reconvenes and decides to appoint substitute counsel to both men from the public ministry, and the trial moves on.

In an effort to avoid the appearance of a show trial, the judges have barred television cameras from recording the proceedings, but in a thoughtless compromise, they allow four waves of still photographers to enter to "guarantee publicity." It has all the seriousness of a red-carpet entrance and all the legal sobriety of a perp walk. About twenty photographers enter and click away, inching close to the defendants' faces for the perfect shot for the next day's papers. A few of the defendants shy away from the cameras and cover their faces, but others—especially Astiz—play up to the attention, feigning stern faces and thousand-yard stares. Their somber faces are splashed all over Argentina's dailies the next morning.

For the rest of the day, the court clerk reads the charging instruments. The clerk's monotonous tone soon loses the attention of most of the spectators, the defendants, and even Judge Obligado, who begins to nod off late in the afternoon.

Astiz passes the time reading a book. As the day draws to a close some six hours later, a small verbal skirmish breaks out downstairs between the defendants and the activists through the bulletproof glass wall. "Sonofabitch," "Murderers!" a few activists yell. Never one to back down from his role as provocateur, Astiz glances back at them as he is escorted out of the courtroom for the day and flashes his book. *Volver a matar* is the title. To kill again.

2

The Argentine Enigma

By the time the armed forces reached the Casa Rosada in the early morning hours of March 24, 1976, Argentina had long since unraveled. For over a year, daily life had been shattered by runaway inflation hovering around 40 percent a month.[1] Shoppers flooded stores on the first of the month to take advantage of the time value of their paychecks. What they didn't use to buy goods, they invested in dollars, which, unlike the peso, held their value until the end of the month.

Pres. Isabel Perón's economic policies had done little to abate the inflation rate of 335 percent from the year before.[2] Indeed, price controls, export taxes, mandatory union wage increases, and a pegged exchange with the dollar had exacerbated the problem, creating wild distortions in prices. Under Mrs. Perón, the government simply printed money to meet its obligations, raising the supply of currency, thereby reducing its value. Two-thirds of the government's expenditures were met by circulating new money, and only 5 percent of its obligations were paid from tax revenues.[3] Interior decorators claimed that covering a wall with the collapsing peso was a less expensive means of home improvement than paying for wallpaper.[4] The government, in several futile last-minute attempts to rein in inflation, had made overtures to the International Monetary Fund about a possible loan, but no lenders were willing to board Argentina's sinking ship.[5]

Argentina's agriculturalists and landed gentry, unsurprisingly, were combative. For three decades, they formed the primary opposition to *peronismo*. Cattle producers threatened to stop supplying beef if Mrs. Perón did not control inflation. Apple and pear producers from the rich agricultural heart of Río Negro refused to harvest, saying harvests would not be profitable with mandatory wage increases, export taxes, and growing inflation.[6] Business associations too announced work stoppages and withheld taxes in protest.[7] Similarly, in a sign of massive civil disobedience, some 70 percent of the country did not pay personal income tax.[8]

Even the unions, historically the unquestioning political backbone of *peronismo*, had turned on Mrs. Perón. There were imminent strikes by the nation's train unions in the days before the coup, following autoworker strikes on March 11 in Córdoba, Argentina's industrial heart.[9] Work stoppages and slowdowns had already reduced the auto industry to just 20 percent of full productivity the previous year.[10] Mandatory government-imposed raises—of 100 percent in May 1975, 40 percent in January 1976, and 20 percent in March 1976, just weeks before the coup—failed to keep pace with inflation. Civil servants' paychecks were lasting just half the month.[11]

The political situation in the days before the coup was no more reassuring. Mrs. Perón had been in seclusion for several months at the end of 1975, suffering from a mental breakdown after a strike by the General Confederation of Labor (Confederación General del Trabajo, or CGT) had brought her government to its knees.[12] The provisional president, Senate leader Ítalo Lúder, had replaced several ministers with more moderate voices while she was away, hoping to ease partisan tensions and fend off a military coup. But shortly after Mrs. Perón returned to service in December 1975, officers from the air force rebelled. She was narrowly saved when the army and the navy refused to join the rebellion, foiling the air force officers' hopes that the other branches of the armed forces would join the insurrection. But even at the time, the failed coup was not considered a government triumph. It was simply a sign of events to come.

Mrs. Perón responded by replacing half her cabinet with party loyalists, doubling down on surrounding herself with yes-men.[13] In early February, she replaced two high-ranking economic aides, including the minister of the economy.[14] The minister of defense, appointed just a month earlier, resigned on February 24, 1976, protesting Mrs. Perón's confrontational stance with the military.[15] Her revolving door cabinet did not instill confidence: Could the national executive get a hand on political deadlock and the runaway economy?

In mid-February, while the major newspapers were reporting Argentina's worst-kept secret—plans of an imminent coup—Mrs. Perón had her head in the clouds. She exhorted Congress to amend the constitution and revise the "mistake" of the previous military regime, which had shortened presidential terms from six years to four, so she could hold on to power for an extra two years.[16]

Congress responded, but not by heeding Mrs. Perón's advice. An impeachment bill was introduced on February 25 by the Popular Federalists, who were joined by the Radical Civic Union, Mrs. Perón's main opposition. Though the measure failed to garner the votes needed—Mrs. Perón's political party, the Justicialist Party, controlled Congress—it was no vote of confidence. Dissatisfied factions in her party had voted against impeachment less out of love for Mrs. Perón than to save the embarrassment of impeaching one of their own, hoping they could survive until the October elections. To split the difference, some dissident members of Mrs. Perón's party intimated that they would support a motion of "incompetence."[17]

Weeks earlier, Mrs. Perón had temporarily closed the offices of a leading opposition newspaper, *La Opinión*, when it suggested that Congress should make such a move.[18] Amid the chaos, Mrs. Perón made overtures about seeking a second term in office.[19] She eventually relented but forced a political stalemate.[20] Fearing further impeachment proceedings, Mrs. Perón withdrew all legislation from Congress.[21] Opposition legislators began to meet over the succeeding weeks to consider Congress's power to self-convene, despite the clear constitutional provisions to the contrary.

Violence, however, overshadowed all economic and political woes and provided the military with its main justification for ousting Mrs. Perón. Incidents in the two weeks before the coup provide a glimpse.

On March 8 and 9, thirteen people were kidnapped in Córdoba, Argentina's second city, including an ex-interior minister, Hugo Vaca Narvaja, whose son was a leading member of the Montonero guerrillas.[22] A few of the abductions were carried out in the characteristic fashion of the paramilitary forces—plainclothes men carrying heavy machine guns stormed their abductees, claiming to be the police, and swept their victims away. In all likelihood, the cadavers would later turn up riddled with bullet holes or burnt beyond recognition. On March 11 the ex-governor of the Salta province in Argentina's northwest, Miguel Ragone, was kidnapped.[23] On March 13 two people died when a confrontation broke out after a group allegedly threw a Molotov cocktail through the window of a restaurant in downtown Córdoba.[24] "Terrorists"—as the coup-supporting *La Prensa* reported—again struck on March 14 against a navy building in Mendoza, but nobody was injured.[25] That same day a "terrorist" from an obscure leftist group known as Brigada Rojas had "confessed" to participating in many acts of terror, including taking revolutionary training trips to France and Cuba and carrying illegal contraband.[26]

On March 15 a car bomb exploded outside the Libertador Central Army Command in Buenos Aires, just a stone's throw from the Casa Rosada in the heart of downtown.[27] Twenty-nine people were injured, and three eventually died from the blast. Gen. Jorge Rafael Videla, the commander in chief of the army, was the target, but he was not in the building at the time of the blast. (Videla became the dictator just two weeks later.) That same day the Montoneros took credit for the assassination of a federal police officer.[28] On the night of March 16, a bullet-riddled body was found on the streets of Pergamino, a suburb of Buenos Aires.[29] Five bombs also exploded across Buenos Aires: one in a mall in the upscale Recoleta district, one in a furniture store, one in an apartment building, and two in a suspected attempt to assassinate the leader of the CGT, Argentina's labor confederation, at his home.[30] Four police officers were reportedly killed by left-wing guerrillas the same day.[31] On March 18 police officers were killed in three separate incidents across the country—one in a bomb explosion in Rosario, one in a firefight in Córdoba, and one in a drive-by attack in Quilmes.[32] On March 19 the central shopping district in La Plata was closed down after several anonymous bomb threats were called in to the local authorities. Later in the day, a blast blew up a bus, killing eight.[33] The bodies of four women—blindfolded and bound at the hands and feet—were also found in Santa Fe after they had been strangled to death.[34] On March 20 three workers and a student were assassinated in La Plata.[35] Two days later four heavily armed people claiming to be police officers stormed into a union meeting of the Tucumán Sugar Industry Workers Federation and shot Atilio Santillán, the union's secretary general, in cold blood.[36]

In all 1,100 people were killed in political violence in 1975.[37] Several hundred more died in the first few months of 1976. It is impossible to know who was responsible for all these deaths. The military's strategy to discredit Mrs. Perón's government relied heavily on military propaganda and overstating the threat posed by guerrillas and other revolutionary groups operating throughout the country. Many news stories reporting "confrontations" were simply transcriptions of military and police propaganda that masked cold-blooded assassinations. Whatever the accuracy of news accounts in the days leading up to the coup, contemporaneous press accounts reflect a society that had become both obsessed with and numb to political violence. Stories of assassinations, kidnappings, and political deaths had become so pervasive that the "news" was typically relegated to the middle pages of Argentina's dailies. Most killings received little attention, just a paragraph or two. The image presented to the average Argentine reflected a society unraveling.

Mrs. Perón had already fled the Casa Rosada as the tanks began rolling down Buenos Aires's Avenida de Mayo and the Costanera Norte in the early morning hours of March 24, 1976. Stubbornly, she refused to believe until the final moments that the armed forces were mobilized to overthrow her government. Reportedly, she rebuked her minister of defense just an hour before the coup when he warned her to leave the Casa Rosada while she was hosting a party.[38] The plans, however, had been several weeks in the making.

A pathetic crowd of about fifty people, mostly middle-aged women, gathered outside the government house to support Mrs. Perón on the night rumors of the imminent coup became public. They pledged to fight to the bitter end. But as the tanks rolled unobstructed through the heart of Buenos Aires and Mrs. Perón's helicopter shuttled her away, the small crowd dispersed. Resistance would have been suicide: the power of the armed forces and, more importantly, the wide social support for military intervention would have overwhelmed Mrs. Perón's tiny cadre of supporters.[39]

The presidential helicopter had transported most of Mrs. Perón's senior cabinet away during the evening of March 23 even as she refused to believe the tanks were coming. When she finally boarded, the helicopter was ordered to take her to Buenos Aires's municipal airport, where a plane was waiting to usher her into exile. But it was too late. The air force had already taken command of the airports; she was promptly arrested while trying to flee and escorted to her summer home to await corruption charges.[40]

The armed forces needed just a few hundred men in the nation's capital to secure political control of the country. Congress conceded defeat: most legislators had already packed up their offices. In the interior province, military units dutifully performed ordinary exercises as the coup unfolded. In Córdoba the governor of the province even considered calling the Third Army Corp chief to resign his post but decided instead to wait for the troops to show up. He handed over power in a five-minute swearing-in ceremony, and citizens awoke to find few outward changes.[41] The headline on the day of the coup, "Military Operations throughout the Country," was received with only slightly more interest than a soccer match between Buenos Aires's popular River Plate team and a visiting club from Venezuela in the Copa Libertador.[42] There was one reported isolated act of resistance to the military takeover at a loyalist union shop; otherwise, there was no public resistance. The battle was won before it began.[43]

What happened to Argentina—at the turn of the twentieth century, a land of promise, economically on par with Canada and Australia; a country of high literacy rates and a large middle class; a land of some of the most fertile and expansive agricultural terrain on earth—that it descended into horrific political violence?[44] The answer, of course, is not a simple one, but any approximation includes—if not begins or ends with—the country's difficult and tepid relationship with liberal democracy. Time and again Argentina's strongest political actors have pushed aside the rule of law and constitutional means of sharing power.

Scholars generally begin to explain the answer by starting as far back as the first encounter between the Spanish *conquistadores* and the native peoples of the Americas. The Spaniards in search of silver who landed on the shores of the River Plate—the expansive river on the shores of Buenos Aires that separates present-day Argentina from Uruguay—were disappointed to find that the region was empty of the precious metal. In lieu of a profitable silver trade, the few Spanish colonialists who stayed established an agricultural colony based on the subjugation and exploitation of the native inhabitants, who provided labor and tribute. Though present-day Argentina is distant from the colonial backwater of the sixteenth century, important traces of this early social structure remain unchanged: a small landed elite continues to control a majority of the country's land and resources and, as a consequence, exercises a disproportionate influence on the fate of the country. Historian David Rock has explained that throughout its history, Argentina "has manifested several obvious colonial features," such as the need to import the bulk of its manufactured goods, a physical structure in which the port city of Buenos Aires dominates the inland and rural areas, a mercantile elite connected to foreign trade that dominates political life, and an inability to adapt to changes in the international order through "self-sustaining and independent direction."[45]

Buenos Aires matured as a place to flaunt the law. Smugglers and counterfeiters traded through Buenos Aires to circumvent the Spanish colonial mercantile monopoly, which required all imports and exports to pass from the Isthmus of Panama and overland to Lima, Peru, which controlled trade to the southern reaches of the Spanish Empire.[46] And while French and American revolutions were brought in the name of liberalism (whether or not they lived up to such a lofty ideal is another question), the Argentine revolution against Spain from 1810 to 1816 was more ambiguous. The postrevolutionary period was marked by civil war between regional strongmen in the interior and Buenos Aires.[47] It took the iron will and extreme violence of the warlord caudillo Juan Manuel de Rosas to unite the country, and it was not until he was finally deposed in 1853 that the country adopted a democratic constitution. Rosas scoffed at the liberal enlightenment document inspired by the U.S. Constitution as a "little notebook," an ominous omen of events to come.[48]

In the late nineteenth and early twentieth centuries, Argentina began to develop as a modern nation. Led by an elite coterie of men interested in "progress," the republican rulers aggressively promoted European immigration after the few Indigenous tribes who remained independent were conquered and viciously exterminated in a genocide in the 1870s by Pres. Julio Roca's forces in Patagonia.[49]

The country boomed, buoyed by a beneficial trading partnership with Great Britain and subsidized immigration from Europe.[50] Argentina became one of the most prosperous countries in the world—some say the seventh richest.[51] It boasted Latin America's first subway line; the world-class Teatro Colón opera house, overadorned with imported Italian marble; free public higher education; a professional army; a modern justice system; and most other markers of an advanced society in the early twentieth century.[52] It was a land of hope and destiny, thought to be among the leading nations in the world, blessed with fertile land and industrious people. Buenos Aires, with its wide boulevards, magnanimous statues, elmwood-lined streets, and beaux arts architecture, was nicknamed the "Paris of the South." So optimistic were Argentina's patrons about its future that the cotton magnate Luis Barolo built a skyscraper on the famous Avenida de Mayo as an interpretation of Dante's Divine Comedy; Barolo believed that because of Europe's decline, Dante's ashes would eventually have to be moved to Buenos Aires and housed in his building.[53] It was also a dynamic society, where waves of immigrants pushed themselves into the swelling middle class, working in factories and textile mills of the country's bourgeoning industrial belt in Buenos Aires and Córdoba.

But alongside this rapid economic growth, political and social tensions grew. Historian Luis Alberto Romero notes that during this period, the country's leaders and intellectuals were preoccupied with the so-called Argentine question. How could this country full of Italian, Spanish, Irish, Scottish, Lebanese, Syrian, mestizo, Jewish, and other immigrants call itself a nation when many of its residents thought of themselves as denizens rather than citizens, there for economic opportunity but not necessarily political identity? What did it mean to be an Argentine? Was it a country rooted in a traditional Hispanic and criollo past, or was it a beacon of Europe in the Americas?[54]

The working out of these existential questions helps explain why democracy never took firm root and why the Dirty War eventually become so ferocious. Liberalism in this context was seen as a liability, a system too flexible and too open-minded to build Argentina as a cohesive nation. Two prominent political strains developed in response.

A republican strain of leaders who controlled the country from approximately 1880 to 1916 was driven to create a more populous and powerful Argentina, full of men of "proper" stock, but was frightened by the plethora of new and radical ideas that came with the immigrants, such as anarchism, syndicalism, communism, and socialism. They believed in a restrained democracy, one in which politics was the preserve of society's upper echelons, who would sustain and nurture the country's special relationship with Great Britain. They were best represented by founding father Juan Bautista Alberdi's belief that the constitution should embody a "monarchy dressed as a republic"; they routinely engaged in vote-rigging and patronage through their political machines to stay in power.[55] Though the country was on the surface a liberal democracy, it was in practice a one-party oligarchy. This line of thinking persisted throughout the century, as time and time again, elites who saw what they thought best for the advancement and development of the country pushed aside constitutionalism when it proved an obstacle to development and growth.

A second—and more radical—group that came to prominence between 1910 and 1930 was attracted to fascist ideas, then in vogue in Spain and Italy, but forged a distinctly Argentine brand of nationalism. These *nacionalistas* were best defined by their vocal rejection of democracy, liberalism, socialism, and communism, which were all characterized as foreign imports from Britain, France, and the Soviet Union and therefore unsuited for Argentina. In place of these foreign influences, the nationalists wrote longingly of Argentina's mythical Hispanic and criollo past, where the Catholic caudillo and his militias ruled triumphantly through force. This harkening back to a mythical past placed Catholicism and the church at the center of the nation as its moral reserve; the armed forces were likewise proclaimed as the country's guardian, a caste "superior" to the people in the words of the leading nationalist poet, Leopoldo Lugones.[56] And unlike the republican rulers, who imitated European customs and longed to be a beacon of Europe in the Americas, the nationalists tried to forge a local and distinct identity. The nationalists spoke of the country's *ser nacional* (national being), a spiritual idea that envisioned the nation as having an organic and natural being, just as real as the fertile Pampas or the unconquerable Andes. The implications of this vision were obvious: "The Argentine state is Catholic in its origins and constitution. Democracy is, by nature, anti-Catholic. Therefore, democracy is incompatible with Argentine institutions," wrote nationalist Rodolfo Irazusta in 1928.[57] The sacred alliance between the church and the armed forces also implied the redemptive beauty of violence; Lugones predicted in 1924 an impending "hour of the sword" that would restore the natural hierarchy of society that had been upended by liberal democracy.[58] As historian Federico Finchelstein has convincingly written in *The Ideological Origins of the Dirty War*, the seeds of extermination in the 1970s were planted in the 1920s and 1930s by these fascist thinkers.

There was a short-lived experiment with popular democracy in Argentina from 1916 to 1930, after the Radical Party—Argentina's first mass populist movement—successfully agitated for universal male suffrage. But in 1930 after the destabilizing effects of the 1929 stock market crash, the critics of popular democracy saw their opportunity, and on September 6, 1930, Gen. José Félix Uriburu led Argentina's first military coup. Backed by the army, the paramilitary Patriotic League, and disaffected republican liberals who wanted to restore the old system of restrained democracy, Gen. Uriburu seized political power amid wide dissatisfaction with the Radical Party administration of Hipólito Yrigoyen.[59]

The coup created a pattern that repeated itself five more times during the twentieth century: when economic crisis ensued, political legitimacy evaporated, and elites called on the armed forces to intervene and reestablish order. The players were different, but the basic script was the same in 1943, 1955, 1962, 1966, and 1976—the years of subsequent military coups—with varying degrees of civilian participation and violence. In the forty-six years before the coup to 1976, the military intervened so frequently that nineteen presidents in twenty-one administrations occupied the Casa Rosada.[60] Only six arrived through open elections. The constitutional term of office is six years, but the average tenure of a president was just over two. Formally, Argentina had been a democracy for over a century, but leaders emerged through free and fair elections for just a small percentage of that time.[61]

In each coup the "liberators" pronounced that it was their duty to "intervene," to "save the nation," or to "restore" the country's institutions, harkening back to the fear of popular democracy that had been at the heart of Argentine thinking since the nineteenth century among Argentina's republicans and nationalists. The Supreme Court even embellished these coups with a veneer of constitutional legitimacy. In 1930, just four days after Uriburu took power, the Supreme Court held that because General Uriburu's government exercised political control and order, the court would recognize his actions as the official actions of the executive branch.[62] Subsequently, the Supreme Court developed an elaborate case law regarding the validity of laws passed by decree during de facto military rule.[63]

But it was not just the military and Argentine political right who rejected liberalism and popular democracy as guiding arrangements for the country. Almost all of Argentina's dominant political actors eventually came to see democracy and liberalism more as tactics than commitments—useful tools that could be disposed of if problematic.

In 1945 these great currents in Argentine politics—Catholic nationalism, fascism, and populism—found their synthesis in Peronism, the transformative political movement led by Col. Juan Domingo Perón. Perón was a singularly Argentine leader, embodying the disparate and contradictory strains within Argentine politics: he was an authoritarian leader thrust into power after a military coup who was then twice popularly elected; his base of support was in the legions of dark-skinned workers, long maligned and dismissed by Argentina's whiter upper classes, but he also managed (for a time) the loyalties of the country's nationalist business leaders by promoting rapid industrialization; and he harbored Nazi exiles at the end of World War II yet spearheaded significant advances for Argentina's Jews.[64] His lexical dexterity allowed him to be many things to many people. One of Argentina's favorite pastimes is arguing over the intractable question of "What is Peronism?" A movement? An ideology? A feeling? An identity? A political philosophy?

Perón's idea of an organized community, inspired by his time as a military attaché in Benito Mussolini's fascist Italy, represented a so-called

Third Way for Argentina between capitalism and Marxism—built on the three pillars of national sovereignty, political independence, and social justice—and served as the ideological base of his administration and movement.[65] Perón rejected strict Marxism because he never believed that workers should control the means of production, only that they should share fairly in the national wealth. (His slogan was "50 percent for the workers," still leaving 50 percent for the capitalists who controlled the factories.) Nor was Perón a capitalist, since he used the heavy hand of state intervention to promote rapid industrialization, manage labor disputes through binding arbitration, and protect the local bourgeoisie. His philosophy, "justicialism," represented a uniquely Argentine phenomenon, a way to both differentiate the country and his movement from European strains of thinking and transcend them.[66] It was a movement rooted equally in the populism of Yrigoyen's Radical Party—which it eventually replaced as the representative of Argentina's popular classes—and the nationalist ideas of the right-wing Catholics and military men.

Perón served as the secretary of labor in the military government that ruled from 1943 to 1946, and it was during this time that he cultivated a base of power by bestowing benefits on Argentina's bourgeoning working class, becoming affectionately known as "Argentina's First Worker." He created mandatory arbitration of union disputes, raised the minimum wage, expanded paid vacation time and workers' pensions, and unionized many workers.[67] For his patronage he demanded loyalty. "For a Peronist, there can be nothing better than another Peronist," he announced upon introducing his "Twenty Fundamental Truths of Justicialism" on Loyalty Day (October 17, 1950), summarizing both the discipline and love required of his followers. Independent communists and socialists were purged from his movement and their unions suspended. When Perón became too powerful for the comfort of his military superiors, they forced him from the government and had him arrested. But on October 17, 1945, thousands of workers across the country spontaneously protested on Perón's behalf, precipitating the fall of the military government and Perón's election as president in 1946.[68]

As much as an ideology, Peronism was a movement, a feeling, and an identity. The movement established *unidades básicas* in virtually all neighborhoods, which served as small centers of localized power. Huge rallies were held to solidify Perón's grip on the country and flex the movement's political muscle in front of the "oligarchy" and other enemies of the people. The cultural symbols of Peronism were as important as its political projects, including the iconography of Perón and his wife Eva "Evita" Perón, the "Peronist March," and the two-finger salute in the form of a *V* for victory.

During the so-called golden years of Peronism, from 1946 to 1951, Perón held together a broad coalition composed of sympathetic officers in the armed forces, the working class, nationalist industrialists, the church, and much of Argentina's middle class. His first term in office saw substantial advances for the working class and a greater distribution of wealth.[69] Indispensable to his rise and success was his wife Evita. She was the symbolic "mother of the workers"—the "lady of hope" who personified the Peronist welfare state through her handouts at the Eva Perón Foundation, funded largely by public dollars and quid pro quo corruption. She also seemed to personally represent Peronism's promise. Despite her humble beginnings, Evita dressed lavishly, a metaphor for the riches Peronism could bestow. Her expensive tastes did not prevent her from lashing out at the country's "oligarchy" and "traitors" during screeds from the balcony of the Casa Rosada, where she convened with her husband and the loyal masses. Her workers, she said, would inherit her jewels when she died.[70]

Perón's opponents—who represented as many strains of divergent political thought as did Perón himself—saw his movement as nothing less than "Nazi-fascism." An odd coalition of the intelligentsia, the socialist and communist left, the conservative upper classes, and the outspoken U.S. ambassador to Argentina, Spruille Braden, all opposed Perón.[71] While the caricature of Perón as a Nazi-fascist was a gross overstatement, his strongly corporatist political style did not leave room for dissent. Though twice popularly elected, Perón's embrace of electoral democracy was a matter of tactics rather than principle. "Paradoxically," historian Luis Alberto Romero has described, "a government that had emerged from one of the few clean elections in the country's history resolutely embarked on the road to authoritarianism."[72] The niceties of separation of powers, independent courts, and checks and balances were anathema to his philosophy and political style. His was not simply a political party but a movement—a movement that represented *el pueblo,* the moral center of the nation itself. All conflict was to be mediated within the Peronist Party or arbitrated by a direct appeal to the state, with Perón as the ultimate arbiter; outsiders, branded *gorilas,* were traitors to his movement and, by extension, traitors to the people. During Perón's rule, Congress became only a shell of constitutional authority; it took to rubber-stamping laws that were written and drafted by the executive.[73] Perón purged the Supreme Court and packed it with judges sympathetic to his program. In 1949 he introduced a new constitution that made his justicialist doctrine the national doctrine and ended term limits so he could spend another six years in office. Perón imposed rigid discipline on his movement consistent with his training as an army officer, with his voice as the ultimate authority.[74]

As a movement rather than an ideology, Peronism showed remarkable dexterity. It embraced social actors and institutions just as quickly as it cast them aside. The church was, at first, a major supporter of Peronism, only to become its enemy by the end of Perón's rule after the church saw that Perón's cult of personality threatened to displace it as the country's spiritual center. The military was an ally until Perón stepped too close to its autonomy. Peronism's strength lay in the dignity it gave to the millions of marginalized Argentines who found their voice through the movement.

After Eva Perón died of cancer in 1952 at the young age of thirty-three (which, as many Eva devotees observe, was the same age as Jesus), Perón embraced even more authoritarian measures of social control. A robust cult of personality grew around the couple. Children read of "Saint" Evita in schools, and officers in the military were required to study justicialism as a precondition for promotion. Perón courted conflict with a once sympathetic church by displacing Catholic teachings in the schools with instructions on justicialism. Opposition politicians were arrested and jailed.

The later years of Perón's administration were marked by increasingly violent conflict. A failed coup in 1951 tried to oust him. This was followed by bombs at a Peronist rally in 1953 and an aerial bombing of the Plaza de Mayo by rebel naval officers in 1955 that killed some three hundred of Perón's supporters. Perón's minions responded in kind. In 1953 they burned the Jockey Club—an ostentatious symbol of Argentina's oligarchy—as well as the headquarters of the Radical and Socialist Parties. In 1955, after the aerial bombings, Peronist mobs stormed the Buenos Aires Metropolitan Cathedral, burned it, and beat many priests. Amid the confrontation, Perón pronounced "five for one": for every Peronist who died, five among the opposition would too.[75]

During his final years in power, Perón began to spend long hours with athletic groups from the Union of High School Students, a Peronist youth group. Rumors abounded that he was intimately involved with a young girl from the group. This solidified church opposition against him, which had already been growing. Lambasted as a dictator and a tyrant, Perón was overthrown in a military coup in 1955, with the familiar alliance of the armed forces, the church, and the upper classes spearheading the revolt. Perón fled into exile and eventually settled in Franco's Spain.

Perón was an outsized leader with a cult of personality to match who was at the center of Argentine public life for a decade. After his exile, the next two decades became an extended conflict over what to do with his legacy. Initially, the leaders of the "liberating revolution" who ousted Perón tried to erase him, an eerie foreshadowing of the disappearances during the Dirty War. Gen. Pedro Eugenio Aramburu, who became the military dictator after Perón's fall, led a process of "de-Peronization." Members of Perón's political party were prohibited from running for office, and the CGT union organization was taken over by the government, its leaders dismissed. Images of Perón and his wife Evita were banned, as was the mere mention of Perón's name, even in private.[76] Aramburu sent Evita's embalmed corpse to a hidden tomb in Milan, preventing the mass of Peronist workers from making pilgrimages to their secular saint. The ban, paradoxically, did more to lionize Perón and Evita than Perón himself ever could have accomplished while alone in exile an ocean away. The working class remained fiercely loyal. They secretly hung iconography of Perón and Evita in their homes, and many named their daughters Eva after the former first lady.

During the "Peronist resistance" of 1955–58, Perón began to stoke combative and revolutionary currents in his movement, particularly in his correspondence with John William Cooke, who Perón appointed as his secret delegate in Argentina while his party was proscribed and he was in exile. As early as 1955, Cooke urged Perón to consider guerrilla warfare and insurrection to return to power. While Perón stopped short of explicitly endorsing Cooke's proposals, he stoked Cooke's desire to lead a revolutionary confrontation against the military dictatorship and placed "blind faith" in the local leader.[77] In 1956, in his "General Instructions to Leaders," Perón endorsed planning for guerrilla warfare and organized terror as a means to bring down the dictatorship. "They are killing us," Perón wrote. "We will not sit around and just pray to the Virgin Mary while they continue their massacres. We must react and kill them, with whatever means are at our disposal, because you have to kill a viper however you can."[78] In 1956 Peronist military officers led a rebellion against the dictatorship in support of the ousted leader. When they were defeated, the rebels were summarily executed—an episode chronicled by Argentine luminary Rodolfo Walsh in his epic book *Operación Masacre*.

But Perón's endorsement of Cooke was short lived, which was in line with his long-standing leadership style—namely, to keep his subordinates guessing as to his true intentions and to keep his options open depending on what the situation called for. In 1958 Perón experimented with an electoral return to power. The Peronists were barred from participating—the generals who ceded power believed that only a restrained democracy that excluded Peronism was a workable solution to the country's problems. But Perón reached a secret deal with Arturo Frondizi, one of the Radical Party's candidates for president, in which Perón promised to support Frondizi if Frondizi promised to legalize the Peronist Party, restore autonomy to the unions, reverse the economic policies of the 1955–58 dictatorship, and promote a Peronist-style economic program.[79] (Perón also had a personal strategic interest in backing Frondizi: he required all "neo-Peronists" running in the elections to withdraw their candidacies so he could retain control over his movement.) With the support of the Peronists, Frondizi easily won the elections.

Perón's trust in Frondizi, however, turned out to be misplaced. The Peronist Party remained illegal throughout most of Frondizi's administration, as did the CGT. Most significantly, Frondizi backed out of a promise to nationalize the oil industry when he signed an agreement with Standard Oil permitting it to search for oil in Patagonia—a symbolically devastating giveaway of Argentina's natural resources.[80] Despite Frondizi's rebukes of Perón, the military never forgave Frondizi for the cardinal sin of negotiating with Perón in the first place. After general strikes in 1961, Frondizi finally legalized the Peronist Party and the CGT as he had promised to do in 1958. In the 1962 midterm elections, the Peronists won many important governorships, including the province of Buenos Aires. The military demanded that Frondizi annul the elections. Frondizi refused and was soon thereafter ousted in a military coup.[81]

When the military called the next elections in 1963, they again prohibited the Peronists from participating. This time Perón refused to back any candidate and encouraged his followers to cast blank ballots. As a consequence the radical Arturo Illia took the presidency with a dearth of legitimacy. (Almost as many ballots were cast in blank as were cast for Illia himself, a symbol of the people's support for Perón.) Another military coup was therefore not long in the making. Illia came under attack from all sides: the Peronists opposed him, hoping to agitate for Perón's return; the army turned against him for his apparent tolerance of the Peronists, who Illia allowed to run in the 1964 midterm elections; and the sensationalist press lobbied against him, nicknaming him "turtle" for his alleged slowness and dim-wittedness.[82]

The military officers who overthrew Illia in 1966, led by Gen. Juan Carlos Onganía, differed markedly from previous military regimes. Whereas the generals who led the coups of 1930, 1943, 1955, and 1962 had nominally taken power to restore Argentine democracy, Onganía's government was self-consciously a dictatorship. Guillermo O'Donnell, a noted Argentine political scientist, dubbed Onganía's approach "bureaucratic authoritarianism."[83] Onganía spearheaded a self-styled "Argentine revolution" for economic liberalization, rapid industrial development, and an end to partisan politics, similar to the program of the military generals who took control in neighboring Brazil in 1964 and orchestrated the "Brazilian miracle." The rulers represented a clique of enlightened dictators who would harness the power of science, technology, and foreign investment on the path to development. To achieve their aims, Congress was dissolved, a state of siege was declared, the universities were purged, censorship was imposed, and decency codes were enacted. But it was also a widely accepted government; with the promise of rapid industrial growth, many of the union movements' leaders initially supported the regime, finding that their interests were better served by close ties to the government than with the protections of a liberal democracy and support for an exiled leader thousands of miles away.[84] (Some were also working for a "Peronism without Perón," projecting their desires for a strong central leader onto Onganía himself and distancing themselves from their own aging leader.[85]) The "revolution" invoked the familiar tropes of Argentine destiny and greatness; it was a project to propel Argentina back to its proper place in the world.

While the early years of the regime were relatively calm, a revolt was brewing below the surface. The political upheaval of the 1960s set the stakes. On the left years of failed electoral strategies, strikes, protests, and organizing had failed to stop the cycle of military intervention, economic crisis, and social exclusion. The Cuban Revolution of 1959 also loomed large in the imagination of a generation of young Argentines who were drawn to agitation and guerrilla warfare as the most promising means for social change. Argentine youth saw in Cuba that a small band of committed guerrillas, properly trained in military and political matters, could topple an American-backed regime. In the intellectual firmament of the 1960s, members of the left began to fuse the theories of Latin American socialism with Peronism, seeing Perón and his party as the Argentine vanguard of a socialist future. Their understanding of Perón was based less on the actual Perón who ruled from 1946 to 1955 and more on an idealized Perón who had been romanticized after more than a decade out of power—a leader whose ideology was malleable enough to be characterized as a socialist. The young members of the generation who gravitated toward Peronism in the 1960s were infants when Perón actually ruled. Despite being a committed anticommunist, Perón tactfully stoked this current within his movement, and the openness of his ideology gave space to those who insisted on his revolutionary significance.[86]

In the midst of this convulsive period, Perón saw an opportunity. ("Me manejo bien en un quilombo" [I do well in a shitshow], he was fond of saying.[87]) By the mid-1960s—after more than a decade in exile—Perón recognized that his distant example was fading in comparison to the rising stars of Ernesto "Che" Guevara and Fidel Castro. In response, he began to present himself as not just the "great conductor" of the organized community but a revolutionary socialist. He took to calling his project "nationalist socialism" and wrote *Latin American, Now or Never* while in exile, a radical tract evoking the tropes of the Southern Hemisphere's socialist left.[88]

But the 1959 Cuban Revolution also grabbed the attention of the Argentine military's strategic thinkers, who saw it as a cautionary tale. Their fear of the spread of communism was informed and shaped by the terminology of the Cold War. But at its core, the Argentine military's response was rooted in the radical ideas of Argentina's nationalistic right—they saw communism and "subversion" as a threat not only to liberal democracy but to the very essence of "Argentineness" and the country's *ser nacional*. While American cold warriors settled on an idea of containment to stop the advance of communism, the Argentine nationalists saw themselves in the opening stages of World War III, with the fate of civilization at stake in their backyard.[89]

Though many leading Argentine military officers were trained in American war schools, it was the experience of the French in colonial Vietnam and Algeria that proved the most useful foreign import. French commandos from these wars had described the global dimensions of countersubversive warfare, recognizing that the psychological component of war was equally or even more important than the military component.[90] "We still persist in studying a type of warfare that no longer exists and that we shall never fight again," wrote Roger Trinquier, the French paratrooper commando, in the preface to his influential book *Modern Warfare*—the Bible for counterinsurgency students in the 1960s and 1970s.[91] He believed that war was no longer the "clash of two armies on the field of battle." It was, instead, "an interlocking system of actions—political, economic, psychological, military—that aims at the overthrow of the established authority in a country and its replacement by another regime."[92] Thus countersubversive warfare had to be directed equally at the guerrillas seeking to overthrow the established order as to the population that was in contention. An army fighting a "subversive" enemy was required to capture the minds and loyalty of the population, not merely subjugate them to its rule. This implied that the impending war in Argentina was not only about fighting with guns; it was about confronting the threat posed by subversive terrorism with sloganeering and propaganda, including confronting pernicious ideas with violence if necessary.

Trinquier also stressed the nonconventional nature of modern warfare. Whereas soldiers in a conventional war squared off in uniform against one another on a battlefield, the terrorists of modern warfare swam like fish in the ocean of a population and used anonymity to their advantage. Hence, Trinquier believed, the laws of war did not apply. As terrorists took no risk on the battlefield, they were not entitled to the humane treatment accorded to captured soldiers under the Geneva Conventions. Once captured, the strategy required that they be "interrogated" so as to give up their comrades. If necessary, torture should be used, as the basic structure of guerrilla opponents was to form small cellular groups that maintained periodic meetings. Infiltrating this infrastructure required quick intelligence, as the cells would break apart if they sensed danger.[93]

The French school proved a useful blueprint for the Argentines, for the French commandoes described warfare that was more than tactics and strategy—it was a fight for the essence of civilization. Indeed, naval officers sometimes displayed *The Battle of Algiers* to prisoners inside the Naval Mechanics School (ESMA) on "special occasions." Raúl Cubas, an ESMA survivor, recalls that one of his captors from the army told him during one such movie viewing, "You are just insignificant nothings who don't understand history. We didn't copy North American intelligence; we copied French counterintelligence, and that's how we've made shit of you."[94]

After army officers took classes in France and French commandoes gave guest courses in the Army War College, army manuals proliferated to spread the French doctrine. These included "Nonconventional Operations" (1968),[95] "Psychological Operations" (1968),[96] "Instruction in the Fight against Guerrillas" (1969),[97] "Operations against Urban Subversion" (1969),[98] "Operations against Irregular Forces" (1970),[99] "Counterintelligence—Military Censorship" (1972),[100] and "Instruction in the Fight against Subversive Groups" (1976).[101] At the heart of these materials was an elastic concept of "warfare" that saw everyone as a potential combatant and every location as a potential battlefield.

As the armed forces feared, by the late 1960s, a number of guerrilla groups had emerged. The first to appear were the Uturuncos, a short-lived coalition of communist and left-wing Peronists who were backed by the Cubans and tried to liberate the rural northwest in 1959. A similar group, called the People's Guerrilla Army, made a similar attempt in 1964, awaiting the arrival of Che Guevara, who was then fighting in Bolivia.[102] Both groups failed, but within a decade, better-organized and more enduring guerrilla groups formed, including the Revolutionary Armed Forces, the Argentine Liberation Front (Frente Argentino de Liberación, FAL), and the Peronist Armed Forces. Whereas their predecessors had focused on rural *foquista* warfare, these groups struck at the heart of urban life. Eventually, these guerrilla groups merged into two larger groups, the People's Revolutionary Army (Ejército Revolucionario del Pueblo, ERP)—a Trotskyite guerrilla force linked to the communist Revolutionary Worker's Party—and the Montoneros, a left-wing Peronist group. The guerrillas mostly engaged in acts of urban sabotage, targeted killings, and Robin Hood–style kidnappings.[103]

When the automotive union in Córdoba called for the nation's first strike under Onganía's rule in May 1969, it was met with repressive force. But at the end of the month, almost spontaneously, a wide cross section of Córdoba's underground left—union members, former politicians, university professors, and students who had been purged from the academy—poured into the streets to support the strike and resist. For two days, on May 29 and 30, rioting shut down the city in an episode known as the Cordobazo. When the police were repelled by protestors' blockades, the army was called in to quell the spontaneous rebellion, an episode that shook the foundations of Onganía's support by unmasking the explosive social tensions festering under his government. In total fourteen people died.[104]

Soon thereafter the Montonero guerrillas burst onto the scene. In May 1970 they kidnapped the aging retired Gen. Pedro Eugenio Aramburu, who was responsible for the execution of Peronist rebels in 1956 and was plotting his own political maneuver against Onganía. After demanding the return of Evita's corpse and holding a revolutionary trial, the guerrillas shot Aramburu in the head and dumped his body. Though Perón had not explicitly endorsed the kidnapping and execution, he later ratified the young guerrillas' action, thereby encouraging the Montoneros.[105]

The strike against Aramburu proved a decisive blow to the regime. Onganía was forced to resign. Gen. Alejandro Agustín Lanusse, Onganía's commander in chief of the army, eventually became president in March of 1971. A close friend of Aramburu's, Lanusse promised "widespread retribution."[106]

With Perón's encouragement, the Montoneros grew and flourished, pursuing their twin aims of bringing down the military government and fighting for Perón's return. They grew from a small band of some twenty young men and women to one of Latin America's largest political and military movements, able to mobilize hundreds of thousands of activists almost on a whim. They gained control of historic Peronist organizations, such as the Peronist University Youth, the Peronist Youth, the Union of High School Students, and the Peronist Workers Youth, which soon came to serve as front organizations for the Montoneros' larger ambitions. Their actions were diverse. There were sporadic killings and bombs to be sure, but they gained traction in the slums, in factory shops, and among left-wing church intellectuals drawn toward liberation theology. Business leaders were also common targets—both as a mechanism to show solidarity with striking workers and to exact ransom from kidnappings to fund the underground network. Most famously, the Montoneros kidnapped the wealthy Born brothers in 1974 and extracted over $60 million in ransom from the family.[107] In all, these attacks netted nearly $200 million for the guerrillas.

The swiftness with which the Montoneros gained supremacy within the Peronist movement seemed to confirm the military's fears of infiltration and subversion. At the same time, it radicalized the orthodox Peronists, who also wanted to engineer their own purge of the "youthful idiots" from their movement, who they saw as Johnny-come-lately traitors. The strengthening of right-wing groups and police repression followed, much of it ironically nurtured and sustained within the

Peronist movement itself. In mid-1970 the first shadow force of the government, known as Mano, appeared, believed to have been composed of off-duty police. They kidnapped union activists and leftist Peronists. Once taken, they were gone without a trace—"disappeared," as the practice came to be known. By early 1971 there was one disappearance every two and a half weeks.[108]

In the face of growing guerrilla activity, Gen. Alejandro Agustín Lanusse declared a state of siege after taking office. He gave the armed forces power to intervene in any area of the country where he perceived a police failure in combating the guerrillas. Citizens arrested in these military actions were shuttled to the Federal Criminal Court of the Nation, a national security court created by Lanusse with summary proceedings and no right of appeal.[109] At the same time, semiautonomous military units were authorized to patrol the country. Top officials, such as Gen. Jorge Rafael Videla, who had served on the Inter-American Defense Board and were familiar with counterinsurgency tactics, were called in as specialists. Their strategy was twofold. The military, in charge of regions of the country under the "state of siege" provisions, fought terrorism by befriending the local population such as by building roads and schools. Already suspicious of the guerrillas hiding in their midst, the local population would turn on the "invading" strangers. Simultaneously, when guerrillas were captured, they were brutally tortured to secure information on the whereabouts of other militants. It was during these years that the military began to test tactics that it would later use during the Dirty War.

But Lanusse's heavy-handedness backfired. He made a pretense of acting within the rule of law (so fragile were Argentina's democratic traditions that dictators always made this claim). In August 1972 sixteen guerrillas attempted to escape from a military prison in Trelew, in the far reaches of Patagonia. They were captured and summarily shot by guards.[110] Public outcry over the Trelew massacre and the failure to curb violence forced Lanusse to schedule elections. With strikes and uprisings in many cities agitating for Perón's return, Perón appeared to be the only man who could save the country.[111]

When Perón's candidate, Héctor Cámpora, won the 1973 elections (Perón was barred from running), his first action was to grant amnesty to the guerrillas who had been imprisoned during the military regime by the national security court.[112] The Montoneros, now acting aboveground, moved to assert their primacy within the Peronist movement. Tensions exploded when Perón returned for good in June 1973. As hundreds of thousands trekked from Buenos Aires to the Ezeiza airport to greet Perón upon his return, a fight broke out between his left- and right-wing supporters. What was supposed to be a triumphant day signaling Perón's definitive return ended in tragedy. Several hundred died, and Perón's plane was diverted.[113] Cámpora soon stepped down as violence between the Peronist factions continued. The slogan had been "Cámpora to Office, Perón to Power," and the able Peronist minion made good on his promise. Perón was elected in October 1973 after eighteen years in exile.

But Perón could not contain what he had unleashed. He had always been a master tactician, adept at favoring the currents of his movement that best suited his immediate aims. So over the course of his exile, he had oscillated between supporting the more revolutionary and the more traditional sectors of his movement. As Richard Gillespie notes, Perón "pragmatically bow[ed] to the Left, Right, or Centre whenever one particular line served his overall aim of a Peronist restoration; and that such gestures in no way negated his traditional beliefs in national development, class conciliation, and a semi-corporatist 'organized community.'"[114]

Soon after Perón took power, the contradictions in his movement could no longer be held together without the unifying rallying cry for his return. In an effort to purge the movement of "traitors" and jockey for power within the movement, the Montoneros assassinated José Rucci, Perón's right-hand man and the leader of the CGT. Perón did not take the attack on his confidant lightly. Right-wing death squads linked to the traditional wings of Peronism began to target the Montoneros and other revolutionaries. The result was fratricide. The left wing of Perón's movement assassinated right-wing members of the movement in an effort to purge the movement and cleanse it of counterrevolutionaries. The right wing assassinated members of the left wing, decrying them as "infiltrators" and Marxists. Both sides shot each other, yelling, "Perón or death!"

Perón ultimately sided with the more orthodox members of his movement. Perón had engineered his return by using the revolutionary left, who provided organizing muscle in the two election campaigns of 1973 and proved a thorn in the side of the military. But once Perón was in power, the revolutionary left became dispensable. The Montoneros had risen to power because of their militancy and their ability to mobilize large crowds among the Peronist Youth and in the universities. But they were a remarkably middle-class movement. The orthodox trade unions wielded much more power and were more important to Perón once in government. During May Day celebrations in 1974, Perón denounced his young followers as "imbeciles" and "babies," and the Montoneros led an enormous crowd out of the Plaza de Mayo. To further purge his movement of the radicals he had used as pawns to facilitate his return to power, Perón enacted a new antiterrorism bill that increased punishment and suspended many due process rights for suspected terrorists. The law was only selectively enforced against the militant left, and Perón overlooked the increasing violence from paramilitaries.[115]

Even as the Montoneros were savaged by Perón, they were unable to completely wean themselves from him, as the pueblo on whose behalf they claimed to be fighting was decidedly Peronist. And so the Montoneros lived in a borderline space, trapped between their loyalty to Perón and his movement and their leader's unbridled hostility.

When Perón died less than a year after being elected, in July 1974, Argentina descended into chaos. He left his third wife, Isabel Perón, as president. Mrs. Perón had never finished high school. Her political legitimacy stemmed entirely from her marriage to Perón. Indeed, she was selected as vice president because Perón did not wish to show favoritism between the various factions in his movement in the run-up to the 1973 election. Perón met her in 1956, a year after he was forced into exile while he was living in Panama (they married later that year in Spain). She was just twenty-five at the time, on tour with a cabaret group. She spent the majority of her adult life living away from Argentina with Perón during his time in exile.[116]

Mrs. Perón's close advisor and Perón's former security chief, José López Rega, known as the "warlock" for his obsession with astrology and the occult, ran the government on her behalf. López Rega began funding the Argentine Anti-Communist Alliance (AAA) out of the offices of the Ministry of Social Welfare to combat the leftist guerrillas. The "Triple A," made up of orthodox Peronists, military officers, and off-duty police officers, was a right-wing death squad. By late 1974 the AAA had killed seventy people, and by 1975 the AAA was killing as many as fifty a week. López Rega was forced out of office when the military made clear to Mrs. Perón that she must back the moderates within her government or face a coup d'état. López Rega left, but the violence did not subside. The Montoneros had joined their brother guerrilla organizations and had gone back underground. They increased their assassinations and high-profile extortion kidnappings, preparing themselves for a war of attrition.

A number of violent conflicts were fought simultaneously. The Montoneros were battling within the Peronist movement for supremacy but were also targeting police officers and the military, including an audacious assault on October 5, 1975, when the Montoneros attacked the Twenty-Ninth Mountain Infantry Regiment in Formosa. The ERP guerrillas were combatting the armed forces as well as bureaucrats in the labor movement. Death squads, often staffed by off-duty police and military officers, were targeting guerrillas but were also going after radical intellectuals, artists, and priests who were sympathetic to the revolutionaries. The lived experience for many was bizarre. To this day the precoup period is little understood, filled with seemingly inexplicable conflicts and contradictions.

Political violence became widespread, and the country descended into chaos. Each of the assassinations tended to have an explanation: a reprisal for the killing of a comrade, a step in the revolutionary agenda toward a new world order, a surgical strike to cripple the institutional structure of the police. But the image presented to the average Argentine in the media cast the violence as random, pervasive, and out of control. Armed gangs of the left and right littered the streets with bodies.

In the face of chaos and political opposition from the Radical Party and the CGT umbrella union organization, Mrs. Perón spent several months in retreat, leaving the government to the president of the Senate, Peronist Ítalo Lúder. Though the armed forces had been discredited after their embarrassing exit in 1973, they began to regroup in the midst of the chaos and political instability. A February 1975 executive decree ordering the army to "annihilate" communist guerrillas in the Tucumán province in Operation Independence signaled the reentry of the military into public life, later solidified in October 1975, when the decree was extended by ordering the armed forces to "annihilate subversion" in the entire country after the Formosa attack.[117]

The military was preparing itself for a war of extermination. Under the previous military regime of 1966–73, extensive counterterrorism measures had been enacted: the country was split into zones, where local army generals were given control over countersubversion activities; a national security court similar to a military court-martial was set up to try terrorists; and a state of siege was enacted so that citizens could be rounded up without probable cause for arrest. But the military saw these measures as a failure. The 1973 amnesty law enacted as Cámpora took office released hundreds of revolutionaries, rendering the security measures from 1966 to 1973 useless. Images of thousands of youth from the Montoneros and ERP descending on the Devoto prison upon Cámpora's inauguration and demanding the release of political prisoners had seared into the military's consciousness an event never to repeat.

Death and total destruction were the only solutions that the military saw to end the growing tide of "subversion." "As many people as necessary must die in Argentina so that the country will again be secure," said Gen. Jorge Rafael Videla, the commander in chief of the army, in 1975, staking out a position that would become the official government policy after the 1976 coup he led.[118]

And so the stage was set for the Dirty War. Violence was spiraling out of control; the economy was in tatters; the Peronist movement, which had historically been able to govern the country, was frayed; the opposition was powerless to oust Mrs. Perón through constitutional means; and the far left had denounced any exercise in constitutional elections as "bourgeoisie," preferring instead to let the contradictions in the system expose themselves to accelerate total revolution.

Most of the population looked on with relief and indifference when the tanks rolled through Buenos Aires on March 24, 1976, believing the military to be the only entity capable of ending the public bloodletting that had crippled the country. Opposition parties welcomed the armed forces, hoping to use the coup to eventually return to civilian rule in a more advantageous position or to populate the ranks of the military administration should the military need civilian allies; the Catholic Church backed the coup because of the military leaders' promise to restore "Western and Christian values" to a country that had spiraled out of control; foreign diplomats offered their support, such as U.S. secretary of state Henry Kissinger, who told the generals, "If there are things that have to be done, you should do them quickly"[119]; and the press largely bowed to the military, finding little reason to challenge the censorship rules that the new regime put in place prohibiting them from reporting on the "War against Subversion."

The *Buenos Aires Herald,* the capital's English-language daily, which would soon become the leading dissident news organization, originally responded to the coup with words of encouragement. In an editorial the day after the coup, the *Herald* noted that the military operation "was not just another coup, but a rescue operation. These are not men hungry for power, but men with a duty, which they have stated with seriousness."[120] Just two days after the military intervention, *La Prensa* was so confident in the leadership of the new administration that the editors devoted the lead editorial to lamenting the halt in the country's beef exports, making scant reference to the military intervention just days before, noting only that economic conditions would finally be "liberated from the politics of demagoguery that had operated until the 24th."[121]

No victory processions were held. The new government was hurried into office—the initial swearing-in ceremony of the junta lasted just fifteen minutes.[122] The message from the quick ceremony was clear: pomp and circumstance would take second place to professionalism and the pressing needs of Argentina in the new administration.

The first glimpse the public received of their new leaders—a photograph from the brief swearing-in ceremony—was similarly reassuring.

The junta's commanders—Gen. Jorge Rafael Videla (commander of the army), Adm. Emilio Eduardo Massera (commander of the navy), and Brig. Gen. Orlando Agosti (commander of the air force)—solemnly stared toward the ground, seemingly reluctant about the roles they had assumed as absolute leaders of a torn and troubled country.[123] Their initial statement outlined the "process of national reorganization," *el processo*, which aimed to "reinstate the essential values that serve as the basis for the integral functioning of the state, with an emphasis on morality, suitability and efficiency. These are indispensable in reconstructing the content and imagination of the nation; eradicating subversion; and promoting economic development. With equitable and responsible participation of all distinct sectors, the goal is to assure the restoration of a republican democracy, representative and federal, adequate to the realities and necessities of the Argentine public."[124]

Comparing the Argentine coup to Augusto Pinochet's ousting of Salvador Allende in Chile just three years before, the *New York Times* cautiously endorsed the Argentine takeover, saying that "General Jorge Rafael Videla and his colleagues have behaved with relative restraint."[125] A week later, a headline assured foreign readers that "bloodshed is absent," a notable exception from the military dictatorships that ruled eight of the continent's ten countries.[126]

In his inaugural speech, Videla reiterated the military's commitment to democracy and human rights: "For us, respect for human rights is not born simply from a legal mandate and international declarations but comes from our Christianity and our profound conviction of the preeminence of man's dignity as a fundamental value. We the army have assumed this authority to assure the due protection of man's natural rights; not to abridge liberty but to affirm it; not to truncate justice but to expand it."[127] Within twenty-four hours the United States, Chile, Brazil, Mexico, Bolivia, Venezuela, Costa Rica, and Spain all recognized the new regime and pledged to maintain diplomatic relations.[128] Within three days Great Britain, Italy, Germany, Greece, South Africa, Turkey, and South Korea followed. *La Prensa* reported that for the first time ever, the European press was evaluating the Argentine military coup not as the outcome of ideological struggle but as an essential step necessary to deal with a national emergency.[129]

Executive power was vested in the junta, a tripartite council composed of the heads of the army, navy, and air force. The junta selected one of their members, Gen. Jorge Rafael Videla, as president. An eight-member cabinet was also created, filled almost entirely with military officers. Congress was dissolved and replaced by a legislative advisory commission of nine officers, essentially acting as the chief advisory council to the junta. The military also replaced the federal ministers, the provincial governors, and the heads of the country's major unions with interim military officials. Political activity was suspended, and some leftist parties were dissolved.[130] All the justices of the Supreme Court were dismissed, and the junta appointed new members. Lower judges followed suit: those who did not pledge loyalty to the statutes of the process of national reorganization were purged. Jurisdiction for national security crimes was transferred to martial law courts, and increased penalties for crimes and terrorism, including the death penalty, were implemented. Many union leaders were arrested; others stayed home from work in hiding. The assets of the major unions were all frozen and workers' activities prohibited.[131] The universities, which had been a major center of radical student activity in the years prior to the coup, were systematically purged of politically active professors and students, and military units occupied the federal universities' main buildings.[132] But politics, in large measure, was perceived to have been the problem, and these radical moves were neither disturbing nor surprising. Mobilized fringes had made the stakes over political battles all or nothing. As politics became a life-or-death struggle, citizens retreated from the public sphere. Amid rampant violence, the radical ideals for social justice on the left sounded just as hollow as the demands for national security on the right. Men in uniform—symbols of professionalism and order—were a welcomed antidote to politics. The long march from a hopeful beginning of the century to a tragic conclusion was complete.

3

The Prosecution's Case

The dimensions of the horror that took place inside the walls of the small officers' club on the leafy compound of the Naval Mechanics School (ESMA) naval base on the northern edge of Buenos Aires can be hard to comprehend. Some have reached to literature to try to find an apt analogy, comparing it to Dante's seventh circle of hell for the dizzying psychological and physical violence that prisoners suffered while on the inside. Others have invoked a historical comparison, calling it the Auschwitz of Argentina because of the thousands of people who were murdered there by administrative decree. Others have simply called it a symbol, the largest and longest-lasting secret detention center maintained during Argentina's Dirty War.

One might presume that the opening statements given by the state would reach for literary metaphors and stirring oratory as an overview of the case to come. The defendants, after all, had routinely criticized the proceeding as a "show trial," and what is worth the price of admission without a gripping introductory scene? But such soaring rhetoric never materialized. There was no memorable exposition comparable to Justice Robert Jackson's at Nuremberg.

This was not the fault of the prosecution so much as a natural consequence of the Argentine procedural code, which requires that the court secretary read charging instruments at the outset of criminal hearings.[1] Given the length of the charging instruments in the ESMA trial—seventeen separate documents totaling thousands of pages—the court's several secretaries took turns to comply. As neutrals, their reading lacked any dramatic flair. Their monotone voices barely changed register, even as they read summaries of gruesome torture and forced kidnappings. Their exposition was targeted for speed and bureaucratic efficiency rather than persuasive effect.

Private human rights lawyers objected to the seemingly empty formalism of this process, which slowed the trial for several additional months after a generation of delay and years of pretrial procedural wrangling. In fact, the secretaries repeated hundreds of pages of the same passages over and over, as each charging document contained a verbatim summary lifted from prior versions filed against other defendants. The documents were also filled with extensive legal citations and were not drafted with a live audience in mind. They were the products of the pretrial phase of the case, which under the Argentine criminal code is rigidly separated from the trial phase. The idea of requiring an open reading of the charging instruments, at least in theory, is to provide the defendants with an overview of the charges against them, but there was little possibility here that the oral lecture provided such a procedural safeguard. Most of the defendants appeared to daydream their way through the months of reading the charges or brought other reading material to pass the time. All the defendants also had an opportunity to read the voluminous documents on prior occasions. It was hard to imagine that this opening procedure provided any benefit. The human rights lawyers asked the court to, at minimum, excise the repetitive passages from the oral summation in an effort to move the case along, but the defendants—despite their apparent inattention—insisted on rigid procedural fidelity. In total, the secretaries required nearly four months of hearings, between December 2009 and March 2010, to complete the task.

Accusations that the proceeding was a show trial were thus quickly dispelled by the trial's opening dramatic failure. After the opening day, attendance quickly dwindled to just a few interested relatives of the missing, human rights activists, and a handful of defendants' supporters. Typically, there were only one or two wire reporters and the left-wing *Página/12* in attendance. Despite the dramatic letdown, however, there was a certain virtue to the tedium. The dull procedure began the trial with a note of seriousness. The opening monotony signaled that the proceeding was an ordinary trial subject to the same burdens as any other proceeding in Argentina.

The heart of the case came from what was titled "Testimonies A," a set of charges that were first filed in 1987 during Argentina's political transition. These charges were abruptly cut short because of the Easter military uprisings that year and the subsequent passage of the due obedience law, which extended amnesty to most of the officers charged in that case. These charges were reopened in September 2003, just days after Argentina's Congress revoked the amnesty laws. Ten defendants were charged in this investigation for their direct participation in acts of kidnapping and torture of sixty victims. In comparison to the universe of defendants and victims who could have been charged, the scope was limited, reflecting the theory prevalent in the 1980s that lower-ranking officers could only be charged in cases where there was evidence of their direct participation in a crime. As a consequence, these original charges did not include any charges for murder or international human rights crimes such as forced disappearances or crimes against humanity. Prosecutors in the 1980s believed that murder could only be charged where there was positive evidence of a killing. Because the dictatorship had disappeared its victims and most bodies remained missing, there typically was no concrete evidence of a murder other than the cruel passage of time. And crimes against humanity were not enumerated as actual charges because there was no penal proscription in Argentina's domestic criminal code for any such crimes. Strangely, prosecutors had also left out other significant charges that could have been leveled. There were no charges of extortion, theft, sexual assault, or—worst of all—kidnapping children. The majority of the charges in Testimonies A were directed at low-ranking officers based on incidents in which witnesses had specifically identified them in the torture room during an interrogation or having participated in a kidnapping raid. Dozens of officers were left out of these original charges owing to the lack of evidence tying them to an individual act of torture or kidnapping—indeed, a great "success" of the ESMA's decision to kill most of its victims.

These charges presented the thorniest due process challenge, as the ten officers in this charging instrument had all received confirmed decisions from the Argentine Supreme Court that the charges were dismissed owing to the due obedience and full stop laws passed in 1986 and 1987. The charges thus seemed squarely an affront to the bedrock principle of *non bis in idem*, known as double jeopardy in the common law tradition.

Testimonies B centered on the responsibility of a group of officers for the kidnapping, disappearance, and murder of the twelve human rights activists taken from the Santa Cruz Church and other areas of Buenos Aires in the raids led by Alfredo Astiz after Astiz's monthslong infiltration of human rights groups. Though the charges were initially filed in the 1980s, after subsequent investigation, the investigatory judge and prosecutor expanded the theory of criminal responsibility in the case and charged all the defendants as coauthors of the crimes, even if there was scant evidence of a given defendant's direct participation in the incident. The theory underlying this expanded concept of criminal liability stemmed loosely from a developing theory in international law known as the "joint criminal enterprise," similar to the concept of a racketeering enterprise in the United States. Under this theory, individual defendants could be held liable for the acts of the group—even without their direct participation in an event—so long as such acts fell within the common plan or purpose of the group.

Testimonies C centered on the kidnapping and murder of journalist and Montonero activist Rodolfo Walsh, who was caught in a firefight with the Grupo de Tareas (GT) 3.3/2 on the first anniversary of the military coup as he was distributing an open letter to the military junta. An additional three cases were added to these main lines of investigation, culminating, in total, in a trial against eighteen defendants for crimes committed against eighty-six victims.

Common to all these cases was the prosecution's assertion that the defendants had participated in a "criminal plan"—conceived at the highest ranks of the armed forces and executed by the lowest-ranking noncommissioned officers—to exterminate the country's "subversive" enemies. This plan, in the words of pretrial prosecutor Eduardo Taiano, was directed by the military junta, perfected by the middle-ranking officers who formed the corps of the bureaucracy of the armed forces, and executed by lower-ranking officers who were given significant discretion in how to carry out the plan.[2]

Taiano identified the plan as emanating from a number of military decrees, written orders, operations manuals, and verbal orders from the military commanders. It began, ironically, under the government of Isabel Perón in 1975—before the military coup—when a series of executive decrees were issued that declared a state of siege and ordered the armed forces to "annihilate subversion." The army, which was given primary responsibility for the campaign, then issued a number of directives that assigned priorities among its various divisions.

In line with their training in French counterinsurgency tactics, the army divided the country into five zones. Corps commanders were given control over each zone of the country, which was further divided into subzones and areas, with officers given responsibility over territorial units of the country relative to their rank.

Simultaneously, the navy issued the Capacity Plan of the Navy (Plan de Capacidades de la Armada [PLACINTARA]). This plan divided the navy into eleven task forces. The task forces were headed by rear admirals. Below the task forces were work groups, so that each task force might have several work groups, such as "Task Force 1" and its several work groups "1.1," "1.2," and "1.3" (in Spanish, Grupo de Tareas, or GT). Below the work groups were work units, given an additional numeral to signify where the groups were in the navy hierarchy. So Work Unit 1.1.1. would be the first work unit in the first work group in Task Force 1. (Work Group 1.1/1 was an alternative way of signifying Work Unit 1.1.1.) The infamous GT 3.3/2, the secret commando unit in the ESMA that took on such an outsized role in the Dirty War, was named that way because it was the second work unit in the third work group under the command of the third task force.

Under this division of labor, the chief of operations of the naval general staff—a rear admiral—was given control over Task Force 3, an area that covered the city of Buenos Aires and its surroundings. Under his command was the director of the ESMA, a large naval academy located at the northern edge of Buenos Aires. The school's director was given control over the GT 3.3, which was housed within the school. Under the school's director was a captain who was put in charge of Work Unit 3.3.2, which became the navy's most notorious antisubversive fighting force as a result of the extent and viciousness of its role in the Dirty War. The GT 3.3/2 had a general staff consisting of a chief of intelligence, a chief of operations, and a chief of logistics.

By regulation, the navy was only charged with combatting subversion in the "areas within its jurisdiction," which were limited to the areas immediately around its bases, the country's navigable waterways, and the far reaches of Patagonia. In all other areas of the country, the navy was instructed to play a supporting role to the army, with a local memorandum of understanding signed between area army and navy commanders to delineate the navy's role in each zone. This was a limited role defined for the navy—under this division of labor, the ESMA was only supposed to patrol the territory around the ESMA and support the local police precincts and the army in the northern areas of Buenos Aires. In fact, the GT 3.3/1—also under the command of the director of the ESMA—was assigned to uniformed street patrols. But the GT 3.3/2 became a clandestine fighting force, given extensive leeway to engage all around the country and, eventually, all over the world.

Despite prosecutor Taiano's focus on the military directives that seemed to shape the navy's involvement in the Dirty War, the official documents only told part of the story. While not specifically mentioned in the charging papers, the case file was full of testimony from survivors who claimed that the ESMA played a special role because of the GT 3.3/2's unique connection to Adm. Emilio Eduardo Massera, who was the navy's first representative on the military junta and the leader of the navy at the time of the military coup.

Massera had dreams of becoming a civilian president when the military regime ceded power. Indeed, it was a playbook pioneered by Perón himself, who used his position within a military government during World War II to catapult himself to popularity and power. A common joke told about Massera was that his biggest political mistake was going into the navy and not into the army. While the army was supposed to take a leading role in the War against Subversion, Massera was not content to let the navy sit on the sidelines; he intended to thrust himself and the institution he led into the center of this "fight"—to bolster his bona fides and exit triumphantly from the dictatorship as the victor over subversion. "If you don't understand Massera's excessive and almost uncontrollable ambition, you won't really understand what happened," ESMA survivor Martín Gras later recalled at trial.[3]

The trouble was that the navy was not equipped to foster Massera's grand ambitions. The navy's institutional intelligence-gathering wing, the Servicio de Inteligencia Naval (SIN), was not prepared to take on primary responsibility in the War against Subversion, let alone sully its "professional" standing to be used for Massera's grand political ambitions. In order to personally ensure the navy's successful participation in the War against Subversion, Massera circumvented the SIN and bestowed on the GT 3.3/2 special authority as the navy's primary repressive unit. Technically, the group was supposed to rely on both the army and the SIN to collect "intelligence" and identify targets, but with Massera's blessing, the GT 3.3/2 assumed all the capacity it needed to operate independently. Rumor has it that Massera himself participated in the baptismal raids of the GT 3.3/2, personally supervising the first torture sessions and wielding the *picana electrica*, an electric shock machine fashioned from an agricultural cattle prod. Massera apparently had direct and frequent contact with the officers who worked at the ESMA, particularly Adm. Rubén Jacinto Chamorro, the ESMA's director; Jorge Eduardo Acosta, the chief of intelligence of the GT 3.3/2; and Jorge Radice, a logistics officer who became Massera's employee as a civilian after both of them retired from the navy in 1979. As a consequence, the GT 3.3/2 assumed an outsized role in the repression relative to the limited role the navy—and the ESMA in particular—was supposed to play under the PLACINTARA.

The GT 3.3/2 was split into three sections: an intelligence unit, an operations unit, and a logistics unit. The intelligence unit was primarily in charge of gathering intelligence, which it gained almost exclusively by torturing detainees, getting them to confess to their "subversive" pasts, and identifying new targets. New victims always arrived in the basement of the ESMA, where they were typically escorted down a narrow aisle with a sign reading "Avenue of Happiness" toward Room 13, one of four small torture rooms at the back of the basement containing perhaps one or two chairs, a metal bedframe with restraining straps, and the electric cattle prod. Only the most highly trained and prized officers were given the sacred duty of wielding this *picana*. The operations unit was the division of the GT 3.3/2 charged with organizing raids. The group was broken down into smaller work teams, generally composed of twelve to fifteen men in three to five cars, which zoomed around the streets chasing targets. The logistics wing was charged with managing everything the GT 3.3/2 needed to operate—storing firearms; repairing cars; registering and tracking war booty; dispensing salaries; making sure there were enough handcuffs, blindfolds, and hoods to properly detain victims; and renovating the interior of the officers' club, as was operationally necessary.

Though there were dozens, perhaps hundreds, of military officers who were left out of the indictments, the state's case included men from nearly every rung of the naval hierarchy. At the very top of the pyramid were Adms. Oscar Montes and Manuel Jacinto García Tallada, who successively served as chief of operations on the naval general staff between 1976 and 1977. They were just two rungs below Admiral Massera. From this position, they were charged under the PLACINTARA with commanding Task Force 3, which covered most of the navy's installations in and around the city of Buenos Aires. There was little direct evidence that connected Montes or García Tallada to the violence, but the prosecution alleged that these were the desk officers who had supervised the GT 3.3/2's actions and had transmitted and perfected orders to exterminate the regime's opponents. (One witness did recall seeing Montes in the ESMA on one occasion, and a group of several ESMA victims was eventually sent to the ministry of foreign affairs as clerks while Montes served as minister of foreign affairs after his retirement from the navy. There was no comparable evidence against García Tallada, who was indicted solely on the basis of his hierarchy.)

Several ranks below Montes and García Tallada, the next-highest-ranking officer was Capt. Jorge Eduardo Acosta, alias "Tigre" (tiger), "Anibal," or "Santiago," who served as the chief of intelligence of the GT 3.3/2 from its formation in April 1976 until his rotation to a new position in 1979. In this capacity, Acosta was charged with overseeing intelligence-gathering activities (read: torture), which gave him tremendous power, as the Dirty War depended on intelligence. What raids would be planned, what officers could expect to encounter on raids, who would be captured, who would be tortured, and who was "guilty" were all matters that intelligence officers determined. Perhaps because of his position, and perhaps owing to his outsized personality, Acosta became the most powerful figure inside the ESMA.

In the dock below Acosta was a group of line officers responsible for the day-to-day operations of the ESMA. In the intelligence wing were Capt. Antonio Pernías, alias "Trueno" (thunder), "Rata" (rat), or "Martín" (who also, for a time, served as an operations officer), a man who gained the faith and loyalty of his comrades by risking his safety in ostensibly dangerous situations and later became one of the ESMA's chief torturers; Capt. Raúl Enrique Scheller, alias "Mariano" or "Pingüino" (penguin), who took over duties from Pernías when the latter was sent to France to infiltrate Argentine exile groups; Capt. Juan Carlos Rolón, alias "Juan" or "Niño" (child), who started off as a temporary officer assigned to the ESMA at the end of 1976 but later came back and oversaw operations in the *pecera* (fishbowl), where prisoners were put to work doing propaganda for the regime; and Capt. Adolfo Miguel Donda, alias "Geronimo" or "Palito," who first served as an operations officer but was later put in charge of intelligence in 1979 after Acosta left his post. From the logistics wing were Néstor Savio, alias "Norberto" or "Halcón" (falcon), who for a time served as the head of the logistics section; Capt. Carlos Capdevilla, alias "Tomy," a navy medic who allegedly oversaw torture sessions and informed the intelligence officers when they could proceed with torture and when the electrocution had been too much and any more treatment risked killing the prisoners; and Lt. Jorge Radice, alias "Gabriel" or "Ruger," who was an accountant by training but also participated in some of the group's operations and was known as a sharpshooter. Pablo Eduardo García Velasco, alias "Dante," was also named among the defendants, but his role was not entirely clear; his twin brother, Miguel, had also served in the navy, and both men were seen inside the ESMA. There was confusion about whether Pablo Eduardo or Miguel was a member of the GT 3.3/2, while the other was a member of the SIN. Pablo Eduardo had even undertaken a hunger strike prior to trial, saying that he had been mixed up with his brother, Miguel, who was part of the GT 3.3/2. Finally, there was a group of operations officers, most of whom were also called upon to perform other duties from time to time: Lt. Alberto González, alias "Gato" (cat) or "González Minotti," who participated in operations but was also a logistics man sent all over the world searching for the money that the Montoneros had collected in ransom and deposited in banks around the globe; Lt. Ricardo Cavallo, alias "Serpico" (snake), "Marcelo," or "Miguel Angél," one of the longest-serving members of the GT 3.3/2 who was an operations man and later given intelligence responsibilities; and Lt. Alfredo Astiz, alias "Rubio" (blondie) or "Angél," the most reviled man at trial for his role in infiltrating a group of human rights activists in 1977 and organizing a raid that ended in the demise of twelve of them, including three members of the famed Mothers of the Plaza de Mayo and two French missionary nuns.

Four of the defendants were not naval officers. Maj. Julio César Coronel, alias "Maco," was a liaison from the army and formed part of the operations team of the ESMA. Despite Coronel's claims that he never worked in the ESMA, Astiz had long ago testified in secret military court proceedings that Coronel had, in fact, worked at the ESMA. Buried deep in Coronel's personnel file was also a decoration from the navy's commander in chief Adm. Emilio Eduardo Massera for his heroism in the War against Subversion. Commissioner Ernesto Weber was a police officer who commanded a team of other officers. Survivors recalled that the police officers played a critical role in the repression—these were the men with the experience and institutional knowledge of the streets. The navy had little practical experience in street patrols, and it was Weber—who headed up a team of police officers—who showed the gentlemen of the ESMA how to do their jobs. Indeed, Weber was nicknamed "220," which, according to the ESMA victims, referred to his aptitude with the *picana,* 220 being the voltage of the outlets in Argentina. (Weber denied this charge, saying that "220" was his numerical assignment when graduating from the police academy.) Below Weber was Commissioner Juan Carlos Fotea, alias "Lobo" (wolf), a former police officer who had fled Argentina after the dictatorship and was hauled back after extradition from Spain, where he had set up shop as a hotelier. And finally, there was Prefect Juan Antonio Azic, alias "Piraña," a former coast guard officer who was only one of two of the eighteen defendants who showed any sort of remorse. (Carlos Capdevilla had slipped into a deep depression with suicidal tendencies. He was diagnosed with prostate cancer in 2003 and refused further treatment in 2007. "He wants to die tomorrow," medical examiners reported.)[4]

Despite the fact that more than twenty-five years had passed since the collapse of the dictatorship, pretrial investigators had not been able to gather much documentary evidence beyond what was unearthed during the democratic transition. The prosecution had compiled a few scattered military decrees and orders (mostly introduced by the military commanders as defense exhibits in the Trial of the Juntas in 1985), but the GT 3.3/2's bulky intelligence files were never located. These included thousands of the GT 3.3/2's files on individual victims, which contained personal data, political affiliations, the officers who participated in the "investigation" leading up to their kidnapping and detention, and the information that lead to their capture. Also missing were the files that the GT 3.3/2 shared as a matter of course with the commander of the First Army Corps and the 601 Intelligence Battalion, who oversaw the army's operations in Buenos Aires. A few of these files had surfaced in individual cases, providing some insight into the organization of the repression and lingering suspicions that the entire trove of intelligence files still existed. Some survivors recall the ESMA intelligence officers burning reams of paper as the dictatorship ceded power to civilians in 1983. Others recall that Jorge Eduardo Acosta ordered all the archives to be microfilmed as he was rotated out of his duties at the ESMA in 1978 and that he kept one of the three copies that were made. (According to survivor Martín Gras, the other two copies went to Adm. Massera and to the ESMA's archives.) Rumors persisted for years that the files still existed—either deep in the navy's archives, on microfilm at Jorge Eduardo Acosta's house, or possibly in a bank in a Spanish safety deposit box. In any event, a few pieces of documentary evidence were tantalizingly candid. The most significant was a list of eighty-one officers who were decorated by Adm. Massera in 1979 for their "heroic valor in combat" and included the names of most of the defendants in the case. The prosecution, with the assistance of a special unit inside the public ministry, also unearthed the defendants' personnel records shortly before the trial, long guarded deep in the navy's archives. These files showed the dispassionate nature of administrative massacre—even though the dictatorship had tried to cover all evidence of the repression, the ordinary workings of bureaucracy had left important traces. The personnel files included annual performance reviews, workers' compensation applications, pension petitions, and psychiatric care records, all of which evidenced the individual defendants' participation in the ESMA. Carlos Capdevilla, for instance, had retired from the navy in 1993 because of post-traumatic stress disorder. In March 1981 the department of military personnel of the navy wrote a memo regarding the "special situation" of five officers—including Acosta, Astiz, and Jorge Perrén—who had served in the ESMA, all of whom had missed key sailing requirements for promotion because of their position there. Both Acosta and Perrén were eventually granted a special exemption by the commander in chief of the navy from promotion requirements in 1981 for "service reasons" and were put at the front of the promotion class. The others were all similarly promoted despite their lack of required experience.

The bulk of the prosecution's evidence came from witness testimony that had been collected over the years: testimony given to human rights nongovernmental organizations (NGOs) and international bodies during the dictatorship; testimony given to the National Commission on the Status of the Disappeared (Comisión Nacional sobre la Desaparición de Personas, or CONADEP); testimony from the trial against the commanders; testimony given to the secretary of human rights; testimony from judicial investigations in Spain, Sweden, and Italy; and testimony from case files of other criminal cases around Argentina. In all, the prosecution intended to put about one hundred ESMA survivors on the stand, in addition to roughly an equal number of witnesses with some relation to the ESMA, such as family members who had looked for loved ones or bystanders to the GT 3.3/2's raids. (Unfortunately, the only ex-ESMA officer to repent and testify in court against his former colleagues, Capt. Jorge Búsico, died years before the trial began.)

Despite the long list of both defendants and victims in the case, it was hard to understand their selection. This was partly a result of the heavy and unavoidable reliance on eyewitness testimony. Without the intelligence files, there was no way to establish a documentary record of all the victims who passed through the ESMA and the officers who participated in each case. It was also a reflection of time, as many of the officers who should have been in the dock had died in the twenty-five years since the fall of the dictatorship. Finally, it reflected poor organization and inadequate investigation of the case in its pretrial phase, which fractured the investigation into multiple parts.

There were hundreds, perhaps thousands, of officers who were assigned to the GT 3.3/2, from the lowest-ranking noncommissioned officers to the highest admirals. The navy had a policy of rotating a group of officers through the GT 3.3/2 every sixty to ninety days to make sure that everyone in the navy took a turn on the so-called front lines. In practice, it was designed to ensure the navy's pact of silence. In preparation for these rotational tours of duty, officers took a training course at the Center for Instruction and Training in the War against Subversion in Puerto Belgrano, the navy's largest base located about four hundred miles south of Buenos Aires. Adm. Luis María Mendía estimated shortly before his death in 2007 that approximately two thousand of the ESMA's six thousand officers were assigned to the War against Subversion at any given time. Not one of these rotational officers had been investigated or indicted.

But even among the permanent staff of the GT 3.3/2, there were notable absences. Adm. Emilio Eduardo Massera was still alive at the time the trial began, but dementia had long set in, and he was declared unfit to stand trial. (He had been convicted in 1985, in the historic Trial of the Juntas, and sentenced to life in prison but was released five years later under Menem's pardon.) Many others had died. Adm. Luis María Mendía, who served as the chief of naval operations and authored the PLACINTARA, died in 2007 awaiting trial. Adm. Rubén Jacinto Chamorro—the head of the ESMA—died in 1986 while under investigation during the early days of the transition. He gave a dying declaration in military court from his hospital bed in defense of his actions and those of his subordinates during the Dirty War. Both Capt. Salvio Menéndez, the first commander of the GT 3.3/2, and Capt. Luis D'Imperio, who replaced Jorge Eduardo Acosta when the latter went to South Africa as a military attaché in 1979, were also dead. Capt. Jorge Perrén had been the GT 3.3/2's first chief of operations, a man who led most of the kidnapping raids during the first and most brutal years of the ESMA and later established an ESMA-sponsored spy operation in Paris designed to infiltrate exile groups in Europe; he too had died just a few years before trial in 2007. Capt. Jorge Raúl Vildoza had been the leader of the GT 3.3, just one rank below Chamorro and a rank above Acosta. Since the mid-1980s, he had been a fugitive, having disappeared with his family and a child kidnapped from a pregnant mother who gave birth inside the ESMA. Years after the trial, Vildoza's "adopted" child returned to Argentina and said his father died in South Africa, where they lived. South African police confirmed that prints of a man named Roberto Sedano, who died on May 27, 2005, matched those in the federal police registries of Vildoza in Buenos Aires. Francis Whamond, a navy captain who came out of retirement to participate in the early torture sessions at the ESMA, died in 2002.

But there were significant absences among a number of former ESMA officers who were still alive. Adms. Julio Torti and Antonio Vañek, each of whom had served as chief of naval operations during the dictatorship and were the only two naval officers who did not benefit from Alfonsín's due obedience law owing to their high rank, were both left out of the case. Adm. Edgardo Otero, who directed the ESMA in 1980, was absent. Capt. Jorge Luis Magnacco, a navy medic who oversaw the births of over a dozen children from kidnapped mothers, was not indicted in the case. (Magnacco had previously been convicted in 2005 for the kidnapping of Guillermo Pérez Roisinblit, a child born in the ESMA whose parents were murdered. The kidnapping of children was one of the few crimes not covered by the amnesty laws.) All these officers had pending criminal charges against them at the time the trial commenced, but in a last-minute decision, the prosecution and the court decided to delay the start of their cases, preferring instead to hold them in abeyance until the completion of a smaller, more manageable case.

Despite the absences, the prosecution's case was strong. The nucleus of the trial from Testimonies A was developed in the 1980s and included some of the most well-identified personnel in the military dictatorship. Save for Julio César Coronel, none of the defendants even denied that they had worked in the ESMA, and most of them openly vindicated their participation. It was based largely on historic testimony and covered well-known territory to those familiar with the ESMA and the history of the investigation.

If viewed as a whodunit, the trial was bound to be a disappointment, as the chronicle of what had happened in the ESMA was well documented. Only in a few instances did the defendants have an alibi defense. For instance, Juan Carlos Rolón, who was indicted for having participated in the disappearance of Rodolfo Walsh and the raid on the Santa Cruz Church, insisted that he was not assigned to the ESMA during either event, which happened in March and December 1977, respectively. He said he had only earlier been assigned to the ESMA for a brief rotational tour of duty at the end of 1976 and later as a permanent officer in 1978. The fact that Rolón and other officers had an alibi at all really only reflected prosecutor Taiano's poor case selection—why Rolón was not charged in cases where there was more substantial evidence still remains a mystery—rather than the defendants' moral culpability. And the fact that the prosecution and the defense might engage in a debate over whether some of the defendants were in the ESMA at a certain date on a certain time when their participation in the navy's war was all but certain reflected the gulf between humanity's moral intuitions about the perpetrators of mass atrocity and the Byzantine tools at the law's disposal.

Nevertheless, for anyone who listened attentively to the reading of the charging instruments over the first four months of trial, it was clear that the prosecution faced several significant hurdles at trial. First, an essential feature of the ESMA, based on the evidence already in the case file, was the murkiness of the lines of command and responsibility (despite the defendants' professional assurances that all was done according to regulation). Who was in charge at any given moment? Who gave orders? Who followed orders? What discretion did lower-ranking officers have? What actions were done according to the criminal "plan," and what actions were taken outside of this plan? All these factual questions were in dispute. Was Adm. Massera a significant force in the direction of the GT 3.3/2, and if so, did he consult with his subordinates in the chain of command, or did he have a direct link to the officers inside the ESMA? If he had a direct link, what was the criminal liability of the intermediate officers who had formal command responsibility over the ESMA but perhaps did not exercise command as a matter of fact? If Jorge Eduardo Acosta exercised significant discretion as the chief of intelligence of the GT 3.3/2 and at the behest of Adm. Massera, what was the criminal responsibility of his superiors? And what was the responsibility of junior officers who worked in the ESMA at a particular time but were not necessarily involved in specific criminal acts while they were there?

These questions mattered, as the prosecution had no direct eyewitness evidence linking the defendants to some of the charged crimes, so it would have to rely on a robust theory of criminal responsibility, grounded in a factual description of the operations of the command structure of the ESMA, to prove its case. In the charging instrument—not authored by the trial prosecutors, which created a number of complications for the trial team—the prosecution had become unmoored from any theoretical anchor to describe the criminal responsibility of the defendants. On the one hand, when describing the responsibility of the higher-ranking admirals in the case, Oscar Montes and Manuel Jacinto García Tallada, the prosecution alleged that the ESMA was a well-oiled and tightly structured machine, where the superior officers exercised complete and effective control over their subordinates. The prosecution rested heavily on legal theories developed by German criminal theorist Claus Roxin in the wake of World War II of an "intermediate author"—namely, that a criminal defendant could be held accountable as the direct perpetrator of a crime even though another person committed the criminal act. In cases where defendants controlled the levers of the state, their underlings were essentially fungible, and the criminal act would be completed regardless of the underling who filled a subordinate position. But in cases alleging horizontal responsibility against junior-ranking officers, the prosecution presented the ESMA more as a loose affiliation of individuals who had collectively agreed on a criminal plan to combat subversion. These two visions of criminal responsibility were not necessarily compatible, nor did the assumptions of the ESMA as either a tightly ordered machine or a loose affiliation of individuals fit neatly with the evidence in the case file. As one of the defense attorneys said to me before trial, "They can prove that crimes occurred, but they can't prove who committed them."

Second, the prosecution faced the challenge of presenting a case based almost exclusively on eyewitness testimony more than thirty years removed from the crimes, under conditions where many of the witnesses were blindfolded, did not know the names of the other victims in the ESMA, and did not know the names of the officers who were perpetrating the crimes. Under ordinary circumstances, the law tended to dismiss such belated testimony as unreliable—part of the justification for statutes of limitation was a judgment that evidence turned stale after the passage of time. In Argentina's human rights cases, however, this concern was cast aside. In reopening the cases a generation after the Dirty War, the courts had determined that under international law, the state had an obligation to investigate and prosecute perpetrators of crimes against humanity and that statutes of limitations could not serve as a bar to prosecution. But the law's judgment that crimes against humanity should never go unpunished still left the prosecution with the task of presenting its case so many years after the fact and contending with the evidentiary burden of belated prosecution.

Paradoxically, the challenge posed by eyewitness testimony in the ESMA case was both that the evidence was stale and that it was too familiar. For decades, the leading activists who pushed to reopen the ESMA trial—many of whom were survivors—had been repeating their testimony to anyone who would listen. In the absence of state investigation, they had taken to documenting what had happened on their own—compiling new testimony, sharing their stories with one another, seeking to identify new victims, assigning names and identities to victims and officers who were only known by nicknames or aliases inside the ESMA and in the earliest years following survivors' release. This process even had a name: *memoria colectiva* (collective memory). As a consequence, by the twenty-first century, much of the eyewitness testimony was muddled between firsthand experience and secondhand hearsay. So many years removed, it was virtually impossible to separate what was lived experience and what was subsequently learned.

Whether the defense, however, would be willing to press this point was an open question. The private defense attorneys, Alfredo Solari and Guillermo Coronel, were so hopelessly committed to discrediting the survivors as ideological enemies—describing their testimony as the "next phase of the revolutionary war"—that they could not trouble themselves with the more mundane questions of the epistemological clarity of the evidence.

Finally, there was the question of what, exactly, the defendants had been charged with and under what law. As a legal matter, the charging documents referenced ordinary crimes under the Argentine penal code—illegal arrest, robbery, homicide, torment, and torture. Citation to these domestic criminal statutes was meant to satisfy the most basic concept of criminal law, *nulla poena sine lege scripta*, or "no penalty without written law"—that is, the state may only prosecute crimes based on prior existing written laws of general applicability, a maxim that had generally been held to prevent prosecution based on vague laws or custom. But Argentina's national criminal code did not include any prohibition on crimes against humanity at the time the defendants' crimes took place. So pretrial prosecutor Eduardo Taiano and investigatory judge Sergio Torres had described these ordinary domestic crimes as having taken place within the "framework" of a widespread and systematic attack on a civilian population, and thus they were effectively the predicate offenses of crimes against humanity. This, they argued, provided the necessary context to strip the defendants of the benefits of any statute of limitations or amnesty, as international law proscribed any statute of limitations or amnesty over crimes against humanity.

But the prosecutors' reliance on a creature of international law effectively added an element to the defendants' crimes that was not codified in the domestic penal code, for a commission of a crime against humanity required an additional element of knowledge of a widespread or systematic attack directed at a civilian population. Surely the defendants had such knowledge—they admitted as much in arguing that their conduct was part of a war and that they were simply following orders to eradicate subversion—but the crimes for which they were indicted did not include this element.

4

Opening Silence

On March 5, 2010—almost four months after the first hearing—the clerk finished reading the charging instruments, and the trial was declared open by Chief Judge Daniel Obligado. After some superfluous motions, the proceedings began with statements from the defendants. (Argentina's legal system has its roots in the European inquisitorial model. Though legal reforms over centuries have implemented numerous protections for the accused, the system still reflects the centuries-old goal of eliciting a confession.)

There was a macabre curiosity about what the defendants would say, if anything. In the nearly thirty years since the collapse of the dictatorship, only one of these defendants had given public testimony in a court proceeding. Spectators had sat through months of the clerks' reading of the charging instruments waiting for the opening moments of the trial when the defendants would take the stand.

Adm. Oscar Montes, the retired former commander of Task Force 3, testified first. He was frail at eighty-five. A pretrial medical report noted Montes's significant health problems, including diabetes and crippling arthritis, which kept him mostly bedridden. (He served under house arrest prior to and during the trial.) While many of the defendants had abused medical diagnoses from friendly navy doctors to evade prison time, Montes was obviously impaired. As he struggled to take the stand, the clerk brought him a portable microphone and he testified from his wheelchair.

Judge Obligado opened the testimony by asking Montes about his basic biographical details, but Montes seemed to have trouble hearing.

When he finally understood the court's questions, he responded with a strained, raspy voice. However, when it came time to say a few brief words in response to the accusations, his voice turned defiant and deliberate. "I am not being judged by my natural judges," Montes told the court, arguing that the civilian tribunal lacked jurisdiction, which he believed was vested solely in military court. He refused to ratify previous testimony he had given in front of military courts in the 1980s, when he was first called to testify, and he denied all the charges against him. (He had informed his medical examiners that he wished to participate in the proceedings so that he could "assume his responsibility and demarcate the responsibility of his subordinates."[1])

As is standard under the Argentine criminal procedure, when a defendant refuses to testify at trial, the court reads prior statements from the defendant from the pretrial phase. But in Montes's case, his lawyers strenuously objected. Those statements, Montes's lawyers argued, were made in front of a military court in the 1980s, and the code of military justice encouraged Montes to testify and tell the truth—a violation, his lawyers argued, of the constitutional right against self-incrimination. Indeed, in the military justice system, it was a matter of discipline for a soldier to tell the truth in front of a military judge. The prosecution argued that the prior statements were constitutionally proper at the time and that they should still be read and incorporated at the current trial. The prosecution also argued that in any event, Montes had later ratified his military statements in front of a civilian court, thus sanitizing the constitutional deficiencies of any of his prior statements.

It was not a mere lawyerly dispute; the prosecution's case against Montes rested in large part on these prior statements. There was little direct evidence against Montes that tied him to the crimes in the charging instruments, but in a series of statements given in military court in 1985 and 1986, Montes had admitted that he visited the Naval Mechanics School (ESMA) for periodic inspections, both scheduled and surprise. While Montes denied in those statements that anyone was tortured in the ESMA, he admitted that he "always found that the orders which I gave under the PLACINTARA [Capacity Plan of the Navy (Plan de Capacidades de la Armada)] had been strictly complied with."[2] The admission was significant in two respects: first, that

Montes had repeatedly visited the ESMA, where he had inspected the operations and intelligence facilities of the Grupo de Tareas (GT) 3.3/2, and second, that he placed himself squarely within the chain of command, meaning that he could not escape liability by arguing that his superior, Adm. Massera, had circumvented the chain of command through his direct contact with Capt. Acosta, his subordinate.

After a tense exchange between the prosecution and the defense over the issue, the court sided with Montes's lawyers, determining that Montes's unequivocal denial of the charges against him constituted a response to the charges, negating the need to read his prior statements.

Adolfo Donda was next. He complained that "none of my bosses are being prosecuted in this case; none of them are here," citing the absence of both Jorge Vildoza and Luciano Becerra, his immediate superiors. His voice cracked as he spoke. He told the court in great detail about the structure of the navy and his allegedly small role in the Dirty War. He said, "This was an institutional fight, the whole navy participated, and I'm here on my own."[3] To underscore the point, he calculated that there were over twenty-five hundred superior-ranking officers above him during the dictatorship. He argued that he was part of the "last chapter"—an allusion to his position as chief of operations during the lighter years of repression in 1979 and 1980—but said the "book's protagonists aren't here." Like Montes, he skirted saying anything about the substance of the charges, refusing to speak in any detail about the victims or addressing any of the accusations head-on. Instead, he told the court he wasn't afraid to convey "[his] truth." So he devoted considerable attention to his personal saga—his brother had been a Montonero, and the victims had long accused him of turning his brother over to the ESMA. He said that in fact, his brother's participation in the Montoneros had caused him troubles. He recalled being cited twice by the Servicio de Inteligencia Naval (SIN), the navy's intelligence service, in the early 1970s. He said that he was still searching for his brother and for answers. "Each one of us took our own path, had our own destiny," he put it mildly. While the issue was completely beside the point—his brother's disappearance was not one of the charges at issue in the case—it was hard to take his account seriously, as his fellow defendant, Juan Antonio Azic, had raised his brother's daughter as his own after his sister-in-law gave birth inside the ESMA and was later killed.

Carlos Capdevilla followed. Like Montes, he was in poor health. He was a recovering cancer patient and suffered severe clinical depression. The medication seemed to impair his full cognitive abilities; on the stand he slurred his words. He warned the court that he tended to forget things but managed to offer a response. As a navy medic, Capdevilla says it was his job to look after the three hundred or so officers who were in the GT 3.3/2, where he was assigned in 1979. He was accused of monitoring torture victims in six instances to ensure that the torture did not kill them. He offered a general denial that he did not know the medical parameters to control a torture session so could not have been guilty as charged. But he also offered more specific defenses. Three of the victims he was accused of torturing had been captured by the ESMA in 1977 and 1978, a period of time, Capdevilla said, when he was not in the ESMA. In the case of victim Thelma Jara de Cabezas, he also said that he was not guilty, as she had previously testified in the 1985 Trial of the Juntas that there were only three people in the torture room when she was tortured, whereas in 1986 she identified a "Tomy" (the slang in the ESMA for a doctor) in the room, an inconsistency that Capdevilla insisted called into question her credibility. Likewise, in the case of victim Víctor Basterra, Basterra had testified that he suffered two heart attacks during his torture session, which Capdevilla monitored. Capdevilla said this would have been impossible and that Basterra could not have identified him if he suffered two such grave medical events.

Most of the rest of the defendants followed a similar pattern. Manuel Jacinto García Tallada, Juan Antonio Azic, Alberto González, Ernesto Weber, and Pablo Eduardo García Velasco all refused to testify or gave only short and curt denials of the charges.

Ricardo Cavallo, who was the only defendant who regularly attended court hearings as he judiciously transcribed the proceedings and circulated blog posts about the trial, read from a lengthy fifty-thousand-word prepared statement, going over the history of terrorism in Argentina and the procedural irregularities in the case.

Jorge Eduardo Acosta gave a rambling speech, recounting small points in his own biography (highlights: he never tortured animals as a youth, he "terribly loved" children), attacking the judiciary, criticizing witnesses, urging reconciliation in Argentina, describing the historical context of the dictatorship, and describing the ESMA in comparison to other wings of the armed forces ("the [GT] 3.3/2 never looked for death").[4] It was all delivered in a flat tone that would have put the audience to sleep if they were not otherwise fascinated with his scattered presentation.

In a series of long-winded letters addressed to his attorneys and filed shortly before the trial commenced, he explained that the charges against him were all lies, invented by ex-Montonero guerrillas who had collaborated with the ESMA task force and later invented terrible stories about what happened in the ESMA in order to rehabilitate their image in front of their old *compañeros* and justify their survival. (No reason was ever given for why these privileged attorney-client communications were filed with the court.) Based on these myths, Acosta explained, a few members of the naval elite met with the Alfonsín administration during the transition and decided that responsibility would fall on a "small number of people for what they hadn't and couldn't have done, with the political objective of resolving a very serious problem on the basis of myths, and many years after their occurrence." Every successive administration, whether from the Radical or Peronist Party, had taken political advantage of "destroying the image of the armed forces" based on these lies and myths. He was convinced from the outset that a trial would end in nothing but a conviction, as the trials were simply a continuation of the "revolutionary war."[5]

It was Alfredo Astiz who gave the most rousing and best attended of the opening statements. He barely mentioned the charges against him but used two hours to denounce the court, to lecture on military and constitutional law, to denounce the victims, and to pay homage to junior officers who had been indicted since the trials were reopened in 2003. He spent a long time expounding his theory that "state terrorism" could not exist because, by definition, *terrorism* was aimed at the state, to subvert the existing order, so the state could never perpetrate terrorism. Such a concept was an oxymoron in Astiz's estimation.

Astiz believed that he would have received a fair trial had he been brought before his "natural" judges in military courts (i.e., those authorized under the military code of justice), but he lamented that he was doomed to conviction because of the political pressure on the civilian courts; he insisted that Pres. Néstor Kirchner's nominees to the Supreme Court meant he was sure to be convicted. He called Kirchner's appointment of a majority of the Supreme Court between 2003 and 2005 a "true coup d'état" without the slightest hint of irony.[6]

While the opening statements dragged on for a month, providing small moments of dramatic intrigue as these Dirty Warriors spoke in public for the first time, very little was actually said. A few nearly inaudible blips crystalized the broader silence. Antonio Pernías—the only defendant to accept a series of questions from the prosecution—made three astonishing admissions during his cross-examination by Dr. Mirna Goransky: he called the disappearance of two French nuns who supported the Mothers of the Plaza de Mayo "an error and a horror," the most anyone would say about the episode; he confessed that Rodolfo Walsh had died in a firefight, though he claimed that he had nothing to do "with the issue"; and he revealed in a moment of off-guard candor that one of the victims, Ana María Ponce, "was dead."[7] These statements, of course, were not news—after thirty years, it was clear the disappeared were dead—but his admission was shocking because of his momentary and fleeting truthfulness. No military officer had ever admitted with such candor what had happened to any of the disappeared.

Still, Pernías's small admissions seemed to offer a cynical and calculated provocation. When prosecutor Goransky asked Pernías how he knew that Ponce was dead, Pernías stopped simply at the fact of her demise; when asked if he knew where she had gone, he demurred and would not further entertain Goransky's questions. As he held on to the information, he sneered at both the prosecutor and the activists sitting behind the bulletproof glass wall separating the spectators from the courtroom floor.

Pernías insisted that he had decided to testify and answer questions because he wanted to be truthful, that he was more interested in leaving a statement for history than in contributing to his own defense, which he argued was a lost cause. To illustrate the point, Pernías placed a copy of Plato's *Apology* on the desk at the witness stand, apparently comparing his ordeal to that of Socrates during his final days. But a pure martyr he was not—he seemed to relish his power over the assembled spectators. In his mind, he was surely in the last phase of the war, and nobody could force him to disclose details that he was unwilling to offer.

Over nearly a month of testimony, the defendants conveyed the same limp clichés that they had been spewing for a generation. Raúl Enrique Scheller—one of the accused torturers—defended his conduct. "Thirty-six years ago the commander in chief of the armed forces—the constitutional president—exhorted the military to 'exterminate the psychopaths one by one for the good of the country,'" Scheller told the court. (He seemed unmoved by the internal contradiction of saying, on the one hand, that all the accusers against him were liars and, on the other hand, that he obeyed orders and did what he did for the good of the fatherland.) But he also stressed that he was just an ordinary soldier who lived an ordinary life. "There was never a unit or position in the navy where you went voluntarily, and nothing was different about the Unidad de Tareas 3.3.2. It was just another position. I went where I was ordered to go," he said.[8]

In the twenty years since their cases were dropped in the 1980s after the due obedience and full stop laws were passed, few of the defendants had voluntarily spoken about the Dirty War, even when fully protected by an amnesty and even when they had insisted on reconciliation. When they were set free in 1987, they were released unconditionally, without a demand for anything in return. They had been allowed to walk the streets, to live their lives, to go to the movies, to frolic in the park, to enjoy their families, to pursue their hobbies, and to enjoy their liberty like any other citizen. Many even enjoyed lengthy careers in the military after the collapse of the dictatorship. Antonio Pernías and Juan Carlos Rolón were only forced from the navy in 1994—eleven years after the dictatorship fell and seven years after they were amnestied—when their promotions went before the Argentine Senate and they were questioned about their use of torture in the ESMA. Néstor Savio somehow escaped public oversight and stayed in the navy until 2003, climbing easily up the promotional ladder in spite of (or perhaps because of) his participation in the dictatorship's repression. Some had been forced into an early retirement, but it was still a retirement—they collected their pensions (some even received hazard pay bonuses for their years in "combat") and found moonlighting opportunities in private industry to lead comfortable lives. Juan Carlos Fotea found obscurity as a hotelier in Spain. A few had offered shreds of an explanation in the 1990s while impunity reigned. But in general their posture had been silence.

Their statements on the stand proved no exception. As a legal matter, this was entirely unobjectionable, even predictable—they were constitutionally guaranteed the right to refuse to testify and even granted the right to lie on the stand if they wanted.

But their silence wasn't the silence of ordinary criminals, as if they were making reasoned choices about the risks of self-incrimination. Rather, theirs was a political silence—a mute statement of principle that their shared refusal to divulge any meaningful details of what they had done was the best course for their country, that a cloak of amnesia and obfuscation over the fate of the disappeared was the best way to move the country into the future. For three decades they had rebuffed attempts to clarify and uncover what they had done; they remained mute about the fate of their victims, falling back instead on cliché defenses that what they had done was all part of a war.

The tone of the defendants' statements, for those who chose to speak, was lecture rather than legal defense, as if they had any moral standing to claim how their fate should be decided. "Article 18 of the National Constitution—indeed, all the guarantees in the constitution—can now be disposed of by any present or future tyrant," Scheller warned the court in discussing the danger of the retroactive application of criminal law.[9] Where one hoped for humility, one found audacity; where one hoped for sorrow, one found boastfulness; where one hoped for repentance, one found disinterest. They were not "silent" in the sense that they refused to talk. They were silent in the sense that their rambling lectures revealed next to nothing about what Argentina needed as a community, politically, to move past the Dirty War, which was some honest recognition on the part of the military about what had happened. They had never failed to take an opportunity to chide the court and the human rights movement for playing politics with law, but their reaction to their indictments had been no less politically charged.

How had the defendants maintained such disciplined silence over so many years? In the 1970s the military commenced a calculated strategy to project the image of an orderly fight against "subversion" and prevent the public from knowing the details of the viciousness of the means to "annihilate subversion." Indeed, one of the first acts of the military junta was to clamp down on any information that might hinder its freedom of action in the War against Subversion. Communiqué 19, issued through the newspapers and on the radio on the day of the military coup, warned citizens of a ten-year prison sentence for "any media which spreads, divulges or propagates news, communiqués or images with the intention of disturbing, prejudicing or discrediting the armed forces or police." The same communiqué also established a punishment of "indefinite detention" for any media news source that published or distributed press releases or images that could be attributed to subversive groups.[10]

For the military secrecy was essential, and once their "war" had ended, they insisted that the country forget. This was not a mafia-style cover-up, as if their interest in ignoring the fate of the disappeared was to hide their crimes and not be caught. Obliterating the past was a moral imperative. "Our difficulties," Adm. Ramón Arosa would later say, "should be settled so that the epilogue is the reunion of all Argentines through the forgetting of mutual grievances."[11] Reconciliation was the goal, but not reconciliation based on the truth about torture and extermination, justice for these crimes, and a request for forgiveness. It was reconciliation based on a claim that the military, guided by the church, understood the best way to preserve social harmony. They wanted the citizenry to overlook the "errors" of the past to live a better tomorrow.

The military's insistence on looking away from the Dirty War was as essential to its terror as the violence itself. It was part of its effort to recreate Argentina, to recover its "Western and Christian values," and to fend off a resurgence of violent and atheist subversion that had threatened the Argentine way of life and, in their view, nearly destroyed the country. The past had to be forgotten because the violent uprisings of the early 1970s did not fit with the military's moralized image of Argentina as an ordered Catholic nation, a land of destiny, where each member of each social class—the workers, clergy, military, politicians, *el campo*, businesspeople—knew their place and worked cooperatively to make the *patria* a great land. This arrangement, based on discipline, national pride, self-recognition, a doctrinaire (and misguided) belief in Christ, an understanding of the limits of politics, and a proper reverence for the armed forces, made their far-off land so much more than a country at the end of the earth. If the disappeared became martyrs, so the military's logic went, then so too would their beliefs. Emotions could be stoked to harbor resentment; resentment, in turn, would turn to political confrontation; confrontation could be manipulated by foreign agents of subversion; and the entire dramatic cycle of civil war would repeat. "The pain of Argentine families cannot be utilized to distort the reality of what happened nor to serve as an explanation for the unexplainable," army chief of staff Eduardo Viola announced in 1980, as if any public discussion of the violence and repression of the Dirty War was nothing more than an attempt to sew division and attack the armed forces—and hence attack Argentina itself.[12]

From the military's perspective, their civilian interlocutors never appreciated that they did not seek a "cover-up," the idea implying that the officers acted as criminals hiding traces of their crimes. The military men insisted they felt the anguish of the family members of those who they had vanquished—the fallen, too, were Argentines—but the proper place for mourning those who were gone was in private, in the home, in the sphere of true and authentic emotions that would not be exploited. "As a Christian and an Argentine, I feel the pain that war and its unfortunate consequences have left in our hearts," dictator Jorge Rafael Videla wrote to a civilian court on the eve of being judged, after overseeing the slaughter of thousands of his compatriots. "I pray to God that this will be the final price that we have to pay to assure authentic national union, peace, and freedom."[13]

The defendants' refusal to provide details reflected a firmly held belief that the confessional, and not the courtroom, was the only place to speak. It was unbecoming—even undignified—to speak of their violence in a public forum. This, of course, reflected a clear limit of the law: the courtroom could not force the defendants to speak, could not change their pernicious ideology. In the face of such obfuscation, though, the law had a simple response—to consider contrary evidence and weigh it accordingly.

5

Trials before the Trial

The Naval Mechanics School (ESMA) trial had a dizzying procedural history. The year 2009 was not the first time that the eighteen men in the dock had appeared in court. The trial, such as it was, was not the result of a single coherent investigation but constructed from bits and pieces that had been cobbled together and separated time and again: allegations in the press lodged as part of the Montoneros' propaganda campaign to expose the crimes of the military regime in the 1970s; hundreds of habeas corpus petitions that were filed during the dictatorship and archived by the courts; denunciations filed with human rights groups, the Inter-American Commission on Human Rights, the United Nations (UN), and the National Commission on the Status of the Disappeared (CONADEP); criminal cases initiated by civilian judges in the convulsive days before and after the transition; an investigation by the military courts in the mid-1980s as part of Raúl Alfonsín's transitional strategy of funneling cases into the military courts; truth trial investigations from the 1990s; dozens of press reports and investigations into the ESMA in the three decades since the collapse of the military government; a series of cases involving economic crimes and the kidnapping of children that were held outside the scope of the amnesty laws; investigations abroad, most notably by Spanish judge Baltasar Garzón; and the investigation by prosecutors and judges since the repeal of the amnesty laws in 2003. The trial that started in 2009, with eighteen defendants and eighty-six victims, reflected this tumultuous procedural history. For more than thirty years, the case had a start-and-stop quality as political pressures, intransigence from the military, and fatigue crippled the investigation.

As the navy would have liked it, there never would have been a trial. But they could not keep the Grupo de Tareas (GT) 3.3/2's activities secret; it was only months after the March 24, 1976, military coup that the ESMA was first identified as a clandestine prison. Owing to the scope of the ESMA's covert undertakings and its central location in the city of Buenos Aires, *militantes* and informed human rights activists quickly heard rumors about what transpired inside. The voluminous and yellowing pages of the case file—chaotically wrapped in hundreds of separate chronologically ordered files, each anachronistically and ritualistically bound with string—attest to the slow but inevitable leak of this information.

The first information to attract limited public attention came from the counterpropaganda initiatives of the Montonero guerrillas. A small group of guerrilla journalists led by Rodolfo Walsh, the renowned investigative journalist turned guerrilla, founded a news agency called the Agencia de Noticias Clandestina (ANCLA) shortly after the 1976 military coup. They distributed crude mimeographed reports in an effort to disseminate censored information. In November 1976 Walsh and his colleagues published the "Secret History of the Dirty War," one of the first reports to provide an inside look at the ESMA, based on Walsh's military and police sources cultivated over two decades of reporting. "The Naval Mechanics School is performing operations beyond its jurisdiction," Walsh reported. "Some of these are done with uniforms, others in civilian clothing, with unidentifiable vehicles with the assistance of the 39th and 45th police precincts."[1] To obtain information for this report, Walsh had cultivated a source inside the ESMA, Sergio Tarnopolsky, who served as an assistant to Jorge Eduardo Acosta while he was a naval conscript. In retaliation for Tarnopolsky's betrayal, the navy disappeared Sergio as well as his parents, Hugo and Blanca; his fifteen-year-old sister, Betina; and his wife, Laura de Luca.[2]

Four months later, on the first anniversary of the military coup, Walsh distributed his prophetic "Open Letter to the Military Junta," a wide-ranging denunciation of the junta (ignored by the mainstream press). Walsh listed "15,000 disappeared, 10,000 prisoners, 4,000 dead, tens of thousands exiled" as "the naked statistics" of the dictatorship's terror. He explained, "With the ordinary prisons full, you have created virtual concentration camps in the principal military bases throughout the country, where no judge, lawyer, journalist or international observer can enter." Walsh cited "more than 7,000 habeas corpuses [that] have been rejected in the last year. In thousands of other cases of disappearances the petitions haven't even been presented because it is already known that they are worthless or because there are no lawyers willing to file them after 50 or 60 lawyers have themselves been kidnapped for doing so." It was the first exposé of the systematic repression of the armed forces—detainees being held incommunicado, executions and mass graves, and the widespread use of the *picana electrica*. Though the military junta had taken power promising to end the two terrorisms, of the left and the right, Walsh denounced the junta as "itself the source of terror."[3]

Walsh's works were not widely cited at the time, owing to Walsh's untimely demise (he was killed while distributing the open letter), the difficulty of distributing information, and the ANCLA's association with the Montoneros. But more accounts about the ESMA soon corroborated Walsh's early reports. In March 1978, a year after Walsh disappeared, Horacio Domingo Maggio escaped from the ESMA. After establishing contact with his Montonero superiors, Maggio distributed a letter about his yearlong detention. In one of the first public accounts from a survivor, Maggio told of torture by an electric cattle prod, scarce food, and days spent hooded and shackled on mattresses in the attic of the officers' club. "When we had to urinate," Maggio wrote, "they brought us a bucket, and they gave us two to three seconds to do it; obviously this was impossible, so we always wetted our mattresses, for which we were beaten." In addition to lucid and horrifying details, he reported the rumors that the prisoners heard about those who had been "transferred" out of the center. In the early months of the dictatorship, Maggio wrote, officers stuffed six or seven people in a car, shot the car with bullets, and then burned the car; later he said that boats left from the ESMA to dump prisoners into the Río de la Plata; finally, he stated that the navy drugged prisoners, wrapped them in burlap sacks, and pushed them out of airplanes into the ocean.[4]

More denunciations followed, and a trickle of information soon turned into a steady stream, and then into a flood. Jaime Dri, a former high-ranking Montonero who was captured by a joint command of the Uruguayan Army and Argentine Navy at the end of 1977, escaped from the ESMA in July 1978, the only other prisoner among thousands of captives to do so. He released a statement shortly thereafter published by the Montoneros that reiterated much of what Maggio and Walsh had said before him.[5] In 1979 three ESMA survivors who had been released the year before—Sara Solarz de Osatinsky, Ana María Martí, and Alicia Milia de Pirles—gave a joint statement to the French Parliament about the state of human rights in Argentina. Running over seventy pages, the testimony from these survivors went into vivid detail about the ESMA's operations from 1976 to 1979, naming dozens of victims who were presumed to have been killed, dozens of other survivors, and nearly one hundred officers who were associated with the ESMA's repressive activities.[6] The women spent weeks before the testimony meeting with other recently freed and exiled prisoners from the ESMA, compiling as much information as they could muster to put into a denunciation. The testimony serves as one of the most extensive early repositories of what happened in the ESMA and has served as a reference point for decades. These early denunciations are full of minor errors—bastardized names of military officers who were not perfectly identified at the time ("Pernia" instead of "Pernías," for example) and only the nicknames of dozens of victims—reflecting the incompleteness of the information that seeped out of the ESMA in the earliest days of the repression and the strained circumstances in which it was collected.

Hundreds of habeas corpus petitions preceded and followed these public complaints. Almost without exception the judicial response to these petitions followed a predictable pattern. The judge to whom the petition was addressed would send requests to the army, navy, air force, police, minister of the interior, coast guard, and president's office for information on the missing person based on allegations in the petition. These various government agencies would send back a negative response, indicating that the person was not being held by that government agency. Without further questions to the government, the judges would then reject the habeas corpus petition. In some cases, the judges remitted the cases to prosecutors to begin an investigation for a "presumptive kidnapping," but in general the petitions were archived and forgotten. Even though some judges received hundreds of these petitions—clearly indicating a widespread pattern of kidnapping and illegal detention—they conveniently looked away. The military dictatorship required judges sitting on the bench to pledge allegiance to the military junta, and judges responded in kind by not interfering in the government's repression.[7]

Even in high-profile cases, such as the 1977 disappearance of the dual Swedish-Argentine national Dagmar Hagelin, the courts closed their doors. Hagelin, just seventeen at the time of her disappearance, was mistaken for another Montonero activist when she went to visit her friend Norma Burgos, who had been disappeared by the ESMA the day before. When Hagelin tried to flee from her apparent captors, they shot her and stuffed her in a car. Alfredo Astiz, the man responsible for infiltrating the Mothers of the Plaza de Mayo, was apparently responsible for the shot. Victims later recalled seeing her in the ESMA nearly dead; she has not been seen since. When Hagelin's father, Ragnar, filed a criminal complaint in 1979—backed by the Swedish government—the civilian judge declined jurisdiction and referred the case file to a military court-martial. In a secret proceeding, the military courts absolved both Astiz and Antonio Pernías of responsibility in the episode (the only two officers identified at that point as having participated in the raid) and declared the case closed.[8] When activists again tried to file a case in civilian courts after the transition to democracy, the military introduced the secret file from the military court and argued that the case was already closed.[9]

Despite the predictable failure of filing a habeas petition, there was a logic to doing so. The contemporaneous denunciations were designed to leave a paper trail once civilian rule returned.

Indeed, by the early 1980s, it was hard for the courts to ignore the petitions. By 1982, when the dictatorship's popularity collapsed in the wake of the disastrous Falklands War, it was impossible for judges to ignore the fate of the disappeared. The ESMA case file is filled with over a dozen investigations into the ESMA *before* the political transition. (Many judges used human rights opportunistically to solidify good graces with future civilian rulers by aggressively targeting military officers, as it proved convenient to do so during the military's disastrous retreat in 1983.[10]) During this convulsive period, judges who served the courts under military rule cited some of the most well-identified ESMA officers to testify, including junta members Adms. Emilio Eduardo Massera and Armando Lambruschini, Vice Adm. Rubén Jacinto Chamorro, and Capts. Salvio Menéndez and Jorge Eduardo Acosta.[11] These early investigations uncovered that the ESMA task force had not only targeted supposed "subversives," as the dictatorship always maintained, but used its power to enact revenge on political opponents of the navy and human rights activists who threatened the regime. The mysterious murders of Héctor Hidalgo Solá—an ambassador to Venezuela who was close to Gen. Videla—and Elena Holmberg—a political officer in Argentina's Paris embassy—drew attention to Adm. Emilio Eduardo Massera and the ESMA henchmen who were allegedly responsible for the killings. The murders suggested that Massera used the Dirty War to further his political career. Solá was reportedly killed after his name was floated as a possible civilian transitional president, a plan that threatened to derail Massera's own ambitions; Holmberg, apparently, was killed after she discovered a meeting between the Montoneros' leadership and Adm. Massera in France to broker a truce between the groups. (Both cases to this day remain shrouded in mystery.) By 1982 Alfredo Astiz had also been identified as the naval officer responsible for the kidnapping of human rights activists from the Santa Cruz Church in December 1977, showing the ruthlessness of the ESMA officers who targeted mothers seeking information on their missing children. The henchmen of the ESMA became the primary targets of these early investigations, backed by an aggressive media campaign against the regime. (Never mind that the press had also remained pliant and silent for years as these crimes transpired.)

Largely in response to the ESMA investigations and the threat of criminal proceedings, the military junta issued in April 1983 its "Final Document of the Military Junta on the War against Subversion and Terrorism." The document was issued on the same day the junta called for national elections, signaling to incoming civilians that it would have no tolerance for investigations into its conduct during the Dirty War. In the most soaring Orwellian language, the junta announced that it "assumed its historic responsibility before the Nation," but no names of the missing were given, and no names of officers were provided. To the extent that there was a problem related to the disappeared, the military explained, "In every armed conflict it is difficult to give complete details. In classic warfare there are many *desaparecidos*. In a war where the enemy doesn't use a uniform and their identification documents are fake, the number of unidentifiable dead increases significantly." The military did admit that "in the apocalyptic context of the fight against subversion, mistakes were made, which may have gone beyond the limits of respect for the most fundamental human rights, as is the case in every armed conflict." But they told the citizenry that it would be "up to God and the conscience and understanding of men to judge."[12]

Accompanying the final document, the military issued an "institutional act" that declared, "All operations against subversion in the national territory brought forth by the Armed Forces and the Security, Police, and Penitentiary Forces . . . were executed in accordance with the plans approved and supervised by the appropriate superior commands of the armed forces, and by the Military Junta from the time it was formed" and hence could not be investigated by the courts. This was accompanied by an order to destroy all documentation related to the War against Subversion.[13]

Six months later in September 1983, on the eve of national elections, the military issued a self-amnesty law. Called a "law of national pacification," it prevented any court from inquiring into the official acts of a military officer during the repression. The law also extended to "subversives" who remained in the country and could still be investigated. (James Nielsen, a lucid commentator for the *Buenos Aires Herald*, said, "It is as though Adolf Hitler, with admirable impartiality, had declared an amnesty affecting Jews and SS officers alike when the Red Army was penetrating Berlin and the British and Americans were sweeping in from the West."[14])

Many of the cases opened in 1982 and 1983 came to a grinding halt with the passage of the military's self-amnesty law—the judges who served under the military regime found themselves in a tenuous position trying to divine the preferences of incoming civilian leaders. Criticism of the military's attempt to close investigations was swift and loud. But society's disgust did not coalesce into firm opposition, and the choice between confronting the military and "moving on" became a central issue of the presidential campaign in the last days of the election. Ítalo Lúder, the candidate for the Peronist Party, said that although he did not support the amnesty law, "its effects would be irreversible, given that in penal law you apply the most benign law."[15] Radical Party candidate Raúl Alfonsín, on the other hand, pledged that he would repeal the self-amnesty law and send the military officers responsible for the Dirty War to court.

The military gambled on Lúder's election and ignored the possibility of a Radical Party victory. Indeed, the Peronists outnumbered the Radicals by a margin of almost two to one, and they had never lost a national election in which they were free to participate.[16] ("Being the presidential candidate of the Peronist Party carries the certainty of being president of the Republic," Lúder bragged after his nomination as the Peronist candidate.[17]) But Alfonsín tapped into a desire among the Argentine people that transcended party politics by articulating a liberal and tolerant vision for the country and courted a generation of youth who had never voted. (It had been ten years since elections were last held.) He drew enormous crowds with what was a moderate—and therefore revolutionary—message: tolerance, civility, and the rule of law. As if to remind the Argentine people that they were capable of more than crass populism and military authoritarianism, he routinely cited the preamble of the Argentine constitution in his stump speech. In September 1983 Alfonsín was catapulted to the presidency in a startling upset.

Euphoria swept Argentina in the wake of Alfonsín's victory. The arts exploded: movie theaters that sat empty under the heavy weight of censorship during the dictatorship filled, and displays of public art popped up all over Buenos Aires.[18] One such display—*Tribute to Democracy*—was a replica of Rome's Parthenon constructed entirely out of books. Subtlety was not the piece's strong suit. Then again, neither was the forceful return of civilian rule.

In his first official act as president, Alfonsín convened a military court-martial for the nine members of the first three military juntas that ruled Argentina from 1976 to 1983. In blunt terms his decree ordering their prosecution stated clearly what the military had long denied:

> The military junta that usurped the government of the nation on March 24, 1976, alongside the military commanders who were functioning at the time, devised and implemented a plan of operations against subversive and terrorist activity that was based on methods and procedures that were manifestly illegal. . . . Between 1976 and 1979, approximately, thousands of people were illegally deprived of their liberty, tortured, and killed as a result of the application of the combat procedures, inspired by the totalitarian "doctrine of national security."[19]

The decree argued that prosecuting the military commanders would reaffirm the fundamental rights of citizens and solidify an independent justice system, both of which were necessary preconditions of "the restoration of democratic life." But, Alfonsín argued, wide-scale prosecutions would be counterproductive, as

> all inhabitants of the country, and especially the junior officers in the armed forces, were exposed to an intense and prolonged campaign of psychological action determined to establish an idea of "anarchic agents of subversion," a diffuse category that encompasses not only the real terrorists but also the mere dissidents, and even those who limited themselves to criticizing the methods employed, who deserved being placed outside of society and even deprived of their human condition, and reduced to objects without legal protection.

As a consequence, Alfonsín believed that lower-ranking officers were, in many cases, driven "to an error about the legal and moral significance of their acts under the coercive system to which they were subjected" and that they should be spared from prosecution.[20]

The same day, Alfonsín sent a package of bills to Congress to reform the code of military justice to implement his transitional strategy. His package included three significant reforms: (1) to repeal the military's self-amnesty law so as to move forward with criminal trials against the military officers responsible for the Dirty War; (2) to create a rebuttable presumption that junior officers who had committed criminal acts did so under superior orders, hence giving them the right to a due obedience defense; and (3) to create an avenue of appeal from any decision of the military justice system in the federal court of criminal appeals to give some civilian oversight to the military justice system.

Congress, however, made two important amendments to Alfonsín's initiative. First, it passed a law giving the federal appeals courts jurisdiction over the Dirty War trials in case of unnecessary or undue delay in the military courts, ensuring that there would be civilian oversight over the military justice system. Second, it carved out an exception to Alfonsín's desired due obedience defense for "atrocious and abhorrent acts." This second amendment seriously undermined Alfonsín's desire to limit the scope of prosecutions, as virtually every action in the Dirty War could be considered "atrocious and abhorrent," so the investigations proceeded with little clarity as to the scope of how many officers might be indicted.[21]

Parallel to prosecutions Alfonsín also insisted that the truth of the Dirty War and the repression be uncovered, and so shortly after signing Decree 158/83, he convened a blue-ribbon panel of notables to inquire into the fate of the disappeared, known as the CONADEP. The commission was designed to take testimony from all over the country and to establish what happened to the thousands who had gone missing. The commission was given a tight deadline—just nine months to collect testimony and issue a report.

Alfonsín's program began to bear fruit nine months after he was elected, when the CONADEP released its *Nunca más* (Never Again) report. The commissioners received testimony from fourteen hundred people; identified or inspected 340 locations that had been recognized as secret detention centers; traveled to fifteen different provinces to take testimony from survivors and relatives of the disappeared; traveled to other countries in Latin America and Europe to visit exiles; collected DNA samples from relatives of the missing to deposit in Durand Hospital to try to identify infants and babies who had gone missing during the Dirty War; received help from foreign governments and the United Nations; and collected testimony from military officers who had been close to the repression.[22]

Summarizing its fifty thousand pages of evidence, the *Nunca más* report definitively put to rest the propaganda and obfuscation that the dictatorship had propagated for seven years. The report identified 8,960 people who remained missing at the end of the dictatorship and said that given the limited time frame in which the commissioners worked, the actual number was probably higher. (Human rights groups have always maintained that the number of missing persons is thirty thousand.) As if there were any lingering doubt, the commission dispelled the military commanders' claims that the violence of the Dirty War was the result of supposed "excesses." "The armed forces responded to the terrorists' crimes with a terrorism far worse than the one they were combatting," novelist and commission member Ernesto Sabato wrote in the prologue. "After March 24, 1976, they could count on the power and impunity of an absolute state, which they misused to abduct, torture, and kill thousands of human beings." It was, in the estimation of the commission, "the greatest and most savage tragedy in the history of Argentina." In 430 pages the CONADEP convincingly outlined the "systematic atrocities" committed by the regime, including torture, murder, and the disappearance of hundreds of infants who were snatched from their parents' hands and shuttled away to families who were sympathetic toward the military.[23]

Four months later a trial against the nine commanders from the first three juntas of the military regime began in Buenos Aires before the National Chamber of Criminal and Correctional Appeals. (The judges had invoked jurisdiction over the case from the military courts after the officers stalled the proceedings for nearly a year. "It was a disaster," one of the architects of Alfonsín's transitional strategy recalled to me in confidence years later, regretting his belief that the military would ever be capable of judging its own officers.) Prosecutor Julio Strassera and his chief assistant, Luis Moreno Ocampo, selected a representative sample of cases from around the country to bring to trial to prove that the commanders had orchestrated a systematic criminal plan, using testimony from the CONADEP as a means to select their cases. Their case was elegantly simple. Though there was little evidence that the commanders had directly participated in the repression, the prosecutors marshaled a case based on the theory that the volume and uniformity of the crimes suggested that the plan was orchestrated at the top ranks of the military and that the defendants could be held criminally liable as the direct authors of the crimes. They argued that during seven years of military rule, there were numerous cases of illegal disappearances, most followed by torture and homicide; that the people committing these crimes acted under the orders of the defendants; that despite a lack of written orders, the repression followed a uniform pattern throughout the country, indicating direction at the highest levels of the armed forces; that the disappeared were taken to clandestine centers that were under the control of one of the three branches of the armed forces commanded by the defendants; that the defendants submitted the disappeared to brutal treatment while in these centers; that the people overseeing the repression and torture had the authority to, and in many cases did, execute the prisoners; that in many cases, the prisoners had their worldly possessions robbed by their captors; that the defendants maintained the repressive apparatus despite numerous objections from foreign governments, the Organization of American States, and the United Nations; that thousands of individual habeas corpus cases had lapsed in the judiciary, which did not follow up on official denials by the executive branch about the whereabouts of thousands of missing citizens under their control; and that members of the armed forces who had objected to the practices of illegal repression were dismissed or, worse still, made into victims of the very tactics they protested against.[24]

Day after day witnesses paraded through the courtroom and told gruesome and tragic stories of what had happened in the dictatorship's secret detention camps. Witnesses came from all over Argentina and from nearly every walk of life. Ítalo Lúder, the former provisional president who signed the decrees to "annihilate subversion," told the court that the decrees in no way meant "physical annihilation or violation of the legal structure of the country. . . . The decrees in no way endorsed repression outside of the law." Theo van Boven, the former UN commissioner on human rights, told the court of the thousands of complaints that the UN received in its investigation of the armed forces in Argentina and said that there had been a "deliberate force to hide the truth." Jacobo Timerman, the famous author of *Prisoner without a Name, Cell without a Number*, told of the confiscation of his newspaper and the antisemitic treatment he received under the power of Gen. Ramón Camps, the butcher who ran the Buenos Aires police force and was one of the dictatorship's most vocal apologists. Clyde Snowe, an American forensic anthropologist, told the court that he had analyzed the cases of unidentified ("ningún nombre," or NN) burials in Argentina from 1976 to 1979 and that they showed a significant increase in young and female deceased, indicating that one of the government's tactics had been to bury their enemies' bodies in municipal grave sites. Adriana Calvo de Laborde testified of her monthslong detention in La Plata. She was kidnapped from her home while six and a half months pregnant and with an infant at home. She was beaten, tortured, and held blinded and handcuffed for months. Eventually, she went into labor and gave birth in the back seat of a police car as they rushed her from the prison. Pablo Diaz told of his arrest when he was just sixteen years old; he and his friends had been protesting an increase in bus fares when they were picked up. He was tortured and subjected to a mock execution; all his friends were executed.[25]

Again, the ESMA played a central role in the prosecution. Thirty-two ESMA survivors and witnesses—including two repentant soldiers—testified in court or by deposition abroad, where many ESMA survivors remained after they went into exile upon liberation from the camp.[26] Víctor Basterra, a survivor who managed to smuggle reams of documents and photographs out of the ESMA, spent longer on the witness stand than any other victim in the case, testifying until nearly three in the morning the day he was called to the stand. The renowned novelist Jorge Luis Borges, who was in the courtroom on the day of Basterra's testimony, commented, "I have a feeling I just witnessed one of the worst things in my life. I hope that the sentence is just."[27]

The court also heard from a parade of subordinate military officers, many of whom described the chain of command in the armed forces and gave defenses of their conduct. Adm. Luis María Mendía, the former commander of naval operations, told the court that his interpretation of "annihilate subversion" meant to "destroy, reduce to nothing . . . the effect caused by destroying the enemy through military actions. . . . The actions of the armed forces are violent. They are destructive; they don't use tear gasses, but lethal gasses." But he insisted that detainees were held under "humane conditions" and that there were standard operating procedures for dealing with detained suspects—they would be released if not guilty or handed over to the executive branch if they were suspected of having links to "subversion."[28] When Jorge Radice was called to testify, he was asked about military operations the ESMA had engaged in and gave evasive answers bordering on the absurd. "I was a soldier. My superiors gave me a target, and I went after the target" was about the extent of what he was willing to admit.[29]

The proceedings were not broadcast, but video without sound was broadcast in snippets on the nightly news, and the entrepreneurial Jorge Fontevecchia published the *Diario del juicio*, a weekly newspaper dedicated solely to the proceedings that ran a transcript of the trial. In all, 832 people testified over four months. Each day's proceedings began at 3 p.m. and lasted until all the day's witnesses had finished, sometimes well after midnight.

The nine military commanders on trial only attended those sessions they were required to—the reading of the indictment, their statements to the court, the closing statements, and the verdict—but a famous photograph of the nine military commanders, dressed in their gala uniforms (except Jorge Rafael Videla, who, refusing to recognize the legitimacy of the court, wore a civilian suit and did not participate in his own defense) and standing before the civilian court, has left an indelible mark on the Argentine psyche. It speaks to not only a repudiation of the past but also the strength and power of the rule of law and democracy. (So powerful is that image that people often assume the commanders attended the entire trial.)

In December the verdict was announced. "Despite the fact that the armed forces who seized power on March 24, 1976, had all the legal instruments and methods available to carry forward repression by legal means, without any detriment to efficiency, they chose to move forward with illegal and clandestine operations on the basis of orders that each of the defendants gave within their respective commands," Judge León Arslanían read in open court. The court then said that as a result, the campaign of the armed forces resulted in a great many crimes committed against "many people, including those who belonged to subversive organizations and many who had nothing to do with them."[30]

Gen. Jorge Rafael Videla and Adm. Emilio Eduardo Massera were sentenced to life in prison. Brig. Gen. Agosti, Adm. Lambruschini, and Gen. Viola were given lesser sentences, while the three commanders who sat on the third military junta were absolved of responsibility for their conduct in the Dirty War, as was Brig. Gen. Basilia Lami Dozo, as the repression had mostly ended before the end of the dictatorship.[31]

The verdict confirmed what the CONADEP had reported and what the commanders had denied—namely, that the War against Subversion was "an operation ordered by the commanders of the three armed forces." The court held that "the personnel under the defendants' control detained a large number of people, held them clandestinely in military bases or other areas under the military's control, they interrogated them under torture, they kept them as captives where they suffered inhumane treatment, and finally, they either legalized them by sending them to the justice system or the executive branch, or they freed them, or they simply physically eliminated them."[32]

Parallel to the investigation of the military commanders, Alfonsín had also ordered the military justice system to investigate army and naval officers who were identified during the tumultuous transition at the end of 1983 and the beginning of 1984.[33] Yet while Alfonsín had ordered an investigation into the ESMA the same day as he convened a court-martial to look into the military juntas, it was not until February 13, 1985, that a military instructional judge, Capt. Roque Pedro Funes, was appointed in the case to open the investigation—more than a year after the court-martial was formally ordered by Alfonsín.[34] Prior to Funes's appointment, the only actions the military justice system had taken with respect to the ESMA were a number of resolutions concerning jurisdiction over the case, placing Vice Adm. Rubén Jacinto Chamorro, the director of the ESMA from 1976 to 1983, in detention and spending an inordinate amount of time considering the veracity of public statements from Raúl Villariño in *La Semana,* which published an interview titled "yo maté y vi torturar" ("I killed and saw torture").[35] Alfonsín had hoped that the military would investigate its own, but the case file from the ESMA military court-martial shows a concerted effort to truncate the investigation. Undoubtedly, the navy was attempting to stall.

Judge Funes, the navy captain appointed to investigate the case, showed little initiative. Immediately after receiving the case file, he took two months to "study" the case.[36] At the conclusion of his study, he issued a ruling questioning his own jurisdiction and holding that he had no ability to take statements from any military officers.[37] It was not until mid-July 1985—four months after Funes was appointed to investigate the case and while the trial of the juntas was fully underway—that he issued his first requests for information, most of which were so basic that it could have been completed in days rather than months.[38]

The navy took months to respond. Its first response was not until October 30, 1985, and it failed to produce most of the information Funes had requested.[39] Funes had asked for registries of prisoners, lists of operations, and lists of "intelligence agents" who worked in the ESMA, none of which was provided. The navy took ten months to simply assemble a list of the positions and ranks of the navy's command (e.g., which officers had filled the positions of commander of naval operations, chief of naval operations on the general staff, and director of the ESMA) during the dictatorship.[40] This information was all publicly available and likely could have been compiled in an hour. The navy also delayed ten months to send Funes a copy of the Capacity Plan of the Navy (Plan de Capacidades de la Armada [PLACINTARA]), the navy's battle command in the War against Subversion.[41] To most of Judge Funes's requests, the navy responded that they could not find the information, that the archives of the information did not exist, or that the archives of the information had been destroyed based on a naval regulation that called for the destruction of documents more than five years old.[42]

This was a ploy to derail the investigation, with Judge Funes actively assisting the navy. Much of the information Funes requested was clearly in the navy's control, as the navy easily responded to Funes's requests if they implicated survivors' credibility. When Judge Funes asked for the criminal background of the witnesses in the case who lodged accusations against the navy, the navy responded in extraordinary detail, information that was most likely obtained in the basement of the ESMA through torture. The navy sent Judge Funes two-page dossiers on two dozen witnesses, detailing the witnesses' histories of political activism, their "terrorist affiliations," their ranks, and their most important political contacts along with lists of terrorist operations they had allegedly participated in.[43] Additionally, when individual officers were called to testify, they summoned precise details about the circumstances of the "arrests" of their captives turned accusers, citing the victims' nicknames, the dates and places of their detention, their revolutionary cells, and the secret codes and security measures they utilized to avoid detection. Antonio Pernías even managed to produce the "confession" that Graciela Daleo had typed and signed shortly after her torture session, an indication that the intelligence files were still accessible at the time of trial. It was highly unlikely that the military officers would have been able to summon such details so many years after the fact if they had not reviewed secret archives shortly before their testimony in military court.[44]

When Judge Funes finally cited twenty-one high-ranking naval officers to testify in February 1986—ten months after taking over the case—the officers were obtuse.[45] Like the military commanders who preceded them in the Trial of the Juntas, the navy's top brass did not divulge any meaningful detail about the Dirty War. Instead, their strategy was to pin political responsibility for the War against Subversion on the civilians who preceded the military and ordered the military to "annihilate subversion" in 1975, to deny that there was any torture or murder in the ESMA, and to claim that their intervention against "subversion" was strictly according to regulation. These were strategies that had already been tested in the Trial of the Juntas and rejected, but the officers hoped that they could stall further prosecutions by keeping their case in military court while a "political" solution was found outside the legal proceeding.

Adm. Luis María Mendía, who had been the chief of naval operations and was the navy's author of the PLACINTARA, explained to Judge Funes that the roots of the navy's actions started long before the military coup in 1976. He traced the growth of "subversion" to a Marxist infiltration of political movements in the 1960s. Mendía told Judge Funes that dictator Gen. Agustín Alejandro Lanusse had tried to combat this enemy through legal means between 1971 and 1973 by instituting a national security court, but the initiative was scuttled by the "political tolerance" shown to subversives when an amnesty law was passed for jailed revolutionaries in 1973. "We were in a complete state of vulnerability," Mendía told Judge Funes. The trials against the military for supposed excesses, said Mendía, reflected nothing more than the fact that the "enemy who lost the armed war [was] continuing it through psychological war, infiltrating culture, education, parts of the government, and journalism."[46]

Adm. Julio Torti, who for a time served as the commander of Task Force 3 and was the commanding officer in charge of the ESMA, explained that there were no "irregularities" in the ESMA, that there were very few detentions, that only in "rare" circumstances were people detained, and that these detentions were brief and according to regulation. "Interrogations," said Torti, "were always performed by personnel equipped in intelligence and were always done with proper treatment." The time to detain people was "strict" and "generally not more than forty-eight hours." The prisoners who were in the ESMA for longer than this period were all "intelligence agents" who were given "economic benefits" and "proper protection." The people who survived the ESMA weren't "survivors" but employees who had left their work at the ESMA after a "mutual agreement about their future" between the leader of the task force and the agent.[47]

Adm. Oscar Montes gave the most extensive defense of the navy's conduct. He explained to Judge Funes that the idea of having small task forces with heavy firepower and mobility was the "heart of the operational theory." Because the war was largely fought by small bands of plainclothes officers, there were "a million lies about 'paramilitary' groups or 'gangs' . . . all the product of a psychological campaign by the enemy." There was no other way of engaging the enemy, as "fighting with uniforms and with conventional battle tactics . . . would have been as useless as fighting guided missiles with mounted horsemen." In fact, not engaging the enemy this way, Montes emphasized, "would have been complete negligence." The poor reputation of the ESMA was the result of a "false campaign of denunciation" spearheaded "by some collaborators who have changed sides for a second time [first betraying their terrorist comrades by cooperating with the military, and then betraying the military by denouncing them before the courts]" and stemmed from the need of the former "intelligence agents" to give some sort of "self-justification in front of their ex-*compañeros*." In other words, Montes explained, the survivors had to say they were brutally treated and tortured to convince their former revolutionary colleagues that they weren't traitors.[48]

In total, twenty-one admirals and captains paraded through Judge Funes's chambers and all offered the same clichés, jingoist slogans, half-truths, and lies about the ESMA—that there had been no torture in the ESMA, that the entire fight was conducted according to regulation, that the denunciations against the navy were part of a well-orchestrated propaganda campaign by former subversives who had to tell stories of horror and torture in order to save face against their former comrades, that all the prisoners were either briefly held and released or promptly handed over to the executive branch for detention, and that the few prisoners who spent longer than just a few days in the ESMA were all collaborators and double agents who had agreed to work with the navy.[49] Equally striking was the fact that Judge Funes accepted these slogans as truth. He never asked obvious follow-up questions, such as "How did the navy determine who was a subversive?" or "Where did all the missing prisoners go?" Judge Funes never confronted the admirals with direct accusations from survivors that were in the case file and on his desk, such as files from the CONADEP and testimony from the Trial of the Juntas. The federal appeals court had convicted Admiral Massera for many of the crimes in front of Judge Funes, but Judge Funes proceeded as if he were starting with a blank slate.

When it was time for dozens of lower-ranking officers to testify, Judge Funes received the same stock answers.[50] "What were the names of your junior officers?" Judge Funes asked Salvio Menéndez, who was the first commander of the GT 3.3/2 after the military coup. "I don't remember," said Menéndez.[51] What about the accusations of pregnant women who were housed at the ESMA and gave birth, only later to be disappeared? "Absurd enemy propaganda," said Jorge Perrén, who had served as the chief of operations of the GT 3.3/2 in 1976 and 1977.[52] And what about the prisoners who had worked for years with the navy, held in long detention? It was a lie. "From the moment they began to collaborate," Perrén told Judge Funes, "they were free."[53] What about the rampant accusations of robbery and pillage and piles of war booty stacked in the attic of the ESMA? It was nonsense, as "everything was inventoried and registered with the commanding officer," said Guillermo Pazos, a military accountant who, for a time, served as the head of logistics of the GT 3.3/2.[54] Was anybody injured, detained, or killed? "These questions should be answered by the navy as an institution," said Raúl Enrique Scheller, one of the GT 3.3/2's chief torturers. What about the use of torture? It was all done according to the "doctrine" that was written for the circumstances, Scheller continued.[55] Did anybody die? They did, admitted Juan Carlos Rolón, but "the details of such should be obtained from the general staff."[56]

In a few instances, Judge Funes and three of his colleagues pursued individual cases brought to their attention. But these "investigations" inevitably absolved the military suspects. Judge Funes and his colleagues treated each case as if it were an individual crime: if there was only one witness, the incident was explained away as lacking sufficient evidence or dismissed because the witness was not credible as a former leftist revolutionary. In one investigation, Hernan Bello was summoned to testify about his kidnapping, torture, and fifty days of detention in the ESMA. The military judge dismissed the case after hearing that the navy had no official information on the kidnapping. Because Bello had belonged to a "subversive organization," the judge reasoned, his testimony against the navy was "disqualified."[57] No effort was made to synthesize these cases, to look for similarities between cases, or to test the veracity of what the military officers said against one another's statements.

Jorge Pinedo, son-in-law of Rodolfo Walsh, was cited by the military courts and years later recalled the atmosphere of what it was like to testify there:

> My first testimony was before CONADEP, in '84 [or] '85. The second testimony—that's really a misnomer, *testimony*—was at CONSUFA [the military courts] because in truth, it was an interrogation. It was before an entity called the Superior Council of the Armed Forces. I received a summons at an address where I was living at that time that nobody knew. . . . They summoned me to an army garage near "Los Patos" in Palermo. I went with a lawyer friend who waited for me on a corner. I

> entered a dark and sordid garage. They took me to an office where two army officers showed up without identifying themselves, sat me at a desk, pointed a lamp at me, and questioned me about what I had testified to the CONADEP. I didn't respond to many of their questions because I was terrified.[58]

Only two officers—Adm. Rubén Jacinto Chamorro and Capt. Jorge Eduardo Acosta—spoke with any hint of candor.[59] Chamorro was disgusted that his military superiors did not give a vigorous defense of his conduct and leadership during the Dirty War, so he took it upon himself to give an explanation. Acosta, likewise, was angry about being forced to retire from the navy. Both of these men recognized that the ESMA held prisoners, that the regulations that supposedly governed the War against Subversion were not followed, and that the "collaborators" were not volunteers but (in their description) former revolutionaries who had chosen to collaborate under pressure to do so. Both men also went into great detail about the structure of the ESMA's GT 3.3/2 and the operational theory behind the repression. Still, neither man went so far as to admit that the navy had tortured and killed its prisoners or executed "innocent" civilians.

When Judge Funes concluded his investigation in September 1986, he gave a soaring defense of the navy. He held that the threat posed by "Marxist subversion" necessitated a response from the armed forces, which had acted with measured and legal force. He said that the naval officers called to testify had acted properly as sailors following superior orders to implement an institutional policy set by the higher command: "Everything was done in a totally regulated fashion with the clear participation of the higher ranks." He also questioned the credibility of the navy's accusers, finding that the witnesses had manufactured their testimony with one another by making up stories to bolster their credibility. According to Judge Funes, the defendants acted in accordance with their "preparation, teaching, and indoctrination." He concluded that he could not formally bring charges against any of the officers.[60]

In early October 1986, the military's supreme council (Consejo Supremo de las Fuerzas Armadas, or CONSUFA)—the appeals court in the military justice system—took the case over from Judge Funes.

They asked Judge Funes to reconsider his decision not to press charges against any of the officers and requested that he press charges where possible. Judge Funes initially rebuffed the CONSUFA by arguing that he did not have the power to formulate charges against the defendants. After further pressure from the CONSUFA, Funes abruptly resigned.[61]

The CONSUFA then took the ESMA case, with instructions from the federal court of criminal appeals to issue an indictment against the ESMA officers where possible. Fifteen high-ranking admirals again paraded through the military justice system in December 1986, this time in front of the CONSUFA.[62] Despite pressure against Judge Funes to formulate charges in October, on December 23, 1986, the CONSUFA also declined to issue charges. It informed the federal appeals court that it did not share that court's conclusions from the trial against the commanders. The CONSUFA told the appeals court that none of the fifteen commanders "received, transmitted, executed, or ordered the execution of orders" and that their orders were "legitimate, clear, and adequate dispositions" to "fight subversion" and were all based on Decrees 2770, 2771, 2772; Decree 1/75; and the PLACINTARA. The orders "did not modify the essence of the PLACINTARA," the CONSUFA held, and "excesses" were impossible given the level of supervision and priority given to the War against Subversion. In conclusion, there was "not sufficient merit to maintain the procedure against the accused," and the fifteen admirals were acquitted.[63] The military was closing ranks to protect its own.

The federal appeals court did not accept the CONSUFA's report. Three days later, on December 26, 1986, it ordered the CONSUFA to continue its investigation in a cursory one-page decision.[64] So in the early days of January 1987, most of the officers who had testified before Judge Funes went once again before the CONSUFA.[65] They repeated their defenses that it was all institutional, that they were following orders, that nobody had been tortured, and that any questions as to the fate of those who were missing should be directed toward the navy.

Time was now of the essence. Before the verdict in the Trial of the Juntas, Alfonsín and a few close advisors met secretly with members of the criminal court of appeals and expressed their desire to limit the scope of future prosecutions.[66] There had been growing unrest in the middle ranks of the military. Bombs had become an increasingly common phenomenon, and Alfonsín had decreed a state of siege near the end of the trial. He asked the appellate judges to clarify the scope of a due obedience defense in their verdict, hoping to quell the unrest by narrowing prosecutions.[67] But the judges refused, saying it was not an issue in the case. So in December 1986, after further military unrest (including a bomb found under Alfonsín's seat when visiting Córdoba to view an artillery display in May 1986) and a successful showing in the 1985 midterm elections, Alfonsín successfully introduced the *punto final*, or "full stop," law in Congress.[68] The law gave courts sixty days to issue summonses against a defendant accused of crimes committed during the Dirty War. Cases were to be filed by February 23, 1987, or dropped.[69]

A flurry of activity ensued. Alfonsín hoped that only a few dozen military officers would be indicted by the February 23 deadline, but human rights activists, prosecutors, and judges ended up filing hundreds of cases. Alfonsín's strategy backfired. The ESMA case file is dotted with dozens of petitions from individual victims seeking intervention; most significantly, all of Argentina's leading human rights organizations filed a joint petition on January 9, 1987, seeking the indictment of 650 officers responsible for state terrorism.[70] While figures vary, approximately 400 officers around Argentina were ultimately indicted by the February 23 deadline.[71]

Among the hundreds of cases to move forward, the ESMA case received a critical push owing to the full stop law. On February 4, 1987, the federal criminal appeals court invoked jurisdiction from the CONSUFA, which had moved at a glacial pace during the nearly five months it retained the case.[72] On February 20, 1987, prosecutors Julio Strassera and Luis Moreno Ocampo, who had successfully litigated the Trial of the Juntas, charged thirty-four defendants from the ESMA for crimes committed against 286 individual victims. The defendants included the commanders of the ESMA task force and the junior officers who had worked at the ESMA on a permanent basis. "Torture and death were notorious," the prosecutors said. They alleged that the methods of the ESMA were so well known, it would be impossible to presume that an operations officer did not know what would happen to a victim once delivered there.[73]

The same day, the federal appeals court ordered nineteen of the thirty-four defendants identified by the prosecution to give statements, the final step toward formal indictment.[74] (The court did not explain why fifteen of the defendants were dropped, especially some notoriously high-ranking officers like Adm. Mendía, who had written the navy's plans for the War against Subversion as chief of naval operations.) To take statements from all the military officers before the expiration of the timeline, the court scheduled long days beginning at 8 a.m.[75] High-ranking officers were questioned about all the victims that passed through the ESMA during their tenure in command; low-ranking officers—Capdevilla, Donda, Febres, Pernías, Scheller, Carella, Azic, and Astiz—were questioned only in those cases where a victim had alleged their direct participation in criminal acts. Of the prosecutor's 286 cases, 103 were prepared to go to trial.[76]

The court concluded statements as the limitations period under the full stop law expired. On February 27, 1987, the court confirmed the indictment of nineteen officers.[77] The officers who were not indicted by this day were formally dropped from the case, and petitions asking them to be indicted were rejected.[78] The trial was set to begin on April 20; summonses were sent out to twenty-seven witnesses who were scheduled to appear in the first week of the trial.[79]

The start date proved tragic.

In early April 1987, a federal court of criminal appeals in Córdoba cited Maj. Ernesto Barreiro for testimony. Barreiro reported to his superiors that he would not appear in court. News of Barreiro's resistance leaked to the press, and the incident soon escalated into a national crisis. Barreiro barricaded himself in his army barracks, and an ambitious young colonel named Aldo Rico at the Campo de Mayo army base outside of Buenos Aires declared himself in open rebellion against the government and in support of Barreiro on April 16. Rico issued a number of demands—an end to the Dirty War trials, an increase in salaries, a sacking of the army chief of staff, and a "restoration of dignity and honor" to the armed forces. Escalating tensions, hundreds of protestors gathered outside the Campo de Mayo army base calling for Alfonsín to tell them whether to storm the base.[80]

On April 16, the day the news broke in national headlines, Alfonsín called for an emergency legislative session, and he promised over national television that democracy would not be negotiated. Four hundred thousand people gathered in the streets in support of President Alfonsín. On Easter Sunday, April 19, hundreds of thousands again gathered in the Plaza de Mayo outside the presidential palace in support of democracy. The General Confederation of Labor (CGT), the umbrella labor organization, called for a general strike in opposition to the rebels, showing that should they sack the government, the military would face terrible opposition. At the last minute, a planned attack on the rebels was suspended to avoid bloodshed, but loyal troops had surrounded Rico's position. That afternoon Alfonsín sent his minister of defense, Horacio Jaunarena, who had the best relationship with the armed forces in Alfonsín's cabinet, to speak to Rico, but no agreement was reached.[81]

Hours later Alfonsín boarded a helicopter bound for the Campo de Mayo army base. Just over three hours later, Alfonsín returned to the assembled crowd and announced,

> Compatriots . . . Compatriots . . . Happy Easter! The rebels have changed their attitude. As it turns out, they will be detained and subject to justice. They are a group of men, some of them heroes of Malvinas [Falkland Islands], who took the wrong path and who reiterated that their intention was not to prompt a coup d'état. But anyway they led the country to this tension . . . through which all of us have lived and in which the Argentine people were the central protagonist. In order to avoid spilling blood, I gave orders to the command of the army not to attack, and now we can thank God. The house is in order and there is no bloodshed in Argentina. I ask the people in Campo de Mayo to leave. And I request all of you: Go to your homes and kiss your children; to celebrate Easter in Argentina in peace.[82]

Alfonsín said that no agreement was reached, but shortly thereafter, on May 13, 1987, Alfonsín introduced another bill to establish a due obedience defense for lower-ranking officers. Except this time, the protection for the military went even further. The law did not allow even for a rebuttable presumption that lower-ranking officers were following orders; it granted them an irrefutable presumption that they had acted under orders and were therefore not criminally responsible for their actions.[83] It was an amnesty for the vast majority of the military in all but name. Opposition to the law was furious but not successful.[84]

Amid the Easter uprising, the Supreme Court suspended the ESMA case on a technicality, seeing that Alfonsín needed room to maneuver.[85] Thus on the eve of the most important trial against lower-ranking officers from the military government, the ESMA case was thrown in limbo.

Within five weeks of the passage of the due obedience law, the Supreme Court declared the law constitutional.[86] The Supreme Court sent the ESMA case back to the federal appeals court to rule on the application of the law. The appeals court ruled that it was constitutional and dropped eleven of the seventeen defendants from the case.[87] When the admirals who were still under investigation appealed the ruling, the Supreme Court found that Oscar Montes, Manuel Jacinto García Tallada, Humberto Barbuzzi, and José Suppicich had not in any way altered or changed the operative plans, and so they were dropped as well in March 1988.[88]

Over the next two years, nothing happened in the ESMA investigation, despite the fact that two defendants—Adms. Julio Torti and Antonio Vañek—were still under indictment and the case had already once been set to go to trial. Whereas the court had previously been prepared to prosecute the naval officers from the ESMA, the amnesty law caused a grinding halt. Several of the members of the federal criminal appeals court had, by this point, resigned or taken other positions—the court was in the thick of reviewing the case against the commanders of the war in the Falkland Islands for negligence and virtually ignored the ESMA case.

Not only was the due obedience law a blow to the trials, but it failed in one of its key aims—namely, to stop further military unrest and rebellion. By the end of his term, Alfonsín faced down two more military rebellions. Alfonsín and his advisors had diagnosed the problem within the military as one of predictability. They believed that the armed forces were resisting Alfonsín's human rights policies because they could never be sure who was a suspect. With the due obedience law passed, that was no longer an issue. But the military rebels still felt attacked. They announced that they had a broader agenda of "defending the honor of the military," as the leader of the rebellions, Mohamed Ali Seinedlín, said. The aims also went to the heart of military life: an increase in salaries, the sacking of many of the top generals who the officer corps felt were not doing enough to protect the honor of the army, and more respect for the institution in national life.[89]

The due obedience law marked the beginning of the end for Alfonsín's government. The law was wildly unpopular, and the Peronists made relentless use of the issue in the 1987 midterm elections. Alfonsín lost his legislative majority, and the Radical Party lost most provincial legislatures. The country became ungovernable, with a firm Peronist legislative opposition. They blocked one proposal after another. At the same time, Alfonsín's austral economic program, which had miraculously halted Argentina's runaway inflation, began to crack. By 1989 inflation was back with a vengeance: it climbed to over 2,000 percent annually, dwarfing the scope of any inflation Argentina had previously seen, even in the months before the 1976 military coup. Food riots became a daily occurrence.[90]

Aggravating the situation, at the beginning of 1989, an obscure group called the Movimiento Todos Para la Patria attacked the La Tablada military base in a guerrilla strike reminiscent of the violent days of the mid-1970s. The leaders of the attack had been connected to the People's Revolutionary Army (ERP) in the past, and a few of the attackers had also worked in the human rights movement. Hebe de Bonafini, the outspoken leader of the Mothers of the Plaza de Mayo, spoke in favor of the attackers. Several conscripts were killed while they repelled the raid.[91]

Inflation had brought down many governments, and Alfonsín's was no exception. Predictably, the Radical Party lost the presidential election in May 1989 to the Peronists. The challenger was a young Peronist from the northern province of La Rioja named Carlos Saúl Menem. During the dictatorship, Menem was detained aboard a prison ship for five years and seemingly came to the job with the appropriate human rights credentials. He was elected largely on an economic program; human rights had receded to the background of electoral concern. There was no reason to think that his human rights program would be markedly different from Alfonsín's. Besides, most issues to this point had been settled: a few dozen officials were still being prosecuted, and the trials were likely to end within several years, bringing the transitional program to a close.

After the election Alfonsín suffered from lame-duck syndrome. Though his party was headed out of office, he still had another six months to govern before Menem stepped into the Casa Rosada, and the economy was spiraling out of control. Instead of waiting, Alfonsín resigned early and passed the reins of government to Menem. Alfonsín stepped down on July 7, 1989, unable to complete his term in office.[92]

The public's tolerance for and interest in the human rights trials had by now almost vanished. Only the most committed pressed for trials to continue. After six years of democratic government and a dozen years' distance from the worst of the crimes, citizens were interested in other issues: the disastrous state of the economy was a more pressing threat to democratic stability and social security.

So three months into his early term, on October 6, Menem issued a series of decrees pardoning over four hundred people still facing trial. The beneficiaries included military officers, guerrillas facing prosecution, and members of several rebellions from the previous two years. Adms. Vañek and Torti—the only two officers in the navy facing trial—were both pardoned. It was an unpopular measure, but Menem saw an opportunity to pacify all sides and settle the issue once and for all so he could move ahead with a program of sweeping economic reforms. He also courted the support of the military so that he could govern without fear of a coup. The pardons were of dubious constitutionality—the legality of pardoning those under investigation was unclear—but Menem had successfully augmented the size of the Supreme Court from five to nine members, who rubberstamped his proposal.[93]

After further military rebellions, Menem's courting of loyal military officers seemed to bear fruit. Whereas Alfonsín had been unable to quash military rebellions with loyal troops and commanders, Menem was able to confront the rebels head-on. In their final 1990 uprising, the rebels were crushed by loyal troops, and the armed forces once and for all seemed to be under civilian authority. For their loyalty Menem responded in kind. At the end of 1990, Menem issued one last series of pardons and released the junta members who were still in jail from the 1985 trial as well as a few junior officers who had been convicted after the Trial of the Juntas.[94]

And so the political transition came to an end. What started off as a virtual certainty that the details of the Dirty War would never be uncovered—fifty years of impunity for military regimes virtually ensured the perpetrators of the Dirty War of this result—yielded to the demands of civil society after the disastrous and humiliating defeat in the Falkland Islands. Propaganda and impunity gave way to truth and justice as President Alfonsín insisted that the country confront its troubling past. But the experiment proved too dangerous for democracy, as it alienated the military, which used brute force and violence in service of impunity.

Human rights activists refused to accept Menem's pardons, and they began to look for cracks in the impunity. These efforts were difficult—public interest in the issue waned as the country set about economic recovery and seemed to prefer a kind of amnesia rather than more engagement with the past—but there were small victories along the way. In 1992 the Inter-American Commission on Human Rights released a report that held that Argentina's passage of the amnesty laws and pardons was incompatible with the American Declaration of the Rights and Duties of Man and that Argentina had "failed in its obligation to guarantee the rights" recognized in the American Convention on Human Rights, which the country ratified in 1984, including the right to a fair trial and judicial protection. The commission recommended that the Argentine government "adopt the measures necessary to clarify the facts and identify those responsible for the human rights violations."[95]

Developments outside of courts had an even bigger impact. In 1994 a former ESMA officer, Adolfo Scilingo, published a wide-ranging confession with Argentine investigative journalist Horacio Verbitsky in which he admitted to pushing drugged detainees from military transport planes into the South Atlantic on two death flights. In first-person detail, Scilingo described the executions. Prisoners were injected with a "vaccine" in preparation for "transfer" to a prison in Patagonia. The injection was an anesthetic. The prisoners were then stripped, loaded onto a cargo plane, and thrown out over the South Atlantic, alive. Every Wednesday for several years, forty to fifty prisoners would "go up." Nobody returned. The report, originally published in *Página/12*, was later published as a book, *Confessions of a Dirty Warrior*.[96]

Confessions made the Dirty War front-page news once again, and international pressure mounted on Argentina to reopen prosecutions. In 1996 with domestic channels blocked, Spanish courts began asserting so-called universal jurisdiction, a legal doctrine stating that any country may indict perpetrators for crimes against humanity if their home countries do not. The Spanish courts requested the extradition of Argentine Dirty Warriors for hundreds of individual cases, not limited to Spanish citizens. Soon France, Italy, and Switzerland initiated prosecutions in absentia for the disappearances of their nationals in Argentina.

Simultaneously, human rights organizations began arguing for the "right to truth," which domestic courts recognized in 1996. This spawned "truth trials"—nonpunitive judicial processes to record testimony about the Dirty War. The federal court of criminal appeals in Buenos Aires eventually opened up a wide-reaching investigation of the ESMA to pursue the right to truth. Dozens of survivors testified in front of the court, a decidedly second-best alternative to the trial that was thwarted in 1987, but a clear way to keep the courthouse doors open. While the victims themselves did not present much new evidence in these proceedings—their testimony largely covered episodes they had previously testified about in front of the CONADEP and the courts in the 1980s—several military officers spoke with more candor than they had in the past. Jorge Radice, for instance, was one of the most obtuse witnesses at the Trial of the Juntas and rebuffed nearly all the court's questions about his role as a sharpshooter at the ESMA. But in the truth trials, he opened up about a part of his bizarre saga, giving a glimpse at how military officers justified their conduct. After leaving the navy in 1979, Radice lent a family property on Zapiola Street to the GT 3.3/2 where ESMA victims labored away for their captors. He had also married an ESMA survivor and former Montonero, Anita Dvatman, who after being captured by the ESMA became an active collaborator. At the truth trial, he acknowledged that the Zapiola property was his family's property (he was born there) and that his wife was "tortured in the ESMA," but he "wouldn't say anything more about the subject." He described Jorge Eduardo Acosta, the chief intelligence officer at the ESMA, as someone who "humanized" things for ESMA victims, stating that "when Captain Acosta arrived, there was less torture, less death."[97] He acknowledged that it was Adm. Rubén Jacinto Chamorro who decided which prisoners would live and which would die (though he refused to name any living officers who might have participated). Nevertheless, he remained steadfast that all accusations of the ESMA's private pillage of property and real estate were "absolutely false."[98] (In 2014 prosecutors opened an investigation into several properties that Radice and his family acquired in 1978, part of a suite of properties that the ESMA task force acquired from its victims and sold.[99]) Judge Horacio Cattani also used the truth trials as an opportunity to investigate and identify the remains of approximately five hundred bodies collected from paupers' graves and other sites throughout the country. The investigation ultimately identified five victims of the raid against the Mothers of the Plaza de Mayo in December 1977, including two French missionary nuns who were disappeared among the twelve victims in the attack.

The Abuelas de Plaza de Mayo (Grandmothers of the Plaza de Mayo) also continued to vigorously pursue the kidnapping and trafficking of babies. In 1998 Gen. Jorge Rafael Videla and Adm. Emilio Eduardo Massera—both of whom had been sentenced to life in prison and then pardoned during the transition—were again arrested and put in pretrial detention for their role in a systematic plan to kidnap children, crimes that were not within the scope of the amnesty law or the pardons.[100] The detention of former Chilean dictator Augusto Pinochet in London in October 1998 on orders from a Spanish court invoking universal jurisdiction over crimes against humanity also proved a turning point, symbolizing international opposition to impunity.

In 2000 the human rights group Centro de Estudios Legales y Sociales (CELS) intervened in a case that the Grandmothers of the Plaza de Mayo were litigating against Julio Simón. Simón was a work group member in Argentina's First Army Corps, indicted on charges of kidnapping Claudia Poblete, who was taken as an infant when her parents were disappeared. (Their "crime" had been subversive disability rights activism.) After their murders she was raised by a military family under a fake identity.

As Verbitsky recounts,

> The Simon case was very special, because, in one operation, a group of repressors had kidnapped a couple and their child. . . . The Full Stop and Due Obedience laws prohibited punishment for the disappearance of the parents, while . . . they were silent on punishment for the kidnapping of the child. . . . All the investigation was done, all the evidence was developed, it was nothing more than a question of law, to decide which law applied. It appeared to us this case would expose these abhorrent laws. How could the law not apply to the disappearance of the parents?[101]

Faced with this paradox at trial in 2001, Judge Gabriel Cavallo declared the due obedience and full stop laws unconstitutional, and Cavallo issued an indictment against Simón for the disappearance of Poblete's parents. Sporadic indictments against other officers followed Cavallo's decision, and a showdown at the Supreme Court over the constitutionality of the amnesty laws seemed inevitable.[102]

"I didn't think the Supreme Court would uphold my decision," Judge Cavallo told me years later about how he felt when issuing his ruling. Though Menem was no longer president, the court was still packed in 2001 with the judges from his "automatic majority" who had rubber-stamped most of his policies and had upheld the constitutionality of Menem's pardons in 1989 and 1990. But events were soon to change the political landscape quite dramatically.

In 2001 Argentina was hit by its worst economic crisis in at least a decade. For years the government had propped up the value of the peso by pegging it to the dollar at a one-to-one exchange rate. This policy, which created *plata dulce*, or "sweet cash," made Argentines extraordinarily rich for about a decade, but it depleted Argentina's reserves as the central bank propped up the value of the peso. On the verge of bankruptcy, the country was forced to depeg the exchange rate, and the peso, practically overnight, lost two-thirds of its value. Argentines found their way of life shattered.

The economic crisis threw Argentina into near anarchy. "Que se vayan todos" (Everybody go) became the slogan of daily protests of housewives, students, and others who banged pots and pans in wide frustration. Five presidents passed through the Casa Rosada in less than six months between 2001 and 2002. When elections were held in May

2003, two candidates—both Peronists—emerged from the first round, Néstor Kirchner and Carlos Saúl Menem (who was running again after four years out of office). Menem won the first round by two percentage points—24 percent to 22 percent—but it was clear he would not survive the second, with Kirchner polling around 63 percent in a runoff. Instead of facing an embarrassing defeat, he withdrew. Kirchner took office with just 22 percent of the vote.[103]

The situation for Kirchner was desperate. As a virtually unknown figure from the far reaches of Patagonia, his chances of survival seemed slim. As governor of the Santa Cruz province, he had governed fewer than two hundred thousand inhabitants—the equivalent of the governor of Alaska running for president of the United States.[104] A columnist from *La Nación*, the country's paper of record, suggested his administration would be weak and proffered that Argentines had only given him a year to govern.[105] Kirchner needed to do something bold and audacious to acquire political legitimacy.

Kirchner had not campaigned as a champion of human rights, and there was little in his background to suggest he would confront the dictatorship. While he and his wife, Cristina, had been part of the *tendencia* (revolutionary wing of Peronism) in college immediately before and after the 1976 military coup, he spent most of his time during the dictatorship growing a powerful and profitable law firm in the Patagonian town of Río Gallegos.[106] Conflicting reports circulated on the eve of his election about whether he would spend political capital trying to annul the amnesty laws, an issue he had left in doubt during the 2003 campaign.[107] But needing a political Excalibur, Kirchner recognized that human rights could provide a powerful political weapon. In his inaugural address to Congress, he told the assembled legislators of his political background: "I form part of a decimated generation, punished with painful absences." Kirchner insisted that the struggles of the 1970s youth were part of the vision he brought to the Casa Rosada as president. He said he would be driven not by pragmatism but by conviction. He told the legislators,

> I come here to propose a dream, to reconstruct our identity as a people and as a nation; I've come to propose to you a dream of truth and

> justice; I've come to propose to you a dream of returning to an Argentina by all and for all. I've come to propose to you that we remember the dreams of our founding fathers and our immigrant grandparents and pioneers, and of our generation who put everything on the line and gave it all believing in a country of equals.[108]

No longer would he permit the country to live with the embarrassing stain of the impunity, of the falsehoods that he and the human rights activists saw as having permeated the last decade of Argentina's life. But his opening discourse also hinted at the broader uses he would make of human rights: drawing a connection between the need for prosecution and the struggles of the 1970s allowed him to paint contemporary critics of all stripes as accomplices of the dictatorship.

He was swift to act. One of his first acts was to meet with leading human rights figures the day before he assumed the presidency, including Estela de Carlotto, the president of the Grandmothers of the Plaza de Mayo.[109] He appointed Eduardo Luis Duhalde, a former Peronist militant and human rights activist, as his secretary of human rights. Hebe de Bonafini, the outspoken leader of the Association of the Mothers of the Plaza de Mayo, went to the Casa Rosada to meet with Kirchner during his second week in office. She had been a thorn in the side of every administration since the transition to democracy, but after meeting Kirchner, she declared, "We were wrong; they're not all the same as we'd previously believed" and confirmed that Kirchner "has begun to do some things that we've dreamed about for years."[110] He pushed for impeachment trials against Menem's "automatic majority" on the Supreme Court with an eye toward appointing new members who might vote to annul the amnesty laws.[111] (Eventually, enough of the justices ultimately resigned instead of facing impeachment trials that Kirchner was able to replace a majority of the court).

During the presidential campaign, the candidates had all been asked to stake out their positions on the extradition requests coming from Spanish judge Baltasar Garzón, who had made international headlines after indicting Chilean dictator Augusto Pinochet and temporarily securing his arrest in London on an extradition request. Upon taking the presidency, Kirchner said that he would consider the extradition requests and that it was under study by his advisors. But in July 2003 he announced that he would do better by sending a law to Congress to repeal the due obedience and full stop laws that had blocked prosecution for more than fifteen years. "We have to judge them in Argentina," Kirchner announced.[112] In late August, with overwhelming popular support, the proposal passed both houses of Congress, and the amnesty laws were annulled.[113]

Kirchner's commitment to confronting the past—in his style—did not end there. In March 2004, on the anniversary of the military coup, he ordered that the portraits of Gens. Jorge Rafael Videla and Reynaldo Bignone—both former dictators—be removed from the Army War College.[114] On the same day, he convened a giant rally inside of the ESMA, where he spoke before thousands of assembled human rights activists:

> We want there to be justice, we want there to be a real and strong recuperation of memory, and we want Argentina to once again remember, to recuperate, and to take as an example those who were capable of giving everything for the values that they believed in, a generation who was capable of doing this, that has left an example, that has left a path, their lives, their mothers, that left their grandmothers and that left their children. Today, they are here in your hands.[115]

When farmers staged a nationwide strike against export taxes in 2008, Kirchner compared the striking farmers to the "task forces" of the dictatorship. When the *Clarín* newsgroup turned its editorial stance from supportive to combative, Kirchner responded in kind by questioning whether the paper's owner had adopted children of the disappeared. Once fiercely nonpartisan human rights groups increasingly came into Kirchner's corner and to his defense, not only siding with his support of human rights but defending his broader governing agenda and style. (Upon his death in 2010, the Association of the Mothers of the Plaza de Mayo declared that they cried for his death "the same as for their children."[116])

Kirchner effectively tapped into a dissident view of the 1980s, of those on the left and close to the human rights movement who felt aggrieved and betrayed by Alfonsín. Though the 1985 Trial of the Juntas seemed, to many, like a great triumph—particularly those outside of Argentina—it was, to a smaller subset, the tragic beginning of impunity by laying the intellectual groundwork for amnesty and pardons. Alfonsín had cast the revolutionary left as "subversives," arguing that their fanaticism and lack of respect for democracy and the rule of law had contributed to the dark times during Argentina's *años de plomo*. Kirchner, by contrast, romanticized the activists of the 1970s. His discourse was obviously an idealized version of what the activists of the 1970s had done (admitting only to "errors" in his inaugural address), but he insisted on remembering the *desaparecidos* as martyrs, examples of activists to inform the struggles of the current moment, in line with his populist political agenda. Kirchner emphasized the singularity of the evil of "state terrorism" as the "one demon" and held that an adequate confrontation with the past had to reckon with the singularity of state violence.

It was, of course, strange that a Peronist president would be the one to spearhead the repeal of the full stop and due obedience laws in the name of human rights, for it was the Peronist left that had taken up arms in a project of social revolution in the 1960s and early 1970s, and it was the Peronist right who had begun the massacre and the disappearances that became the official government policy under the dictatorship, and it was a Peronist candidate in 1983 who pledged to respect the military's self-amnesty law and turn the page on the Dirty War, and it was a Peronist president who pardoned the military in 1989. But this was the great political strength of Peronism—it was able to continuously update and reinvent itself, always the vanguard and expression of the pueblo.

Many have accused Kirchner of naked political opportunism, stating that his lack of interest in the issue before becoming president reveals that his embrace of the cause was nothing more than a political calculation. Whatever Kirchner's personal reasons for embracing human rights, he undeniably tapped into a profound feeling of resentment within Argentina. On the one hand, Kirchner came to power after the convulsive economic collapse of 2001. "These neoliberal economic crises have a profound impact on the social scene," Beatriz Sarlo, one of Argentina's leading public intellectuals, told me. "They are not just economic crises but political and social crises."[117] Among a generation of

Argentines who came of age in the 1990s and for whom the dictatorship was not even a distant memory, the collapse in 2001 was a moment of collective soul searching. What had gone wrong in the country that led to such a destabilizing moment? The answer, many of them found, was in the impunity that prevailed beginning in the 1990s; Argentina owed a great moral debt because of its past.

The initiative to repeal the full stop and due obedience laws proved popular, but was it legal? Congress was ordinarily prohibited from declaring laws constitutionally null and void, this being the provenance of the courts. And throughout the 1990s, the Supreme Court—packed by the justices of President Menem's "automatic majority"—had repeatedly upheld the constitutionality of these laws. But when the issue reached the Supreme Court in the 2005 *Simón* case, the court—now controlled by a majority of Kirchner's appointees—held that the due obedience and full stop laws were unconstitutional. Though the reasoning was elusive—in a seven-to-one vote, the justices issued seven separate opinions—the justices converged on the idea that international human rights law prohibited crimes against humanity from being subject to amnesty, pardons, or statutes of limitations. This rule was expressed in customary international law as well as a host of international instruments, such as the Universal Declaration of Human Rights, the Convention on the Prevention and Punishment of the Crime of Genocide, the Geneva Conventions, the Convention on the Non-applicability of Statutory Limitations to War Crimes and Crimes against Humanity, and others. The international law governed Argentina under Article 118 of Argentina's constitution, which gave international human rights norms the force of constitutional law. (The amendment was passed in 1994.) The court reasoned that other constitutional principles, such as the prohibition on ex post facto laws and the principle of legality, should yield to the moral imperative of prosecuting the military and fulfilling the country's obligations under international law. Said differently, the court found a universal duty on states to prosecute crimes against humanity. The court held that in Argentina, the due obedience and full stop laws violated this principle, and they could not serve as an impediment to prosecution. (Later cases would hold that Menem's pardons were equally constitutionally offensive.) The holding did not apply to crimes committed by the guerrillas, as these were not crimes committed by the state and hence could not be considered crimes against humanity. And so by 2005, all three branches of government had repudiated the amnesty and endorsed a full-scale revision of the past.

In September 2003, just days after Congress had repealed the full stop and due obedience laws under Kirchner's leadership, the federal criminal appeals court in Buenos Aires reopened the ESMA investigation.

But the decision to reopen the case presented dozens of legal issues beyond those addressed by the Supreme Court in the *Simón* decision. What would be the effect of double jeopardy and *non bis in idem* for defendants who had their cases thrown out of court after the passage of the full stop and due obedience laws? What was the proper venue for the trials? The military courts, as seemed to be required under the military code of justice? The federal courts of criminal appeals, as was required under Alfonsín's 1984 amendments that placed the federal criminal appeals courts in charge of human rights cases? Or would the cases be sent to the *juzgados federales*, the pretrial lower court chambers? And would the cases be prosecuted under the old criminal procedure used prior to Argentina's 1994 constitutional amendments, which were inquisitional and conducted in closed chambers, or would they move forward under the reforms that created public trials? Would prosecuting the cases under the 1994 reforms violate the constitution's guarantee to a "natural judge" established by prior law?

As ESMA officers were haled back into court for charges first investigated in the 1980s as well as new charges, this thicket of legal questions generated seemingly endless motions and appeals. While Julio Strassera and Luis Moreno Ocampo had filed charges in February 1985 that were scheduled to go to trial on April 20, 1985, it took years before the "reopened" cases reached a similar procedural posture. The first case ready for a trial in 2007 involved only one lower-ranking coast guard officer, Héctor Febres, for only four cases.

Many within the Argentine judiciary have embraced the trials. "We are bringing truth and justice to an enormous quantity of victims and victims' families, most of whom have never confronted or learned about their deaths," Judge Daniel Rafecas, one of the investigatory judges charged with looking into the crimes committed by the army inside of

Buenos Aires, tells me. Echoing the thoughts of many of his colleagues, he argues that investigating and sanctioning the military is the most important work in the judiciary. He says that the importance of the trials is providing truth and justice for the victims—that after years of disinformation, the state can gain support and legitimacy through the trials. "The decadence in Argentina in the last decade had its roots in the dictatorship," he tells me, referring to the *plata dulce* of the 1990s and the freewheeling spending and corruption of the time. "We need to own up to our history."[118] Indeed, Rafecas argues that only by confronting the military—even a generation after the fact—can Argentina build a true democracy:

> I'm certain that the moral, economic, and political collapse of the country is related to the lack of truth and justice. All throughout the twentieth century, we have been authoritarian—antiliberal, antidemocratic. The elites in the country—the military, the judicial branch, the church—have all been heavily influenced by fascism. It explains why we had the most repressive dictatorship in the region. This process, these trials, is meant to break that. We have to construct a real democracy, and we can't do that without looking at the worst of our past.[119]

To underscore the point, he asks me rhetorically,

> How can I send someone to jail for making fake IDs when the perpetrators of the worst crimes in our history live on the fancy Calle Bulnes? I don't know yet that this will improve our institutions, but I'm betting that by demonstrating the gravity of the crimes—showing the sadism of what was done, the *despersonalidad* of the repressors—that justice will break this terrible chain of our history and help build a more serious country. My sensation is that Argentina does not yet have a consensus on the gravity of the crimes committed by the dictatorship.[120]

Judge Gabriel Cavallo, who as an investigatory judge was the first one to declare the due obedience and full stop laws unconstitutional in the *Simón* case, concurs. For him the balance between the rule of law and the necessity of prosecuting these crimes falls clearly on the side of the prosecution. "You come from a consolidated democracy; we don't," he tells me, comparing the United States to his country. He admits that the "trials against state terrorism are an exceptional response to an exceptional situation," not typically a defense you hear in legal circles but certainly one that resonates in this context, where the ordinary expectation of the court of law as an institution of stability might need to yield to the greater project of democracy building and historical justice. He says that the due obedience and full stop laws were not about consolidating democracy; they were "excuse[s] to cover up what happened. [Implementing them] was a political decision to pacify everyone." But now that the state has the power to prosecute, Cavallo argues that investigations should proceed: "Only now are we in a process of truly consolidating democracy. We are correcting an error."[121]

Still, not all of Argentina's bureaucrats involved in the trials have been so cavalier in their assessments. Federico Delgado has been at the forefront of prosecuting the military, but he hesitates to commend the strict "legality" of the prosecutions, preferring instead to focus on the historical justice of the trials rather than their procedural merits. "I haven't decided if these prosecutions are just," Delgado tells me in his office over maté, an Argentine tea sipped from a gourd. "You just know that these crimes are so awful, you have to prosecute them. These guys were like the Nazis. They kidnapped people and threw them, defenseless, into the ocean. They stole children. There are certain things you simply cannot do in the name of the state," he says, adding, "The desire for truth and for justice among the victims is very strong." But he does admit unease: "Argentina has a culture of vengeance; we don't have deep democratic values. You can also see these trials as a form of vengeance."[122] Delgado says that the country's problem is that it has always been deeply divided, and human rights are no different. He explains that the military was not just "four crazy generals." The regime was backed by wide social consensus and support. The debate over human rights in the country reflects similar divisions. Was it just the top generals who were responsible? Was it the entire military? Was the military in cahoots with big business, the church, the media, and right-wing labor leaders and the Radical Party? Was it the fault of the left-wing revolutionaries who opted for violence instead of electoral mobilization? And should these discussions of social responsibility map strictly onto criminal liability?

Others see less-than-benign forces that have coalesced to make the recent wave of trials possible. While the Kirchners rhetorically insisted that the trials are necessary to impose the rule of law on a country so often governed by the whims of those in power, some of those propelling the trials forward have obvious ulterior motives. "When the trials first opened, I was surprised at many of the judges who decided to push forward," Pablo Parenti, who served for a time as the head of a special unit in the public ministry to coordinate and oversee the human rights prosecutions, told me in 2008.[123] It was not always committed liberals and constitutionalists who pursued human rights trials but judges with questionable ethics and rumors of corruption; they saw in human rights a way to whitewash their reputations. Some argue that the Kirchners too have made skillful use of the trials to impose their will on the judiciary. Corruption charges have circled the couple for decades, most of which they have managed to avoid by also weaponizing human rights as a skillful pressure point against many judges with numerous skeletons in their closets.

Graciela Fernández Meijide, former secretary for the CONADEP, is skeptical of the utility of the recent trials. She has decades of experience in the human rights movement but has sharply disagreed with many of her former colleagues and associates over her view of the trials and the Kirchners more generally. She tells me that the main challenge to Argentina in the twenty-first century is building better democratic institutions and tackling corruption and that, on some level, the trials are actually hurting Argentine institutions and the rule of law rather than helping. She cites as an example the 2007 Supreme Court decision that repealed the pardon of a general who had been released from punishment by President Menem in 1990. "From the most progressive standpoint," she explains, "you can't commit double jeopardy, even if the prior court to decide it was a shitty court. You can't just change the law every time a new sector takes power." She also says that the one-sided nature of the trials has obscured rather than illuminated history, and she dissents from the idea that the generation who was disappeared at the hands of the military was a group of "young idealists." "The Montoneros have never undergone a self-criticism," she tells me. "They have never gone out to the streets, block by block like the Tupamaros did in Uruguay, and talked to their supporters about where they went wrong. The Montoneros didn't fight for human rights and democracy; they fought for revolution." She says the lack of self-reflection in Argentina on the part of the left has hindered the development of a liberal society and that the trials—which, in theory, are supposed to fortify democracy—are having the opposite effect. "If you ask me," she says, "if there's a risk of military intervention in Argentina, I'd say no. But if you ask me about the quality of Argentine democracy, I'd say it is very poor. We can't pretend people live with issues from the past, they're interested in issues of today, of life."[124]

6

The Brutality of the ESMA

"Where is the last place you want to be?" the interrogators were fond of asking new captives. "The ESMA," the captives would say if they had heard the rumors of what transpired behind the iron gates of the Naval Mechanics School (ESMA). "Well, here you are!" their captors would gleefully reply.

The rumors, of course, were true: those who "fell" into the ESMA were beaten, tortured, humiliated, held incommunicado, and usually killed, tactics that were common in the Dirty War. But the rumors did not prepare the ESMA's victims for the psychological minefield that began after the physical torture was over. According to Martín Gras, a former Montonero guerrilla held at the ESMA for over a year and who provided extensive testimony on the internal workings of the Grupo de Tareas (GT) 3.3/2, the naval officers who ran the torture center at the ESMA bragged of their little fiefdom as being "the Sorbonne of antisubversion."[1] It was not enough that the ESMA officers successfully infiltrated the Montonero guerrillas, broke their captives, and exterminated most of their victims (whether they were guerrillas or not). Parallel to their brutality, the officers chose a small group of prisoners for survival and put them through a psychological experiment known as the "process of recuperation," which owed as much to French counterinsurgency theory as it did to the Spanish Inquisition. The process was designed to reshape the ESMA's captives into God-fearing and patriotic Argentines by exploiting their victims' terror and disorientation from having been captured by the navy and allowed to live. The *militantes* had prepared themselves to die—many carried cyanide pills to commit suicide instead of being taken alive—but they had not prepared themselves to live after capture. Could they survive? What would they have to sacrifice to do so?

The detainees became nonentities sucked up into the military's black hole, held in a macabre limbo between life and death. Just outside the walls where they were held, survivor witnesses at trial recalled hearing the sounds of ordinary life—children playing at a school across the street from the ESMA; commuter trains barreling past, taking thousands of office workers to their jobs in downtown Buenos Aires; airplanes flying overheard as they made their final descent to Jorge Newbery Airfield; the yells and screams of throngs of enthusiastic fans who cheered the River Plate soccer team from the iconic stadium just down the road. But inside the prisoners were subordinated to the whims and fancies of the officers who controlled their fate. The logic of the camp was to "obliterate the identity of the detainees," according to Martín Gras. "The central technique was to absolutely deny the prisoners their free will. Nothing, absolutely nothing that we prisoners did inside was done as a matter of right."[2]

Death was never far away. Prisoners were rarely killed inside of the camp—it was usually an accident if they were—but a rotating cast of anonymous hooded and shackled prisoners routinely populated the camp and just as quickly disappeared, leaving behind only shoes and used clothing. These anonymous figures haunted the trial, populating the testimony of the eighty-two survivors who took the stand. The prisoners chosen for survival were sometimes given small benefits—at first it might be a cigarette or a swig of whiskey, later it might be a visit with a family member, a trip to a soccer game, or a night on the town—but these sweet tastes of life were always soured by the constant reminder that they lived in perhaps the only condition worse than slavery, as a living disappeared. The ESMA was, in the words of the prosecution, "a place where schizophrenia was a major part of the structure: it was death before death, or life between death."[3]

What happened at the ESMA has been known for years. But the trial was the first time the ESMA was presented to the public in all its destructive dimensions. Over the course of more than a year between April 2010 and April 2011, survivors took the witness stand one by one, spending considerable and painful emotional energy by pouring out their experiences from thirty years prior. As a legal matter, some of their testimony was superfluous, and at times it bordered on the irrelevant. But as a matter of "justice," both the prosecution and the victims' lawyers agreed that it was essential. In their minds, the issue of justice went far beyond proving just the limited set of charges in the case; the trial was an opportunity to show what had happened at the ESMA and record the catastrophe for history.

It was a compelling case.

The ESMA task force would kidnap its targets from their homes, their workplaces, or on the streets—typically marked by another comrade who had broken under torture (though few witnesses admitted to having done so). Detainees were stuffed into a vehicle, usually thrown hooded onto the back seat or floor of the car, and raced off to the ESMA. Once there they were escorted down a staircase from the parking lot at the back of the building to the basement of the officers' club at the far end of the school. A sign above the central hallway of the basement read "Avenue of Happiness." At the end of the corridor were several rooms, including the famous Room 13, where the interrogations took place.

Martín Gras dryly recalled his first moments in the ESMA at trial:

> Among the *militantes*, some information circulated about the ESMA. When I walked down the steps that lead to the basement, and I heard the music . . . I knew that I was in the ESMA. . . . A man appeared who was clearly the boss, because he asked for details about me, the person who had just been kidnapped. [My captor] gave them details. [The boss] hugged me and kissed me through my shirt, and said to me, "I love you! I love you!" I thought to myself that I had fallen in a very bad place.
>
> The first thing that happened, curiously, was a conversation. They took off the improvised blindfold that they had put on me, and I had a conversation with a man about forty years old, with gray hair, with a tidy appearance, in slacks, a shirt, and silk tie. He had an authoritarian and firm tone, and he explained to me "the rules of the game" of the place. He explained to me that I had surely been trained to resist pain . . . but that I was now confronting an unprecedented situation. They had unlimited time and unrestricted means to get the information that they wanted.

That, before, a dissident who was detained for a short time had to be presented before the justice system, but that was no longer the case.[4]

Silvia Labayrú, who was nineteen at the time she was kidnapped, recalled with much more terror the day she was kidnapped:

> I was driven without a hood in the back seat of a car. When I got in the car, they told me, "You lost." They took me up Avenue Figueroa Alcorta, to the entrance of the ESMA, and they put a hood on me, put my head down, and threw me on the floor of the car. From there we entered the ESMA, and they drove me to a small parking lot. They got me out of the car and took me down into a basement. They told me I was number 765, and they directed me to a small room. Later I saw that they called this the "Avenue of Happiness." It was five or six rooms that were used to torture. They took me to one of these rooms, and inside was Captain Whamond and several other officers who I didn't know. [Whamond] started to beat me with a stick. After the beating, they took my clothes off, they put me naked onto a metal bed frame, and he started to interrogate me and electrocute me on the legs and feet.[5]

She was given the same treatment as everyone else despite being five months pregnant.

Witnesses recalled that the interrogators were obsessed with making sure that their procedures went to the most sensitive areas of a man's or a woman's body: the genitals, the nipples, and inside the mouth. The interrogations were usually accompanied by loud music to disorient the torture victims and drown out the sounds of the screams. Doctors were on call to monitor the torture and make sure that the detainees did not die from electrocution. The torture victims were overcome with involuntary convulsions during electrocution with the cattle prod. Two opposite responses were common. Some recalled the tremendous pain of the electricity and the beatings. Others, however, testified that the torture put them into a kind of meditative state, and they were able to separate their minds from the physical experience of the pain. A few even managed to beat the torture—it is rumored that Jorge Caffati, a longtime Peronist militant, proudly sang the "Peronist March" as his interrogators tried to elicit information from him.

Detainees might spend a day or two in the interrogation room in the basement, sometimes longer if the task force believed a captive was withholding valuable information. The interrogation was designed to break the prisoners and get them to "sing" on their revolutionary colleagues, as was the parlance on the inside. The Montoneros had established an elaborate security system in which members of each guerrilla cell made periodic contact with one another through a telephone answering service or prescheduled meetings. If contact was not made during one of the controls, the cell would "lift up," and members were prohibited from contacting one another or going to future meetings, the assumption being that the missing cell member had been detained or kidnapped and had compromised the security of the rest of the group. The bulk of the ESMA's "intelligence" work was aimed at infiltrating these meetings, capturing prisoners and torturing them until they broke and gave up information on other members of their cell.

"Every war has a decisive weapon," testified Martín Gras. "The GT officers were convinced that they were fighting the Third World War against an evanescent and phantasmagorical enemy: subversion. Because of this, the central problem was how to identify the enemy, who could be anywhere and be any person. To [identify] this enemy, the only efficient way was torture, which became the decisive weapon in this particular type of confrontation."[6]

But the ESMA task force utilized much more than pain to extract information from their captives; they played a complicated mental game with their prisoners. As the ESMA survivor Pilar Calveiro notes in her book *Poder y desaparición*, submitted into evidence, the naval officers knew that most of their victims expected to die when they were captured—many carried cyanide capsules to commit suicide rather than run the risk of confessing under torture—but they had not necessarily expected to live. The navy exploited this expectation of death and convinced some of their captives that they could live, and to prove that survival was possible, they often brought other captives into the torture room who had long been taken for dead. Sometimes these were heroic and well-known members of the Montoneros, such as Norma Arrostito, one of the founding members of the Montoneros, and Roberto Ahumada, the former leader of the Peronist Youth and one of Perón's delegates on his return from Spain after nearly two decades in exile. By showing off these important prisoners to new captives, the ESMA task force reduced the new captives' will to resist. *If others had succumbed and given up information,* the prisoners would think, *why should I make myself a martyr?* Jaime Dri remembers that when he arrived at the ESMA, the officers brought Beto Ahumada to the torture room. "It was the first great blow I received," recalled Dri. "To me, Beto Ahumada had been dead for a while—this was the first dead person I saw alive."[7]

There were other methods to extract information from the prisoners. The ESMA task force also knew that most members of the Montoneros were desperate and demoralized. Their struggle had a glorious beginning, culminating in the months before Perón's return when they seemed to be the most powerful political force in Argentina and were able to mobilize hundreds of thousands of Argentines in just a matter of days. But after their split from Perón, the growth of paramilitary organizations that specialized in hunting them down, and their loss of political support among Argentina's mainstream, members of the Montoneros increasingly felt that their fight was for naught. This was especially pronounced among the lower-level activists, who often remained committed to the organization because of personal loyalties to fellow *militantes* rather than their belief that their cause would succeed. Their desperation and demoralization were especially pronounced after most of the Montonero leadership left the country in exile in late 1976 and early 1977, leaving the *perejiles* (low-ranking activists) to fend for themselves against the ruthless tactics of the dictatorship, with little or no organizational support from their once powerful bosses. The ESMA was well aware of this internal frustration, and so after they tortured their detainees for information, they often found that these detainees were desperate to survive—to live any way but constantly on the run and in hiding—and when offered the opportunity to collaborate and survive, they were willing to do so. If they could survive, perhaps the other prisoners they turned in could also.

Carlos Muñoz testified that a fellow prisoner put pressure on him to "sing"—that is, to turn in other comrades. He continued,

> Part of the "intelligence work" of the operations group was to try to use your friends, your *compañeros,* your brothers, and your family to break

> the kidnapee. It was a mechanism, it was habitual, daily—any one of the *compañeros* who were kidnapped can tell you that in the middle of your torture or post torture, someone would come and say to you, "Look, why don't you sing . . . ?" And these weren't the officers who told you this; these were people who were tortured, who obviously were used to do this. And how could you refuse to do so? That's another question . . . refusing to do so meant that you weren't collaborating. Not doing so . . . it was to get yourself into a complicated situation.[8]

It was, of course, humiliating. The interrogations and torture were aimed at destroying their solidarity with fellow activists, their dignity, and even their will to live. "On the one hand," recalled Arturo Barros, a former Montonero militant, "it was the destruction of the will to resist the interrogation. On the other hand, it was the destruction of the individual as a *militante politico*; it was designed to remove your will to confront the injustices that you saw in the world."[9]

Torture was the mechanism to feed the camp with new detainees. At the end of the torture sessions, when the new detainees were disoriented, broken, dejected, and desperate to make it end, the officers would take them out in shackles in a patrol squad on a *paseo* or *lancheo*—a fishing expedition. They would be taken where the ESMA officers believed that they had a meeting with a fellow *militante*, and they would be required to mark that person if they saw them. Many resisted by silently refusing to mark their comrades on the streets, but the ESMA took the prisoners out in pairs to make sure everyone was telling the truth. If one victim marked their comrades and the other did not, they would know that the victim who did not mark their comrades was withholding information.

After the interrogations and *paseos* were over, the prisoners were taken into the *capucha* (hood), an area of the attic with little ventilation or light where they were kept on mattresses on the floor separated from one another by particleboard dividers. "If torture was something insufferable, the *capucha* was truly terrifying," testified Ana María Martí. "I saw hundreds and hundreds and hundreds and hundreds of people that I didn't know who they were; I couldn't remember more than a handful. The orders were not to talk, not to cry, not to scream."[10]

Because the prisoners were hooded while they were there, most of the testimony of this confinement focused on the sounds and smells of the place—the moving chains, the screams and panic attacks of new arrivals, the whispers from other prisoners as they tried to figure out who else was being held there and what was going on.

Life in the *capucha* was complete degradation. The guards randomly beat prisoners. "One guard played soccer with our heads," recalled Martín Gras.[11] The "bathroom" was usually a small bucket. Both men and women used the bucket the same way—hooded, cuffed, and shackled, they bent over the bucket to urinate or defecate and then went back to lying on their mattresses after relieving themselves. When the prisoners were permitted to use the real bathroom, they were escorted in a single-file line as a group. The guards watched as everyone performed their necessities. "Sometimes they took us five or six times in a day," testified Ana María Martí. "Other times it was once every two days. Many of us urinated in *capucha*, the smell of *capucha*—it was like there was no oxygen. . . . There was the smell of excrement, of urine, of vomit, of blood, of death."[12] Food was scarce and repetitive. They were given *maté cocido* (Argentine tea) in the morning, bread and meat during lunch and dinner—a "bife-naval," as it was called in the lingo of the camp. In the winter, the temperatures plummeted; in summer, they soared. Rats crawled on the floors. At one point the guards brought in cats to chase off the rodents. Some prisoners recall that they watched the rats below their hoods as a way of passing time while they lay motionless and confined to their small boxes and mattresses. Silvia Labayrú, who was pregnant at the time she was kidnapped, recalled, "I had the feeling that they were simply waiting for me to give birth—they themselves said that our kids were innocent and didn't have to pay for the errors of their parents. There were clear indications [that] they didn't see me as a human being. They didn't look me in the face."[13]

Fernando Kron recalled life while hooded twenty-four hours a day:

> Being there on the inside was a strange dimension between life and nonexistence. Being hooded meant being objectified—not only because we were numbers, but because we were paralyzed, we had no relationship to anything. That is to say, being hooded meant being part of an

> absolutely inhumane process in which we had no ability to make any decisions about anything that was going to happen in what I would call our bizarre lives. Being hooded, being in these conditions was a type of limbo where our life completely depended on someone else. What was left to us was our internal world, and sometimes they even tried to completely destroy this too. It was very difficult not to drive yourself crazy while hooded, chained, and kidnapped.[14]

Mario Villani, who spent three years in several of Argentina's prison camps, including the ESMA, recalled at trial,

> For me, the physical torture wasn't the worst. The worst torture was daily life in the camps, surrounded by the screams of those being tortured, constantly thinking that tomorrow they would kill me, thinking that I would never be able to have a future—to not say to yourself, "When I get out of here, I will rejoin my family, my wife. I will look for a job, I will leave the country." You couldn't do any of these things. I told myself to just get to the next day, and every time I did, I said to myself, "I made it." But you heard the screams of those being tortured, being treated like animals, seeing people die, falling into a coma. You had to continually simulate in front of the officers that everything was okay, that nothing was wrong. This, this life, for me, was worse than the *picana*, especially when those I loved disappeared.[15]

Many other victims similarly remember the physical torture not being the worst part of life in the ESMA. Miguel Lauletta said,

> Sometimes people believe that torture is nothing more than when they tie you to a bed and give you the *picana*, but all of us who passed through the ESMA know that the entire time there was torture. I was in the room where they kept all the documentation, and sometimes they would enter, put a hood on me, chain me, take me out of the room, and sit me on a bench right outside the door. I felt people entering and I heard the screams of someone inside, and when I returned, I smelled the smell, the smell that stays on someone's body after they have been tortured, what a smell. I saw hair stuck to the wall with blood. This too is torture. Torture isn't just being hit by someone. It's every day that we suffered there inside. Torture is the sensation we got on the days of the

transfers, when we heard the numbers. I, a devoted atheist, prayed to God that they didn't call mine.[16]

The "lucky" victims were released soon after being moved to the *capucha,* usually within a week or two. While it is impossible to say why these survivors lived and hundreds of others were killed, they were apparently the "mistake" cases, people with not a significant enough connection—real or imagined—to the revolutionary left to be worth holding or killing.

Most of the rest of the victims were "transferred," a euphemism that many of the captives did not initially understand. At first some believed that the transfers were sent to supposed recuperation camps in Patagonia where they would be held for a time before they were released. "During one transfer before December 1976," recalled Lisandro Raúl Cubas, one of the early ESMA detainees, "they started to call the prisoners. All the prisoners were identified by a number. I was 571. They kept calling out those who were to form a line, and I desperately started to yell 'Me, me, take me, 571!'"[17] But the tense environment and violence of the transfer days belied the idea that "transfers" were beneficial.

"We knew that every Wednesday," recalled Marta Álvarez at trial, "the guards got very nervous. . . . You couldn't ask to go to the bathroom. Everyone was very nervous. In *capucha,* they called everyone by number, and you heard the sound of chains going down the stairs. On these days, it was very rigid for everyone."[18]

Martín Gras recalled a similar climate:

> It was very strange: every Wednesday, the officers disappeared. This particular task they left to the junior officers of the work group. Specifically, the level of a set of junior officers of particular trust, who were called the *pedros* in the code of the work group. The *pedros* would appear in *capucha* with a clipboard and a list of numbers—remember that they used numbers and not names—accompanied by some *verdes. Verdes* were young kids, young kids. I guess that some of them were students at the ESMA, probably *cabos,* very young. So they'd stop at the door of the *capucha* and yell out numbers. Immediately, a group of the *verdes* would descend upon a person and grab them. They didn't leave time for them to get their shirts. If they had taken off their shoes, they didn't

> give them time to take their shoes. It was very violent. They immediately took them away. It was . . . there was an air, a tremendous air of tension and violence. You smelled it.[19]

Gray or white hoods were placed over those prisoners chosen for transfer, and they were marched out in a line generally fifteen to twenty people long.

The officers kept the destination purposefully vague, treating the victims like cattle hidden from the slaughterhouse floor. In truth, the "transfers" meant certain death. The prisoners were walked to the basement and given what they were told was a vaccination. The fluid was actually a dose of the sedative sodium pentothal, dubbed "pento-naval" by the officers. The dose was just enough to let the victims walk under their own power but not enough for them to resist. The prisoners were loaded onto trucks, driven to the airport, loaded onto airplanes, and pushed out alive over the South Atlantic.

Martín Gras recalled that he first heard that the transfers meant certain death from Silvia Labayrú when the two were taken to the bathroom together and Labayrú told him that Officer Alfredo Astiz told her never to request being transferred. Gras received confirmation when a prisoner was taken on a transfer and later returned to the ESMA. Recalled Gras,

> Detained and kidnapped next to me in *capucha* was a former noncommissioned officer [NCO] of the navy—I don't remember his name, he was known by the pseudonym "Tincho." Tincho had been tortured and later taken on one of the transfers. He returned from the transfer. He was returned from the transfer because he had been a noncommissioned officer in the navy, and the SIN [Servicio de Inteligencia Naval] had a right to question him, but the SIN had not yet questioned him. So they made him return from the airport. . . . He told me about his experience: he had been taken to the basement, to the infirmary. In the infirmary a noncommissioned officer had given him an injection, which he said was a vaccine against a bunch of diseases. . . . They gave him that injection and told him that he would have some dizziness, probably until he lost consciousness for a moment, because it was a very strong injection to guarantee his health in the new detention center where he was

> going to be taken. . . . He remembered that there were people lying on the floor, that they had vomited. Tincho is . . . was, he was a big person, 1.90 meters tall, 100 kilos heavy. What we reconstructed later is that the injection they gave him in the basement was pentothal. . . . Pentothal must only be effective in relation to the amount of drug injected per kilo . . . Tincho apparently did not fall asleep completely, but he became drowsy and exhausted. They put him on a truck—he says that he recognized the ESMA, that he had previously served at the ESMA—they drove through the interior of the ESMA and then ended up at the airport, where a plane was waiting. When they're there, while the guards were moving the sleeping prisoners from the truck to the plane, the guards got a call on the walkie-talkie and ordered the NCO in charge to return [Tincho]. The ESMA NCOs treated him with some . . . I wouldn't say softness, but maybe a little more flexibility because at the end of the day, Tincho had also been an ESMA NCO. The guards finished transferring the prisoners and then brought Tincho back in the front of the truck. Tincho then told them, "How unlucky I am, I thought I was leaving here! And that the interrogations had ended, now the SIN is going to grab me back!" The two NCOs stopped the truck, looked at him, and said, "Kid, you don't know what you were saved from. All those guys in the truck with you will be dead in an hour; you're the only one still alive."[20]

In 1995, a former naval officer named Adolfo Scilingo came forward to journalist Horacio Verbitsky and recounted in vivid detail his participation in two of these death flights. Once on the plane, Scilingo explained, a doctor injected the prisoners with a second shot to put them to sleep. The doctor then left the cabin—"something to do with the Hippocratic oath"—and then, "in their unconscious state, the prisoners were stripped, and when the commander of the airplane gave the order, which happened according to the location of the plane, the hatch was opened and they were thrown out, naked, one by one." Scilingo continued,

> That's the story. A gruesome story, but true, and no one can deny it. I can't get the image of the naked bodies lined up in the plane's aisle, like something in a movie about Nazis. It was done from Skyvan planes belonging to the Coast Guard and Electras belonging to the Navy. In

> the Skyvan, it was through the rear hatch, which slides down to open. It's a big door, but it has no intermediate positions. It's closed or it's open, so it was kept in the open position. The noncommissioned officer kept his foot on the door, so that there would be about 40 centimeters opening onto empty space. Then we started to lower the subversives through there.[21]

The suffering that the ESMA's prisoners experienced was, tragically, no better or worse than prisoners in the extensive network of 340 clandestine prisons that were set up all across Argentina throughout the dictatorship, where torture, kidnapping, sexual humiliation, execution, and forced disappearance were official government policies. But the depth of the evil at the ESMA—or was it the humanity?—was characterized not by the beatings, the sexual humiliation, the torture, the solitary confinement, the sensory deprivation, or the executions but by birthday cakes, family visits, Christmas and New Year celebrations, fancy dinners, nightclubs, and Argentina's victory during the 1978 World Cup held in Buenos Aires. This was the "insanity" of the place, as the prosecution repeatedly said in their closing argument at trial. Those who were chosen for survival were put through a dizzying "process of recuperation," an idea apparently invented by Capt. Jorge Eduardo Acosta, the chief of intelligence, to save some of the detainees while most were discarded.

Why had the navy become so involved in the War against Subversion in the first place? And why was it an officers' club at a naval junior officers' school that became the seat of the strangest psychological "antisubversive" experiment of the dictatorship? By regulation, under the Capacity Plan of the Navy (Plan de Capacidades de la Armada [PLACINTARA]), the navy's role in the War against Subversion was limited to the areas within its jurisdiction—the navigable waterways, the bases where they had significant troop presence, and the maritime borders of the country.[22] The focus of the navy's "antisubversive" efforts was, by regulation, to be concentrated in the sparsely populated areas where they had a significant presence. The ESMA was only supposed to be in control of a small area of Buenos Aires around the school itself, cooperating with the two local police precincts. They had been relegated to a subordinate role to the army, which was assigned the primary responsibility of fighting the War against Subversion. Indeed, Adm. Chamorro, the director of the ESMA, was supposed to report to the First Army Corp about the ESMA's operations.

This was the most obvious way to divvy up responsibility for the War against Subversion. "The navy prepared itself to defend the fatherland in the sea," Capt. Jorge Eduardo Acosta, the head of the ESMA work group, put it in a declaration in military court in 1985. Argentine naval officers prior to the March 1976 coup held themselves out as the seafaring elite, the great inheritors of the British Imperial naval tradition, known largely as the more democratic of the service branches. They were ill-prepared to fight an urban counterinsurgency. It was the army that was better trained to fight the War against Subversion—French and Argentine specialists had taught in the Army War College, and the army had written the operations manuals that guided the counterinsurgency campaign. Indeed, the military background of most of the officers who worked as part of the GT 3.3/2 shows that they had little or no counterinsurgency training. Antonio Pernías, one of the task force's "intelligence" officers, was trained as an infantryman. Even those officers who came from an intelligence background, such as Raúl Enrique Scheller, said that they mostly learned to fight "subversion" on the job, that their formal training had not prepared them for what they were assigned to do.

But the truth was, the ESMA officers were men of initiative. "We learned how to do it during the war," said Jorge Eduardo Acosta, the chief intelligence officer at the ESMA. They were men who took it upon themselves—as a matter of military honor, patriotic pride, and personal duty—to fight the War against Subversion. In fact, a number of the officers volunteered to be there; some even came out of retirement. (Outside of the courtroom, I heard rumors that the army personnel who migrated to the ESMA made their way there because they felt constrained in the army; the most creative work, so to speak, was taking place within the ESMA, where they felt the War against Subversion was being won.)

It was, apparently, thanks to Adm. Emilio Eduardo Massera, alias "Cero," that the navy assumed for itself the outsized role of full-blown Montonero hunters. Recalls Martín Gras, "Theoretically, the Junta divided the power of the state 33 percent for each service branch, but this was a fiction. The army was the army, the navy was the navy, and the air force was the air force. As the formal justification for the coup was repressing subversion, power was obtained in direct relation to the efficiency of the War against Subversion."[23]

With this division, the army would inevitably have more power than the navy or the air force, as the army was to have primary responsibility in the War against Subversion. But according to Gras, Massera saw this as an opportunity. Massera was an ambitious admiral—a common joke was that his biggest mistake in life was going into the navy rather than the army, where all the previous military presidents had come from. The army was a much more powerful institution than the navy, but Massera was determined not to let his membership in the wrong service branch determine his future prospects as president of Argentina. As a way of both furthering his own political ambition and raising the profile of the navy vis-à-vis the army, Massera insisted that trusted men close under his command spearhead an effective campaign against subversion on behalf of the navy.

To inspire his underlings, victims testified about rumors that Massera participated in some of the earliest raids conducted by the GT 3.3/2 and even supervised one of the earliest torture sessions. At a speech several months after the military coup in front of officers at the ESMA, Massera told those gathered to "employ the maximum violence possible, without tripping up over the means," a maxim that was frequently repeated by Jorge Eduardo Acosta, Massera's trusted underling and the intelligence chief of the GT 3.3/2. "We are not going to fight until the death," Massera later told an assemblage of officers in November 1976 at the height of the Dirty War. "We are going to fight until victory, whether or not it is beyond death."[24]

In order to make the navy a more effective fighting force in the War against Subversion, Massera sidelined the traditional navy bureaucracy. Theoretically, the SIN was supposed to gather and analyze intelligence, but Massera was dubious of their ability. "From what Tigre [Acosta] told me," recalled Andrés Castillo, "the SIN told Massera that they weren't prepared because they were a smaller force than the army. But because Massera wanted to be more important than the other service branches, he created the GT 3.3/2, without paying attention to what the SIN had said, and he named people who he trusted or gave him prestige within the navy. Acosta was a man he trusted." Other officers were appointed to the GT 3.3/2 to lend credibility to Massera's project. Castillo stated, "[Alfredo] Astiz was there because his father had been a very important officer who was passed over and forced to retire when Massera was promoted [to commander in chief.] . . . Because of this, they assigned Astiz, which gave [Massera] prestige within the navy."[25]

Jorge Eduardo Acosta, one of the more candid officers, recalled the origins of the ESMA. In January 1976, before the military coup, the ESMA participated in preparations for the coup. Prior to the formation of the GT 3.3/2, the officers at the ESMA had limited themselves to patrolling the streets and arresting a number of Peronist leaders who were on a list as suspected opponents of the military coup, known as "Operation Garaffa." But the operation was not successful, as the navy failed to locate most of its targets, so in April "a special group denominated as the Unidad de Tareas 3.3.2 was formed." Acosta recalled that on April 14, 1976, during a ceremony in the Salon Dorado of the ESMA, when Capt. Burgos was laid to rest after being killed in a Montonero attack, Adm. Rubén Jacinto Chamorro, the head of the esma, pressed Adm. Massera to plunge the GT 3.3/2 into the fight against the Montoneros, and the members of the task force were eager to do more.[26]

Apparently with Massera's blessing, the GT 3.3/2 then devoted itself to attacking the Montoneros. The first few months of operations were not successful. "We'd go in our uniforms, we'd knock on doors, and out came the grenade," recalled Jorge Eduardo Acosta. During the initial phase, until about July 1976, Acosta said that the task force "acted in a conventional way" and "did not obtain practically any terrorist alive, and if it happened, it was by accident." There were "very few successes in obtaining information." By changing their tactics to "increase the weight of the actions of the intelligence agents," Acosta bragged that the GT 3.3/2 began to have "important successes."[27]

According to some of the earliest survivors, a turning point came when Capt. Salvio Menéndez, the commander of the GT 3.3/2, was injured in a firefight in June 1976, leaving Jorge Eduardo Acosta in charge. Prior to Acosta's tenure as leader of the task force, the detainees were routinely and quickly exterminated. But according to Marta Álvarez, who was kidnapped in June 1976 and saw the early development of the GT 3.3/2, Acosta saw that the detainees were significant assets—not just for intelligence purposes but to help the navy articulate political doctrines and also to gain a better understanding of the revolutionary movements they faced. Acosta began to require all the new detainees to write their life histories—long confessions detailing all their activist and guerrilla activities.

In a rambling statement in military court in 1986, Acosta explained it this way:

> According to the Occidental and Christian conception, war is the continuation of politics by other means (the political *hecho* par excellence). According to the Marxist concept, war is the interim between two moments of peace (the political *hecho* par excellence). In the end, the different types of war—conventional, nuclear, revolutionary, limited, galactic—are only in essence different in the politico-military charge of the moment—in other words, what percentage of 100 percent is it political or military. As a consequence within the idea of "judicial reasonableness" you can't respond to a conventional war with nuclear war, and likewise, without going into great detail, you can't respond to a revolutionary war with a conventional or a nuclear war. This would affect "judicial reasonableness," and this is in fact what we respected. We responded to the methods of a terrorist revolutionary war . . . with the methods of revolutionary war of the legal forces and within the juridical framework to which I have alluded.[28]

Marta Álvarez testified,

> After Acosta took over, they put the detainees in contact with one another who were there, and for the new detainees, and who knew who we were, they started to bring us to show off to each person they detained. They took us to chat with them . . . like two or three *compañeros* who were kidnapped named me, thinking that I was dead, and they told them, "Do you want to see her?" They couldn't believe that I was alive, so they brought me to see them.[29]

Acosta also made the prisoners analyze information, look at newspaper clippings, and track what the foreign press was saying about subversion and human rights. Shortly after Acosta put these first survivors to work, Álvarez says, he started talking about a process of recuperation. "He said that 'Jesucito' would decide who would live and who would die," Álvarez told the court. "He told us that he needed a team and that we were a good option to be this team—that the idea was to engage in politics, that they couldn't just go out and kidnap people, that they had to change their project, that they had to have a political project."[30]

Acosta recalled that the intelligence agents were selected for three criteria: first, if there was a real possibility of tactical success and obtaining information; second, if there was an opportunity to "show a criminal" that "terrorism wasn't the path to solve the problems of the Argentine community," a lesson that could be taught by the navy itself; and third, if the individual had the capacity to adapt to being an intelligence agent for the length of the war.[31]

The navy's top brass had all testified for years that the intelligence agents had been voluntary collaborators, but when asked about this issue, Acosta offered to "clarify." He told a military court in 1986 that "all the intelligence agents were in some way deprived of their freedom for a prolonged period. But it's important to stress that they weren't deprived of their freedom; rather, they tacitly accepted this type of live-work situation where this pseudodeprivation of freedom meant security to avoid being murdered by their organization, as happened to Señora Gerardini, who was murdered by the Montoneros organization because her husband had previously agreed to be an intelligence agent."[32] He explained that the intelligence agents (his way of describing his prisoners) were given the possibility of "doing something constructive for the nation in such a difficult moment when they had just worked very shortly before to destroy it." They were also "given the chance to reconnect to their families without fear." In sum, Acosta told the court, "to determine if they were deprived of their freedom, you have to evaluate the spirit and moral conviction behind this necessity," which he didn't think was illegal.

For the first two years while the ESMA operated, corresponding to the time that Jorge Eduardo Acosta was in charge, the detainees chosen for survival were split into roughly two groups. At first, a "ministaff" was created. Many survivors recall that the ministaff were active collaborators with the military, though the extent and significance of that collaboration have gone through significant revision and reanalysis over the years. The members of the ministaff were the detainees who routinely went out on raids with the ESMA task force to mark other *militantes* and the ones who showed an exaggerated sympathy and identification with the military after they broke under torture. (One of the members of the ministaff, Anita Dvatman, married officer Jorge Radice.) Later, the GT 3.3/2 formed a "staff" among the prisoners, which was a larger group of detainees who worked in an office in the attic of the ESMA known as the *pecera*, or "fishbowl," because of the glass walls that segregated the area from the rest of the attic.

The staff was put to work to bolster the political ambitions of Adm. Emilio Eduardo Massera, who was then campaigning for an electoral exit from the dictatorship and was hoping to cast himself as a populist president and the rightful heir to Juan Domingo Perón. The staff members summarized press reports from foreign agencies, wrote histories about Argentine trade unionism and the militant left, and even did coursework for their captors for their studies at the war school. They were used as a kind of left-wing think tank to bolster Massera's political ambitions.

Juan Gasparini, a member of the staff, explained why the navy wanted them:

> They used to tell us that they were interested in our manner of thinking. They thought that the political experience that we had gained through the revolutionary tendency of Peronism, in which we had mobilized two to three million people in the great mobilizations of Ezeiza and the ones that proceeded and succeeded it. . . . That is to say, they thought that we had a kind of magic formula.
>
> They thought we knew the magic formula, so they wanted to know how we thought, how we reacted to the day's news, our opinions on what we read in the newspapers, and in some cases—not in my case, but in the case of those who they thought had some sort of political importance—they asked them to write the story of their lives. It seems as though they copied this from the experience of the United States in Vietnam. That is to say, to know the thinking of your supposed enemy,

> you had to make him tell about his life. After they told the stories of their lives, they could find the secret laws that these people lived by in their lives to know them better and, obviously, to be able to combat them better.[33]

Gasparini recalled that he was asked about the day's news and what he thought of the political transition. "It wasn't military collaboration—that is to say, we didn't give them details about people so that they could go out and repress—rather, it was an exchange of ideas. . . . It wasn't about collaborating with them militarily," recalled Gasparini. "It wasn't about giving them information so that they could go out into the streets and repress people; rather, they wanted to know our ideas."[34] Jaime Dri told the court, "We were going to be the center-left for Massera's government. Those of us who survived weren't *perejiles*." He also noted that most of the survivors were significant members of the Peronist and Montonero leadership.[35]

When asked about the ESMA's connections to Massera, Captain Acosta explained in military court in 1986 that it had nothing to do with Massera's political objectives but was in order to fully realize the "mother objective" of the antisubversive fight—to "go deep into" the "global aspects" of the war through policy by focusing on education, culture, and unions. He said the intelligence agents under his command were required to study and analyze each of these objectives so as to enable the GT 3.3/2 to predict the activities of the subversives and outmaneuver them. Massera, Acosta explained, was a "complex political figure" who the task force used, in part, as a replacement for the Montoneros' Mario Firmenich (the leader of the Montoneros). By replacing one idol with another, Acosta said, they were able to "defantasize the intelligence agents."[36]

Some of the officers also exploited the captives. For them, the impunity with which they operated became a chance to pillage, to steal, to rob, and to rape. They seemed to enjoy their work and the power that came with it. Though not formally part of the charges, witnesses recalled officers using their female captives as sex toys, abusing them at will.

Graciela García, a member of the ministaff who was for years ostracized by many of her fellow survivors, was thought by many to have been Jorge Eduardo Acosta's girlfriend. But at trial, García explained the situation:

> One night I was taken down to Acosta's office and . . . he offer[ed] me a piece of cake. He was "kind" that day, so to speak—not the worst version of himself—and he told me that he'd take me out. The next day, I was taken out, taken to a car, and when I opened my eyes, [Acosta] was driving. I don't know if there was another car. We entered a building on Olleros Street, near Libertador, which I understood they used for certain purposes. They called it "Guadalcanal," and there began the sexual abuse by Acosta. It was not violent because violence wasn't necessary. I was already kidnapped; I experienced violence every day. From there they took me back [to the ESMA] to shackles and handcuffs.[37]

Both the close connections between Massera and Acosta as well as the "extra" activities of some members of the GT 3.3/2 caused tension among the officers who formed the task force. According to Martín Gras, Antonio Pernías was

> the most prominent among the intelligence officers but would not hesitate to put his body on the line during operations. He came from the navy infantry; infantrymen are trained to get rough. . . . He was very respected within the logic of the work group. Acosta wasn't. Acosta was considered not serious. . . . There were Perni-istas within the *grupo de tareas*. In fact, he had a very bad relationship with Acosta; there was a lot of tension between them. But Acosta had to tolerate it because [Pernías] was a man who could guarantee the success of operations. They were two completely different personalities.

Likewise, Lt. Juan Carlos Rolón was "an intelligent man," according to Gras. "He was more informed than your average officer, who [was] in general poorly informed. He was a man who read, he understood the international context, and he was worried about the future consequences of what they were doing." Gras thought that Rolón "did what he did because he understood that this was his obligation under the sacred concept of due obedience. But it didn't seem like he felt particularly satisfied by what he was doing, in contrast to Acosta." Rolón was someone who tortured because he had to, according to Gras, while Acosta was one who tortured because he wanted to.[38]

Whatever the internal divisions, the ESMA's operations under Acosta's intelligence direction quickly bore fruit. In just over a year, the navy went from being a relatively insignificant and ineffective part of the War against Subversion to being perhaps the most effective of the three service branches, at least from the internal logic of the Dirty War. Miguel Lauletta, an early detainee known as "Cain" (survivors recall he earned the nickname because of his extensive collaboration with the GT 3.3/2 and his propensity to turn over former *compañeros,* but Lauletta says it was a nickname that came from before he was in the ESMA), recalled many of the ESMA's "successes" at trial in infiltrating the Montoneros. By October 1976, just eight months after the military coup and only four months after Acosta effectively took control of the group, the ESMA discovered the Montoneros' *citas nacionales,* a series of national meetings for *militantes* to reconnect with the organization and facilitate an exchange among the regional columns of the organization. Dozens of important *militantes* fell into the hands of the ESMA after October 20, 1976, which provided the ESMA with a comprehensive picture of the Montonero organization.[39] Lisandro Raúl Cubas, a victim who was kidnapped that day, recalls that he ingested a cyanide capsule before he was captured, but it did not work, and he awoke on top of a pile of dead bodies.[40]

After the *citas nacionales,* the intelligence officers drew a diagram of the organizational structure of the Montoneros on the wall of the torture room so that they could show newly arrived detainees where they were in the structure and overwhelm them with the amount of intelligence they had on the organization—the four columns around Buenos Aires and in the capital. As more *militantes* were sucked up, the intelligence officers filled in the chart with details on individual cells—who belonged, who was whose *responsable,* what were the *militantes'* nicknames and real names, and what activity they were assigned to do. It quickly caused the unraveling of the Montonero organization in Buenos Aires and its surroundings. The ESMA soon infiltrated the *pies telefonicos,* a pre–answering machine service that the Montoneros used as a security system to control meetings and to ensure the safety of individual cells. In November 1976 the ESMA kidnapped most of the lawyers who lent support to the organization. A month later the ESMA infiltrated and kidnapped most of the military section of the Montoneros' Columna Norte, the brigade based in the northern suburbs of Buenos Aires. In January 1977 the ESMA kidnapped most of the members of the Montoneros' finance section, giving the GT 3.3/2 a trail to the millions of dollars that the Montoneros had collected in ransoms held in bank accounts around the world. In February the military structure of Columna Capital was captured, and in March the logistics section of the Montoneros followed. Hundreds of activists were kidnapped in the months between October 1976 and September 1977, when the pace of the kidnappings began to slow, as few targets remained.[41]

As the ESMA "succeeded," the makeshift operations in the officers' club of the ESMA expanded. In the beginning, the improvised space in the basement was just an empty room; kidnap victims were chained to the columns when they were held prisoner. But the space was soon built out—first a room for the guards to sleep in; later an infirmary and a documentation lab. The sophistication of the building and its ability to accommodate various uses expanded as the GT 3.3/2 became more entrenched. Eventually, by late 1977 and early 1978, there was a documentation and photography lab in the basement and a glass-walled "office" in the attic known as the *pecera* (fishbowl) in which the task force housed the staff as they worked during the day. In the Salon Dorado, the task force set up the heart of the intelligence operation, housing intelligence archives and weapons in a room that was ordinarily reserved for ceremonies.

The "process of recuperation" that these survivors were put through as they were put to work for the navy revealed the elaborate extent to which the navy controlled the lives of their captives. They psychologically, physically, and emotionally destroyed them and then tried to bring them back to life in their own image. The process began with a few privileges—a hood might be replaced by a blindfold, shackles might be removed, a cot on the floor might be replaced with a bunk bed in a room. Over time the privileges increased—phone calls to family members, visits with loved ones, work during the day, jobs outside of the ESMA, supervised release. The naval officers wanted to remake their prisoners into good Christian citizens, modeled after their own families and backgrounds, with submissive women and God-fearing men. Each stage of "recuperation" seemed to be a test: with each successive benefit, the prisoners were supposed to prove yet again that they had renounced their revolutionary commitments and no longer sympathized with their former *compañeros*. At any given moment, though, the prisoners knew that if they acted wrong or said the wrong word, it could all be revoked, and they would be "sent up to talk with Jesus," as Acosta would remind them.

Alberto Girondo, who was captured in May 1977, recalls the process. The idea was to "completely change us," he told the judges at trial, "to turn us into converts of the navy's own repressive ideology. They believed that after staying in the *capucha*, after torture, after the *pecera*, we would convert into a certain type of person. They took us to restaurants, allowed us to call our families, made us go out and mark comrades. This was the basis of the process of recuperation that they made certain prisoners go through."[42]

To survive, the process required considerable psychological dexterity from the victims. The guards and officers began to treat the prisoners in the process of recuperation "as if everything were normal," recalled Graciela García, one of the earliest survivors and a member of the ministaff.[43] One day the guards might hit and kick the prisoners; the next day the same guards would serve the prisoners dinner and invite them to sit down for a meal. Miriam Lewin said, "Even though we constantly heard the screams of pain, we had to pretend that nothing was going on, because any sort of solidarity or empathy with someone who was being tortured was interpreted as a sign that we weren't in the process of being recuperated."[44] The prisoners had to be on guard with everyone around them. "The *represores* didn't have uniforms, the prisoners weren't in striped uniforms," recalls Graciela Daleo about her initial confusion when being kidnapped in the ESMA. "The repressors were dressed just like us, and many of us were the same age."[45] Even if one was eventually able to distinguish who was who, not all the prisoners were to be trusted. A wrong word could get passed to the officers, and one's commitment to the process of recuperation might be called into doubt.

During sojourns on brief family visits, some of the victims' families did not know that their relatives had been detained by the military. Preceding their detention, many of them had already gone into hiding and had lost regular contact with their families. The ESMA officers continued this subterfuge, making the prisoners periodically call or write to their families to maintain the veneer of "normalcy" that had preceded their kidnapping. Nilda Noemí Actis Goreta recalled at trial, "My family never knew, neither did my friends. They never knew I was kidnapped because I hardly ever communicated with my family by the telephone. I would write to them and . . . well, they had me continue to write to my family. For my family, I wasn't disappeared, I wasn't kidnapped, I wasn't a prisoner, nothing. I just continued to live in some place."[46] For other family members, the ESMA officers were actually saviors—men who had saved their children from the clutches of subversion. Miriam Lewin recalled at trial that her father gifted Capt. Jorge Eduardo Acosta a bottle of Chivas Regal whiskey after he brought her home and explained to the family that she was going to be recuperated.[47]

Perversely, the officers began to "help" their detainees under the twisted normalcy of the camp. There were two classes of prisoners: the new arrivals, who lay hooded and shackled in the *capucha,* and the prisoners in the process of recuperation, who might live in bunks, were able to periodically bathe and change their clothes, and spent their days doing tasks for the ESMA. All of these were little advances toward a "normal" life, but with death always lurking closely in the background. Alongside the daily pain and destruction, the officers took the prisoners under the process of recuperation out to eat, they celebrated birthdays together, and they helped the victims with family problems should they arise. After the naval officers encouraged Miriam Lewin and Carlos García to marry—two detainees who had started a relationship while on the inside of the ESMA—the officers bought them a vacuum cleaner as a gift. Many of the women were taken to Los Años Locos (The Crazy Years), an aptly named dance club. Alfredo Ayala recalled that during a national holiday, the ESMA officers once set up a long table with a tablecloth down the central hallway of the basement, just outside the torture room, and served churros, chocolate, and *medialunas*. There were also weekend trips to a *quinta* allegedly owned by Antonio Pernías's father, where victims and officers squared off in games of soccer and dined over an *asado* together after the game. "We developed a very complicated relationship," recalled Martín Gras at trial. Over time "it became hard for these officers to order us killed because we had been with them and speaking with them for over a year. It was easier to kill an unknown face."[48]

It was, perhaps, Silvia Labayrú who best embodied this perverse existence as both captive and object of the ESMA's generosity. A former low-level Montonero activist, Labayrú came from an upper-class family and was five months pregnant when she was kidnapped. This did not stop the ESMA officers from torturing her, but soon they began to treat her marginally better than the other prisoners. Officer Antonio Pernías, who was her *responsable*, said at trial that she was "special," though he did not elaborate on what he meant by that. In any event, while most of the mothers who were pregnant at the ESMA were eventually killed and their babies turned over to military families in secret, Labayrú was saved after her pregnancy, and her baby was given to her family. Recalls Martín Gras, "Silvia Labayrú had a special effect on us, as much for the detainees as the repressors. In the midst of this crazy world that was the GT, to see a pregnancy develop was something that in some way touched the most basic fibers of everyone. In a way, unconsciously, the baby that was developing inside of her was, in a peculiar way, all of our child."[49]

As the officers devoted long hours to their captives, the line between prisoner and captor sometimes blurred, and many survivors have spent the better part of three decades trying to redraw that line. Some have speculated that the naval officers needed this human contact with their prisoners as much or more than the prisoners needed the small overtures of generosity. Most of the ESMA officers lived twenty-four seven in the ESMA. After so many years of torture and killing, they needed these prisoners as a psychological escape valve, to make themselves feel that in the midst of extermination, they were "saving lives"—hence Capt. Jorge Eduardo Acosta's constant admonition that the ESMA prioritized life.

Two prisoners eventually escaped—Horacio Domingo Maggio on a trip to a store, where he rushed out a back entrance, and Jaime Dri when he was taken to the Paraguayan border to mark fellow *militantes* returning to the country from exile during the 1978 World Cup. But why didn't more prisoners escape, given that most of them were taken out of the ESMA at some point and surely would have had the opportunity? Ana María Martí recalled the pressures that bore down upon the victims in this situation:

> I lived terrorized that something would happen to my family. Because there, inside, you realized that there were no limits—that they had all the power, that they could do what they wanted, when they wanted, to whom they wanted, and where they wanted. And they showed it every day, with permanent threats. . . . When they took me to see my family for the first time around October, my mother was dying. After that they took me every month, every two or three months. If I could have tried to escape, I'm not sure I would have been successful. But living under the horror of the ESMA, everyone thought about escaping, but I didn't escape because of the terrible consequences that could happen. There was nobody to protect my family, there was nobody to protect my sisters, my parents, my children, nobody to protect the people who were inside in the *pecera*. . . . It was terrible. This is why I say we were bodies and brains without any autonomy. We were overwhelmed by total and absolute terror.[50]

Nilda Noemí Actis Goreta had a similar explanation. She says that even after the guards allowed her to sleep outside of the ESMA and work at a real estate office set up by the ESMA, she was still "kidnapped" because an elaborate system of checks and controls remained in place:

> There were still so many *compañeros* inside, and I thought that their lives depended on our behavior—or, looking on the bright side, that if I was working on the outside, they might choose one of them to work on the outside. The weight of them [the ESMA] knowing where my family lived, who they were, who were my friends—because of all of this, it never crossed my mind to escape, either on the inside or the outside. What's more, our documents wouldn't have worked; we didn't have them. It never crossed my mind.[51]

Maggio, one of the escapees, was subsequently detained and given a savage death. Once he was captured, Capt. Jorge Eduardo Acosta made sure to remind all his prisoners of the price of escape. Andrés Castillo, who knew Maggio from before their detention, recalled what happened:

> When I first arrived [at the ESMA], Maggio was already kidnapped. I had known him for many years because he had been the general delegate of the Santa Fe provincial bank. . . . Maggio, like other prisoners, including me, were taken to places—this was around the time of the World Cup—many prisoners were taken to the border to mark *compañeros*. Of course, we didn't do it; they never brought anyone back from the border. . . . Maggio was taken to the post office one day and escape[d]. A few months later, they take us down and take us to where the cars were parked in front of the *Jorges*. There was an ambulance with the door open, and there was Maggio's body. I could only recognize it because I knew him well. He was missing half of his face. I don't remember if it was the right or left side of his face. They told us this is what happens to anyone who escapes. . . . The terror began when they stopped torturing you, beating you. The terror was every day.[52]

For many years, the fact that more of these people did not escape was taken by those on the outside as evidence that the survivors were, in fact, collaborators—that at some point, they chose to cooperate with the ESMA and saved their own lives by sacrificing others. But "there weren't even rules to survive," says Martín Gras about who was chosen for survival. He continued,

> There are those who think that those who survived did so because they were traitors, or they gave up information. But the statistics show the opposite. A large number of the survivors acted ethically correct. Why? Because if it was possible to establish rules of the game—that if I give up a certain number of people, I survive, I would be an equal, I would be negotiating. But by definition, in a concentration camp, equality . . . between people doesn't exist—it's only absolute and complete arbitrariness, the complete denial of anyone's rights.[53]

Indeed, it seems that many of the ESMA detainees survived not because they collaborated but simply because their captors took a liking to them. María Eva Bernst de Hansen recalled her relationship with police officer Ernesto Weber. She recalled being nearly propositioned by

Officer Raúl Enrique Scheller (who she knew by his nickname "Mariano") while she was his captive:

> [A] few days later Mariano came to talk to me—he asked how I was doing, how I was doing with work, things like that, very ordinary, normal life things—he told me that I was a beautiful woman, that he wanted to sleep with me. I told him, "Look, sir . . . you tell me that I am a war detainee, I am a lady that you took me out of my house while I was breastfeeding my baby. I'm not a prostitute; you didn't find me on the street." And he told me, "Don't worry, dear, forget it, pretend that I didn't tell you anything." But he sent me back to *capucha*, and they left me lying there, on his orders, and they gave me no more work. . . .
>
> [Later] they took me out to mark people . . . with "220" [Weber]. On one of those occasions . . . I told [Weber] that I had been working, that Mariano had told me that he wanted to sleep with me, and he replied, "Kid, the truth is that you have some ovaries, because for much less than that, there are people who are no longer with us." From then on he had a closer relationship with me, he told me that I looked like a daughter of his, he gave me T-shirts, he brought me cigarettes, chocolates.[54]

She recalled that Weber even helped her father obtain work while she was still a prisoner when he heard that he was out of work and in poverty. At one point, Weber learned that Acosta wanted to "transfer" Bernst de Hansen. "Look," Weber told her, "we are in a meeting, and I'm trying to save you. They wanted to transfer you, and I told Tigre [Acosta] that if they transferred you, I was going to quit and take all my people with me."[55]

By 1979, after Massera retired from the navy and Acosta was getting ready to retire from his duties as head of the GT 3.3/2, the task force decided to release the remaining prisoners who had been in the process of recuperation. Gasparini recalled,

> In this process, as these *señores* called it, they were sent out to repress with the idea that their supposed enemies—the terrorists, the subversives, as they thought of me—that we were a species of savage animals who went around killing children on the streets. But after twenty

> months of our forced lives together, they noticed that at bottom, we weren't the people that they had been told about but that we were Argentines. That they thought differently than us but that we weren't criminals or terrorists.[56]

In some cases, the prisoners were released in Argentina. The ESMA task force helped many of the captives find work, or they simply put them to work in institutions close to the navy, such as the ministry of social welfare or the ministry of foreign relations. Others were sent abroad, oftentimes with plane tickets paid for by the navy and foreign contacts arranged by the ESMA officers themselves. It was Father Emilio Grasseli, the secretary to the military vicariate bishop, who helped many of the ESMA detainees flee to Venezuela. In the navy's version of events, they got them out of the country for their own good, to protect them from the other armed service branches who might still kidnap the detainees. But even from abroad, many of the victims did not feel out of control of the ESMA. Silvia Labayrú recalled how several of the officers came to visit her in Spain.

Raúl Cubas would recall years later at trial, "When Rolón freed us—in my case, he took me to Ezeiza [Airport] on January 19, 1979. . . . Rolón told me, 'Okay, remember that when the Argentine Nuremberg comes, you will tell the truth, that we saved you.' Thirty-four years later, I tell Rolón—I'm sorry he's not here today—that I'm completing that promise, and I am saying the truth and nothing but the truth."[57]

Victor Fatala told the court, "Anybody who wasn't in this situation can't understand what someone lived there on the inside. It's so difficult, because everything, including all the interpersonal relationships, were conditioned by the need to survive. So all the relationships that were formed weren't formed with free will, implying that I had [an] affinity for someone or something; rather, they were all formed in [the] function of the desperation that each one of us had to cling to life."[58]

Once freed, many of the victims could not free themselves from the ESMA. At first, the officers would follow them, check up on them; they even visited them in exile in Europe. But it was also the fact of having survived that trailed many of the survivors. "Surviving is something that is very difficult, especially in the first years, when we had to repeatedly explain why we were alive, when even I couldn't understand why I was alive," recalled Ana María Martí at trial. She continued,

> People didn't trust us. How could we leave the ESMA alive? [They ask,] "Why are you alive and the others aren't?" I spent many years of my life explaining this until I decided to isolate myself. It continues to be difficult—like on days like this, it is very uncomfortable to be alive . . . I'm sometimes embarrassed to be alive. I can't help but think that some *familiares* must question why I am alive and their family members are dead.[59]

A question, of course, that the naval officers have yet to answer.

1. Gen. Jorge Rafael Videla (*center*), Adm. Emilio Eduardo Massera (*left*), and Gen. Orlando Ramón Agosti (*right*) appear at a March 28, 1976, press conference shortly after the March 24, 1976, military coup. Licensed from Getty Images / Keystone / Hulton Archive.

2. Protesting Mothers of the Plaza de Mayo, demanding answers from the dictatorship regarding the whereabouts of their missing children, are confronted by mounted police during the March for Life on October 5, 1982. Licensed from Getty Images / Horacio.

3. Argentina's military commanders appear in the Federal Criminal Appeals Court of Buenos Aires to stand trial for crimes committed during the military dictatorship. *Top to bottom:* Adm. Armando Lambruschini, Gen. Jorge Rafael Videla, Adm. Emilio Eduardo Massera, and Gen. Omar Graffigna. Videla, dictator from 1976 to 1979 and sentenced to life in prison before he was pardoned, was the only commander to appear in civilian clothing. Licensed from Getty Images / AFP / Dani Yako.

4. The "Four Columns" building of the Naval Mechanics School, or ESMA, behind an iron gate bordering the compound. The officers' club, where the GT 3.3/2 held its prisoners, is located just to the north of this iconic building, just to the left outside the frame. Author's collection.

5. The attic of the officers' club of the ESMA, known as the *capucha*, or "hood," where prisoners would spend days or months hooded and shackled. Licensed from Getty Images / AFP / Juan Mabromata.

6. After Néstor Kirchner was elected in 2003, he renewed social interest in the human rights abuses of the military dictatorship. Here, the portrait of former dictator Jorge Rafael Videla is removed from the portrait room of the Army War College in Palomar on March 24, 2004, the anniversary of the coup, after President Kirchner ordered its removal. The portrait of Gen. Reynaldo Bignone was also removed. March 24 is now an official holiday known as Memory Day. Licensed from Getty Images / AFP / Ali Burafi.

7. Pres. Néstor Kirchner embraces Hebe de Bonafini, leader of the Association of the Mothers of the Plaza de Mayo, during a ceremony on the thirtieth anniversary of the military coup, March 24, 2005. Licensed from Getty Images / AFP / Juan Vargas.

8. Defendants appear in the federal courtroom in Buenos Aires for the first day of the ESMA trial. *Left to right:* Adm. Oscar Montes, Maj. Julio César Coronel, Lt. Alfredo Astiz, and Capt. Pablo Eduardo García Velasco. Astiz, the "blond angel of death," shows his disdain for the tribunal by wearing a house cardigan and jeans to the proceedings. Family members and human rights activists sit behind the wall of bulletproof glass downstairs; upstairs the press and military supporters observe the proceedings. Licensed from Getty / AFP / Daniel Garcia.

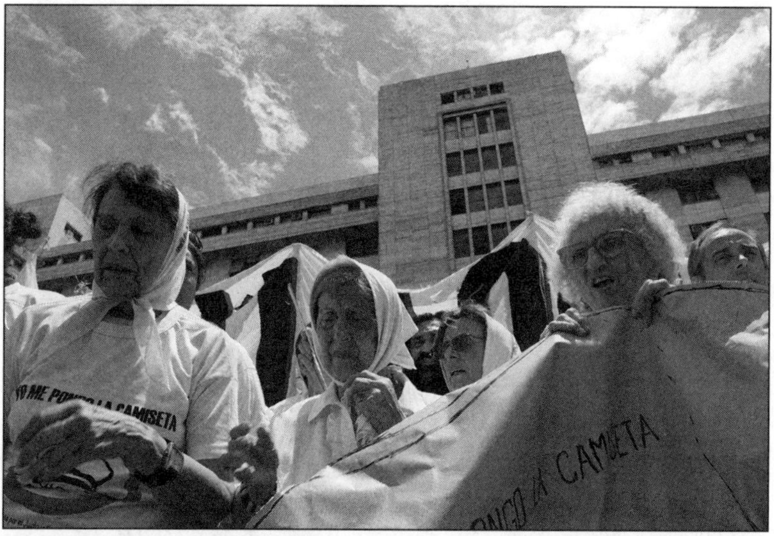

9. Protesters gather outside the federal courthouse on Comodoro Py in Buenos Aires in November 2009. Author's collection.

10. Protesters gather around a banner adorned with images of the disappeared, which they will carry down the Avenida de Mayo through the heart of Buenos Aires on Memory Day, March 24, 2010. Author's collection.

11. Cardinal Jorge Mario Bergoglio, now known as Pope Francis, testifying from the diocese of Buenos Aires during the ESMA trial. Bergoglio refused to testify in open court, so closed hearings were held at the Buenos Aires diocese. Author's collection.

12. Protesters gather outside the federal courthouse on Comodoro Py in Buenos Aires on October 26, 2011, to watch the reading of the verdict in the ESMA case on a giant screen erected outside. Alfredo Astiz, wearing an Argentine blue-and-white lapel pin, appears on the screen under a banner that reads "Jail for all the genocidas of the ESMA." Licensed from Getty / AFP / Juan Mabromata.

7

Rodolfo Walsh

The Naval Mechanics School (ESMA) trial was brought in the name of justice. Activists, prosecutors, politicians, and judges all insisted that the trial satisfied procedural due process, that it was an example for Argentina and the world because the perpetrators of the Dirty War were pursued using the law. The defendants were investigated and indicted by the public ministry and given the opportunity to defend themselves against the charges in open court.

I had heard repeatedly from public defense attorneys in the case, however, that this rosy picture was not accurate. In the thicket of the case file, they told me, I would find a number of irregularities, mostly small and slight injustices, but so common and numerous that they added up to an unfair procedure and trial. They told me that the rules were continuously bent with an eye toward jailing and punishing the accused. Jorge Eduardo Acosta's pretrial ordeal was the worst example: he had spent more than eleven years in pretrial detention before his day in court. Though the limit to pretrial detention was two years, investigators continuously filed new charges as each two-year limitations period approached, ensuring Acosta's lockup. Other defendants had spent similarly lengthy periods in pretrial detention before being brought to trial, though some, like Ernesto Weber, benefited from house arrest.

After sitting through the trial, pouring through the case file, interviewing witnesses, and reading the verdict, I came to the conclusion that the problem was equally as conceptual as it was administrative. The trial of the ESMA officers was not a beacon of procedural fairness as the architects insisted. But the problem in large measure stemmed from the fact that the law was only loosely equipped to confront the task of prosecuting mass atrocity, especially in a context like the Dirty War, where secrecy was central. The law required proof beyond a reasonable doubt to sustain a conviction. But in reconstructing the Dirty War, the best that investigators had to work with in many cases were second- and thirdhand versions of events that survivors heard from one another or from military officers while on the inside of the camps. Evidence that linked an individual defendant to an individual act—the kind of proof ordinarily required in a criminal case—was the exception rather than the rule. Prisoners were blindfolded and largely kept isolated from the torture and violence; to the extent that they had contact with one another, it was usually outside the areas where the ESMA officers tortured their prisoners. Likewise, the task of assigning individual guilt to individual defendants—the requirement of the criminal law that there be an *actus reus* as part of a crime—was at odds with the dynamics of mass atrocity and the moral culpability of the defendants. Their guilt seemed reflected as much in what they had done (wielding the *picana*, kidnapping a victim, driving a car on a raid that ended in someone's capture and torture) as in their mere participation in the bureaucratic machinery of death. For even if they had not participated in every criminal act charged in the indictment by providing some material support to a specific crime, the defendants seemed morally blameworthy for lending their energies to a *system* that they knew would result in the widespread suffering, torture, and murder of its victims. And so the prosecution was trapped by a legal framework that required proof of individual action in individual cases, but most of what the prosecution could prove centered on group liability. Nowhere in the trial was this tension more on display than in the case of Rodolfo Walsh, where the prosecution only had direct evidence against half of the defendants charged with his disappearance.

Rodolfo Walsh is a hero of the Argentine left, owing in large part to his mythical status as a prophetic martyr of the dictatorship. His image is painted in murals across the country, his works and prophetic voice are cited routinely by activists, and his name is invoked as a symbol of the power of intellect fused with action. He made his name as a young investigative journalist by exposing crimes committed by previous military governments against Peronist rebels and workers, writing in an accessible narrative style that foreshadowed the New Journalism wave of the 1960s. He was a dogged reporter with a towering intellect and an unwavering commitment to the Peronist masses. By the early 1970s, Walsh committed himself to revolution and joined the Montoneros, eventually ascending to the group's intelligence chief. He had proven his skills in Cuba, where he reportedly helped decode U.S. communiqués to rebels during the Bay of Pigs Invasion. Later he helped found *Prensa Latina,* a Latin American communist newswire, with the Colombian novelist Gabriel García Márquez. During the dictatorship he cultivated sources deep inside the military—including Jorge Eduardo Acosta's personal assistant at the ESMA, Daniel Tarnopolsky—and he published the first account of what happened inside the naval compound. In addition to his skills as a military strategist, the prosecution observed that Walsh was a threat to the dictatorship because he represented a challenge to the military's campaign of secrecy. He put his reporting skills to effective propaganda use for the movement, starting the ANCLA news agency while in hiding and periodically issuing mimeographed reports that would not be released by other news sources. (His historiography does not include his alleged involvement in the bombing of a federal police mess hall in July 1976.)

As a consequence, Walsh was a significant target for the dictatorship both because he was an important figure in the Montoneros and because of his network of contacts and his dogged reportorial skills. "He was a man of tremendous strategic and tactical capacity," recalled Capt. Jorge Eduardo Acosta at trial.[1] The dictatorship had pursued him for months. An intelligence file unearthed from the archives of the Buenos Aires police force and submitted into evidence in the case showed that Walsh had been tracked by the intelligence services since at least 1973. After the 1976 military coup, the armed forces raided a house where he had previously stayed, and in October 1976, his daughter Maria Victoria died in a confrontation with the army. (She reportedly shot herself in the temple after a prolonged firefight rather than give herself up and face the terrible ordeal of trying to not give over her comrades—an episode memorialized in Walsh's famous "Letter to Friends.")

But despite the military's best efforts and Walsh's high profile, the dictatorship was unable to capture him. He moved around with a fake identification as Norberto Freyre. He moved from house to house and adopted the security measures of a high-ranking Montonero. Though he would eventually criticize the leadership of the Montoneros for their excessive militarism, their isolation from the working masses, and their failure to better protect low-level activists, he was a committed revolutionary. In his wrenching "Letter to Friends," written three months after the death of his daughter, he praised her revolutionary ideals and her "mature" decision to commit suicide rather than give herself up and face the terrible possibility of breaking under torture. "Walsh was almost like a legend for some of the intelligence officers at the ESMA," recalled Martín Gras at trial. "They talked about 'Walsh's ghost'; they spoke of how he walked the streets disguised as a priest so he could avoid the street controls."[2]

On March 25, 1977—one day after the first anniversary of the 1976 military coup—Walsh went with his *compañera* Lilia Ferreyra from their safe house in San Vicente to Buenos Aires. Ferreyra recalled at trial that the two parted ways when they reached the Constitución train station. Ferreyra went to meet Walsh's daughter Patricia and son-in-law Jorge Pinedo; Walsh went to attend several meetings he had planned for that afternoon to distribute his open letter. Walsh and Ferreyra were scheduled to reconvene later that day in the Palermo neighborhood near Patricia's house, if they had time; otherwise, they would meet the following day at their home in San Vicente along with Patricia and Pinedo, a chance to see his daughter and son-and-law and their new baby boy, who Walsh had not yet met.[3]

One of Walsh's scheduled meetings that afternoon was with José María Salgado on the corner of San Juan and Entre Ríos Streets. Salgado was a former police officer who had allegedly planted a bomb in the mess hall of Coordinación Federal police station the year before in one of the most high-profile and deadly terrorist attacks by the Montoneros. Unbeknown to Walsh at the time he set up the meeting, Salgado was already kidnapped. The meeting was "poisoned," in the parlance of the time—the ESMA was using it as a trap.

When Walsh showed up at the scheduled time, around 2 p.m., a coterie of officers was waiting for him. One of them apparently shouted

"Stop! Police!" and in the convulsive moments afterward, Walsh was gunned down. According to one version of events, the officers shot him multiple times from behind after someone saw him reach into his briefcase for what they thought was a gun. In another version, Walsh died while firing on the officers with his .22-caliber Walther PPK. In yet another version, someone apparently yelled "Pepa, pepa!"—slang for "grenade"—and the officers shot Walsh. The moment of Walsh's death is also a matter of dispute; the evidence from the trial never conclusively established whether he died on the spot, in transit to the ESMA, or in the ESMA. Two witnesses—Martín Gras and Silvia Labayrú—testified that they saw his body in the ESMA. His remains are missing; rumors persist that his corpse was burned in the sports field behind the ESMA complex in an *asado*, the method for disposing of the bodies of prisoners who died before they could be dumped into the sea.

The next day, when Ferreyra returned to their house in San Vicente with Patricia and Pinedo, she found the house ransacked, with Walsh nowhere in sight. Ferreyra explained, "I said, 'Let's go.' I don't know what I yelled, what I said—I can't remember it word for word. And from there we hurried away over the dirt roads, in deep anguish and really impacted that Rodolfo wasn't there and that the house was destroyed. That's when another phase started . . . which always happens with a forced disappearance: uncertainty, anguish, and desperation trying to understand what happened."[4]

In 1985, when Walsh's case was included in the charges in the Trial of the Juntas, the court declined to hold Adm. Emilio Eduardo Massera responsible for the episode, saying that there was not enough evidence to prove that Walsh had been apprehended by the ESMA. But in the intervening years, statements from military officers made at the height of the amnesty laid that doubt to rest. "He defended himself and died in a firefight," Admiral Massera said in a television interview in 1995, rebuffing the claim by his interviewers that Walsh had been kidnapped. Massera's admission was followed by statements by Roberto Gonzalez, who admitted in the truth trials in 1998 that the ESMA was responsible for Walsh's death. The minutes of Gonzalez's testimony read as follows:

> [Gonzalez] also remembers a case in which the man the witness knew as "Neurus" or "Estaban" died in a shoot-out, who in fact was Rodolfo Walsh. The case involved a meeting, when the [Montonero] organization ordered one of their members to a particular place. This meeting was discovered by the task force, but he doesn't remember how—that is to say, "For [Walsh] it was set; for us no." [Gonzalez] was not at the episode with "Neurus." . . . He also remembers, and the members of the Montonero organization would remember, that in the firefight, a neighbor was injured . . . eight, ten, or fourteen people participated in the operation, taking into account "Neurus's" important position in the organization, chief of intelligence of the Montoneros, he was a very important person, and nobody knew if he would be accompanied by other members of the organization even though he ended up being alone. In the operation Rodolfo Walsh ended up dead and his corpse was brought to the task force, which was the normal procedure. The witness personally felt frustrated that Walsh wasn't detained alive, as he was an important figure within the Montonero organization. He knows that the operation in which Walsh died was in Capital Federal [the city of Buenos Aires], but he can't specify the day or the date. He knows that [Walsh] resisted, that he was armed, and that he died.[5]

Antonio Pernías also confirmed at trial that the ESMA oversaw Walsh's capture. In his words, the operation was "meticulously planned and efficiently coordinated by [Captain] Yon," though Pernías claimed he was "not involved in the issue." (Yon, the only member of the Grupo de Tareas [GT] 3.3/2 that Pernías identified, was dead by the time of trial.)

So the case proceeded in a strange space between the certainty that Walsh was one of the ESMA's victims and the considerable haze surrounding which officers participated. In 2007 prosecutor Eduardo Taiano and pretrial judge Sergio Torres charged ten members of the ESMA task force with Walsh's disappearance, alleging that they had "directly participated" in the "planning and execution of the operation" that ended Walsh's life. The charges included his kidnapping and the robbery of his belongings.[6] They declined to indict the ESMA officers for homicide, instead only opting to indict them for his kidnapping.

At trial there was little evidence presented to show that some of the defendants had "directly participated" in the planning and execution of the raid against Walsh; in fact, in five of the ten cases of the defendants charged in the incident, there was no evidence at all that connected them to the raid other than their membership in the GT 3.3/2. Only one witness—the prisoner Miguel Lauletta, who says he was taken by the GT 3.3/2 in one of the cars in the raid against Walsh—was a witness to the events in question.[7]

The state's best evidence was against Juan Carlos Fotea, a former police officer and a peripheral member of the GT 3.3/2. Lauletta recalled seeing Fotea in a car during the melee between Walsh and the task force, one of a handful of officers Lauletta identified. Lauletta recalled that someone thought Walsh had a grenade and yelled "Pepa, pepa!" Upon hearing the screams, Walsh reached for a folder, and he was shot dead before firing any shots himself. Lauletta said that upon returning to the ESMA, Ernesto Weber stated, "I was behind him and tried to grab him, but some idiot from a car yelled 'Stop! Police!' and he turned around and put his hand in some plastic folder that he had" and that they had to shoot him.[8] (None of the other officers Lauletta identified were defendants at the trial. The most radical victims' groups in the case declined to use Lauletta's testimony and privately denounced him as a collaborator who could not be trusted. "He'll lie to protect the navy," Carlos Lordkipanidse told me of their decision to ignore Lauletta's statements. The private attorneys who represented Walsh's daughter Patricia did not present evidence of Lauletta's statements in their closing argument.)

Against five other defendants, the prosecution managed to elicit testimony from survivors connecting them to the episode, though none of them saw the defendants at the scene of the crime. Juan Gasparini, a victim, recalled that "Dante" (Pablo Eduardo García Velasco) was the officer who finally elicited information from Salgado that led to the meeting with Walsh. Gasparini's mattress in the *capucha* was next to Salgado's, and he reported that "Dante" would come to visit Salgado repeatedly to take him down to the basement, where they tortured him to get information on Rodolfo Walsh. He continued, "I didn't see [Walsh's] body, but based on what García Velasco told [Salgado,] who was right next to me, I knew that they killed Rodolfo Walsh in March '77."[9] (García Velasco claimed it was a case of mistaken identity—that it was his twin brother, Miguel, who Gasparini had identified. Before trial he had gone on a hunger strike to protest his pretrial detention.) Lisandro Raúl Cubas recalled that Ricardo Miguel Cavallo, a naval lieutenant, had asked him and two other prisoners several months before the kidnapping if he knew Walsh, suggesting that Cavallo was one of the officers involved in the investigation to locate Walsh and hence must have participated in his kidnapping.[10] Miguel Lauletta and Ricardo Coquet, two victims, recalled a conversation they had with Ernesto Weber, a police officer and another one of the defendants in the incident. According to both Lauletta and Coquet, Weber told them that when the officers spotted Walsh, someone screamed "Stop!" Walsh made a gesture at getting something from his portfolio, and they opened fire. (Coquet testified that Weber had also said that Walsh "defended himself with a .22."[11]) According to this story, Weber was shot from behind, along with other officers, and Walsh was riddled with bullets. "We pumped him full of bullets, and he wouldn't go down, that sonofabitch," Coquet recalls Weber complaining.[12] Lisandro Raúl Cubas and Martín Gras also recalled that Alfredo Astiz complained that they had been unable to capture Walsh alive—that it was a shame that a figure of such renowned importance was shot.

Against the remaining four defendants, the evidence of individual direct participation was thin. In the case of Antonio Pernías, the prosecution eventually admitted at trial it was unable to identify any action that Pernías had taken in the incident. They were only able to allege that one witness had seen Walsh's papers near Pernías's office. So the prosecution lurched through explaining Pernías's liability. At one point during its summation, the prosecution argued that given Walsh's importance, as well as Pernías's place within the GT 3.3/2, it would have been "irrational" to conclude that he had not participated. This was an argument that Pernías had "directly participated" (in the words of the charging instruments) by inference. But as Pernías's defense pointed out, there was plenty of evidence suggesting otherwise. On the day of the raid, Martín Gras testified that Pernías had coincidentally brought him down to the basement to be interrogated while the raid was taking place; this suggested that Pernías did not, in fact, participate in the raid and that the raid did not consume the attention of the entire GT 3.3/2. Furthermore, Pernías's defense pointed out that Mercedes Carazo, a former Montonero activist who became Pernías's "lover" while detained in the ESMA, said nothing about Pernías's involvement in the episode, despite spending over a year living with him while he was on a mission in France and professing to be Rodolfo Walsh' friend. While the prisoners recalled that the officers often spoke of the important Montoneros they had captured, Pernías's silence on the subject seemed to put his participation in the episode in doubt.

At another juncture the prosecution said that Pernías was responsible because of his position as an intelligence officer and that the ESMA had worked on the case for many months and then later spent months analyzing the items collected from Walsh's house. This might have been true, but the evidence for this charge was simply an extrapolation from Pernías's presence in the ESMA—there was no additional evidence to draw a connection between Pernías and the Walsh episode. It was, perhaps, a reasonable inference to make, but this description of Pernías's criminal participation in the event seemed at odds with the description of the case in the charging instruments, which had not identified his illegal participation in the incident as having anything to do with the intelligence work before or after the raid on Walsh but was based on his participation in Walsh' kidnapping on the day he was taken by the ESMA.

Finally, the prosecution argued in its summation that Pernías's involvement in the Walsh incident—and any of the officers' involvement in any of the individual incidents—was, in fact, irrelevant. All that mattered was proving their presence in the ESMA on a particular date when a particular crime happened; any additional evidence was nothing more than a "plus." This too conflicted with the description the prosecution had offered in the charging instruments, which described the defendants' "direc[t] participat[ion] in the planning and execution of the operation that culminated in the kidnapping of the victim." But it was really all the prosecution could say about the matter in light of the pretrial investigation and charging instruments authored by a different legal team.

The charges against Jorge Radice and Juan Carlos Rolón were similarly indirect, as the prosecution was not able to make a direct connection between the defendants and the Walsh episode. Rolón, in fact, had claimed he did not even work in the ESMA at the time of the Walsh raid; he had been on rotation at the ESMA in early 1977 and did not return until months later.

The case was also muddied by the differing descriptions of the case offered by the prosecution and the victims' lawyers, who put forward different interpretations of the event in their summations. To the state, Walsh had been gunned down on the spot, but to the victims' lawyers, he had died in a firefight while resisting arrest. The defense protested vigorously that the case was so muddy that the prosecution had forced them to respond not to evidence about the incident but to a series of hypotheses—that there was so much uncertainty surrounding the incident that it was difficult to know what they were supposed to defend against. Was Walsh killed on the spot, or was he shot and then taken away? Was it a kidnapping or a murder? Did Walsh fire at the officers, either first or in self-defense, or was he gunned down in cold blood? Who was at the scene of the crime, and what evidence was there that they were there? Who participated in preparations leading up to the crime, and what were the preparations? What, exactly, were the defendants being charged with in the episode? Were they supposed to respond to a charge that Walsh was kidnapped, as was charged by the pretrial prosecutor? Were they supposed to respond to the charge that Walsh was murdered, as charged by the trial prosecutor and victims' lawyers? Were they supposed to respond to a charge that they had "directly participated" in the episode, as charged in the charging instruments of the case? Or were they supposed to respond to the charge that they were criminally responsible because of their membership in the GT 3.3/2, as charged by the prosecution at the conclusion of the trial?

In the end, the court absolved three of the defendants in the Walsh incident: Juan Carlos Rolón, because the prosecution couldn't prove that he worked in the ESMA during March 1977; Pablo Eduardo García Velasco, because the prosecution had mistakenly indicted Pablo when it was in fact his twin brother, Miguel, who used the alias "Dante" and had discovered the route to capture Walsh; and Julio César Coronel, who was injured in a firefight the same day of the Walsh kidnapping but successfully argued that it was a different firefight in a different area of the city where he was injured (at least enough to throw his participation in the Walsh episode into doubt). But the court was never able to adequately explain how it arrived at the conclusion that several of the defendants, like Antonio Pernías and Jorge Radice, were responsible in the case, other than simply being members of the GT 3.3/2. There was no evidence at trial that they had "directly participated" in the planning or execution of the Walsh operation.

But focusing on the legal aspects of the Walsh case—whether the prosecution's theory of criminal responsibility was correct, whether there was enough evidence to indict and convict the defendants for their direct participation, whether it was unfair to change the charges (and thus the factual foundation required to convict)—suggested that the primary interest driving the Walsh case was strictly legal. Over the course of the trial, however, it seemed as though the focus was more about sanctifying Walsh as a martyr—a victim who had given his life in solidarity with the pueblo, first through his courageous investigations and later joining the Montoneros—rather than just presenting him as a tragic victim ruthlessly gunned down by a group of some twenty men who outnumbered him and murdered him in cold blood.

References to Walsh's famous "Open Letter to the Military Junta" during the trial were routine. The document was transcribed in the charging instruments and read in its entirety during the opening moments of the trial, admittedly one of the few instances that broke the tedium of the clerks' reading of the case. During their summation, the prosecutors and the victims' lawyers, especially the group of lawyers representing Walsh's daughter Patricia, made extensive use of the open letter, sanctifying it as a kind of courageous and prophetic denunciation of the dictatorship and its agenda writ large. There were also long references to his lost works, apparently stolen by the ESMA and only seen by a handful of people. His former *compañera* Lilia Ferreyra (they were never married, as Walsh had a prior marriage and divorce was illegal) spent considerable time during her testimony in court summarizing as best she could one of his lost unfinished stories, *Juan se iba por el río*, a fictional account of one of the last of the Argentines who, nearing the end of his life, sets out to cross the expansive River Plate on a horse (an impossible feat in real life, "but the important thing is that he had the courage to try," Ferreyra reports Walsh as saying). Even the testimony about Walsh had a kind of cinematic quality to it; Lilia Ferreyra, one of the last people to see Walsh alive, recalled his last moments in a guayabera shirt and linen pants as they parted ways at the train station, never to reconvene.

8

The Santa Cruz Raid

Beyond disappearing their victims, the officers of Grupo de Tareas (GT) 3.3/2 went to elaborate lengths to cover their tracks. On several occasions, they tried to convince prisoners to give public press conferences and renounce the Montoneros. When these overtures failed, the Naval Mechanics School (ESMA) task force once sent Humberto Barbuzzi, an intelligence officer, to give one of these conferences pretending to be a repentant Montonero. In 1978 the ESMA sent a group of officers to both Paris and Madrid, where they set up counterpropaganda operations to try to arrest the tidal wave of negative reports that were coming out of Europe and infiltrate Argentine exile groups who were spreading the news about human rights violations in Argentina. The navy also planted fake stories in the local newspapers, the most famous of which was the December 10, 1976, report that Norma Arrostito, one of the legendary founders of the Montoneros, had been killed in a confrontation with security officers. The report even included photos of blood-stained walls where the confrontation had allegedly taken place, but Arrostito was actually detained in the ESMA for over a year before she was killed by the GT 3.3/2. When officers from the task force discovered that friends or relatives of their captives had filed habeas corpus petitions in the courts, the officers would do everything in their power to get the complainants to retract their cases, including putting their captives in touch with their families to encourage them to withdraw their filings. The prisoners never alluded to where they were, saying only that their best chance of survival and "recuperation" would be if their families abandoned any legal redress. In 1979, when the Inter-American Commission on Human Rights visited Argentina in October to report on the status of human rights in the country, the GT 3.3/2 took all its captives housed in the ESMA and transported them for several weeks to a weekend home in the Tigre delta known as El Silencio, or "The Silence." When the commission was given access to the ESMA officers' club, where commissioners had heard reports of a clandestine detention center, the commission reported that they found no conclusive evidence of prisoners being held there.

But none of these initiatives seemed to compare with the sinister and ferocious attack on twelve human rights activists at the end of 1977, one of the central cases at trial that took up much of the court's attention.

By mid-1977 relatives and friends of the disappeared had few options. The dictatorship had been in power for over a year and remained popular. People who wanted to know what had happened to their missing friends, family members, and colleagues had virtually nowhere to turn. Political parties were suspended, and their leaders had little interest in raising human rights as an issue of political opposition at the height of the dictatorship's power. The courts had closed their doors to petitioners seeking information on missing loved ones. The church hierarchy did not raise a voice in protest of the brutal repression in the country, and many of its most important members were openly sympathetic to the dictatorship and its War against Subversion. The press remained largely indifferent to the widespread human rights violations occurring in Argentina. The interior ministry (run by the army) opened an office to accept claims from relatives and friends of missing persons, but nothing ever came of these complaints.

With no other options, a small group of women—all mothers of the disappeared—began to meet in Buenos Aires's Plaza de Mayo in April 1977. At first they were a small group, an informal gathering of women who had met one another on their Kafkaesque journey to police stations, courts, the interior ministry, military barracks, churches, and everywhere else they could think to go to try to locate their children. As time passed their numbers and their profile grew. They went from one dozen to several dozen women and attracted the attention of the international press after they started to don white headscarves and courageously defy the dictatorship's prohibition on public gatherings and political activity. For their safety they discouraged men and younger people from participating. They believed that the mounted police who watched them from the edge of the plaza and often forced them to leave would be less likely to attack a group of older housewives than they would a crowd full of men and young people. The *Buenos Aires Herald*, one of the few newspapers in Argentina that published information on the disappeared, started calling them the "Mad Mothers of the Plaza de Mayo," but the pejorative was eventually dropped from the title, and the group came to be known as simply the Mothers of the Plaza de Mayo.

The group did not have an official leader, but Azucena Villaflor de De Vicenti stood out. A rotund and loud woman, the disappearance of her son, Néstor, had destroyed her, and she dedicated herself completely to finding out what had happened to him. Other mothers recall that she was often the one to propel the group to do more, to have courage, to protest more loudly. She often hosted meetings at her Avellaneda house just outside the Buenos Aires city limits where the mothers would strategize.[1] A few months after the mothers first organized and began to hold weekly vigils in the Plaza de Mayo, a young man named Gustavo Niño showed up claiming to be in a desperate situation: his sibling (some witnesses recall it was a brother, others a sister) had disappeared, and his mother was too sick to travel from their hometown of Mar del Plata to Buenos Aires to search for him. "He became close to us," María del Rosario Carballeda de Cerruti, one of the mothers, recalled at trial. But his ability to join the group was unusual: "He was the only young man to do so, because we didn't want our kids to come and [march] with us. We were afraid they too would be taken." She remembers that Niño was "very nice. He used to tell us that he had a brother who had disappeared. We tried to tell him to leave, that he was compromising the rest of us, but he said that he wanted to look for his brother because his mom was in Mar del Plata and couldn't come."[2] Cecilia De Vicenti, Azucena's daughter, recalled at trial that the young Niño held many of the other mothers as if with a spell.[3] He was just about the age of many of their children who had gone missing. A few times, he brought along a younger but equally dashing girl with fair skin and strawberry-blonde hair. He told everyone it was his sister;

she tended to be reserved, sad, and quiet. He seemed to win the mothers' confidence when one day, he stepped in between the mothers and a police officer who was threatening them.

Niño and Azucena grew close. At the marches Niño was constantly at her side. "Everyone thought that he was her son," Cerruti said at trial.[4] One day when the mothers had planned a protest for early the next morning, Niño asked to stay at Azucena's house for the night, claiming that he had nowhere else to go. Azucena took the proposal to her husband, but he refused. Cecilia De Vicenti, their daughter, says that her father did not want a strange boy in the house with their daughter. He also argued with his wife that her activism was putting her in danger: she was signing documents with her name and address. He told her that Néstor had disappeared, but she still had two other children to think about.[5] But she remained close to Niño and took him under her wing. Niño was there at the marches, at meetings in people's homes, at churches—a desperate young man seeking his sibling.

Along with the mothers, Niño also met two French missionary nuns at the Thursday marches, sisters Alice Domon and Léonie Duquet. The nuns joined the mothers on their Thursday walks around the Plaza de Mayo for spiritual and moral support. They were not your typical nuns; consistent with the radical winds blowing through the church in the late 1960s and early 1970s, both refused to wear habits so that they could be closer to the people. Domon had also spent years in the impoverished north of Argentina helping peasants organize themselves in agrarian leagues before she was forced to leave because of persecution.[6]

Niño also joined a group of younger activists connected to the Communist Vanguard who were in charge of the party's human rights wing, most of whom also had relatives who either had gone missing or were held in executive detention. The group was composed of about thirty people. Niño often went to meetings at Remo Berardo's house, a painter in the La Boca neighborhood who had a brother who was missing. Berardo and some of the other activists, including Eduardo Horane and Horacio Elbert, were in the early stages of starting a newsletter with information about human rights in Argentina, where family members could learn what was happening and write articles. Ruth Chonchol, one of the members of this group whose husband was detained at the time, recalled at trial that Niño was "very available. He was very active within the group. . . . We could always count on him, and on his car . . . I remember one time, I went to the *Buenos Aires Herald* to see how much it would be to publish an advertisement and whether we could publish the ad that we wanted to, and he [took me] in a white Peugeot 504." Chonchol recalls that the affable Niño was "well accepted in the group. Nobody suspected anything of him. He was just like any other *compañero*."[7]

Not everyone remembered Niño as trustworthy and affable. Cecilia Vázquez de Lutsky, another member of the communist vanguard, was suspicious: "It was so strange the way he used to speak recklessly about his brother being in the Montoneros. We were generally much more discreet. There wasn't any need to say things so openly, so abruptly, so imprudently." She recalls getting a ride home one day from Niño and his sister:

> He had a car, which was very strange because the majority of young people our age in Buenos Aires didn't have a car. We were students or we worked. . . . He took me toward the botanical gardens where I lived at that time, on Charcas Street. . . . He talked a lot. He told me that he was soon going to leave the country, [that] he had a family member who was waiting for him in Holland, and that it was a good opportunity for him. I didn't want to ask him a lot of questions and didn't want him to tell me about other things because I didn't want him to ask me things about my life: where I lived, what I did, nothing. I didn't feel calm around him; in truth I didn't really know him. I had met him a couple months before, and I didn't get the sense that he thought the way I did.[8]

By mid-1977 the dictatorship was declaring victory in its War against Subversion. Dictator Jorge Rafael Videla had traveled to the United States that year and conveyed in a press conference that he hoped for a "Christmas in Peace." Human rights activists saw it as an opportunity, and they launched a campaign to collect signatures and identity card numbers from people with relatives who were missing or were being held by the executive without trial. "For a Christmas in Peace, all we ask for is the truth" was to be the slogan, and the activists began collecting money and signatures for an advertisement. The goal was to publish the advertisement in one of Argentina's major newspapers on

December 10, Human Rights Day, with a list of names of those demanding information on the missing.[9]

In the weeks and months leading up to December 10, activists, including many of the mothers and some members of the communist vanguard, launched a campaign to collect signatures. One of the few locations to welcome the group was the Santa Cruz Church, a progressive church that had often been a safe haven for refugees from other dictatorships in Latin America and had been one of the few churches to open its doors to human rights activists during the dictatorship. Uki Goñi, a journalist for the *Buenos Aires Herald* who wrote the first book about Astiz and the Santa Cruz kidnapping, recalled at trial that he would often meet with the younger activists working on this campaign, as they would come to him with information and press releases. "They asked me to go to the meetings in the church, but I never went," Goñi recalled at trial. "It seemed to me they were like kamikazes; they were so exposed."[10]

December 8, 1977, was the final day to compile signatures and collect money to place the advertisement in the newspaper on December 9 so that it would run the next day. There were several meetings around the city that day as organizers collected lists of signatures and consolidated funds to pay for the advertisement. At the end of the day, a group of activists was scheduled to meet at the Santa Cruz Church. Azucena Villaflor de De Vicenti was not there that day—she had gone to the house of Emilio and Chela Mignone (other leading rights activists searching for their daughter Mónica) and was expecting activists from the Santa Cruz Church to meet her later in the day.[11] But the nun Alice Domon was at the church that afternoon as well as several of the activists from the Communist Vanguard and several other mothers. Nélida Fiordeliza de Chidichimo, one of those mothers, also remembered the young Niño being there. Niño, she said, was there "all afternoon. He'd come and go; he always wanted to know where Azucena was. He'd ask for Azucena." Shortly before the meeting was over, Niño left, saying that he did not bring any money and he would soon return with the funds.[12]

That's when the raid occurred. "I saw [Esther] Careaga the moment she was leaving the church, and someone said, 'Esther's got the money, let's go,'" recalled María Cerruti at trial, speaking about one of her fellow Mothers of the Plaza de Mayo. She continued,

> Careaga exited with another woman who I could never identify. . . . [They were] walking out the door and walking toward the corner of General Urquiza Street . . . I was about five meters behind them—five or six meters behind them—with María Ponce de Bianco [another mother]. I was closer to the fence; María Ponce de Bianco was closer to the curb. I saw a man in long sleeves. He took María Esther Careaga and threw her into one of the cars. I screamed, "What's happening, what's happening?" Another man appeared at my side and grabbed María Ponce and threw me against the fence . . . I screamed, "They are taking us!" Another man appeared and pushed [me] away. He told [me] to carry on, that it was an antidrug operation. It all happened in a second; I couldn't see anything because it happened so rapidly.

By the time Cerruti gained her composure, the men had driven off with Careaga and Ponce de Bianco.[13]

Cecilia Vázquez de Lutsky was there as well, a few paces behind the rest of the group at the door, walking an older man down the stairs to the church office:

> There were cars parked in a line very close to one another, and more cars parked in a second line behind them. As we were leaving, I heard someone say, "They are taking Sister Alice." As I was trying to walk down the stairs and helping this older man, I lifted my head, and I saw . . . Sister Alice from behind. I think I also saw Ángela Auad with her hands behind her, either tied or cuffed, and I saw a man—a huge strong man with a gun, a very large gun. I don't know anything about guns, but this seemed to be enormous. I was completely paralyzed, disoriented, and shaken up.

She recalled at trial that the man on her arm struggled to support himself: "It was all so fast. . . . They pushed [Sister] Alice [Domon] into a car as well as other people who I couldn't identify."[14]

Roxana Salomone, who was seven at the time and at the church with her brother, recalled looking at Ángela Auad, who was her nanny:

> When the sun started to go down, at some point Ángela started to gather us up to leave, and at this moment, it all happened so fast. Screams. We started leaving the church, but everything I'm about to say happened on the street. I saw how they pulled Ángela by her hair, they dragged

her along while she reached toward us, they dragged her to a car that was parked nearby, just at the door to the gate of the Sacarist. . . . We were abandoned on the street, crying.[15]

By the time the (supposed) narcotics officers drove off with their captives, seven people had been detained: two Mothers of the Plaza de Mayo, Esther Ballestrino de Careaga and María Ponce de Bianco; four young activists, Ángela Auad, Raquel Bulit, Eduardo Horane, and Patricia Oviedo; and Alice Domon, the French missionary nun who had worked with the mothers and tried to give them spiritual support during their search for their children.

Earlier that day Remo Berardo was also kidnapped from his studio in the La Boca neighborhood.[16] And around the same time as the raid on the Santa Cruz Church, two other activists, Horacio Elbert and Julio Fondovilla, were kidnapped at the Bar Comet near the offices of the *Buenos Aires Herald* where they were supposed to meet with the paper's journalist Uki Goñi.[17] And two days later, Azucena Villaflor de De Vicenti was kidnapped from her house as she went to buy a newspaper after making lunch for her daughter.[18] Léonie Duquet, who lived with Alice Domon, was also kidnapped.[19]

In the chaos and confusion after the raids, many people thought that Gustavo Niño was also kidnapped. In fact, his name appears in the list of missing persons in the advertisement that the activists eventually published. When several of the mothers saw him approaching them at a bar at their weekly vigil a week later, they were stunned. But they told him to go away, that he was putting himself in too much danger, that a young person shouldn't be seen near them after what had happened the week before.

As it turned out, Niño was not who he said he was. He was, in fact, Alfredo Astiz, a member of the ESMA task force. For months he had been infiltrating the Mothers of the Plaza de Mayo and other activist groups to gather intelligence. His "sister" who accompanied him on occasion was, in reality, one of the ESMA's detainees, Silvia Labayrú, who testified years later about the infiltration.

How was Astiz identified? The following year he was sent on a spy mission to Paris as "Alberto Escudero" to infiltrate Argentine exile groups in Europe. When he showed up at a meeting to organize a campaign against the dictatorship, several people from the Santa Cruz Church recognized "Alberto" as "Gustavo," and Astiz quickly fled. Years later, his face donned the cover of every major newspaper in Argentina when he surrendered the South Georgia Island to the British in the Falklands War in 1982, complete with his name and rank, and activists positively identified the man they knew as "Gustavo."

In the months leading up to the kidnappings, the captives inside the ESMA were aware of what was going on. Silvia Labayrú told some of her fellow prisoners that Astiz had taken her out to meetings of human rights activists, and they were spying on them.[20] But Astiz also told some of his favorite prisoners about his infiltration. "We knew what was happening from Astiz himself," said Ana María Martí at trial. "Astiz was a young guy. He liked to talk about what he was doing; he talked to us about a lot of things. He loved the work that he did. He told us that he was infiltrating various organizations."[21] But there was little to nothing his prisoners could do to stop it. "If I had to redefine 'impotence' in the dictionary," testified Graciela Daleo at trial, "I would explain it to mean what we felt inside knowing that all of this was happening and that we couldn't do anything—we couldn't do anything to warn those on the outside that Astiz wasn't the brother of a disappeared person."[22]

It seems as though the ESMA did not initially infiltrate the human rights groups with the intention of kidnapping the mothers; rather, they hoped to find the "subversives" that they believed were behind their movement. "It was clear that the dictatorship and the navy couldn't understand the fact that there were people who wanted to organize themselves to demand to know what happened to the disappeared. They believed that someone had to be behind them, like the ERP or the Montoneros," recalled Labayrú. There are several versions of what ultimately prompted the ESMA to move from monitoring and infiltrating the human rights groups to actually kidnapping their members. Labayrú recalls that at a meeting in the La Boca neighborhood at Remo Berardo's house, someone handed Astiz a flyer from a communist party. "This was the cause that sparked the massacre," she said. "It was what they were looking for. As they said, 'International Marxism is behind human rights in Argentina.' Astiz went crazy because of this pamphlet, and this ended in the terrible decision, the decision to kidnap everyone. It was immediate . . . I don't know if they ever found out that the Marxist-Leninist Party was unarmed, was a nonviolent party, and was very small."[23] Andrés Castillo, another ESMA captive, explains the raid differently: it was all designed to stop the publication of the advertisement in the newspaper on December 10.[24] (It failed to do so.) Juan Gasparini, another captive, has yet another explanation: the decision to kidnap the family members was disorganized and impromptu. Antonio Pernías, who was substituting as chief of the ESMA's task force while Jorge Eduardo Acosta was away, ordered the raid when Astiz came back one day with news that he feared his cover had been blown.[25] (For his part, Antonio Pernías, who denied any participation in the incident, called the raid "an error and a horror" but did not elaborate further.)

Witnesses recall that the members of Grupo Santa Cruz were put through the same awful process of detention as anyone else who was taken inside the ESMA: they were hooded, shackled, tortured, and thrown into small boxes where they were forced to sleep. Ricardo Coquet recalled the day when they were brought in; he said at trial that he saw eight to ten people sitting on a bench—hooded, waiting to be tortured—in the hallway of the basement.[26] Many witnesses recall seeing an older lady, who they presume now to be Sister Léonie Duquet, walking with difficulty, as if she had been tortured.

Whatever the genesis of the kidnapping, it quickly became a political liability for the navy. Denunciations came in from around the globe, particularly from the French government, which was alarmed about the attack on its citizens. Despite the fact that the regime claimed to be fighting seditious terrorists and attacking "subversion," a group of activists seeking information on their missing loved ones was sucked up in the repressive dragnet.

Survivors recall that the kidnapping of the French nuns caused such concern for the dictatorship that calls began pouring into the ESMA from the other service branches; the army, and particularly dictator Jorge Rafael Videla, were worried about what had happened and called the ESMA to see if they were capable of doing such a thing. Silvia Labayrú testified that this was what ultimately prompted the ESMA to kill the group.[27]

In response Jorge Eduardo Acosta, the ESMA's chief intelligence officer, devised a plan to deflect attention from the armed forces: he was going to stage the incident as if the Montoneros, rather than the government itself, had kidnapped the French nuns. A few days after the kidnappings, the two nuns were brought down to the basement and put in the *huevera,* a sound-recording studio that was constructed to film and edit propaganda material. A detainee who was a former Montonero, Ricardo Coquet, spray-painted a Montonero banner, and Marcelo Hernández, who worked in the ESMA's documentation wing as a prisoner, took a photograph of the nuns in front of the banner. The image was sent to *Agence France-Presse* along with a letter of demands to the French government for the release of the nuns. The image circulated in the local and international press a few days after the kidnapping.[28]

Within days of the kidnappings, survivors from the ESMA recall that they no longer saw or heard any members of the Grupo Santa Cruz in the ESMA; they had all been "transferred." For years a version circulated that after the photos were taken, the Grupo Santa Cruz was ushered away in a special "transfer." Several witnesses said that they had seen Héctor Febres and Antonio Pernías return from a special outing late at night with mud on their pants and boots, and they had spoken about dropping off a package. Survivors deduced from this that the nuns had been taken to the Tigre delta and dumped in the swamplands north of Buenos Aires. This was the most widely held theory of what had happened to the nuns and the Grupo Santa Cruz until 2004, when forensic anthropologists excavated several paupers' graves south of Buenos Aires. The unidentified bodies had been interned at the General Lavalle Cemetery after washing ashore in December 1977. The bones displayed injuries consistent with falling from a great height with little possibility of directional control, such as broken pelvises. In a standard investigation launched by the local police in the 1970s, it was determined that one of the bodies was Ángela Auad, one of the activists kidnapped from the Santa Cruz Church on December 8, 1977.[29] For an unknown reason, Auad's family was never made aware of her identification, so she remained missing from her family for nearly three more decades after her kidnapping, despite the fact that the local authorities had identified her. (A forensic anthropologist who worked on the case explained to me that the "left hand often did not know what the right hand was doing" during the dictatorship, so despite the military's best attempts to cover up what they had done, other parts of the state bureaucracy functioned as normal.) After her identification the forensic experts were able to work from the hypothesis that some of the other bodies that washed ashore around the same time were also from the Grupo Santa Cruz. Over the next year, Esther Careaga, Azucena Villaflor de De Vicenti, María Ponce de Bianco, and Léonie Duquet were identified as four of the remaining bodies from the paupers' graves.

The identification of Astiz by activists, the identification of the bodies through DNA analysis, and the testimony of former prisoners left no doubt at trial that the nuns and the family members were kidnapped by the ESMA task force. But giving any more certainty to the story—who participated in the raids, what happened to the group while on the inside of the ESMA, and where they were held—proved a more difficult endeavor.

In all, eleven officers were indicted for their involvement in the Santa Cruz raid. The raid on the church was perhaps the best documented, most researched, and vigorously investigated crime of the Dirty War, but even still, significant details about the event remained murky, highlighting just how effective the military had been in hiding their conduct and the difficulty of establishing proof.

The closest witness to events, Silvia Labayrú, who accompanied Astiz during part of the infiltration, could not specify all the participants. Over the years, she had recalled being both at Remo Berardo's studio and at the Comet Bar on December 8, as she was used to lure the activists into the navy's hands. But at trial she could not recall which victims were taken from which locations, apparently misstating that both Alice Domon and Ángela Auad were taken from Remo Berardo's house, when in fact they were taken from the Santa Cruz Church. In 1984, when she testified before Argentina's truth commission, she said that "Pantera" (a nickname for Jorge Perrén), Julio César Coronel, and "Norberto" (a nickname for Savio) had participated in the raid at Remo Berardo's house. Years later when she testified at trial, she did not remember Norberto as having taken part in the raid but did again mention "Pantera" (Perrén's nickname) and "Maco" (Coronel's nickname).[30]

While numerous witnesses placed "Gustavo Niño" at the scene of the Santa Cruz raid on December 8, 1977, one witness actually believed that Astiz was there at the time of the kidnappings. Roxana Salomone was seven years old at the time and playing in the church courtyard while her nanny, Ángela Auad, was inside for the meeting. She claims that at one point, an officer grabbed her to push her in the car with Auad, but another man stopped him and told him it wasn't necessary. Salomone says that when Astiz's photo appeared in the press years later, she recognized him as the man who had pushed her out of the car.[31] Yet all the other witnesses at the Santa Cruz Church recall that Niño had left the scene before the raid. Other mothers recall that they also saw him the next week when he tried to join them again at the Thursday march. It is difficult to believe that Astiz would have exposed himself and revealed his identity in public by interacting with one of the other officers on December 8 if he still planned to operate afterward.

The testimony from other witnesses was similarly inconclusive when taken as a whole. Many witnesses recall that Acosta spoke frequently of the Mothers of the Plaza de Mayo before the raid in December 1977. It seems unquestionable that he was responsible for the affair. He apparently ordered the infiltration and was one of the most powerful figures within the camp. But whether he was there on the day of the raid could not be established. According to both Juan Gasparini and Alberto Girondo, Acosta was away from the ESMA the day that the raid was ordered. Gasparini maintains that Antonio Pernías made the decision to kidnap the family members and the nuns. But he also says that Acosta came back and took charge of the situation once he learned of the kidnappings.[32]

But others recall that Acosta was there as soon as it happened. Both Carlos García and Ricardo Coquet, who were in the basement at the time the group was brought in, recalled Acosta going in and out of the interrogation room.[33] Labayrú said that she heard that Acosta personally participated in the interrogation of the nuns, suggesting he was there on the day of the raid.[34]

The prisoners who were in the basement of the ESMA on the day of the raid—Daleo, Girondo, Coquet, García—all testified that both Pernías and Astiz were there. Many of them also remember "Maco" (Julio

César Coronel) in the basement, and a few mention Raúl Enrique Scheller. But it is difficult to trust any single memory, for the stories of the Santa Cruz raid have been processed, told, reprocessed, and retold so many times over so many years that it can be difficult to distinguish between what is a fact, what is an implanted memory, what is a memory of a memory, and what is a repetition of a story or rumor that feels like a memory. Many witnesses, for instance, claim to have seen the nuns in the ESMA bathroom. That one or two of the prisoners might have seen them in the bathroom is certainly believable. As Ana María Martí explained, "I tried during these days to go to the bathroom as much as I could, because the bathroom was a privileged place where you could find out things, because people weren't hooded in the bathroom."[35] But it seems implausible that despite the admittedly tough security measures that the ESMA put in place after the Grupo Santa Cruz was kidnapped, so many people would see the nuns in or on the way to the bathroom. It seems more likely that one or several people saw them in this circumstance, and the story circulated, and some prisoners eventually adopted the story as their own.

Some captives had an explanation for why some of the stories of what happened to the Grupo Santa Cruz seemed contradictory and incoherent. Miguel Lauletta chalked it up to counterintelligence work by the ESMA. Lauletta told the court,

> For instance, with the French nuns, a version circulated that Pernías and Febres had been seen with mud, with their boots all muddied up, and that they had buried the nuns somewhere in the Tigre delta. But later the facts showed that they had been thrown into the sea like everyone else, because one of them appeared. These were counterintelligence measures. We kidnapped people—they already knew that we were going to be freed—they hoped that at the least we would have contradictory information to make it more difficult to divulge what really happened.[36]

He told the court that memory "is very difficult. I have spent years trying to get names together, through the memory of other *compañeros*."[37] In a more honest moment, Alberto Girondo, who says he was in the basement on the day the GT 3.3/2 returned with its first prisoners from the Santa Cruz raid, recalled how difficult it is and has been to remember what happened to the Grupo Santa Cruz. "My information is fragmented and difficult to organize," he told the court. He continued,

> I had been completely convinced, based on the statements of others—not because I saw it—I was convinced that the Grupo Santa Cruz had been transferred, that they had been in *capuchita* and *capucha* and had been transferred in two groups. That the nuns had been transferred separately, not with the principal group . . . I was also convinced because of things that I heard that [the Grupo Santa Cruz] was "transferred" to the Delta, in the River Plate. It was said that Febres had come back at night with his boots all muddied up [the day of the transfer]. . . . These were the versions of events.[38]

9

Between Memory, Truth, and Justice

Cases like the Santa Cruz raid and the kidnapping of Rodolfo Walsh raised a fundamental question: Were the witnesses' recollections credible? In broad brushstrokes, the answer was undoubtedly yes. The defense's attempts to deny what happened—to say that it was all enemy propaganda, to insist the testimony against them was a vast left-wing conspiracy—sounded as stupid during the trial as it had been frightening in the 1970s. But pouring through thousands of pages of testimony, books, newspaper clippings, and memorials and sitting through hundreds of hours of interviews and court testimony, I came to appreciate the constraints on the survivors' recollections. Their memories are, first and foremost, limited by biology. Unlike mechanical or digital equipment that is able to preserve and record, the human mind is plagued by an inability to perfectly absorb what it has seen, heard, and sensed. And over the years, despite the best attempts to preserve memory through repetition, discussion, writing, and sheer will, uncertainty has fogged the clarity of the testimony. Names are forgotten, times and places confused, details dropped. Paradoxically, the problem also runs in the other direction, as the need for clarity and consistency in response to a secret campaign of extermination has compelled many to be assertive where there is in fact doubt. Sometimes minor asides became central concerns, and doubt is slowly transformed into confidence and certainty. As Primo Levi noted of his own experience after surviving Auschwitz, it is sometimes in the very act of remembering that information is both lost and twisted—that in sorting one's recollections, memory tends to become a script, with deviations from the central story hard to recall.[1] In the Naval Mechanics School (ESMA) trial, there were instances where survivors did not testify in their early statements in the 1980s as to who was in the room while they were being tortured; others could only name their captors by a nickname or bastardized versions of their real names. But by the 2000s, they had created a coherent and consistent story of their ordeal, complete with the full names of the responsible defendants.

This ordinary problem of memory was heightened in the case of the ESMA's survivors. Many details were unknown at the time of their captivity—names of both victims and victimizers, locations, dates, times, physical descriptions—and those who have bestowed upon themselves the unenviable task of bearing witness have sought refuge with other witnesses. Many survivors have spent hours and hours with one another going over their stories and recounting as many details as they can recall to order the madness of their individual experiences and to identify victims who were tossed into the sea like trash. But in this collaborative process, the memories of each individual have been inevitably and sometimes irretrievably impacted by the moods and thoughts of others; in the effort to reconstruct, preserve, present, and bear witness, the survivors have incorporated the accounts of others into their own recollections so that the distinction between memory and hearsay has been blurred. For the writing of history, of course, this has been mostly advantageous: perpetrators and victims have been identified by name, times and places have been corroborated, and stolen children have been found. But for justice, this collective synthesis poses a fundamental challenge, for it is ordinarily prosecutors and courts who are responsible for synthesizing numerous firsthand accounts into a coherent narrative, not witnesses themselves. At this late stage—more than thirty years after the crimes were committed—the survivors' testimonies have been stripped of the disoriented, partial, and raw immediacy of their experience. In converting from individual memory to "collective memory," it has become difficult in many cases to separate what was seen, heard, felt, and spoken by an individual witness from what was learned from others.

When I asked one journalist—a longtime observer of the ESMA who has interviewed dozens of survivors—about finding "truth" from inside the ESMA, he told me, "Welcome to the twilight zone." He continued, "The question of who saw what is a very delicate one with ESMA survivors. Often, to grant greater credibility to their statements, survivors would relate being eyewitnesses to events that were actually seen by another fellow survivor. Especially in their early testimonies."[2]

There was also a gulf between what the survivors knew to be true and what they were willing to share in open court. Guilt, shame, doubt, fear, and misunderstanding had piled on top of insecurity, mistrust, anxiety, and apprehension. The survivors, aware or not, almost uniformly tweaked their recollections based on their audience. The stories told before the court were distinct from those told before *compañeros* and trusted fellow *militantes*; the stories told in public were tailored to the painful necessities of the moment rather than speaking to the universal historical interest in the Argentine tragedy. One witness, for instance, told me outside of the courtroom (she asked me to withhold her name to speak candidly) of the awful choice she faced while being tortured: admit that she was a Montonero and give up the names of fellow members of the organization, thereby risking her own life and the life of anyone else she gave up, or claim no connection to the guerrillas and say that she was just a member of the Juventud Peronista (a Montonero front group) disgusted by the Montoneros' break with Perón in 1974. She chose the latter strategy, and to bolster her story, she gave up the names of four *compañeros* who she knew stayed loyal to Perón and never joined the armed movement of the Montoneros. Although they might be kidnapped and tortured, she believed that she might be saved and they would be released once the ESMA confirmed her friends were not Montoneros. Tragically, one of the four men she turned over to the ESMA died of a heart attack from the electric shock of the *picana electrica*. Wracked with guilt over the episode, she did not mention any part of this ordeal (or her membership in the Montoneros) at trial, preferring instead to edit the death of her former friend out of her testimony and avoid both the painful and judgmental stares of her former *compañeros* who might see her as weak or as a traitor and the judgment of her friend's family members, who might be angry that she had saved her life in exchange for his.

The existential condition of the ESMA survivors has been learning to live with the barrage of "whys" that came after their release—Why did you survive? Why did you not do more? Why did you not escape? The problem with answering these questions is that the explanation requires revealing an entire universe that is far beyond our ordinary experience; explaining every tiny action taken inside the camp requires context. This is true not only for the large questions of torture and death but for the trivial concerns of day-to-day life on the inside, such as the moral significance of sharing a meal with a military officer or being released from the ESMA and later checking back in. Acts we would all forget in ordinary life are felt as profound failures or compromises inside the twisted moral universe of the camp. One survivor, María Eva Bernst de Hansen, told me of the guilt she has carried for nearly forty years since being freed from the ESMA for forgetting someone's name. Thrown next to her, inside the depths of the *capucha,* was a man from Mar del Plata. She learned where this man was from—that he had a wife, that he had two children—but she did not remember his name. She tells me that perhaps because of this tiny error, she imagines that his family has never discovered what became of him and that his children are stuck in an interminable limbo of living as the descendants of a *desaparecido*. If only she had been able to do more.

This simultaneous fear of not being understood—of lacking the vocabulary or the creativity to convey the experience—and the anxiety of bearing witness and being judged as a consequence both guides and constrains the survivors' testimony. We do not live in a world where the survivors can demand an audience but free themselves of the inevitable responses of sympathy, remorse, empathy, and compassion but also of anger, disbelief, and judgment. "It wasn't so bad," "This was a war," "What did *you* do to survive?" "You must be exaggerating"—some of the statements uttered by the defense and their supporters at trial—are just a tiny sampling of the responses the survivors receive for the very fact of having survived.

"Surviving is difficult," recalled Ana María Martí at trial. "I've had to repeatedly explain why I am alive when even I myself don't know. People mistrusted us. I spent many years of my life trying to explain this until I decided to isolate myself. On days like this, it's very uncomfortable to be alive."[3]

The reluctance to speak at trial was most acute in the survivors' treatment of their activism and connection to the revolutionary left. It was here where both fear of judgment and strategic editing were at their apex. The survivors told countless stories at the trial of being sucked up into the clutches of the ESMA, of torture and death, but they almost always skillfully skirted around the details of their *militancia*.

Why the omissions? It was certainly different for every victim, but there were some common reasons that explained the general avoidance. For some it was a reflex left over from the 1970s, when members of the Montoneros were required to hide their organizational identity as a matter of security. For others it was prompted by a fear of future prosecution; some of the witnesses had been indicted in the 1980s for their alleged terrorist activities, and while the logic of the law would seem to spare them from prosecution (only crimes committed by the state were not subject to statutes of limitations, so the crimes of the guerrillas were all prescribed), the fickle quality of the rule of law in Argentina had convinced some that it was better not to risk prosecution. For still others it seemed to be a kind of moral imperative—the discourse of "two demons" had to be fought on every front. Bringing *militancia* into the trial was not only irrelevant; it threatened to dilute the moral clarity of the trial, which was intended to prosecute state terrorism. And finally for others the reluctance to talk about their *militancia* seemed to stem from a reluctance to discuss the brutality of their experience. If they mentioned, for instance, that they had formed part of a particular Montonero cell, the next questions might be "Who gave you up?" and "Who did you give up?" Though these questions might have been legally relevant—drawing connections between victims helped corroborate evidence and might have strengthened the case for the criminal liability of the defendants for participating in days' long operations—both the witnesses and the prosecution preferred to ignore the issue as not essential to the case.

The reluctance to speak about *militancia* in any concrete way also showed that the narrative arc of the trial hinged on misdirection, and it was here where the trial showed that the twin aims of "truth" and "memory" were not necessarily compatible. For if the trial was supposed to establish the singular quality of the horrific violence of the ESMA—which was undeniable—any evidence of the revolutionary affiliation of the victims threatened to dilute the moral clarity of the lesson.

The trial, in the words of the prosecution, was meant to analyze "crimes that were committed from the apparatus of the state." The testimony and the accompanying documents proved this theory by outlining the structure of repression and terror that was organized and implemented at the highest levels of government and executed by low-ranking enforcers, focusing on the undeniable sadism, brutality, and viciousness of the defendants. The ESMA was, in the words of the prosecution, a place where "schizophrenia was a major part of the structure: it was life before death or life between death." But in describing the ESMA as schizophrenic, the prosecution avoided speaking about the revolutionary affiliation of the victims, and as a consequence, the trial tended to leave spectators wondering why it had all happened.[4]

To be sure, some answers were offered, generally by linking the actions of the small men in the dock to the grand ambitions of the dictatorship itself. "The object," said the prosecution at one point, was to "usurp state power and perpetrate an extreme liberal economic model."[5] The dangerousness of the supposed enemy was "exaggerated" so that the dictatorship could go forward with its criminal plan. But these explanations seemed too forced, written with an eye toward the politics of the moment rather than a penetrating examination. Did the men in the dock really care about economic liberalization? In fact, in the case of the navy, these answers not only seemed misguided but were actually wrong, as Adm. Emilio Eduardo Massera was one of the most vocal critics of the economic policies of the military regime in his bid to secure the presidency on a populist platform after a democratic transition, a stance that landed him in jail several times for criticizing the military. Missing in all the explanations of why the ESMA existed and what happened inside was the fact that the central objective of the Grupo de Tareas (GT) 3.3/2 was to eradicate the revolutionary Peronist left by hunting down and annihilating Montonero guerrillas and their front groups. Inside the torture room was not a battle between the bourgeoisie and the proletariat but a war over Argentineness itself.

In the thousands of pages of multiple charging instruments, as well as the days' long closing arguments by the prosecution and victims' lawyers, there was barely a mention of the Montoneros. Individual cases were presented as exactly that: individuals divorced from the larger revolutionary movement to which they belonged and isolated from one another so that it was difficult to make sense of what had happened. There were some notable exceptions to this rule, such as the case of Rodolfo Walsh, but in the cases where the prosecution did mention the revolutionary affiliation of the victims, it was done more as hagiography than factual description. Instead of being described as revolutionaries, the victims were recast in two ways: as "political activists," with little explanation as to what that category meant or what group they belonged to, or as "the disappeared," reduced to homely categories like "student," "mother," "worker," and "lawyer" that neutered them of any political affiliation. The stories of kidnappings generally started with a sudden and apparently unexpected encounter with the ESMA task force on the street, at work, or at home, as if the kidnapping was entirely random. And to bolster this idea of neutrality, the prosecution and the victims' lawyers stressed the suffering of the family members who were left behind and did not know what had happened to their relatives, of the children who lost parents, of the parents who lost children, of the siblings who still longed to celebrate birthdays with their brothers and sisters. The stories told rose to the level of mythology; according to the prosecution, the perpetrators were able to commit these crimes because they were "mediocre and insignificant men who found in the ESMA a place to become gods."[6] It was a story that explained the repression based on the psychology (and psychopathy) of the perpetrators.

The fact is there *was* a logic (twisted as it was) to what the navy had done, a fact that a robust history of the ESMA will someday explain. The GT 3.3/2 had considered as "subversive" any person with a faint connection to the Montoneros and, more generally, anyone from the revolutionary Peronist left. The GT 3.3/2 sowed terror and recognized few, if any, limits to their actions. But behind this ruthlessness was a calculated logic: to do away with the "subversive" threat posed by the revolutionary Peronist left. To that end, the navy terrorized anyone with a connection to send a message.

Of course, this did not mean that the testimony presented at trial was not truthful—only that in the gray areas of the survivors' testimony and the prosecution's presentation of the case, there was a gap between what an academic historian might describe and the lesson of "memory." Justice required moral certainty, and there was a fear that complicating the story of the ESMA by hinting at the revolutionary and sometimes violent affiliations of the witnesses might obscure that lesson. The architects intended the trial to correct an "error" from the 1980s, when the Dirty War was framed as a confrontation between leftist guerrillas and a right-wing military dictatorship; they hoped that by focusing exclusively on the ruthlessness of the state's violence, the singularity of "state terrorism" would be properly revealed. The purpose of "truth" was to unmask the violence of the Dirty War and lay the blame squarely at the feet of the military and their civilian allies. "Justice ends up writing history, so you have to do politics with justice," one ESMA survivor told me.[7]

This vision of the trial is not shared by some liberals in Argentina, who believe that the proceedings have become too infected by a partisan agenda. They see that the emphasis has strayed too far from justice and too close to "memory building" so that the law itself—and hence Argentina's institutions—ultimately suffer. In a country ravaged by clientelism and a weak rule of law, many see the utilization of the law for a larger political agenda as more of a threat to Argentine democracy than the impunity itself.

Beatriz Sarlo, a former communist revolutionary and one of Argentina's leading public intellectuals, tells me that the trials in some cases have obscured history. She is mostly supportive of the trials but has critiqued the discourse surrounding them. "Our history is fixated on trauma," she tells me. "We can't move on without a realistic account of the past." She insists that the country suffers from the left's inability to undertake a profound self-criticism: "We had ideas—we wanted to fight imperialism, even if it meant with an atomic bomb—and we have to analyze how those ideas lead us to embrace violence. But the left won't touch this until the last little old soldier from this era dies."[8]

Graciela Fernández Meijide, who was a member of the Permanent Assembly for Human Rights (Asamblea Permanente por los Derechos Humanos, or APDH) and a secretary for the National Commission on the Status of the Disappeared (CONADEP), has also become a critic of the recent wave of trials, despite her human rights bona fides. "The victims have wanted to preserve a heroic memory of this period," she tells me, "so the trials haven't been able to clarify history. The Montoneros, and also the human rights movement, say it's not time to analyze the violence of the left. They accuse you of propagating the theory of 'two demons.' Demons? What demons? This is a stupid analysis. Things aren't just good or bad."[9]

Sergio Bufano, a former guerrilla and now the editor of *Lucha Armada*, a small but important journal that tries to grapple with the left of the 1970s, says that the Kirchner administrations sought to glorify the 1970s for their own purposes. He says that you can either exalt the past or look at it critically, and he has chosen to do the latter. He says in this glorified vision of history, "It's as if *Kirchnerismo* was the result of what we fought for in the 1970s."[10] It's an invented idea that links the Kirchner administration's policies to political ideals of 1970s revolutionaries and, by extension, the Kirchners' enemies with the enemies in the past. All opponents are cast alongside the military dictatorship itself.

It is a fair criticism. Not necessarily one that undercuts the project of the trials entirely, just one that insists on a fuller and or more expansive critique of the social responsibilities of Argentina's history and one that places less emphasis on defending the "marvelous youth" of the lost generation. One that believes trials should be about justice rather than the consecration of an incomplete memory and the propagation of a bowdlerized history.

A source close to the investigation tells me,

> In Argentina there are a lot of taboos. People don't talk about the *lucha armada*, or activism. There isn't much political space to talk about it. Things are so black and white. If people recognized that they were guerrillas, it might complicate the trials. There's fear that there might be a debate about the armed struggle. But history isn't black and white. We can't put things below the rug that don't mesh with our way of thinking.... People love to talk about revolution, but there aren't many ways to do it. You have to fight an army, the oligarchy. You have to kill people. Nobody assumes responsibility for this.[11]

He takes pains to point out that one cannot equate the violence of the state with the violence of the guerrillas. The guerrillas did not steal babies and did not torture people; the scope of their violence pales in comparison to the violence perpetrated by the state. He says, "We are a society that wanted order, but they didn't like it when cadavers started appearing."

Still, Horacio Verbitsky, a prominent supporter of the trials from his column in *Página/12* and the president of the human rights group Centro de Estudios Legales y Sociales (CELS), disagrees: "The talk about leftist violence has expired. For seven years during the dictatorship, all we heard about were the 'subversives.' Even under Alfonsín and Menem, we had a discourse about the 'subversives.'"[12] He says that the emphasis is finally in the right place—that the recent wave of justice has done an admirable job of finding and convicting the direct perpetrators and has finally created a public culture where other perpetrators and accomplices in the judiciary, in powerful economic sectors, and in the church might also be called to account. Though these efforts have not gone as well as prosecuting the military itself, he says that there has been a change in the social consensus about the past.

"What do we mean by truth?" Hugo Vezzetti asks me. "There is a juridical idea of truth, which is what is proved at a trial. It's normative. Historical truth is different and is subject to debate. It changes over time. The vision of the judge is different than the vision of history."[13]

10

The Jesuits

During the late morning hours of May 23, 1976—a Sunday—security forces stormed the "Villa Evita" neighborhood of the Bajo Flores slum in Buenos Aires.[1] It was one day shy of the two-month anniversary of the military coup, just as the ferocious repression of the Naval Mechanics School (ESMA) was reaching its climax. On that May day, two progressive Jesuit priests—Orlando Yorio and Francisco Jalics—were the targets.

In the military's delirium, Yorio and Jalics's proximity to the poor and liberal spiritual practices were subversive. In 1975 the two opened a small religious base community just outside the slum.[2] Such communities were in vogue in the wake of the Second Vatican Council, a way of living closer to the poor and inserting the church among the people of God.[3] Yorio was a slender, quiet, and deliberate theologian who was called to direct pastoral work among the legions of Paraguayans, Bolivians, and Argentines from the country's interior who populated the slum. He believed that the church should devote itself to divine liberation and construct an authentic socialism for Argentina. Initially, this was an academic concern. From his positions at the University of Salvador and Colegio Máximo, the Jesuits' seminary, Yorio lectured on liberation theology, national consciousness, and the theology of socialization. His writings reflected a religious commitment to Peronism—he wrote of Perón's return from exile and his status as a uniquely Argentine political figure as a divine signal that Argentina was on the cusp of liberation.[4] In 1974 his interests became more practical. With the help of Mónica Quinteiro, a nun who later left religious life to devote herself to politics, Yorio arranged for a group of missionaries to teach catechism in the slum.[5] He saw evidence of the divine among the dispossessed who inhabited the area. He was, according to his brother Rodolfo's testimony at trial, "doing nothing more than obeying the conclusions of the Episcopal Conference of Medellín, ratified by the Argentine Episcopate," meaning that he worked with the poor.[6] But at the time the dictatorship did not draw neat lines between missionary zeal, political theology, and "subversion." As one of Yorio's captors explained to him during his six months in captivity, "You're not a guerrilla, you're not violent, but you aren't aware that a man of your cultural level, [in going] to live [in the slum,] you unite the people, you unite the poor, and uniting the poor is subversion."[7]

The Hungarian-born Jalics did not devote his missionary work solely to the slum, but he was nevertheless a target because of his liberal spiritual outlook. An adherent of the calls for reform in the wake of the Second Vatican Council, Jalics pushed for far-reaching religious revival. To Jalics, Vatican II—which upended the traditional liturgy, invited priests to recite mass in vernacular languages, and called upon the church to dialogue with other faiths—had been an opening to undercut the rigidity and dogmatism of classical prayer. In his prayer retreats organized at their base community, Jalics incorporated eastern practices such as yoga. Father Enrique Rastellini, who lived with Yorio and Jalics from 1973 to 1975, told me that Jalics's religious progressivism at times went so far that others accused him of not really being a Jesuit.[8] Given the times such accusations were life-threatening. The military was steeped in traditional Catholic practices, viewing anything unorthodox as inherently subversive and corrosive of the country's "national being." Such religious fault lines, in fact, became the fault lines of the Dirty War.[9]

Yorio and Jalics were detained in the May raid, taken to the ESMA, and held for six months. Initially, they went days hooded and shackled without food or water and were forced to relieve themselves in their clothing.[10] Measured against other human rights abuses committed by the regime, Yorio and Jalics's treatment was tragically common. Neither was beaten nor subjected to electrocution. And unlike thousands of others, they survived to relate their experiences.

Nevertheless, their ordeal has attracted international attention for decades as symptomatic of the enigmatic role of the Argentine Catholic Church during Argentina's dark years, which failed catastrophically in denouncing abuses of the Dirty War. Yorio and Jalics later interpreted their six-month detention, in part, as punishment for their progressive spiritual practices—a way of separating them from the church. It has come under renewed scrutiny decades after the fact, as on the day of the raid, the priests had been in a yearlong dispute with their provincial superior, Father Jorge Mario Bergoglio, who the world now knows as Pope Francis.

Bergoglio's role in their kidnapping and subsequent release has been a source of controversy and intrigue for four decades, heightened by Bergoglio's meteoric rise within the church. After his release, Yorio came to believe that Bergoglio was the source of malicious rumors that trailed him and Jalics for several years before their kidnapping, including the idea that they were connected to the guerrillas. Both Yorio and Jalics came to blame Bergoglio for their kidnapping.[11] The year before the raid, Bergoglio had ordered Yorio and Jalics to abandon the base community in the slum and return to live with their Jesuit brethren in larger dormitories. Bergoglio has insisted that his decision to dissolve the base community was not meant to interfere with their work in the slums; instead, it was part of a policy to centralize the Jesuits in larger dormitories (and, as a consequence, increase his control over the order). One of the special charisms of the Jesuits is a duty of obedience to the pope and superior orders; the Jesuits' founder, Saint Ignatius, was a former military leader, and his disciples remain organized around quasi-military chains of command and obedience. Yorio and Jalics saw Bergoglio's directive for them to leave their base community as a betrayal of their commitment to both the slum dwellers and their work in the base community. Rather than obey Bergoglio's order, Yorio and Jalics "represented," a formal challenge to Bergoglio's command. A few weeks before the raid, they received a decision from the Jesuit superior general in Rome: they must dissolve the religious community.[12] Rather than obey, Yorio and Jalics decided to begin the process of leaving the Jesuits—a decision they say was forced upon them by Bergoglio, who worked for years to isolate them and tarnish their reputations. Days before the raid, in the midst of their transition from the Jesuit order to the "secular" clergy, Yorio maintains that his ministerial license was revoked by Cardinal Juan Carlos Aramburu, then the archbishop of Buenos Aires.[13] (Bergoglio denies their licenses were revoked and says that he, in fact, continued to give them permission to minister during their period of transition.[14]) Yorio claims that while he and Jalics sought refuge in a new diocese, Bergoglio frustrated their efforts by speaking negatively about them behind their backs.[15] While in captivity, Yorio's anonymous interrogators asked him about the suspension of his ministerial license, telling him that a truthful answer regarding why his license had been revoked was the key to his survival.[16] Based on this statement, it appears the military was familiar with Yorio and Jalics's standing within the church.

Human rights activist Emilio Mignone, whose own daughter Mónica worked in the Bajo Flores slum and was disappeared just two weeks before Yorio and Jalics were detained, wrote in his classic book *Iglesia y dictadura* (Church and dictatorship) that the revocation of their licenses was a "green light" to the dictatorship, a signal that Yorio and Jalics were personae non gratae in the eyes of the church. Mignone accused Cardinal Aramburu—and possibly Bergoglio—of being responsible for giving the military the go-ahead.[17] In a series of exposés published in 1999 about Bergoglio—who had just ascended as archbishop of Buenos Aires and was in line to become a cardinal—Argentine investigative journalist Horacio Verbitsky singled out Bergoglio for his responsibility in Yorio and Jalics's kidnapping. "I have no reason to think that [Bergoglio] did anything for our freedom, to the contrary," Yorio told Verbitsky in 1999. Verbitsky, quoting Yorio, wrote that Bergoglio had been responsible for malicious rumors surrounding Yorio and Jalics that they were Marxists and connected to the guerrillas. Verbitsky even insinuated that Bergoglio had visited the priests during their captivity, quoting Yorio as saying that he suspected Bergoglio had seen them in an operations house where the navy kept the priests detained for six months.[18] (In several court statements in the 1980s as well as in a secret letter authored in 1977 to Jesuits in Rome about Bergoglio's conduct, Yorio never made this specific accusation.)

Jalics also blamed Bergoglio. In 1995 he included a passage about his kidnapping in a section of a book he wrote on forgiveness and pardon.

"During a long period where I was kidnapped, I performed an important internal process that will help us understand the means of achieving redemption through spiritual exercises," Jalics wrote. He continued,

> It was a time of civil war between groups of the extreme left and extreme right in Argentina; university students were rowdy because of the events of the moment. They felt a great pressure to join the guerrilla. At the time I lived with a *compañero* [Yorio] right next to a slum in Bajo Flores, Buenos Aires. We were both theology professors at different universities. We wanted to bear witness that, even though misery existed, it was possible to do something for the poor through peaceful means. The official church and our superiors had ordered us to go live amongst the poor. But many people held extreme right political views and looked suspiciously at our presence in the slums. They interpreted our presence there as support to the guerrilla and they tried to denounce us as terrorists. We knew where the wind blew and who was responsible for such slander. I went to talk to the person in question [a reference to Bergoglio] and I explained that he was playing with our lives. The man promised me that he would let the military know that we weren't terrorists. But from subsequent declarations from an officer and the information in thirty documents that I was able to access later, we proved, without room for doubts, that this man had not done as promised and, in fact, to the contrary, had presented false charges with the military.[19]

Jalics also discussed Bergoglio's role in the incident with Emilio Mignone. According to Mignone's memorandum of the conversation, Jalics said that Bergoglio "knew [I] was detained by the navy, but [he] did not do anything to free us. What's more: once we were freed, Bergoglio opposed us staying in Argentina and spoke with all of the bishops to ensure that they would not accept us in their dioceses in case I left the Society of Jesus."[20] After Bergoglio was named pope, Jalics spoke publicly for the first time about the issue. In an ambiguous statement released the day after Bergoglio was named pope on the German Jesuits' website, Jalics said that he had been able to speak with Bergoglio years after the event. "Following that, we celebrated Mass publicly together and hugged solemnly. I am reconciled to events and consider the matter to be closed." He added, "I cannot comment on the role of Father Bergoglio in these events."[21] A week later, however, he released a second statement to clarify allegations that Bergoglio had been involved in his kidnapping. "I myself was once inclined to believe that we were the victims of a denunciation," Jalics said, "[but] at the end of the 90s, after numerous conversations, it became clear to me that this suspicion was unfounded. It is therefore wrong to assert that our capture took place at the initiative of Father Bergoglio."[22] Privately, however, Jalics implied to Yorio's sister, Graciela, that he did, in fact, continue to believe he had been denounced by Bergoglio.[23]

Undoubtedly, Bergoglio played an ambiguous role during the years of the military government—as did the overwhelming majority of Argentines. Unlike some courageous clergy and laypeople, Bergoglio did not publicly speak out against the regime. But his defenders say that he nevertheless acted prudently: he protected the Jesuits in his flock during those turbulent years, and he privately helped people where he could. Some have even characterized Bergoglio as an Argentine Oskar Schindler because he helped shepherd dozens of at-risk priests and laypeople to safety. (A book by a sympathetic Italian Catholic journalist, Nello Scavo, titled *Bergoglio's List: How a Young Francis Defied a Dictatorship and Saved Dozens,* makes the connection explicit.) Mignone's and Verbitsky's accusations have therefore not been without their detractors. In his 1999 exposé, Verbitsky featured the testimony of Alicia Oliveira as a counterpoint to Yorio's accusations. Oliveira spent years as a human rights lawyer under Emilio Mignone's tutelage and is a close friend of Bergoglio's. She explained that Bergoglio in fact worked to save Yorio and Jalics by securing multiple meetings with the dictatorship's highest authorities. She explained that Bergoglio's decision to order the priests to leave their base community was part of an order-wide policy of removing priests from the slums during a convulsive and dangerous moment in Argentine history and that Bergoglio acted prudently in insisting that they leave the slum for their own safety and the safety of the Jesuits at large.[24] After Bergoglio became pope and the accusations regarding Yorio and Jalics resurfaced, a number of priests came forward and stated that they had been saved by Bergoglio, who provided them refuge in Jesuit dormitories and helped them go into exile.

Bergoglio did not speak publicly about the incident or his role during the dictatorship until 2010, when he opened up to two sympathetic interviewers for an authorized autobiography, *El Jesuita: Conversaciones con Jorge Mario Bergoglio* (The Jesuit: Conversations with Jorge Mario Bergoglio).[25] "If I said nothing at the time," Bergoglio told his interlocutors, "it was so as not to dance to anyone's tune, not because I had anything to hide." He says that he tried to protect Yorio and Jalics. He encouraged them to abandon their pastoral work in the slums, which he says exposed Yorio and Jalics to the dictatorship's "witch hunt." About his behavior in general, he says, "I did what I could for my age and, with the few contacts I had, to plead for people who had been kidnapped."[26] In other words he prioritized discreet engagement with the military and quiet resistance rather than open denunciation. In Bergoglio's self-presentation, one can question his tactics but not his moral compass.

Since Bergoglio became Pope Francis, the overwhelming majority of Argentina's most important human rights figures have been taken by the "Francis effect" and become his supporters—likely a result of genuine skepticism over Mignone's and Verbitsky's accusations and an accommodation to the pope's power and influence. Estela de Carlotto, the head of the Abuelas de Plaza de Mayo (Grandmothers of the Plaza de Mayo), and Hebe de Bonafini, the head of the Association of the Mothers of the Plaza de Mayo, are the most famous examples. But prior to Bergoglio's ascendance to the papacy, the Argentine human rights community largely (though not universally) saw Bergoglio as an accomplice—both because of his alleged involvement in Yorio and Jalics's disappearance and also because of the church's wider resistance to support the human rights movement throughout Argentina's thirty years of democracy. Under his tenure as cardinal of Buenos Aires and president of the Argentine Episcopal Conference, the church's archives remained virtually sealed, and the church had not provided any meaningful support to investigators. Bergoglio had even sent a message of support to right-wing marchers calling for a general amnesty and an end to the human rights trials—a far cry from his statement to the Grandmothers of the Plaza de Mayo to "count on [him]."[27] (Human rights activists are not the only ones who have done a 180-degree turn concerning Bergoglio; Cristina Fernández de Kirchner was locked in a yearslong conflict with him while she was president from 2007 to 2013. Neither traveled the several blocks between the Buenos Aires Cathedral and the Casa Rosada, both on Buenos Aires's central plaza, to see the other. But Cristina became a Bergoglio supporter later in her tenure from 2013 to 2015, including travels to Rome for several private audiences with the pope in addition to trips to Paraguay, Brazil, and Cuba to see him.)

And so when Yorio and Jalics's case came up for consideration, there was a strong desire to subpoena Bergoglio to testify. Technically, his testimony bordered on the irrelevant. The only defendant charged with Yorio and Jalics's kidnapping was Adm. Oscar Montes. There were no allegations of Montes's direct participation in the incident and no suggestion that Bergoglio had any contact with Montes. (Mignone did testify in the 1980s that in the search for his daughter, he had secured an interview with Montes in which Montes admitted that Yorio and Jalics had been taken by the navy, but the prosecution did not allege that Montes had directly participated in Yorio and Jalics's kidnapping beyond his command responsibility.[28])

Bergoglio initially resisted his citation, which has variously been interpreted as evidence of his true opposition to the calls for justice in Argentina or as a shrewd maneuver to avoid being drawn into the sometimes toxic politics surrounding human rights. (At the time of his citation, Bergoglio had been enmeshed in a bitter dispute with the Kirchner administration. The Kirchners had made effective use of branding their political opponents as collaborators with the dictatorship. Bergoglio's supporters saw the citation as a way for the government to sling malicious accusations at him.) In resisting the subpoena, he cited an obscure provision of the Argentine penal code that allows high-ranking government officers and church officials to respond to written interrogatories rather than testify in person. (That the penal code still recognizes such privileges for church officials is one of many legal preferences provided for the Argentine Catholic Church, which remains a quasi-official state religion.) Bergoglio eventually agreed to testify but not without significant compromise: he secured an agreement from the court that the entire tribunal—three judges, numerous law clerks, and dozens of lawyers—would relocate to his chambers inside the archbishopric offices in downtown Buenos Aires to take his testimony under seal. As a consequence, I was unable to attend Bergoglio's examination, but I obtained two contemporaneous transcripts of the proceedings taken by persons authorized to attend as well as a video recording of Bergoglio's testimony.

"He played an ambiguous role," Bob Cox told me the day of Bergoglio's nomination to the papacy. Cox edited the *Buenos Aires Herald* during the last dictatorship until he was forced into exile for flouting the government's pressure to censor the *Herald*'s coverage of the disappearances. At the time, Cox told me that Bergoglio's role during the dictatorship "hasn't been clarified" and that Bergoglio has done little to explain his role, or the role of the church more generally, during the Dirty War.[29]

The highest authorities in Argentina's Catholic Church did not wait long to announce their support for the military after the March 24, 1976, coup. Minutes after the commanders in chief of the army, air force, and navy swore themselves in as a three-member ruling junta before "God and the evangelical saints," they took the time to meet with Bishop Adolfo Tortolo, then the president of the Argentine Episcopal Conference and the military vicar. After the encounter Tortolo told the press that the church would "positively cooperate" with the new government in the hopes of "definitively reinstating an authentic national spirit and a frank and loyal coexistence between Argentines."[30] Tortolo observed that the gravity of the country's national crisis required the church to lend support to the new government even though governing was a state and not a church matter.[31] Five days later, when Gen. Jorge Rafael Videla was sworn in as "president," Tortolo was on hand for the short, austere, and exclusive ceremony along with Buenos Aires archbishop Juan Carlos Aramburu and papal nuncio Pio Laghi.[32]

Before the coup Bishop Tortolo had stumped in his sermons for a "holy and purifying war" against guerrillas and Marxism; after the military took power, he frequently appeared at military installations and spoke of the unity of the "Cross and the Fatherland."[33] Bishop Victorio Bonamín, the military vicar of the army, stated that the armed forces were involved in a fight for "morality, human dignity, and ultimately a struggle to defend God."[34] While these two bishops were among the most enthusiastic supporters of the regime, the message from the institutional church was not much clearer. In May 1976, after the bishops became aware that dissidents were being kidnapped, tortured, and disappeared, the Episcopal Conference released a statement to the country calling upon Argentines to "contribute to the recuperation and salvation of Argentina." The church ambiguously stated that "the State can never renounce its duty to exercise legitimate and necessary authority, including coercive measures, even though at the same time everyone in society must conserve their liberty, in the manner in which this does not cause risk of harm to the common good."[35]

The coup leaders went out of their way to court church authorities, who in turn were drawn in by the military leaders' moderate and moralistic language. Nine months after the coup, Pio Laghi—the pope's ambassador in Argentina—described dictator Videla to visiting American diplomats as a "basically decent, sincere man."[36] He repeated his assessment four months later, in March 1977, when he told U.S. diplomats that Videla was "a good Catholic, a man deeply aware of and concerned over the personal religious implications of his responsibilities."[37]

The military got the message. The enemy, according to Videla, was not only someone "with a gun or a bomb, but anyone who encourages their use through ideas that are incompatible with Western Christian civilization."[38] The Tucumán provincial military governor Gen. Antonio Bussi said in a press release several weeks after the coup that "the Argentine Army combats subversion so that we may continue to believe in God."[39] This religious fanaticism made its way into the depths of Argentina's torture chambers. In the ESMA, Capt. Jorge Eduardo Acosta, the chief torturer, told those who did not cooperate that they would go speak with "little Jesus," a euphemism for death. Silvia Labayrú, one of the ESMA's prisoners, recalls that Capt. Antonio Pernías once escorted her to a talk by Archbishop Marcel Lefebvre, a reactionary priest who spoke out against Vatican II and was ultimately excommunicated by the church. Stories abound of priests entering secret prisons and giving confession to the prisoners; one such priest, Christian Von Wernich, was convicted of human rights crimes in 2007 for converting the confession into an interrogation tactic.[40] (Despite being convicted to life in prison, Von Wernich has not been excommunicated from or sanctioned by the church, even under Pope Francis's watch.)

There were a few public denouncements of the military during the dictatorship by the Argentine Episcopal Conference, but they were timid at best. The church's criticisms of the military government read as critiques among friends rather than prophetic denunciations of mass repression, arrests, and disappearances. In 1977, when the bishops denounced torture, prolonged arrests, and disappearances, they nevertheless addressed the military leaders as "your excellences" and invited the military to "dialogue," suggesting that the issue was a matter over which reasonable men could disagree.[41] A year before he died, in 2012, dictator Videla told journalist Ceferino Reato during a jailhouse interview that the military and the church had a "very good relationship." He continued, "The Church was not addicted to us, we had our clashes, but, as an institution, it acted prudently: it said what it had to say without creating an unlivable situation."[42]

The historical debate over the role of the Catholic Church will probably go on for decades, maybe even centuries. To its critics the church is guilty of more than a sin of omission; it was actually an accomplice of the regime by providing theological justification and support for the military. "There was a true identification," writes Rubén Dri in *La hegemonía de los cruzados*. "The Bishops behaved as the true legitimizers of the Process, as spiritual guardians of the sword of the soldiers."[43] Others suggest a more nuanced view—that one cannot speak of "the church" as being an accomplice because the church, like so many other institutions in Argentine society, was fractured and in a state of crisis. Internal divisions among those who supported the military, those who denounced it, those who did not get involved, and those who prioritized private pleading in place of public denunciation prevented the church from forming a unified opposition. In the church's official history, it has been unfairly criticized. As Pope John Paul II said on a visit to Argentina in 1987, the country's bishops had engaged in "selfless acts" that "saved lives," most of which had been "forgotten or ignored."[44]

This history of the church at large frames any view of Bergoglio, who did not make the dictatorship an important theme of his bishopric. In fact, as archbishop, he showed considerable resistance to confronting the past: During a 2007 homily, Bergoglio spoke of the need to "bless the past" and not speak badly of it. He encouraged his followers to embrace the sins and injustices of the past with pardon, remorse, and reparation: "To bless the past is to speak well of God, of our fathers, and our grandfathers." He also warned, "He who speaks ill of the past surely does so because he is planning to obtain an advantage in the present or the future, an advantage that is not a blessing for others."[45]

"There was not a clear distinction between the social, political, and spiritual divides of the era," says Loris Zanatta, a leading historian on the Argentine Catholic Church in the twentieth century.[46] An existential crisis brought the Argentine church to crippling paralysis. In 1959, largely in response to the great tragedy of World War II and the sweeping technological changes of midcentury, Pope John XXIII called for an aggiornamento—a breathing of new life—into the Catholic Church in an effort to reconcile the two-thousand-year-old institution with the modern world. Convened in 1962, the three-year gathering of cardinals, bishops, and other religious luminaries was an effort to "look to the present, to the new conditions and new forms of life in the modern world, which have opened new avenues to the Catholic apostolate," as John XXIII announced at the beginning of the council.[47] The liturgy was reformed, priests were encouraged to say Mass in vernacular languages, laymen were given greater prominence. The church proclaimed its desire to dialogue with other faiths, thereby showing itself more tolerant of non-Catholics.

In Europe, Vatican II was generally received as a call for democratization, harmony, peace, and nonviolence. Two world wars within thirty years had decimated the continent; modernity and industrialization had atomized the faithful and alienated them from church life. But in Latin America, the reforms were received with a more drastic interpretation. When the Latin American Bishop's Conference was held in Medellín in 1968, sometimes referred to as the Vatican II for Latin America, the bishops issued a call to action. The peoples of Latin America were plagued by "the lack of material goods for minimum sustenance"; "oppressive structures, that invite the abuse of having and the abuse of power"; "the exploitation of workers or the injustice of transactions"; and cultural imperialism. This misery—nothing short of "institutional violence"—was "an injustice that cries out to the heavens." The Latin American bishops prophesized a time when "consideration of another's dignity would increase," when the continent would be "oriented towards a spirit of poverty" and the "acquisition of culture." So the bishops announced "with dramatic urgency" that it was "the hour of action." It was time for the "meaningful gestation of a new civilization."[48] Like the Israelites in Egypt, the bishops prophesized that the peoples of Latin America were on the verge of divine liberation.

The Latin American bishops called for a "true liberation" wherein all people would realize the "reign of justice, love and peace." The bishops spoke on behalf of families, workers, and *campesinos*, against the rich and elite classes that dominated the continent, and put their own interests—and those of foreign powers—ahead of their compatriots. Political change was a prerequisite of divine liberation. The bishops called out political systems that frequently "attacked the common good and favored privileged groups." The bishops also issued a warning: "We should not be surprised that the 'temptation to violence' has been born in Latin America," they said. "The patience of the pueblo that has tolerated a difficult condition for years that those with a greater appreciation for human rights would not accept should not be abused." The church said that if the privileged of the region failed to embrace the "profound transformations that are necessary," they themselves would become responsible for the "explosive revolutions of desperation." Nevertheless, while the bishops recognized the legitimacy of insurrectional revolution in cases of "evident tyranny," they concluded that dynamic popular organization was the better path to peace and justice. The bishops called upon the church to organize and foster social consciousness among the masses. "An aesthetic and apparent peace can be obtained through force," the bishops said. "An authentic peace implies struggle, inventive capacity, permanent conquest."[49]

The pronouncement received a less-than-enthusiastic response from the most important figures in Argentina's Catholic Church. The Medellín document assumed that the church was an institution outside of the state—in a position to criticize it, to vocalize opposition to oppressive elites—but in Argentina (often the enigma of Latin America) the church was functionally part of the state. It had considered itself the spiritual center of the nation and was closely linked to Argentina's most conservative and traditional sectors, including supporting nationalist military coups throughout the twentieth century. The first major document released after Medellín by the Argentine Episcopal Conference reflected its unease: "We live in an hour of renovation in the life of the Church, of worry amongst some of its children, of transformation in contemporary mentality, of the relaxation of social mores, the acceleration of human activity, of hope that the Church will show itself in all its manifestations more conscious of its mission, more free of temporary interests, more committed to radiate the Gospel of Salvation that it carries."[50] Though the bishops recognized that Argentina, then under a military dictatorship, suffered from an "unjust structure," their call for reform was modest and presented no direct challenge to the military. The church needed to reach individuals; liberation would come through teaching the powerful word of the gospel to virtuous people: "It is our duty to work for the total liberation of man and illuminate the process of change in unjust and oppressive social structures generated by sin."[51] And they announced the importance of working with the poor, but not necessarily in opposition to the rich and powerful—the call was for the church to identify with the poor as part of the nation. "The action of the Church should not only be oriented towards the pueblo, but rather it should also, and principally, be from within the pueblo itself," the bishops said, meaning that the church should "love the pueblo, penetrate within the pueblo and understand it"; "trust it in its creative capacity and its transformative force"; "help it express and organize itself"; "listen to it, capture and understand its expressions even though they come from a culture a level apart"; "know its hopes and aspirations, its anguishes and pains, its needs and values; know especially what it wants and desires from the Church and its ministers"; and "discern in all of this what should be corrected and purified, what is current but only transitory, what has permanent values and seeds of the future." The Argentine bishops warned against importing "problems, attitudes, norms or values that are far and foreign, especially when they take away or weaken their reasons for living and reasons for hope."[52] Indeed, the document seemed to warn about the dangers of working with the poor more than it directed concrete action in accordance with Medellín: "He is not poor who feels superior, secure, and strong. . . . He is not poor who feels pride in his poverty and makes an ostentatious manifestation of it. . . . [Poverty] does not plant resentments, it does not engender bitterness, it does not provoke violence, and it is not a definite state."[53]

But the Argentine church was not homogenous. A small but vocal group of younger radical priests both foreshadowed and insisted on the revolution prophesized in Medellín. In 1967, a year before Medellín, a loosely knit organization called the Movimiento de Sacerdotes Para el Tercer Mundo (Movement of Third World Priests) formed in Argentina with the express purpose of "overcoming the antagonism between Christianity and socialism" and rejecting "capitalism and international imperialism."[54] In numerous public statements, magazine articles, speeches, and pastoral activities, the movement attempted to articulate a synthesis of Christianity, socialism, and Peronism. The priests saw their role as one of prophecy, to denounce the manifestly unjust situation of the poor and the oppressed and to accompany the masses on whatever path they chose for liberation—even violent revolution. In May 1969 they issued a statement of principles that was "strongly in support of a revolutionary process, of radical and urgent change in [the country's] structures and our formal rejection of the current capitalist system and all types of economic, political and cultural imperialism." They saw "armed fight of the people for their total liberation and for the installation of an authentic socialism" as the most efficient way out of the national crisis. The other paths—converting the oppressors or "active nonviolence"—were evaluated and rejected as unviable. Indeed, in 1970, when the Montonero guerrillas kidnapped and executed former dictator Pedro Eugenio Aramburu, the Third World Priests all but endorsed the execution. They declared that "every man has the same fundamental value" and said it was "not Christian to underappreciate the life of a man," but at the same time, neither was it Christian to "overvalue" one in relation to all the others.

It was not long before hostilities erupted between the Argentine Catholic hierarchy and the Third World Priests. In 1969 the Third World Priests declared themselves in open conflict with the church authorities. Church unity, they announced, should never be accepted "at the price of betraying a revolutionary process."[55] The bishops' conference did not hesitate to publicly reprimand the scofflaw priests: "The children of light are not afraid of walking in the light of day; they don't hide their steps nor do they want to remove themselves from episcopal favor."[56]

It was here that the battle lines of the Dirty War began to be drawn—the priests in rebellion nurtured many of the revolutionaries who would swell in the radical Peronist movement's ranks over the coming years. As recounted by Richard Gillespie in *Soldiers of Perón*, many of the leaders of the Montoneros had formative experiences as Catholic activists before accepting the dogma of revolution and the legitimacy of armed struggle.[57] The hierarchy, for its part, saw the rebellion as nothing short of a Marxist infiltration of the church and, hence, the soul of the nation. Its mission was to "plainly and simply adapt the Church to the modern world, rather than try and convert and save the world within the Church," according to right-wing Catholic Carlos Sacheri in his book *La Iglesia clandestina* (The clandestine church).[58] In other words, the clandestine church was trying to "instrumentalize everything that is Christian in service of a Marxist inspired social revolution."[59] (Sacheri was murdered by People's Revolutionary Army [ERP] guerrillas in 1971.) The progressives were doing nothing less than fighting a "psychological war" within the church, one leading to the "self-destruction" of the institution.[60] In fact, the "progressive" priests were dangerous because they could "soften" people who were "spiritually less developed" and who were "dazzled" by them, thus leading part of the faithful to heresy.[61] Such a worldview came to form the military's own view of "subversive" undesirables, those who would be targeted during the Dirty War.

For both the "renovation" priests and the "traditionalists," the *patria* was endowed with divine significance and should represent God's reign on earth. For the traditionalists, the church should retain its traditional place within society as the arbiter of moral values (against divorce, in support of religious education in schools, training leaders with proper Catholic education); for the renovation priests, the church should insert itself among the masses to create an authentically Argentine community where the spiritual practices of the pueblo would reveal a local divine order. Explicitly, both were antiliberal. For the traditionalists, liberalism had dangerously separated the public from the private life and relegated religion to secondary private importance; for the "renovation" priests, interested in the mood and idiosyncrasies of the pueblo, liberalism was an imperialist concept implanted on Argentina to justify an exploitative capitalist system.[62] "One of the characteristics of modernity," wrote Lucio Gera, a leading renovation theologian, "is that it has pulverized, it has dissociated all human experiences, and has replaced man as a sum of experience, not as a profound unity, but rather something quantitative, as a mathematical fact, as the sum of all things."[63] The project of liberation theology—and by extension, the church—was to overcome this dissociation and unify politics and religion so that all Argentines could achieve their dignity and self-determination as members of a pueblo.

The jump from searching for an authentically Argentine political organization to bestowing the Peronist movement with spiritual significance was not great, as Perón was seen as an authentically and uniquely Argentine, the true leader of a pueblo. If the project of liberation theology was to ensure the pueblo's historical self-expression, to free it from oppressive foreign structures, then figures like Perón—who had articulated an Argentine Third Way—were politico-religious saviors. "If we believe that we should work from inside the pueblo, attentive to the fact that [the pueblo] is Peronist," the Third World Priests wrote after their fourth national convention in 1971, then it was necessary to work for "economic independence, political sovereignty and social justice"—the three pillars of Perón's justicialist doctrine—and to "prophetically criticize deviations or betrayals of the party with respect to these." This led them to sympathize with revolutionary Peronist groups, who saw themselves as the vanguard of a revolution. "The pueblo is revolutionary," the priests wrote, "and the pueblo is Peronist. Therefore Peronism is intrinsically revolutionary."[64]

By the time Bergoglio was called to trial on November 8, 2010, Yorio and Jalics's kidnapping had been thoroughly investigated. As early as 1977, Yorio's and Jalics's names appeared in court papers when Emilio Mignone recounted a conversation he had with Yorio shortly after Yorio's release in a case connected to the disappearance of his own daughter

Mónica, who was kidnapped just two weeks before Yorio and worked in the same slum.[65] During the democratic transition, Yorio was cited to testify five separate times. Yorio's and Jalics's cases were ultimately among the 709 cases considered by the federal criminal appeals court in 1985. The court found that Yorio and Jalics had been kidnapped by the navy and taken to the ESMA.[66] (In those earlier investigations, several priests, including Rodolfo Ricciardelli, Jorge Vernazza, and Gabriel Bossini, had all testified. Bergoglio had never been cited to testify and had never volunteered to give testimony.)

On the day of the raid, Yorio was supposed to be leading Mass at a modest sheet metal chapel in the Bajo Flores slum. But that Sunday, owing to the revocation of his ministerial license, he watched the raid through the window of his house just outside the slum while he was meeting with a group of Paraguayan priests and nuns.[67] The soldiers skipped by Yorio and Jalics's house and went straight to the chapel (about fifty meters from their house), where Yorio's replacement, Father Gabriel Bossini, was performing Mass.[68] A teenage missionary assisting with the Mass who had worked with Yorio in the slum remembers several green army trucks full of soldiers, as well as police cars and vans, approaching the chapel.[69] Witnesses guess that at least one hundred heavily armed soldiers dressed in green camouflage participated in the operation as well as a smaller group of men dressed in civilian clothing. As the soldiers descended upon the chapel, the parishioners heard boots marching, trucks and cars moving, and orders being yelled. Children inside the chapel began to cry. Curiously, the soldiers did not stop the Mass as they surrounded the church; in their twisted religious devotion, it was apparently unethical to breach the Sunday ritual but not to kidnap defenseless teenagers and two priests.[70]

When the Mass was over, the soldiers shouted orders at the parishioners: the slum dwellers were told to return to their homes, and the teenage catechism students assisting the service were lined up against a wall outside the chapel.[71] Some had come that day to show solidarity with Yorio, who they believed had been unjustly punished. Over approximately two hours, the students were interrogated about their activities and Yorio's activities in the villa, after which point they were loaded onto a bus and hooded and taken to the ESMA.[72] They were released after being detained overnight, but the episode inflicted substantial and lasting trauma. One of the teenagers recalled years later that she was groped and harassed by guards while she was captive. Another remembered that on the day of her release, she was blindfolded and set in a field when an officer fired a gun. She thought she was being executed.

Yorio and Jalics weren't so lucky. After the soldiers spent approximately forty-five minutes to an hour with the catechism students at the chapel, several officers told Father Bossini to take them to Yorio and Jalics's house. When the officers barged into their home, Yorio was separated from his guests as well as from Jalics. Yorio's visitors were ordered against a wall, and Yorio was taken to another room while the soldiers ransacked the house.[73] They interrogated Yorio, asking him about what he thought of Augusto Pinochet in Chile and of Angola and whether he had taught the slum dwellers to show adequate respect toward the military. They asked him if he had been friends with Carlos Mugica, a revolutionary priest who had been outspoken in the years leading up to the coup and was assassinated in 1974. When the soldiers searched the house and found several pamphlets from the Montonero guerrillas, Yorio explained that he was a theology professor and sometimes collected political materials for his classes and research. Undoubtedly, however, the discovery confirmed the soldiers' suspicions about Yorio's "subversive" connections. They also asked him about Mónica Quinteiro, whose picture they found among his belongings. Quinteiro had disappeared the week before. She had worked with Yorio and Jalics in the slum helping organize missionary work until about a year before the raid, when she announced to Yorio and the group of catechism students that she would have to separate from their missionary group because she had decided to do "political" work that was inconsistent with being a missionary. (One of the catechism students who was at the meeting when Quinteiro announced her resignation told me it was clear Quinteiro was joining the Montoneros.) One of the officers approached Yorio and told him he had known Quinteiro, who came from a military family, since she was little. Yorio's impression years later was that the officer was trying to help Quinteiro escape from certain death.[74]

To Yorio there were strange aspects of the operation. The soldiers addressed one another with army ranks such as *major* and *captain*, but

Yorio—who grew up an army brat, as his father was in the army—did not believe their mannerisms were typical of army officers.[75] Jalics later recalled seeing an anchor on the belt of one of the officers, which he recognized as the distinctive sign of the navy.[76] While the soldiers apparently tried to mask their identities, the federal court of criminal appeals held in 1985 that the navy, in fact, detained Yorio and Jalics.[77]

The soldiers remained at Yorio and Jalics's house until about 3 p.m., when they released Bossini and Yorio's guests. (Father Luis Dourron, who lived with Yorio and Jalics at the base community, escaped by bicycle as the raid descended on the slum; he was not detained in the dragnet that day.) Yorio was loaded into a car and, after several blocks, was hooded.[78] When he first testified about his captivity, in August 1983—before the dictatorship collapsed—he recalled being taken down a stairway and led into a basement with a cement floor; there he was required to sit hooded on the floor with his hands tied behind his back. He heard other people in the room, some of whom plead to go to the bathroom. He also recalled hearing guards and music coming from a small radio or portable music player. This was before Argentina's National Commission on the Status of the Disappeared (CONADEP) investigation, but survivors later corroborated all these details as consistent with the standard arrival at the ESMA.[79] Jalics, separated from Yorio, underwent a similar "arrival": he was hooded and cuffed from behind and, after a drive that he estimates was twenty to sixty minutes long, taken into a basement.[80]

Inside, deprived of sight, Yorio believes he heard a woman, possibly Quinteiro, say, "Ay, Orlando," though he was never certain who called his name. Soon he was taken up a stairway, placed into a small dark room (still hooded), and shackled with a ball and chain.[81] Some of the details of his testimony remain murky. When first called to testify in 1983 and 1984, he alternatively stated that he was then either taken up a flight of stairs or accompanied up an elevator. He also variously recalled receiving no food or water within his first several days in detention but also recalled receiving coffee.[82] Such small inconsistencies are common among survivors' testimonies.

Yorio was kept in solitary confinement for what he believes was two to three days, the isolation broken only by the occasional insult or threat from a guard. When Yorio asked to go to the bathroom, his guards refused, and he relieved himself in his clothing, which he was not permitted to change.[83] Cut off from human contact, Yorio later testified that he focused on meditation and a "need to communicate with Jesus so as to be able to go to heaven."[84]

About three days into his detention, Yorio says his captors injected him in the thigh with a sedative. "I want to go with Jesus, I want to go to heaven," he meditated to himself as he slid into a drug-induced semi-conscious state. Amid his stupor, he remembers his anonymous interrogators asking him about Argentine history, his theological writings, and his activities in the villa. They also asked Yorio about "Mónica," and he began telling them about Mónica Quinteiro, though he was unsure initially whether they were asking about Mónica Quinteiro or Mónica Mignone, who he also knew.[85] He says that they asked "dirty" questions about the intimate details of Quinteiro's sex life.[86]

A day or two later, Yorio was taken to another room where he was placed on a bed. There he thought he would be electrocuted as his guards had threatened on several occasions.[87] Instead, a serious man with a calm demeanor entered the room and identified himself as a "practicing Catholic."[88] In contrast to the threatening behavior of the other guards, this man addressed Yorio with the formal *usted*. Yorio's hands were retied at his front.[89] The man told Yorio that he wanted to help him, that he wanted to save him, but that it was fundamental to explain why he did not have his ministerial license. Yorio told him that he did not know; his superiors had told him that there had been threats against him and that it was a secret.[90] Yorio said that he assumed the question "referred to an ongoing conflict, about conversations I had with the father provincial of the order [Bergoglio], who asked the members of this community to leave there, informing them that the reasons were secret but that they came from Rome and Argentina."[91]

After this interrogation Yorio was taken back to his cell, where he slept, probably for an entire day. Yorio was given food for the first time in days—a sandwich and a Coca-Cola—and was told that he was going to be set free, but on the condition that he distance himself from the poor and that he avoid ministering in public for a year.[92] According to Yorio an interrogator told him,

> Look, Father: Know that taking you has been a great trauma for us. Know that we were looking for a Montonero chief, and as it turned out, we found a man who we have to give work. I'm not a soldier, and I would like to talk with you; we could talk if you stayed here. But I understand that you are most interested in leaving here, and I am in a position to say that you can leave with your freedom—but on the condition that, because of human problems, you are going to have to spend a year in a college. You should not appear in public. You are an idealist priest—I would say a mystic, a *piola* priest—with only one error . . . you have interpreted the doctrine of Christ overly materially. Christ speaks of the poor of spirit, and you have given a materialist interpretation of this, surely influenced by the Marxist infiltration of the Latin American church, and you have gone to live with the materially poor. In Argentina the poor of spirit are the rich, and you, going forward, should dedicate yourself to help more with the rich who are spiritually lacking.[93]

After approximately a week, Yorio and Jalics were taken out of the ESMA by their captors to a different location. In the new location, they were housed in the same room and had contact with each other for the first time since being kidnapped. Jalics told Yorio that he had discovered that they had been in the ESMA based on an Independence Day speech he heard out of the window in the cell of his room in which the orator stated, "Here, in the Naval Mechanics School."[94] At this new location they were treated better: Their hoods were replaced with blindfolds, they were handcuffed in front, and their legs were no longer shackled together. They were regularly fed and allowed to bathe occasionally. The guards who rotated through the house did not treat them as poorly as they had been treated in the ESMA. Still, they were kept in isolation from other prisoners, provided no opportunity to move, and kept in near total sensory deprivation for six months.[95] Jalics later recalled that he survived the ordeal by focusing on his spiritual exercises, finding an opportunity in the punishment to meditate.[96]

The man who had first interrogated Yorio in his house came back and again inquired about Mónica Quinteiro, including whether she was "recoverable."[97] (As one of the many inexplicable questions around the trial, Mónica Quinteiro was not among the victims in the prosecution's case. Her case was ultimately included in a follow-up trial that began in 2012.) At their new location, the interrogators expressed some apparent remorse. Yorio recalls that one of the interrogators told them, "You will hold on to hate, but know that there is a great problem in Argentina, know that this is a war, and that in war sometimes the just pay for the sinners." The interrogator also tried to tell the priests that he was on the "good side": "Know that amongst us [the military] there are people who only want to kill."[98]

While it is unknown why Yorio and Jalics were taken to this new location, it was not the usual treatment. Perhaps having been discovered at the ESMA, the navy wanted to move them to a different location so they could not be identified; based on what the interrogators told them, they also clearly saw Yorio as a valuable intelligence asset, a man who could explain the political reality of the country and help them identify infiltrators in the church.

On October 23 officers gave Yorio and Jalics a slumber-inducing injection and loaded them onto a truck. Over the course of their journey in the truck, they were given two more injections. Yorio recalls that the next thing he remembers is waking up in an open field, in the fresh air, without chains or handcuffs. After fifteen minutes he got the courage to take off his blindfold and saw Jalics next to him.[99] Though still woozy, the two priests walked about a kilometer before finding a small house; the resident told them that he had seen a helicopter fly overhead the day before. Yorio and Jalics then took a train back to Buenos Aires and hid in the first church they could find, the Church of the Sacred Heart. From there the parish priests at Sacred Heart paid for a taxi to take Yorio and Jalics to Father Jorge Vernazza, and from there Yorio spoke on the phone with Bergoglio.[100]

"Did Father Bergoglio tell you what he had done in your and Father Jalics's favor?" prosecutor Luis Moreno Ocampo asked Yorio at the 1985 trial of the Juntas. Yorio replied,

> Yes, he told me something, not much, or . . . I don't have everything so clear in this moment, I know he communicated with Commander Massera, this he told me . . . about names, that's all I remember. I also know that the cardinal of Buenos Aires intervened . . . and I know that

> the Society of Jesus intervened, this yes, when I was in Rome, the secretary to the general of the society in this moment, he told me yes, that they did *gestiones*, including the fact that there had been a report from the embassy of Argentina in the Vatican; they had informed the Society of Jesus about me.[101]

Soon after their release, they received word that the police were seeking them. With assistance from the papal nuncio, Yorio and Jalics went to a police station under diplomatic cover to give a statement about their ordeal. They went into exile shortly thereafter; Jalics to the United States, where his mother lived, and Yorio to Rome, where he began his studies at the Jesuit theological seminary in the Vatican.

"From a young age, life pushed me into leadership roles," Bergoglio told his biographers in 2010.[102] In 1971, just two years after he was ordained, Bergoglio was selected as master of novitiates of the Argentine Jesuits and given responsibility over incoming seminarians. Two years after that, in 1973, he was again catapulted forward and selected as "provincial" of the Argentine Jesuits, the title given to the superior of the local order, known as a "province." At just thirty-six, he was one of the youngest priests ever selected for the position. Reflecting on that decision, Bergoglio would later describe it as "crazy" that he was promoted at such a young age.[103]

Bergoglio's meteoric rise owed equally to his unusual charisma and his unique position between the warring factions within the church. The older Jesuits saw promise in the young Bergoglio—they accelerated his spiritual formation to groom him for leadership. He took his final vows years before the time when most Jesuits commonly take such vows. When he was appointed master of novitiates, he rose to the occasion. He reversed the decline of novitiates entering the order. (The year before Bergoglio was appointed, not a single novitiate had entered.) While the world now knows Pope Francis as a reformer and a liberal, his outlook as a young priest was decidedly more orthodox. He guided his students through a rigid and disciplined classical formation, focusing on spiritual matters rather than politics and social issues. Bergoglio did focus on the poor but not through the prism of liberation theology, as did so many of his contemporaries.[104]

When the time came to name a new provincial in 1973, Bergoglio emerged as a leading candidate. Associates recall it was his seeming ability to bridge the divide between younger and older priests that propelled his rise. While the older Jesuits felt comfortable with his traditionalism, the younger Jesuits were excited by the prospect of one in their generation becoming the leader of the local order, whether or not he shared their views. "He was our candidate," recalls Father Ignacio García Mata, who was two years ahead of Bergoglio in seminary. "All of us young priests greatly admired him; he was extraordinarily capable."[105]

The enthusiasm, however, was not universal. Father Ignacio Pérez del Viso, also two years Bergoglio's senior, told me what he thought when he heard Bergoglio's name floated as a possible leader: "No way, he's too young! He's going to get burned!" Even though Bergoglio had been a master of novitiates, Pérez del Viso worried that Bergoglio's experience would not translate well if he were called upon to supervise older ordained priests, who are much more self-assured than impressionable novitiates. "The conflicts of that period divided people deeply; they were very severe," Pérez del Viso told me.[106]

Bergoglio's predecessor, Father Ricardo "Dick" O'Farrel, stepped down so that Bergoglio could take over before the Jesuit General Congregation 32, scheduled for the end of 1974. The Jesuit leader in the Vatican, the superior general Father General Pedro Arrupe, had put social justice at the heart of his pastoral activities, and the congregation was expected to push the Jesuits toward solidarity with the oppressed, like the apostles of the early church after Christ's death. (It was Arrupe who, in 1968, had coined the term *option for the poor*, which became a cornerstone of liberation theology in the 1970s and 1980s.) "Bergoglio was chosen at a very difficult moment to play a very complicated role," says Jorge Scuro, an ex-Jesuit from Uruguay who was a classmate of Bergoglio's in seminary.[107]

But shortly after ascending as provincial, Bergoglio demonstrated he had different priorities. In a series of speeches in 1974, Bergoglio announced that church unity—not social justice—would be an "absolute priority" of his tenure. Without unity, he warned that the church itself risked "disintegration," the "final stage of a process born in atheist individualism and disbelief." He showed little tolerance for the spiritual analysis of many of his contemporaries like Yorio, who flirted with partisan politics and embraced a Marxist analysis of the gospel.[108]

In a speech to Argentine theologians in April 1974, for instance, he chastised those who failed to recognize "what is viable." He accused priests among his flock of being interested in "false solutions," "passing ethical postures," "elitisms," "abstractions," and "dialogues with ideologies that are foreign to us"—a not-so-veiled critique of liberation theology and the renovation priests among the Jesuits such as Yorio and Jalics. He never invoked the vocabulary of liberation theology, such as *preferential option for the poor, the oppressed,* or *class structures.* Rather, he was squarely within a long line of Argentine Catholic nationalists who saw the mission of the church as promoting harmony among the country's social classes.[109] "Our most authentic liberation projects privilege unity over conflict," he told a congregation of Argentine Jesuits in February 1974, "because what is at stake is the project of a Nation, and not the accommodation of any particular class." It reflected Bergoglio's embrace of popular religiosity (itself reminiscent of conservative strains of Peronism), an alternative to liberation theology—a religious practice that connected the church to the poor but did not foment emancipation. Bergoglio explained that the

> faithful pueblo does not divorce its Christian faith from its historic projects, nor does it mix them with revolutionary messianism. This pueblo believes in resurrection and in life: it baptizes its children and prays for its dead. Our pueblo prays, and what does it ask for? Health, work, bread, and familial understanding, and for the fatherland, peace. Some think this is not revolutionary, but the same pueblo that asks for peace knows that on top of this is the fruit of justice.[110]

At the end of August 1974, a year into Bergoglio's six years as provincial, he released an evaluation of the province. He recognized that there had been a "crisis" in the church as a consequence of the aggiornamento. The challenge, he told his brethren, was to "consolidate the body of the province" and have a "clear vision of the ends." He also insisted on ending the antagonism between the younger renovation priests and the church hierarchy, which had exploded in recent years: "I believe that today it is an absolute priority to think of the Argentine

Church as an institution, and the Argentine Society [of Jesus] as an institution in this Church. This is not simply a juridical or legal problem, rather it is an attempt to see through the depth of the ecclesiastical problem that affects the institution." He insisted that unity was nothing less than "a matter of survival" and commanded his brethren that "either we insert ourselves into the body, where God the Savior goes, embracing there—with the attempt to resolve them—all contradictions, or we will destroy ourselves in disintegration."[111]

As Pope Francis, Bergoglio is often portrayed as a liberal reformer—a humble servant of God and the first Jesuit to ascend to the papacy. (By tradition, Jesuits are prohibited from aspiring to or offering themselves for higher ecclesiastical offices.) But the young Bergoglio is remembered quite differently by his contemporaries. One of Bergoglio's former Jesuit brothers complained of Bergoglio's tenure to me, "There was a very strong feeling of brotherhood among the Jesuit orders in Latin America, but we lived isolated. It took us a long time to repair the relationship with our brothers in Latin America." (He wished to remain anonymous so as to speak candidly, "otherwise they'll send me to Mars or the moon.") He told me that Bergoglio was obsessed with Marxism, almost to the point of being paranoid.

Bergoglio's tenure was so full of conflict that he was all but banished from the Argentine Jesuits following his six years as provincial and his subsequent tenure as dean of the Colegio Máximo, the Jesuit seminary outside of Buenos Aires. He was first sent to Frankfurt to complete his dissertation and, upon returning to Argentina, was sent into internal exile in Córdoba to keep him away from the center of power in Buenos Aires. When he became an auxiliary bishop in Buenos Aires in 1992—an odd trajectory for a Jesuit, as Jesuits typically do not become bishops—he was banned from living in any Jesuit houses.[112]

Bergoglio's laser-like focus on unity, his desire to accommodate the church hierarchy, and his distrust and disdain for liberation theologians put him on a direct collision course with priests like Yorio and Jalics. Yorio firmly embraced the theology that Bergoglio decried as "elite," a "false abstraction," and a "passing ethical posture." Over the course of the early 1970s, Yorio's academic writings in journals such as *Teología*, *Stromata*, and *Revista Biblica* reflect an ever-increasing interest in divining the religious significance of revolutionary Peronism. In 1973, for instance, Yorio began divining a closer unity between the church and national liberation movements: "Throughout history, each time the Church has truly identified itself with the poor and made itself poor, the Church has inaugurated, or been witness to, or collaborated in creating a new politics." Liberation theology, Yorio wrote, was a theological sign of this new politics. It was a way that the church "identifies with the poor and takes charge of the new political potential that the poor have inaugurated." He attempted to articulate how the church could facilitate and accompany the poor on their path to an authentic socialism, showing clear support for the Movement of Third World Priests. Yorio recognized that there were certain questions over tactics—who should control the means of production, the question of violence, and whether to form alliances with groups with atheist ideologies—but these were ancillary to the central need for the church to accompany the people on their path of liberation. He identified the Peronist model as the clearest vehicle of the people's capacity for self-organization and self-determination and believed that the "Christian faith has a special role" owing to the poor's loyalty to and comfort with the church. And Yorio insisted that liberation would not come through legal reform: "A socialist model for Argentina must be prepared to go through clandestine situations, secretly or publicly outside of the law." While Peronism was the clear vehicle for liberation in Argentina, the project of a *patria grande* throughout Latin America—where many other countries gravitated toward Marxism—necessitated a "greater openness to the language and use of Marxist instruments." Looking at history, Yorio divined that at some point, the people would need to go through a "violent fight" to construct a new socialist system. He described the "Peronist special formations and other armed groups inspired by Marxism" as a means of having an armed forces to "guarantee the reality of popular socialism." The primary path to liberation, Yorio wrote, was not military but political. Nevertheless, the armed groups were necessary for the defense of the people's political project: "War and just violence are a path towards the self-organization of a people."[113]

Topics that Bergoglio considered as "abstract" and "foreign" to Christianity Yorio considered fundamental. He wrote about the control of the means of production, the need for realistic political alliances on the path to liberation, the legitimacy of unjust legal structures, the morality of subverting the law, and the conditions under which "just violence" could be "unleashed."

When lawyers explored these conflictive and heady days within the Jesuits, Bergoglio largely glossed over the deep divisions of the era and his place within them. He skirted any honest discussion of his conflicts with Yorio and Jalics. At trial Bergoglio described his relationship with the two priests as "a normal relationship as between two Jesuit brothers. We weren't friends, we weren't enemies, but we had a good relationship." He recalled them as "good priests, very intelligent both of them, good professors. Jalics had a special gift for spiritual direction; I had him as a spiritual advisor for two years in theology. Yorio had an exquisite sensitivity united with intellect. He was an above-average intellectual, and with this synthesis, his theological classes were enriching." In response to a judge's question about their theology, Bergoglio highlighted that Yorio and Jalics had "a balanced and orthodox position, in line with the framework of the two instructions issued by the Holy See." By this he meant that neither of them used a Marxist hermeneutic.[114]

But his conflict with Yorio and Jalics wasn't just spiritual; there was a personal divide as well. "I remember people's main criticism was that Bergoglio insisted he had the only correct interpretation of Saint Ignacio de Loyola," says José María Poirier, who is now the editor of the liberal catholic magazine *Criterio* and spent much of the 1970s in exile in the Vatican.[115] Several former associates described Bergoglio as "authoritarian." Indeed, Bergoglio has elsewhere acknowledged that his "authoritarian and quick manner of making decisions" led him to have "serious problems" and to be "accused of being ultraconservative."[116] When Father Pérez del Viso described Bergoglio that way, I asked him to elaborate. In careful terms he told me that "some people are called to exercise power; others are there to advise, to teach. We weren't all born to be president of the republic. Bergoglio, temperamentally, was born to lead."[117]

Bergoglio was both strong-willed and young, two characteristics that certainly would have clashed with Yorio, who suffered from a not-so-small dose of vanity. This divide—intellectual, spiritual, and personal—slowly grew into a chasm as Bergoglio asserted his authority over the province.

Almost as soon as Bergoglio took over as provincial, conflict began. In a secret 1977 letter Yorio wrote to the Jesuit superiors in Rome shortly after his release, which private lawyers in the case had reviewed before taking Bergoglio's testimony, Yorio recalls a painful saga of delaying the taking of his final vows to become a full professed Jesuit.[118] Asked directly about whether he could recall if Yorio had any problems with his vows at trial, Bergoglio said that he was not aware of any problems Yorio had with his vows.[119] But in his 1977 letter, Yorio recalled that Bergoglio originally stated that Yorio could take his final vows within six months of his ascendance as provincial, yet when that six months arrived, Bergoglio told Yorio that there had been problems with his final vows. Yorio claims Bergoglio says he had received significant negative feedback from his advisors, who warned them against Yorio's aptitude. Yorio says that Bergoglio took a second round of advice, and though the results were not as grave as the first, the advice remained negative, including that he had "errors and misconceptions" in his conception of God, insecurity in his theology, a lack of physical health, mental illness, and disobedience and disloyalty to Bergoglio; that he divided the province; that he wasn't worthy of taking his final vows; and that he shouldn't continue being a Jesuit because it would do damage. Yorio says at the time, Bergoglio assured him that he did not share these concerns, that it was a problem within the province and among other Jesuits, but they decided to postpone his vows yet again. Later Yorio says that he asked some of Bergoglio's advisors about these allegations, and they said the advice they gave Bergoglio about him had been the opposite of what Bergoglio suggested, and they didn't think there was so much pressure against him within the province.[120] (Yorio did not apparently consider that when confronted, these advisors declined to reveal their confidential criticisms conveyed to Bergoglio.)

Yorio also claims that shortly after Bergoglio became provincial, he was sacked from his teaching positions. When asked about the reasons for Yorio's departure from the Máximo, Bergoglio said at trial that "people came and went because courses were cyclical. It's hard to say. Perhaps he left because that year, the course wasn't offered and he would take it up another year."[121] Again it seemed like an instance of Bergoglio downplaying the sources of tension and conflict between him and Yorio.

Regarding Bergoglio's most controversial decision with respect to Yorio and Jalics—his order that they leave their base community on the edge of the slums—Bergoglio testified that it was never meant to stop their work in the slums. He described it simply as part of a policy of "reorganizing the Argentine province [of the Jesuits] where the small communities would dissolve to fortify specific jobs, schools, residences, and missionary outposts. At that time I think there were eight small communities that were redistributed among the Jesuits." As Bergoglio presented it, it was a managerial decision on his part to redistribute priests among the province to help fortify other activities in other locations, something he said is habitually done in all religious orders. He said that the order to close the community was not meant to interfere with Yorio and Jalics's pastoral work: "It was not a parish, it was not a prayer house; it was where Jesuits lived who worked all around. One of those places was [the slum]." He continued, "They lived there, nothing more"—as if his concern were merely the address of his priests in his flock. Bergoglio insisted that even if he ordered them to leave their residence in the base community, he never ordered that they stop work in the slums; they could continue their work from their new residences.[122]

This was only half true. It is certainly true that Bergoglio wanted to reorganize the province and bring priests closer to him, but even his staunchest defenders acknowledge that part of his motivation was to get priests out of the slums and out of harm's way. Bergoglio says that in response to his ordering them to dissolve the community, they did what they were allowed under canonical law: they "represented." His tone at trial did not convey the fact that there had been a conflict; he described it all as if the process were normal. He said they represented properly, though at the time, he must have seen their maneuver as a serious challenge to his authority—made particularly difficult by the fact that Bergoglio was junior to Yorio and Jalics, both of whom had been his professors during his formative years as a young Jesuit. Bergoglio says that the entire process lasted for over a year and that Father Pedro Arrupe (the Jesuit superior general in Rome) had to intervene.

Bergoglgio eventually told Yorio and Jalics that they would have to dissolve the community or find another path.[123]

It came to a head, according to Yorio, in February 1976, when Bergoglio advised them to leave the Jesuits because of the serious pressure against them coming from within Argentina and Rome (which Yorio says Bergoglio never clarified). Yorio asked for some time to make the decision, but Bergoglio said there wasn't time because he was getting pressure from the superior general in Rome regarding Yorio and Jalics, and his position was firm. (Yorio says he privately hoped that a little time would help him clarify some of the rumors that circulated regarding him and that he would not need to leave the Jesuits.) Shortly after their February 1976 meeting, Yorio says Bergoglio left for Rome to meet with the superior general of the Jesuits. Yorio says he gave Bergoglio a letter that described the context of everything that happened to him and included a request for a period of absence from the Jesuits so that the rumors trailing him and Jalics might be clarified and their positions restored. Yet when Bergoglio returned, he transmitted an order from Superior General Arrupe that Jalics go to the United States and that Dourron and Yorio go to other places in the province and dissolve their community. "I was surprised that there was not even minimal reference to my report, nor my request for an absence," recalled Yorio in his 1977 letter. Bergoglio told him they could request to leave the Jesuits as a solution and try to find a bishop who would accept them as a community.[124]

At that point Yorio recalls, "It appeared clear to us that the Society had blocked all paths. The rumors and accusations trailed us for four years, at minimum, without our ability to clarify them, nor to defend ourselves, not to know who accused us, and with what proof." After several years of hearing such rumors and Bergoglio's statements of significant pressure against them, Yorio stated that Bergoglio "did nothing to defend us and we started to suspect his honesty. We were tired of the province and totally insecure." Yorio continued, "It appeared to us the most urgent thing was to save our priesthood and our lives. The most secure would be to get a bishop. It also seemed to us the easiest path because [Bergoglio] showed signs of wanting to smooth this exit for us."[125]

Yorio says that Bergoglio offered to help and that he would give good reports to local bishops about them and secure a fast path to a bishop. When Yorio went to speak with Bishop Miguel Raspanti, he says Raspanti received them well and seemed ready to accept the group: "We even understood that we already had parishes assigned." But when Bergoglio's report arrived, Yorio later recalled, "everything stopped." Raspanti ultimately accepted Dourron, but not the entire group.[126] At trial Bergoglio explained that he spoke for a long time with Raspanti over the phone and that Raspanti asked a lot of questions about each one of them. Bergoglio testified that based on his interpretation, and the conversations he had with Raspanti, Raspanti did not want to accept the three as a group.[127]

As they were leaving, Bergoglio says that he advised the three of them to speak with any bishops they knew. He advised them to talk to Bishops Novak, Raspanti, Zazpe, and others.[128] Yorio says he tried to get acceptance from several other bishops but was rebuffed each time, hearing secondhand that Bergoglio had given bad reports about him and Jalics, which prevented their transition. He stated, "It became clear to us that it would be impossible to get a bishop if the secret accusations against us weren't clarified, and that our priesthoods and lives were in grave danger."[129]

Bergoglio suggested, without quite saying so explicitly, that Yorio and Jalics had, in fact, been a bit reckless. "I believe there was great exposure," said Bergoglio. He continued,

> I believe so, but also I would say relatively because they knew they had access to the provincial *curia* of the Jesuits and that they could live in the *curia provincial* of the Jesuits and that they were in dialogue with the Church, with the Provincial [Bergoglio] to find a path. There was greater risk, but relative. . . . I even offered for them to come live in the *curia provincial*. Everyone was already discussing that there might be a coup. Come live here while you look for a friendly bishop.[130]

Bergoglio stated that in response to this offer, they said, "Thanks, we'll take it into consideration."[131] Human rights lawyer Luis Zamora did ask whether Bergoglio knew Yorio and Jalics felt like they were being left exposed by the church, to which Bergoglio categorically said no. "To the contrary," Bergoglio testified, he thinks it was the opposite "based on the conversations they had with me."[132]

As for the revocation of Yorio and Jalics's ministerial licenses—which Mignone always maintained was the green light to the military to go ahead with Yorio and Jalics's kidnapping—Bergoglio says, "I don't believe their licenses were suspended. That they were allowed to do pastoral work in [the slum] would indicate that they could do it. It would be difficult for a parish to admit someone as a helper if they had their license formally suspended." Bergoglio zeroed in on the minutiae of church doctrine: Zamora asked on whose authority a ministerial license would depend, and Bergoglio stated that it would be the local bishop. Given that they were in a period of transition looking for a new bishop, Bergoglio says that he told them they could continue celebrating Mass while they looked for a bishop. He says that if Cardinal Aramburu, who was the archbishop of Buenos Aires, had taken action on their ministerial licenses, he would have communicated that to Bergoglio, but Bergoglio never received such information. Bergoglio acknowledged some ambiguity in his granting Yorio and Jalics permission to continue to celebrate Mass during their transition; Zamora asked if it was authorization to celebrate private Mass or celebrate like any other priests, and Bergoglio said that he "left it a little to their interpretation."[133] Subsequent to his testimony, Bergoglio transmitted to the court a copy of the granting of Yorio and Jalics's ministerial licenses in 1975 and stated in court papers that he was unable to locate any files suggesting that those licenses had ever been revoked, but he did acknowledge in court that suspensions are not always documented and that sometimes they may be verbal.[134] Yorio says he was informed by Father Serra that his license has been taken away after Bergoglio informed the archbishopric that Yorio was leaving the Jesuits. Yorio says that when he went to ask Bergoglio about the issue, Bergoglio gave him a license to celebrate private Mass. This was approximately seven to ten days before the kidnapping.[135]

When Yorio and Jalics were kidnapped, Bergoglio remembers that he learned about it the same day. Bergoglio recalls receiving a phone call from someone from Yorio and Jalics's neighborhood, though the caller did not provide a name (or Bergoglio refused to divulge it).

As soon as he heard the news, Bergoglio said, "I began to move—to talk to priests who would know those who had access to the police and the armed forces. We acted immediately." He says initially they didn't know where the priests were, "but in time people started to say that it had been the navy." He says he informed all members of the Jesuits immediately, and also the archbishopric and the apostolic nunciature.[136]

Perhaps the most intriguing part of Bergoglio's testimony was that he strongly suspected both Yorio and Jalics had been detained by the navy within days of their kidnapping, a fact that would not have been publicly known at the time. Asked where he obtained this information, Bergoglio was reserved. He refused to divulge the source or state whether any priests close to him within the Jesuits or another part of the church had been able to secure this information. "It was said, vox populi," Bergoglio told the court. "People brought bits of information; it appeared as though it was the navy. This is what we started to learn as we searched and asked. It pointed there." Asked for clarification on where his information came from, Bergoglio did not provide any specifics: "The people that one asked said it was the navy, that it was the naval infantry." Human rights lawyer Luis Zamora pressed Bergoglio for more details—"Who did you ask?"—to which Bergoglio evasively responded, "The people that could have some influence, the people that I consulted with, that had connections to judges, with some military officer, with some police, with the ministry of the interior, with the government. They all pointed to the navy."

Zamora pressed further: "Do you remember a single name among these people that would have such easy access to power?"

"No," said Bergoglio.

"Were they church authorities, the cardinal?"

"It was everyone one could go to in such a moment of desperation, you know? It was friends, acquaintances—'I've got an acquaintance and I'll try and find out,' that type of thing."

Zamora pushed hard: "That you discovered that they were kidnapped by the navy is enormously important information. Let's see if you can make some effort, Mr. Bergoglio. It's a very important fact that you are conveying and would allow us to know the origin—someone that signaled, someone that you thought was trustworthy, so much so that you told Massera. The source was serious; it wasn't just anyone, am I right?"

"The whole world was in agreement about this," said Bergoglio. "It wasn't just one person who said it; the whole world said 'It was the naval infantry.'" Pushed several times to reveal a name, Bergoglio finally said one of his sources may have been Father Fernando Storni, who was dead at the time of trial.[137]

Whether or not Bergoglio was avoiding revealing his source or had simply forgotten over so many years, testimony from the 1980s seems to make it clear that Father Bossini, who replaced Yorio as a priest in the slum's chapel the day of the raid, was likely the source of this information. In 1984 both Fathers Rodolfo Ricciardelli and Jorge Vernazza, who also worked in the slum, testified that Bossini had managed to obtain information from his naval contacts, including Adm. Mayorga, that the priests had been detained by the ESMA.[138] Yorio also testified years earlier that he had received communion inside the ESMA, which Father Bossini had arranged to deliver to him while in captivity. (Bossini, who was called to testify in 2010, stridently denied that he had ever been to the ESMA. He recalled very few details about the raid itself. So evasive was his testimony that the prosecution asked the court to open a perjury case against him during its closing argument. When I called Bossini after the trial to ask him about Bergoglio and the priests, he told me he did not want to talk about the incident.[139]) Emilio Mignone had also obtained the same information and, in his search for Mónica, secured an interview with Admiral Montes, who confirmed that Yorio and Jalics had been taken by the navy.[140] When asked about Bossini, Bergoglio said that he only knew him by name and was not sure what he was doing in the slum on the day of the raid. Asked if he ever spoke with Father Bossini, Bergoglio said, "I don't remember."[141]

Bergoglio explained, as he had to his biographers and to Verbitsky years earlier off the record, that he had gone to see Adm. Massera and Gen. Videla on two occasions each to plead for Yorio and Jalics's lives. As for his first meeting with Massera, Bergoglio says, "I told him these priests weren't involved in anything unusual, and I waited for an answer. As he didn't answer, at the end of a few months, I asked for another interview while I took other steps, where I became basically sure that they had them." The second meeting with Massera lasted fewer than ten minutes, and Bergoglio recalled it as "ugly." He admonished Massera, "Look, Massera: I want them to appear." The first meeting with Videla was more formal. Videla took note and promised to look into it. Bergoglio says he secured the second meeting by asking Videla's priest to call in sick so that he could substitute and meet the commander at his official residence; again Bergoglio says he asked Videla for information, and he promised to look into it, but nothing came of it. About these meetings Bergoglio says he went alone on all four occasions and never made written notes, though he claims that he immediately called the superior general of the Jesuits, Father Pedro Arrupe, in Rome on the telephone. He did so "because of the urgency . . . in that time, there was no mail, no fax, there was telex. I did it by phone." He says he did it from a public phone in order to avoid using the phones at the curia.[142]

Bergoglio also testified about other steps he took to keep others informed about Yorio and Jalics: he says that he wrote to Jalics's mother and to his brother informing them of the steps he was taking and that he met with either Yorio's brother or brother-in-law. In his testimony, Bergoglio also said that he kept his advisors informed of what he was doing, including Father Victor Zorzín. (When I called Zorzín, he remembered it differently. He defended Bergoglio's actions and said he did work to help free Yorio and Jalics, but at the same time, his memories did not jibe with Bergoglio's recollections of his involvement; he recalled getting involved on Bergoglio's orders the day Yorio and Jalics were freed.[143])

Once Yorio and Jalics were freed, Bergoglio helped get them out of the country. He arranged for the Vatican ambassador's office to accompany Jalics to the police station to get his passport so that he could leave. With Yorio, he arranged for incardination with Bishop Jorge Novak (one of the few courageous priests during the dictatorship) and for him to study at the Pontifical Gregorian University in Rome (the Jesuit seminary in the Vatican). About his departure from Argentina, Yorio wrote of Bergoglio that

> with respect to the process of incardination and my transfer to Rome, I understand that he acted properly and diligently. My bishop was very grateful for that. But explanations of what happened beforehand, he could never give me. He cut it short and asked me to please not ask for them because in that moment, he felt very confused, and he didn't know how to give them to me. I didn't ask for them either. What could I say to him?[144]

Human rights lawyer Luis Zamora pressed Bergoglio on what he did once Yorio and Jalics were freed and informed him of the precarious situation in which they had lived in for six months. Bergoglio said that he informed the church hierarchy but did not file any legal papers, instead preferring to let the church hierarchy handle the response.

When asked about what Yorio and Jalics thought of his actions, he said that "neither of them ever told me that I could have done more.... They didn't reproach me." But he did acknowledge that he heard through others that Yorio had his doubts. Bergoglio mused, "[Yorio felt that] maybe I had not protected them enough, that I hadn't done everything possible. I don't remember if that's exactly what it was, but it was as if I hadn't protected them enough, [and] by not doing so, I had left them exposed.... I never heard the word *betrayed*; at least that never got to me." Bergoglio thought Yorio's opinion was "conditioned by the suffering he had to go through."[145]

Yorio's siblings, Graciela and Rodolfo, describe Bergoglio as the "intellectual author" of their brother's kidnapping. Graciela told me that she and her brother are "convinced" that "Bergoglio was one of the participants in all the intrigue and rumors that circulated around [Yorio and Jalics] within the society." She continued, "We are also convinced that he didn't do anything to protect them." They say the fact that Yorio was kidnapped immediately after his ministerial license was suspended means that someone in the church was an accomplice to their kidnapping, and they fault Bergoglio.[146]

Yorio's siblings do not accuse Bergoglio of actually turning Yorio and Jalics over to the military, but Rodolfo says, "You might not directly kill someone, but you might feel happy when someone who you hate ends up dead." They tell me that Bergoglio's ideological opposition to their brother, combined with both his indifference and his spreading bad reports about their brother to other members of the church, makes him responsible for the kidnapping.

They both told me about meeting with Bergoglio during Yorio's disappearance and say his attitude confirms their suspicion that Bergoglio was insensitive to Yorio and Jalics's fate. Rodolfo recalled going to the Jesuit seminary shortly after Yorio's kidnapping to meet with Bergoglio for help. Not more than five minutes after arriving, Bergoglio asked him to leave, telling him that officers from the intelligence services were on their way. Rodolfo left but stuck around the large leafy campus to verify whether officers were on their way. He says that a military car arrived, which to him "implied that there was a relation between Mr. Bergoglio and the people who took over the government." Rodolfo says Bergoglio later told him on the telephone that the officers did not have any information, and they attributed the disappearance to another service branch with which they did not have contact.[147] (Bergoglio recalled at trial meeting one of Yorio's siblings but did not remember any details.)

The Yorios met several more times with Bergoglio, always unsatisfied. Rodolfo recalls that Bergoglio visited their mother's house twice. On the second occasion, Bergoglio insinuated that Yorio was dead. "They still talk about Jalics," Bergoglio said without mentioning any names, "but they don't speak about Orlando anymore." Rodolfo says this crushed his mother's hopes. Rodolfo felt like Bergoglio was not really trying to help. "He never had any information, he never had any sources," he testified in 2011.[148]

I heard other people express a similar criticism. After the raid, when eight of the young missionaries were detained for a day, Bergoglio did not seek any of them out or meet with them. "I was doing work that had been started by the Jesuits," says Silvia Guiard, one of the missionaries. "It had to do with the church, with religion. They should have worried about us. They had no preoccupation for us." She tells me that in his dispute with Yorio and Jalics, Bergoglio "didn't care that there were people working with [Yorio and Jalics]. We were collateral damage; we didn't matter to him."[149]

Verbitsky has been Bergoglio's harshest critic. He claims to have found what he considers a smoking gun. In 1979, while Jalics was in exile in Germany, Jalics solicited Bergoglio for help renewing his Argentine passport. Under the existing regulations, Jalics was required to return to Argentina to renew his passport. Jalics asked Bergoglio if Bergoglio could use his connections in the government to help Jalics arrange to renew the passport from the embassy in Germany, fearful of a return trip to Argentina. Verbitsky found a letter in the foreign ministry archives that Bergoglio sent to the ministry asking that they give Jalics special dispensation to renew his passport from abroad, explaining that the cost of the return trip to Argentina was prohibitive. But in a memo alongside the letter suggesting that the petition be denied, an official from the ministry notes that Jalics had "conflicts with obedience" and was "accused alongside Father Yorio of suspected contact with guerrillas." The official concluded, "No bishop in Greater Buenos Aires wanted to accept them." The source for this information, according to the memo, was Bergoglio, who put in a "special recommendation not to allow for what was solicited." In other words, Bergoglio told Jalics that he would help him secure a new passport and wrote a favorable letter on his behalf, but then told the ministry verbally that they should do the opposite. To Verbitsky, the letter is conclusive proof that Bergoglio betrayed the two priests: it reveals a man who told his subordinates that he would do one thing but then did the opposite. This portrait is a key part of Verbitsky's accusations because Yorio claimed that in the run-up to his kidnapping, Bergoglio repeatedly told him that he would try to stop the barrage of dangerous rumors about him but did otherwise behind his back.[150]

The authenticity of the document is not in question, as Bergoglio admitted at trial both filing the letter on behalf of Jalics and also having a conversation with one of the foreign ministry officials. But in his defense, Bergoglio says that the foreign ministry official did not record that Bergoglio had told him the accusations were untrue.[151]

Though the letter does not reflect well on Bergoglio, it does not necessarily imply that he was complicit in the priests' kidnapping. The letter was sent two years after Yorio and Jalics were freed, when they were both living abroad. "If Yorio and Jalics survived, it's because there was very strong pressure," says Father Ignacio Pérez del Viso, a contemporary of Yorio, Jalics, and Bergoglio. "Who did this, the Bishops? They had no relationship with Yorio and Jalics. If anybody, it was Bergoglio, who represented a great international order."[152]

When Yorio's siblings gave me the letter that he had sent to Rome in November 1977—the same letter that provides the basis for many of Verbitsky's accusations—they assured me that I would "see who Bergoglio really is." But the letter muddies the waters as much as it clarifies. Yorio makes a number of accusations against Bergoglio, mostly based on second-, third-, and fourthhand accounts of what Bergoglio was allegedly doing behind his back. They are impossible to confirm, as most of the priests mentioned are dead or infirm. Yorio seems unaware of his own precarious position within the church and the legitimate criticisms against him. When he confronts Bergoglio about rumors he heard from within the Jesuits about him and Bergoglio will not reveal the source, Yorio leaps to the conclusion that Bergoglio himself was the source. He overlooks the possibility that Bergoglio would not name his sources to prevent further confrontation and conflict.

I shared Yorio's letter with six Jesuits and one ex-Jesuit, some of whom I knew to be hostile to and critical of Bergoglio because of lingering anger over Bergoglio's tenure as provincial in the 1970s. They had all heard the accusations against Bergoglio for years, which circulated like family gossip amid the close-knit order. After reading the letter, all of them ended up feeling more sympathetic toward Bergoglio. Father Pérez del Viso told me that he came to the conclusion that Yorio "wasn't aware of what he symbolized for another sector of the church." He says that Yorio was a "clear reference for all the people who put an accent on Medellín, on a church for the poor," but was not capable of recognizing that others might have legitimate criticisms of his theological positions and pastoral activity or that they were concerned his pastoral style might put others at risk.[153] Father García Mata had a similar criticism. He told me that Yorio was incredibly smart, nice, and warm—"like an angel without original sin." But he also said that Yorio could be "naive."[154]

Jorge Scuro, a former classmate of Bergoglio's and a friend of Yorio's, thinks Yorio remained suspicious of Bergoglio not because of what

Bergoglio did but because of who he was and what Yorio thought he should have done: "Many times we didn't think of the agents of the dictatorship as the traitors; we thought of those closest to us as traitors, those who weren't faithful, who were less animated, who were more talkative." He says that many victims of Latin America's dictatorships focus their energies not on the anonymous security agents who kidnapped and tortured them but on those who were closer to them, those who might have whispered in the wrong situation that someone "has an image of Che Guevara in his office."[155]

Some stated that Yorio's suspicions of Bergoglio grew over the years. "When they were freed, they never mentioned it," Father García Mata told me. "I spoke with Yorio the day after he was freed. He told me everything about his captivity . . . Yorio thought absolutely nothing of [Bergoglio's role in his kidnapping] at the time." In the late 1990s, a number of incidents caused Yorio to fear for his life. An assistant priest from his parish was murdered, and his house was broken into. He came to believe that corrupt police officers or drug dealers in the slums where he worked were targeting him. Eventually, he decided to leave for Uruguay, around the same time Bergoglio became the archbishop of Buenos Aires. Several of Yorio's associates told me privately they believed he suffered from a "persecution complex." (His siblings told me he had a genuine fear for his life.)

Together, the evaluations from Bergoglio's former Jesuit associates portray a personal dispute among Yorio, Jalics, and Bergoglio that was misinterpreted by the regime. But their own relationship with Yorio and Jalics was not so much different from Bergoglio's. When I asked many of them individually where they were or what they did when Yorio and Jalics were kidnapped, most of them did not remember any significant details, if they remembered anything at all about the kidnapping. There is also another explanation for Yorio and Jalics's kidnapping: the ESMA likely zeroed in on the priests after kidnapping Mónica Quinteiro, an ex-nun who had worked with Yorio in the Bajo Flores slum but left religious life to join the Montoneros. Yorio has always testified that his captors asked him about her, strongly suggesting that the ESMA's "intelligence" that Yorio and Jalics posed a threat came from Quinteiro.

Shortly after Bergoglio became pope, I spoke with Miguel Petty, an Anglo-Argentine Jesuit who speaks flawless English with the patrician accent characteristic of his clan. I had expected Petty to be critical of Bergoglio. During the dictatorship, Bergoglio thinned the ranks of the Jesuits' Center for Research and Social Action (Centro de Investigacíon y Accíon Social, or CIAS), a social policy think tank, and exercised greater editorial control over their academic journal. Bergoglio sent Petty, one of the center's leaders, to Córdoba, Argentina's second city, in 1978—similar to the order he had given Yorio and Jalics to abandon the slum. Petty told me that Bergoglio wanted to "eliminate" the center.[156]

"It was very painful. I remember me and my staff, we spent a whole week crying. These were very painful decisions," Petty told me. But he says that the vow of obedience he took when he became a Jesuit required him to follow the order. "You suffer it," Petty tells me, "but you don't question it. It was his decision." I asked Petty what he thought about Yorio and Jalics's situation, given that they had also received a difficult order. "They were somewhat hotheaded to refuse," Petty told me. "The proper thing for them would have been for them to say, 'Okay, if you don't want us here, we will leave.' . . . To work in a slum is a wonderful thing to do, but it wasn't the time and place. [Yorio] should have waited a few years, and Bergoglio would have pushed him back into the slum, but it was just so damned dangerous."[157]

Petty told me that it was probably best for everyone that Bergoglio ordered Yorio and Jalics to leave their religious community. He illustrated it with an example from his own life. Petty himself narrowly escaped death a month after Yorio and Jalics were kidnapped. On July 4, 1976, three priests and two seminarians were gunned down in the nave of Saint Patrick's Church in Buenos Aires. The men who carried out the assassinations wrote on the church that the priests had died for "indoctrinating innocent minds." Petty was scheduled to be at the church to visit the priests, who were his friends, just hours after the assassination. Petty told me he got the true story of what happened on the day the priests were killed:

> One of the seminarians had joined a guerrilla group, and his guerrilla boss later admitted it, that he had him down as a member of his

guerrilla group. And the priests had gotten to know this about the priest, and they told the boy he had to choose between the guerrilla and the seminary. But they didn't say, "Pick up your bags and leave the damn house now! Right away." Instead, they said, "You've got to go." That night they were all killed.[158]

He hesitates to criticize Bergoglio: "Bergoglio must have had no end of all sorts of different pressures—from Rome, from Jesuits, from the military, from the Bishops. And there were lots of things that, obviously, he could not repeat to people like Yorio . . . Yorio was in a terribly dangerous situation that he didn't seem to be aware of." He adds that in general, Bergoglio's behavior was to "get the Jesuits out of the firing line." He acknowledges that the issue is "terribly complex," but he tells me that "it's very easy to read things into it so many years later."[159]

It was an evaluation I heard over and over. Father J. L. Caravias, a Jesuit priest who was expelled from Paraguay in the early 1970s, had a long history of solidarity with the poor. He worked with unions in Paraguay, with *campesinos* in the north of Argentina, and in the slums in Buenos Aires. "I'm sure [Bergoglio] didn't agree with what I was doing to organize the people," Caravias wrote in a blog post in April 2013 shortly after Bergoglio was named pope. But several months after his arrival in Buenos Aires, Bergoglio warned Caravias that he had received a tip that Caravias was on a paramilitary death list. Bergoglio urged him to leave the country, which he did. Caravias wrote, "Maybe Bergoglio, like every man, made certain errors. Sometimes unwisely. He let his fears and prejudices guide him. But we all do this. The poison gases of the dictatorships made us all crazy."[160] When I spoke to Caravias over the phone, he told me that he is forever grateful to Bergoglio because Bergoglio "helped [him] escape a certain death."[161]

Even one priest who had negative things to say about Bergoglio told me he did not believe Bergoglio was responsible for Yorio and Jalics's kidnapping. He told me that he appreciated Jalics's recent statement absolving Bergoglio of responsibility in the kidnapping. "Jalics could say a lot of other things about Bergoglio that he apparently prefers not to say," the priest told me. "We all have a personal story with our superiors, be it Bergoglio or anyone else." He allows that Bergoglio might have been "imprudent" in how he handled Yorio and Jalics, but ultimately Yorio and Jalics were involved in pastoral work that they wanted to pursue.

Father Pérez del Viso told me that both sides were right: "Bergoglio was right to say, 'They're going to liquidate you; it's very dangerous.' And the others, they said that 'if we leave the poor, they are going to say we abandoned them. We have a commitment with them. They'll say we are just trying to save ourselves.' And who's correct? Both sides are correct."[162]

I told Miguel Petty that I sensed some callousness among Yorio and Jalics's former colleagues. He gave me a very frank answer: "Everybody was having problems somewhere or another. It was yet another incident. . . . It wasn't a unique thing, I don't think." He added, "I hate to think of it, but we were sort of used to this [kind of] thing happening."[163]

Focusing on Yorio and Jalics reduces Bergoglio's complicated behavior during the dictatorship to a simple, legalistic question: Did he betray them or not? "There's been too much emphasis on Yorio and Jalics, rather than the Dirty War as such, and the support of the church hierarchy for the military Junta," says Federico Finchelstein, a history professor at the New School in New York who has written extensively about Argentine fascism. Finchelstein says Bergoglio's actions should be evaluated in historical terms. In Finchelstein's estimation, Bergoglio was an "iconic member of the church of the 1970s, a Cold War church that was identified with the ideology of the junta." He says that even though Bergoglio is not one of the most extreme examples of this church—friends say that he was privately against the regime—"his open silence represents an Argentine pattern." Finchelstein argues that Bergoglio's public silence was not neutral and that Bergoglio has "advanced in an institution where you are rewarded for not speaking out."[164]

Until he became pope, Bergoglio resisted speaking about the past, particularly the role of the church. In 2007 he put it most bluntly when he said in a homily that it was the obligation of all good Christians to "bless the past, not slander it." He charged those speaking ill of the past with "attempting to obtain an advantage in the present or in the future," a thinly veiled attack on the Kirchners, who made prosecuting the military a centerpiece of their populist administrations.[165] Bergoglio's evaluation of his own role is one of confusion rather than engagement: "I was thirty-nine years old at the time and had been provincial of the Jesuits beginning in 1973. I had a very partial vision of what was going on; my role was very different from being the bishop of a jurisdiction."[166] His explanation of the broader role of the church during those years tends to be apologetic rather than searching and critical. In his autobiography he separates the clergy into three groups: those few who publicly spoke out against the repression, those who "did a lot but spoke out less" (presumably where he places himself), and those who were "naïve or lazy." He does not criticize the wing of the church that actively supported the military dictatorship and provided theological justification for their Dirty War.[167]

But just as Bergoglio's role in Yorio and Jalics's kidnapping is subject to multiple interpretations, so too is his relationship to the past. One explanation for his silence is that presidents Néstor and Cristina Fernández de Kirchner put the past to effective and opportunistic political use and dogged many of their political opponents with charges that they were complicit with the dictatorship. During his tenure Bergoglio was one of the Kirchners' primary adversaries—they clashed over abortion, gay marriage, corruption, and social programs. Argentine sociologist Marcos Novaro, who has written two volumes on the modern history of Argentina, told me that the debate about the past at the present is "poisonous," and it is understandable that Bergoglio has avoided it because he is more interested in "not losing the cultural war of the present." Novaro says that criticizing Bergoglio for not speaking out, for not doing more, and for refusing to engage with the past is a criticism that can be launched at many other sectors in Argentina: the unions, the press, and the millions of ordinary citizens who remained silent as their brethren were secretly carted away and executed.[168] In other words, Bergoglio acted a lot like everyone else.

11

Closing Arguments and Verdict

After twelve months of testimony, the summation of the case began in April 2011. Four major issues presented themselves during the closing arguments: witness credibility, the prosecution's theory of criminal liability, procedural conflicts, and alibi defenses.

In its summation the prosecution went into precise detail in each of the eighty-six individual cases at trial by summarizing twelve months of testimony and documentary evidence into coherent individual narratives. Most interesting to those sitting through the closing arguments was the prosecution's citation of the defendants' personnel records, which had been buried deep inside the tribunal's archives and were not accessible to the public. These documents filled out the prosecution's case by incorporating contemporaneous bureaucratic papers into the trial. In most cases these files listed the assignments of the Grupo de Tareas (GT) 3.3/2 during the Dirty War, though some of these records were obviously altered or had gone missing. They also included glowing praise from most of the defendants' superiors for their valiant professional conduct during the War against Subversion. The most interesting document from this trove of material was Adm. Emilio Eduardo Massera's review of Capt. Jorge Eduardo Acosta in 1979, giving his underling "excellent" marks across the board. Massera was not supposed to write the year-end review of someone so many ranks below him in the chain of command, so the assessment tended to show that the tight link between Massera and Acosta was not an invention of the survivors but a fact of the Dirty War. (Ironically, this evidence tended to undercut part of the prosecution's case, as the direct link between Acosta and Massera gave credence to the defense's argument that Massera exercised outsized and direct control over the GT 3.3/2 outside the chain of command.)

The most controversial aspect of the state's closing argument was its theory of criminal liability. The prosecution argued that criminal liability could be based simply on a defendant's membership in the GT 3.3/2 at the time of one of the crimes enumerated in the charging instruments. The prosecution argued that the defendants had conceived and implemented a "criminal plan," according to which there was a predetermined division of labor, and each defendant was responsible for perfecting the criminal plan by playing their small part in the larger machine. The mere fact of being a member of the GT 3.3/2 was enough to prove criminal liability, and anything beyond that was simply a "plus." Though they had amassed significant evidence of many of the defendants' individual and direct participation in crimes and spent more than two days at trial summarizing this evidence, at the end of the day, the prosecution saw this as merely additional or superfluous evidence.

As far as the quality of eyewitness testimony was concerned, the prosecution argued that traumatic episodes were seared into human memory in such a way that recollections were strong and credible. They even suggested that like cases of child molestation, memory might improve over time, especially with the help of therapy, though they never presented an expert witness or cited academic studies to substantiate the argument.

The victims' lawyers' summations did not differ much from the prosecution's in terms of the substance of their presentations. The Centro de Estudios Legales y Sociales (CELS) filled out the prosecution's arguments by spending considerable time explaining the internal organization of the navy, clarifying that each level of command had its own general staff, and augmenting the case against the Naval Mechanics School (ESMA) officers by seconding the prosecution's argument that they were criminally responsible for the mere fact of having occupied roles within the formal structure of the GT 3.3/2.

But there were two areas where the victims' lawyers' summations diverged from the prosecution. As part of CELS's closing statement, a lawyer for the Abuelas de Plaza de Mayo (Grandmothers of the Plaza de Mayo) made a long and impassioned speech that the trial court should declare that there was a clandestine maternity ward in the ESMA. The trial had revealed some information about the issue, and the grandmothers had made a point of asking the witnesses about clandestine births in the ESMA, but the request seemed out of place. The issue of stolen babies was not raised in any of the charging instruments and was not formally part of the factual basis of the case. The defendants were not on notice that this would be part of the charges and thus had no incentive to challenge the grandmothers' description of the ESMA as a clandestine maternity ward. The interjection illustrated that the demand for "truth" and "memory" had inserted itself into the trial, reflecting the premise that the proceedings were supposed to be a chance to confront not just the charges at issue but the ESMA itself—that any criminal case confronting the ESMA must reckon with the dozens of mothers who were brought to the room on the third floor where they gave birth, only to have their children snatched from them and handed over for secret "adoption" by families who were more sympathetic toward the military. As horrendous as this behavior was, it was not part of the prosecution's case (and was, in fact, the principal subject of another parallel trial against most of the same defendants).

Three other lawyers—two private attorneys (Myriam Bregman and Luis Zamora) representing victims' groups and attorneys for the secretary for human rights—also argued that the court should characterize what happened in the ESMA as acts of genocide. The argument seemed at odds with the Genocide Convention's definition, which prohibits acts undertaken with the intent to destroy a group on the basis of national, ethnic, religious, or racial categories but excludes political persecution. The secretary argued that the Argentine dictatorship had targeted part of a "national group" and therefore committed genocide. The secretary recognized that the principle of legality prevented the court from charging the defendants with genocide (the crime was nowhere in the Argentine penal code), but he urged the court to acknowledge the issue in the verdict as a framing device, to leave a written record for history that what had happened in Argentina rose to the level of that singular form of violence. Myriam Bregman and Luis Zamora went further and actually asked the court to convict the defendants of genocide.

Zamora argued that the defendants could be convicted of genocide because there had been an international *jus cogens* custom prohibiting the practice when the crimes were committed and that this custom went further than the language of the convention by prohibiting extermination on the basis of political affiliation. Bregman urged the court to convict the defendants of genocide not necessarily because it was legal to do so but because doing so would bring "juridical truth in line with historical truth."[1]

All the defense teams repeated the legal deficiencies they saw in the case that they had been arguing for years: violations of the prohibition of ex post facto criminal laws, violations of the norms against the retroactive application of criminal law, violations of the defendants' right to a natural judge, lack of criminal responsibility on account of due obedience to superior orders, and the legality of detaining suspects under the state of siege provisions. The lawyers acknowledged that these arguments ran counter to Argentine Supreme Court precedent, but they persisted nonetheless as a matter of professional protest.

The two private defense teams were aggressive in their attacks on both the court and the victims. Guillermo Coronel, who represented his father, Julio César Coronel, alleged that the trial had "transformed monsters"—referring to the victims who had joined any of the various Argentine revolutionary groups in the 1970s—"into good little altar boys." Echoing the attacks made by the defendants themselves, he said that the trial had been partial and stripped of its context, a political tool of revenge by the government. He faulted the prosecution for basing its case on testimony from Montoneros, who had "for a long time been enemies of the republic, a fact that everyone now wants to forget."[2]

Alfredo Solari presented a similar defense. The witnesses "weren't 'young idealists,' neither were they a 'wonderful youthful generation.' They were seditious terrorists, antisystem, and they attacked the nation instead of participating in a passive electoral political process outlined in the national constitution." The threat of subversion, he said, had "created in the authorities the inexcusable duty to defend the fatherland. What else could the national government have done? Leave the armed groups to take power through violence, abrogate the constitution, supplant all individual and political liberties, and submit the country to a collectivist Castro-Guevarist dictatorship? This would have been fulfilling their duties?"[3]

Many of the defendants, especially those who were well identified and against whom there was considerable evidence of their direct participation in acts of kidnapping and torture (such as Jorge Eduardo Acosta, Antonio Pernías, Raúl Enrique Scheller, and Alfredo Astiz), invoked the defense of following superior orders. But they refused to explain the orders they followed or who issued them; they only alluded to a vague plan issued by Decrees 2770, 2771, and 2772 to "annihilate subversion." They did not say, for instance, that they had been ordered to torture so-and-so and that a specific superior officer had given that order in this context. Their individual identification with the larger purposes of the Dirty War belied their defense as little soldiers in a giant machine who were simply following orders.

But in a few areas, the defense teams presented compelling cases that seemed problematic for the prosecution. The first was challenging the prosecution's description of criminal responsibility. The defense attorneys all roundly lambasted the prosecution's theory, calling it a form of strict liability or "objective" liability, which was prohibited under criminal law. They argued that charging the defendants for mere membership in the GT 3.3/2 amounted to charging their clients with omissions rather than criminal acts.

The defense also attacked the prosecution and the victims' lawyers in several cases where they said the final accusation violated the principle of *congruencia* (convergence) between the charging documents and the final accusations in the case. The Argentine penal code (unlike U.S. law) allows prosecutors and victims' lawyers to change the categorization of a crime as long as the change is based on the same facts that are presented in the charging instruments. The defense argued vigorously that in at least five cases, the prosecution's change of charge violated this principle, as the new charges seemed to extend beyond the facts outlined in the charging instruments. In the case of María Cristina Lennie, for instance, Adm. Oscar Montes had been indicted for "illegal deprivation of liberty," but CELS argued his crime constituted a homicide. According to CELS, the facts at trial showed that Lennie had ingested a cyanide pill while on the verge of being captured. Thus her suicide was induced and therefore constituted a homicide because it was provoked by her knowledge of the fate that awaited her if she was captured. Montes's defense argued that this violated the principle of *congruencia*—that in changing the legal description of the case, the victims' lawyers would need to prove why she had committed suicide and to connect that decision to the actions of the defense, but Montes had not gone to trial prepared to respond to that accusation. The defense argued that the new charge of homicide was too much of a surprise and the charge should be rejected as procedurally improper.

The defense team that represented Adms. Oscar Montes and Manuel Jacinto García Tallada also attacked the heart of the prosecution's description of the ESMA as a tightly regulated machine. Both these admirals were accused under a theory of *autoría mediata* ("mediated authorship"), meaning that as superior officers, they had exercised control over the will of their subordinates and were therefore liable as coauthors for the actions of their subordinates. But the trial did not uncover any orders written or issued by either Montes or García Tallada, so the prosecution's case against the two admirals was based entirely on their position within the chain of command as well as on other defendants' statements that the GT 3.3/2 was tightly regulated and functioning within the naval chain of command. Montes and García Tallada's lawyers argued that the trial had not uncovered evidence to prove beyond a reasonable doubt that the orders regulating the navy prior to the 1976 military coup remained in place afterward. To bolster their defense, they cited extensive testimony from the survivors themselves who attested to the direct link between Adm. Massera, the commander in chief of the navy, and Adm. Rubén Jacinto Chamorro (Montes and García Tallada's immediate subordinate) and Capt. Acosta. This suggested that the ESMA responded more to the whims and fancies of Adm. Massera and less to the organic structure of the navy. In some of the earliest testimonies from the 1980s, the first accusers cited many of the names of the defendants and perpetrators of the Dirty War but omitted mention of Montes and García Tallada. The lawyers also cited Massera's apparent command over the GT 3.3/2 even after his retirement, suggesting that the ordinary naval chain of command was not respected. They cited the fact that a group of ESMA prisoners was moved to a house owned by Jorge Radice, a logistics officer in the ESMA, to work on Massera's political campaign but remained under supervision and in close contact with members of the task force during this period. Montes and García Tallada's lawyers also cited witness testimony indicating that after Adm. Massera's retirement, the GT 3.3/2 wanted to keep information from the navy's new commander, Adm. Armando Lambruschini.

Furthermore, Adm. García Tallada had a compelling defense against a subset of the charged crimes. The prosecution did not distinguish between prisoners held by the GT 3.3/2 and prisoners held by the Servicio de Inteligencia Naval (SIN). All the prisoners were held inside of the officers' club of the ESMA, but the task force prisoners were allegedly held in the *capucha* and the SIN prisoners in the *capuchita* (a small room above the attic.) García Tallada was charged with a number of cases of prisoners who were supervised and held by the SIN, which was reputed to have had an intense rivalry with the ESMA's GT 3.3/2. García Tallada's lawyers argued that he could not be responsible for these prisoners, as he was not supervising the officers who held the SIN's prisoners. The SIN was a branch of the intelligence chief of the naval general staff. Though the SIN formally became the intelligence wing of the GT 3.3/2 under an amended Capacity Plan of the Navy (Plan de Capacidades de la Armada [PLACINTARA]) issued in 1980, the prosecution could not show that the SIN had been the intelligence wing of the GT 3.3/2 prior to this date.

The final issue that the defendants presented was eyewitness credibility. Was witness testimony really credible thirty-five years after the fact, especially when some of the details were specific enough to identify the very day or week of an alleged incident? How could the court adequately separate what the victims had seen and experienced from what they had heard over the years? How could the court determine whether the identifications by the victims of both fellow victims and the perpetrators were correct, especially when they often did not know the names of either at the time of the crimes?

Alfredo Solari, a private attorney representing four of the defendants, pulled together many of the contradictory statements from the witnesses in his ideologically charged final summation of the case. He pointed out, for instance, that when Ana Testa first testified in the 1980s, she identified three people in the torture room only by their aliases. (Each military officer used an alias instead of his real name while on operations and inside the ESMA.) But at trial, she identified six officers in the torture room, each one by name. This was just one of many instances where the testimony of the survivors had shifted and become more confident over the years.

Three of the defendants also had strong alibi defenses. Julio César Coronel, who was charged in the Rodolfo Walsh case and the Santa Cruz Church case, argued that he had been injured in a separate incident on the same day Walsh was kidnapped. Only one witness, Raúl Cubas, had identified him as part of the Walsh raid, and Cubas had said at trial that Coronel told him several days after the event, "What a disaster, Walsh died on us!" But Coronel's lawyer argued that this would have been impossible because Coronel was in the hospital undergoing surgery. Indeed, it seemed that Cubas's recollection would have been mistaken even if the prosecution's theory that Coronel was injured in the gun battle with Walsh was correct, as he would have been not in the ESMA several days after the raid but in the hospital. His defense entered into evidence a certificate of his entrance into the hospital on March 25, 1977. The medical records said that he had been in a gunfight in San Fernando, far removed from the raid on Walsh, which took place near downtown Buenos Aires. Coronel was also injured by a 45mm bullet, but Walsh was said to have been carrying a .22-caliber pistol. As for the Santa Cruz case—the only other case that Coronel was charged with at trial—his defense argued that he was still recuperating from his injury in March and therefore could not have participated in the Santa Cruz raid.

Juan Carlos Rolón, who was also only charged in the Walsh and Santa Cruz cases, had a much more straightforward defense: he was not in the ESMA when either of those crimes was committed. He had said for years, and continued to maintain at trial, that he was only in the ESMA as a rotational officer in December 1976 through January 1977 and again as a permanent officer in 1978. The Walsh kidnapping took place in March 1977 and the Santa Cruz raid in December 1977, so his defense said he was not criminally liable for either episode.

Finally, Pablo Eduardo García Velasco's defense argued that he should not be found guilty because his was a case of mistaken identity. His twin brother, Miguel, was also a naval officer—Pablo claimed that he worked for the SIN and that Miguel worked for the GT 3.3/2 and that the victims had gotten them mixed up.

In the weeks leading up to the verdict, a nervous tension descended on the courtroom. The trial had lasted almost two years, and over that period, monotonous routine had characterized most of the hearings, even amid the horrendous testimony presented by the survivors. But with the moment of reckoning drawing near, the sensation of normalcy grew into unease among both the human rights activists and the defendants themselves. As the prosecution summarized its case, two of the hearings were canceled when two of the defendants fainted in the courtroom. When Néstor Savio took the stand to offer his final words, he lost his composure and began to sob before the judges. (They were not tears of repentance.) The human rights activists also began to fear that after two years, the case might be derailed and the defendants absolved. The last trial in this courtroom had ended with absolutions for the majority of the defendants, and they feared a similar verdict would be reached in this case.

The anxiety was compounded by the impending presidential election, scheduled for October 26, 2011. Both sides were convinced that somehow the court was playing politics: The defense attorneys were convinced that the tribunal would release a verdict just days before the election to ingratiate themselves with Cristina Fernández de Kirchner, who was running for reelection and would certainly champion a set of convictions in the ESMA case. The human rights activists were equally convinced that the verdict would be delayed until after Kirchner was reelected, as they believed there would be a large number of acquittals, and the court would only have the political cover to issue the acquittals after the elections.

On the day of the verdict, eventually scheduled for October 22, 2011—days after the elections—the courtroom was packed, with more people in attendance than on any other day. As the 6 p.m. hour approached for the verdict to be handed down, a huge crowd of thousands of people gathered outside of the courthouse to watch the proceedings on a giant screen that had been set up to transmit the final moments of the trial. A *cumbia* band played to the assembled crowd outside, with a photoshopped portrait of Alfredo Astiz in a prison-striped uniform behind bars, projecting what they hoped would be the verdict.

Inside the courtroom, we waited anxiously for the judges to enter. Minutes grew to more than an hour and a half until they finally entered, apparently delayed by a last-minute visit from the *consejo de la magistratura,* a controversial public agency charged with the appointment and removal of judges, which often brandished the specter of hearings to put pressure on judges in politically sensitive cases.

When the verdict was announced, it came as a surprise—all but two of the defendants were convicted on virtually all counts charged by the prosecution, a tremendous win for the prosecution and the human rights organizations. Oscar Montes, Antonio Pernías, Alfredo Astiz, Raúl Enrique Scheller, Jorge Radice, Alberto González, Néstor Savio, Ricardo Cavallo, Adolfo Miguel Donda, Julio César Coronel, and Ernesto Weber were all sentenced to life in prison. Manuel Jacinto García Tallada, Juan Carlos Fotea, and Carlos Capdevilla received twenty-five years in prison, and Juan Antonio Azic received eighteen years. Only two defendants were acquitted of all charges—Juan Carlos Rolón and Pablo Eduardo García Velasco—but they were not released because there were still pending charges against them that would soon be brought to court. (Their acquittals were eventually overturned on appeal.)

So was the verdict just?

Ordinarily, it would be an easy question to answer, as the response turned on whether guilt had been established beyond a reasonable doubt through the consideration of evidence in open court. If that was the criterion used to evaluate the trial, then the answer was a qualified yes. The charges had been proven by evidence that was introduced over the course of the trial. Though there were a few cases where the court might have erred by stretching the limits of criminal responsibility, such as the convictions of Ricardo Cavallo and Juan Carlos Fotea for their involvement in the Santa Cruz case (there was no evidence presented at trial linking those two men to the kidnappings), the court's general conclusions were correct. Perhaps they had not been proven to satisfy a philosophical definition of certainty, but the convictions seemed to pass the lesser legal hurdle of proof beyond a reasonable doubt. The judgment was also undoubtedly informed by the intuition that even if there were a few individual cases where the evidence had resulted in a false positive, there was so much that the defendants were not charged with that a conviction was warranted nevertheless. (Not that this was the *proper* thing to do—only that it was a realistic reading of the court's decision.) Besides, many of the defendants had only half-heartedly defended themselves against the specific charges; their real objection to the proceedings was the fact that they were charged at all.

As a procedural matter, the defendants' treatment, however, was not a model of judicial fairness, and this called the justice of the verdict into some doubt. It was not an issue that came up in the day-to-day proceedings of the trial, but it was reflected in the long arc of their legal saga since the transition to democracy in the 1980s. If the law was supposed to provide clear rules and be an institution of stability, the treatment of the military defendants fell short. They were first given an amnesty by the military government, then called into military court to answer for what they had done, and then transferred to civilian courts. Then some were released from investigation after it was determined under the full stop law that their cases were prescribed and others were indicted, then they were released from judicial scrutiny under the due obedience law and Menem's pardons, then they were haled back into court in truth trials to testify in a theoretically "nonpunitive" forum (though one activists had used as an incremental step in breaking the amnesty), then they were indicted by European judges under a theory of universal jurisdiction and for crimes committed against European dual nationals. Then they were once again accused in cases of robbery, baby kidnapping, and rape that fell outside the amnesty laws, and then finally prosecuted under the full weight of the criminal law after the amnesty laws were voided. It was not a strong testament to the rule of law in Argentina, and their legal saga revealed a judiciary where rules and holdings bent to the larger political agenda of the moment. Their treatment since 2003, when the amnesty laws were repealed by Argentina's Congress, underscored the point. Many had been detained for years before trial; their pretrial detentions stretched well beyond the two-year limitation set by statute. (Jorge Eduardo Acosta spent thirteen years in prison before a guilty verdict was finally handed down in his case.) The investigation and the structure of the charges against the defendants had been broken up into so many little pieces that the verdict itself also ended up having no impact on the liberty of the defendants. The two men who were acquitted in the case—Juan Carlos Rolón and Pablo Eduardo García Velasco—were both nonetheless kept in prison despite being absolved of the charges against them because both men had more charges pending in a future trial to come. Time and time again, the rules and procedures yielded to keeping the defendants imprisoned.

At trial the defendants lost virtually all the legal arguments they lodged in court. On the question of the competency of the court to judge the case, the court sided with the prosecution; on the question of double jeopardy and estoppel, the court sided with the prosecution; on the question of validity of the due obedience and full stop laws, the court sided with the prosecution; on the question of the legality of the charges under the figure of a "crime against humanity," the court sided with the prosecution; on the question of prescription, the court sided with the prosecution; on the question of the constitutionality of the law 25.779 (repealing the amnesty laws), the court sided with the prosecution; on the question of the validity of the defendants' pretrial statements given to investigators, the court sided with the prosecution; on the question of the admissibility of prior testimony of absent witnesses, the court sided with the prosecution; on the question of whether some of the defendants' prior statements in military court were admissible, the court sided with the prosecution; on the question of whether the investigation and trial had violated the guarantee of a speedy trial, the court sided with the prosecution; on the question of *congruencia* (the requirement that pretrial charging instruments match the final posthearing charges), the court sided with the prosecution; on the question of the veracity of witness testimony, the court sided with the prosecution; on the question of a defense of due obedience to superior orders, the court sided with the prosecution; and on the question of "genocide," the court recognized what had happened as a genocide and held that the violence was perpetrated in a framework of genocide, though it did not actually convict the defendants for the crime. Not that this reflected poorly on the tribunal—many of these issues had already made their way to the Supreme Court, which had routinely held against military officers raising legal challenges to the reopening of the prosecutions—but it highlighted how many legal arguments, many of them grounded in ancient legal principles, had been foreclosed as "obstacles" in aid of the great project of doing justice.

But an analysis of the evidence presented at trial and the fairness of the legal holdings only began to answer whether the trial and the verdict had been just. The ambition of the trial, and of the human rights trials more generally, had been to reckon with the past, and that was an ambition that could not be judged on the legal merits of the case alone. As this sort of exercise, it was much harder to determine whether the trial had been "just" because the ambitions of the trial, to the extent that they were clear and identifiable, did not lend themselves to easy analysis as "right" or "wrong."

If the ambition of the trial was to show not just the crimes in the case but what the ESMA had done, the trial was a success. The prosecution's powerful closing argument, read over three weeks in mid-2011 and summarized by the court, was a damning description of what the ESMA had done. Many of the victims and activists I spoke to after the verdict were satisfied with the result. After thirty years their torturers and kidnappers were finally behind bars. And so if the trial was supposed to provide some measure of restitution, then it succeeded here as well.

But was it satisfactory as an answer to history? Unfortunately, after attending months of the trial, my suspicion that the judges overseeing the case were unworthy scribes was confirmed when the judgment was released. The two-thousand-page judgment revealed a court that was lost among the competing purposes of the trial—between memory, truth, and justice. Was the judgment supposed to reveal the "truth" about the ESMA? Was it supposed to be a document reflecting what was to be remembered? How were these ambitions to be weighed against the competing task of rendering justice if the judges found those ambitions in tension? Unfortunately, there were no strong answers to any of these questions in the verdict, which read like a document written by committee, clearly drafted and cobbled together by the judges' various clerks. The court spent considerable energy in the verdict trying to "explain" the ESMA, but its various explanations seemed to contradict one another and also seemed tangential to the central significance of the ESMA. The judgment included a long description of the history and the growth of the left-wing revolutionary movements and the military's embrace of French counterinsurgency tactics, which culminated in the Dirty War, but it also included a long discussion of genocide, which seemed at odds with the historical description of the Dirty War as the result of a political conflict. The most awkward section of the judgment was the court's attempt to "explain" the survivors, who the defendants had targeted as being collaborators and traitors. The court rejected this characterization but spent pages and pages "explaining" the survivors' behavior as if it had all been a matter of Stockholm syndrome, the psychological condition made famous by Patty Hearst, who identified strongly with her captors after her release. One could excuse this foray into irrelevancy if it proved illuminating, but it was as useless as it was wrong. (It was also hard to see why the court considered the issue in the first place, as neither the prosecution nor the defense raised the issue, and nothing of legal significance seemed to hinge on the survivors having that condition.) There may have been one or two instances of Stockholm syndrome in the ESMA, where female prisoners fell in love with their captors (one victim ended up marrying one of the officers), but the great majority of cases were not explained by this psychological phenomenon. Indeed, the very fact that the witnesses had testified *against* the navy was the best evidence against their having the syndrome.

The judgment also included an unbalanced treatment of many of the factual issues in the case. The court actually ignored some of the most challenging arguments presented by the defense. The court, for instance, never addressed García Tallada's argument that he was not responsible for the kidnappings of the SIN because he was not in the chain of command in control of the SIN. The court also devoted hundreds of pages to discussing criminal authorship and dismissed the prosecution's theory of criminal liability as being too expansive but never articulated an alternative vision that explained the convictions, such as in the cases of both Ricardo Cavallo and Juan Carlos Fotea, where there was no direct evidence connecting them to the Santa Cruz raid.

On the question of witness credibility, the court did not address the challenge presented by the defense. The court acknowledged the "absolute clandestinity" in which the repression took place as well as the obstacles to witness recollection, such as being hooded and blindfolded, being isolated, and not knowing their fellow captives' names, all of whom used aliases. The court also acknowledged that many of the witnesses only reluctantly appeared in court, having done so many times over the years, as reliving the experience caused "anguish" and anxiety. This had the effect of leading the witnesses to "forget details, names, nicknames, places, circumstances, and much more." But at the same time, the court held that in other cases, "distance" had allowed the victims to "remember more clearly" now that they were far removed from the occurrence and felt safe. The court did admit that "witnesses who are called to testify long after the fact can combine their real observation with creations of their imagination" but ultimately held that this in "no way invalidates the testimony."[4]

After the trial the defendants' lawyers bitterly complained that the judgment reflected nothing but the political nature of the case—that the defendants were bound to be convicted from the beginning because of the court's bowing to the political pressures of the moment. They were correct to complain about the seriousness of the judgment, but to me it seemed as though the court was less trapped by the politics of the moment and more confused by the cross-purposes that were supposed to be served by the trial. The court had tacitly assumed that it could reconcile the goals of "memory" and "truth" alongside its pursuit of justice but had become unmoored in the process, not fully satisfying any of the three. In its treatment of the witnesses, for instance, it seemed that the court's reluctance to try to analyze the veracity of the witnesses' statements was a way of prioritizing the ambition of "memory" over justice; the court intuited that the voices of the survivors had to be sanctified because challenging their memories would threaten to unravel the entire project. At the same time, there also seemed to be an impulse to find against the defendants based on an inkling that historical justice had to be done despite the fact that in some cases, there was not overwhelming evidence to convict. And the rambling sections of the verdict unconnected to the charges at issue (approximately one thousand of the two thousand pages of the verdict) indicated that the court had become lost in the pursuit of "truth" even though its central task should have been justice.

Ordinarily, the one-sided treatment of the legal issues would have signaled a trial that did not reach the right result. But it was also hard to shake the feeling that the ESMA trial and Argentina's human rights trials were different. It was not that they were strictly and technically perfect proceedings, but the result represented an important step for the country to finally put the past into its proper context. While politics had infected the trial and the victims' insistence on using the trial for memory had taken time and resources, it was important to celebrate the judgment for what it had accomplished. Despite small areas of doubt, the men who had run the ESMA during the worst years of the repression in Argentina had finally been brought to justice for kidnapping, torturing, and disappearing thousands of people, and such a conviction was important for society.

The judgment seemed tragically correct. It was impossible after so many years to approximate any sort of platonic ideal of justice. This was both procedural—since the transition, the defendants had accumulated a number of procedural protections that had to be cast aside to put them on trial—and substantive, as time had taken its toll on the witnesses' memories and also robbed the prosecution the opportunity to prosecute many of the dictatorship's most important figures who had died before standing trial. But at the same time, the verdict represented Argentina's insistence that certain conduct must be demarcated as outside the scope of permissible behavior—that no state, no matter the reasons, may turn on its own citizens and discard them like trash.

So was justice done? It was a question that could be asked but not so easily answered.

Epilogue

Over the course of the trial, I tried to get in touch with the defendants. I imagined that their trial performance was, in part, a show—that they too were following an unrehearsed script, written subconsciously to convey what they were supposed to say in front of the judges and their military colleagues. Perhaps privately they would offer some repentance or speak more candidly about their role in kidnapping, killing, torturing, and murdering. Did they feel any remorse? Any regrets? How did they explain the strangely intimate relationships they developed with the victims after so many years of living together in the Naval Mechanics School (ESMA)? How did they see the dancing, the drinks, the long conversations?

I first attempted to contact Ricardo Cavallo after meeting his father, Oscar, at one of the first hearings in the case. "I'm sure he won't have any problem seeing you," Oscar wrote to me in an email, assuring me that he passed my desire to speak with his son along to him. He told me that Ricardo speaks and reads English and French and understands both Italian and German in addition to his native Spanish and that I could write him in any of those languages.

Sure enough, I received a note in late January 2010, weeks after the start of the trial, via email from Ricardo Cavallo a few days after his father told me he would probably speak with me. Dated January 28, 2010, from Ezeiza Federal Prison, Cavallo wrote a formally worded inquiry. He told me he would have no problem in granting me an interview but explained that information on the subject had been "in the best of cases unilateral and doesn't take into account the entire context." He told me that it was better to say nothing than to have one's words altered or taken out of context. He asked me to send him anything I had written about the issue and continued, "I don't assume that you take or will take a position on what happened in my country in the 70s. To the contrary. I myself as an Argentine and one who lived this era even though I was very young, I did not agree with what happened in those years, almost with nothing."[1] He encouraged me to study the "real context" of the situation in the country and thanked me for my interest in the issue.

I sent him a response letter, along with several articles I had previously written, and received a follow-up (a scanned copy of a handwritten letter) from him on February 2. In a similarly politely worded letter, he told me that the interview would not be possible because either I was too superficial or I had taken sides and was pushing a point of view. He did insist, however, that he had no involvement in the raid on the Santa Cruz Church, and he complained about his lack of access to the case file. He said that he had read forty of the sixty-four two-hundred-page files in the Santa Cruz case, "and my name has not come up once." He thanked me once again and was sorry that, for now, we would "not be able to organize [the interview]."[2]

I had a similar experience with Alfredo Astiz. Several lawyers close to Astiz told me independently that they thought he would be amenable to a conversation, off the record, and they told me they would encourage Astiz to speak with me. But they all received a negative reply. "He just doesn't think anything good would come of it," one of the lawyers told me. Astiz's sister, Lucrecia Figueroa, gave me a similar explanation of why her brother no longer wanted to talk to anyone in the media. "They always pervert his words," she told me. "There's no point in him speaking to anyone anymore." He had given an interview to the journalist Gabriela Cerruti in the 1990s, which was later published. Astiz insisted that Cerruti had given him assurances that the interview was off the record, and he later sued her in court for misrepresenting his statements.

My luck with most of the other defendants was the same. Oscar Montes's daughter told me that he was too ill to speak with anyone. (He subsequently passed away under house arrest, where he was serving his life sentence.) When I called Manuel Jacinto García Tallada's house, a woman answered the phone and told me that he was not interested in talking about the case. I went to Ernesto Frimón Weber's house, where he was serving time under house arrest in a middle-class Buenos Aires neighborhood, and knocked on his door. He was home and spoke with me for a few minutes at his door but would not open the door completely and did not let me in. "I won't speak without the court's permission," he told me. "I don't want to jeopardize my house arrest." He suggested that I should go get a coffee. "There's a nice place around the street," he said, "but I haven't been there for a while, as I can't leave."[3]

I frequently spoke with Guillermo Coronel at the courthouse throughout the trial. He represented his father, Julio César Coronel, and told me that his father, who was under house arrest, would be amenable to speaking with me. I scheduled appointments with Guillermo on three separate occasions at his law office in downtown Buenos Aires, but he was absent each time I visited. Julio César Coronel died shortly after the trial.

Six months after the verdict was released, I was told by one of the defendants' supporters that some of them would finally be amenable to speaking with me from inside the Marcos Paz prison, where most of them were serving out their sentences. I would sign up to meet one of them in particular, but the military supporters assured me that once inside the prison, several of them would likely speak to me. "He is a sailor par excellence," one of his former associates told me of the man I was supposed to meet. (I was asked to withhold his identity.) "He's a man that always did what he was supposed to" and a man who "raised a nice family."

I woke at 5:15 a.m. on a cold winter's day hours before the sun rose to meet several former naval officers who travel to visit their former colleagues twice a week. They asked me not to identify them or to reveal where exactly we met. "Not that we are doing anything illicit; it's just that it could cause problems for us," my chaperone explained. They visit on days when male visitors are permitted at the Marcos Paz maximum security prison, where most of the country's human rights defendants are held in the *pabellón lesa* (crimes against humanity pavilion). It was a holiday, and the streets were mostly empty except for a few partiers who had stayed out all night under the orange glow of the streetlights.

The prison is a three-hour drive from Buenos Aires over potholed country roads. We traveled in a small twelve-person van. About two hours into our journey, just after sunrise, we stopped at a roadside bakery to pick up snacks to share with the officers for the visit. "There's nothing we can do for them politically, so we buy them *medialunas*," one of the retired naval officers told me as we checked out from the pastry shop, clutching a bag of the Argentine version of a croissant.

We arrived at the prison, in the middle of the expansive Pampas, around 8:30 a.m. A large group of people was already waiting for the guards to open the gates, casting long shadows in the winter's sun. A number of women also made the journey with their husbands and siblings, though they would not be permitted entry on this all-male visitation day. Dew consolidated from the night before was now thawing, and water dripped off the sheet metal roof of the waiting area outside where visitors announced themselves at the entrance. I stood in line for about half an hour. My companions had all been to the prison before and were quickly let in. I waited outside for about two hours before my name was called and I was informed I had been approved.

I was told that if the prison guards asked me any questions about my relationship to the prisoner, I should tell them that we had met years ago when he was visiting a relative in the United States. He had put my name on the list as an approved visitor. Journalists and researchers, apparently, were not given easy access to the defendants, I was told, as the government had disapproved of an interview given by former dictator Jorge Rafael Videla, which had just been published as a book.

Though nominally maximum security, the security was sparse. I set the metal detector off on my entrance, but nobody made me empty my pockets or pass back through. I was given a superficial full-body pat down. I noticed that guards checking pastry bags and other items gave them only a cursory glance. I had left my recorder home after being told that it was not permitted, but it is clear I could have entered with it.

On the other side of security, I loaded a bus with two retired military officers, and we drove to the cell block where the military officers were held. The two men talked privately about their travels to the United States. It was not an ordinary prison situation—these visitors appeared well off and were light skinned, a stark contrast to the more marginal and Indigenous-looking prison population I had seen on a visit to the Devoto prison a few years before.

The prison was nice, relatively speaking. The cinderblock walls were painted with baby-blue trim (Argentina's national color). On our way to the cell block, we passed a statute of the Virgin of Luján, Argentina's patron saint, as well as a two-story cross. On the inside, there was an atmosphere of an *asado*. Hundreds of men were gathered eating pastries and smoking cigarettes in plastic chairs around plastic tables covered with plastic red checkered tablecloths. A smaller group gathered outside on the patio, where they strolled in the cool morning air. Argentine prisons are notoriously overcrowded, but here the men appeared to have plenty of space and a large patio and interior hall in which to move around. Months later the magazine *Tres Puntos* published an exposé on the cells where these men lived, including photos of their televisions and cell phones—sort of like a room at a standard hotel. Alfredo Astiz's mother had told me when I met her a few months before that she delivered fresh linens to her son during her weekly visits. She told me that he treated prison like a military assignment. The men on the inside were disciplined and rose early to keep the facilities tidy as if they were on a ship.

When I entered I saw most of the defendants from the case circulating somewhere in the room as well as dozens of other defendants from other human rights trials. I sat down with the officer I had been scheduled to see, within earshot of two others, and he agreed to talk to me on the condition that I not reveal his identity.

"I've never been prosecuted for anything," he told me shortly after we exchanged pleasantries. "I've never even run a red light." Indeed, except for the fact that we were meeting in a prison, he seemed like an ordinary older Argentine gentleman. He was well groomed, with neatly combed hair parted at the side, a windbreaker, and a V-neck sweater. (Prisoners in Argentina do not wear uniforms.)

I told him that I had come to talk to him to try to understand his version of what happened in the ESMA. He told me that Argentines were facing the problem of communism, a problem "in all of Latin America." He said the problem of worldwide communism was worse in Argentina because there was a Peronist guerrilla movement alongside the People's Revolutionary Army (ERP). He told me that the military leadership should be judged, "but not us little guys [*pibes*], who were twenty-five to thirty years old at the time."

"You're getting here too late. There's a democratic tint to this government, but it's authoritarian. It will end up as a dictatorship," he said without a hint of irony. He told me that the government uses "fear and terror" to control the population. "This woman [Cristina Fernández de Kirchner] has no limits."

He insisted that the claims of torture were overstated: "There were other methods of getting information. Many Montoneros felt repentant for what they had done and cooperated freely. Collaboration was essential."

When I asked him directly about torture, he insisted, "It wasn't torture; it was interrogation." He explained that in a normal war, the military never would have tortured people. But in a war where the enemy uses infiltration among the population as its primary weapon, it is a different story: "In your war on terror in the United States, you are lucky, because you know who to suspect. You can look at the face of a Muslim and know. But when the enemy has blond hair and blue eyes, you have to resort to other methods." He told me it was a "huge lie" that everyone who was detained in the ESMA was tortured. "It did happen in some cases," he admitted, "but only in a few."

I asked why the GT 3.3/2 killed defenseless prisoners. He responded, "They [the Montoneros] understood these were the rules of the game. They understood that if you were captured, you'd be killed." He told me that lots of people were freed after two or three days. In any event, he insisted that it was not his call to make: "The decision wasn't at our level. Well, if they had come to me and said, 'Take them all to the hospital,' I would have said, 'That's ridiculous!' But I would have done it." He told me that of the two thousand people who were detained in the ESMA, one thousand were freed. Unsaid was his admission that one thousand died.

He did admit to a logic behind the disappearances: "If someone disappeared for thirty days, it caused a lot of desperation in the Montoneros. But thirty years? We can't have this." I asked why he didn't give the names of those he saw go through the ESMA if disappearance was still a problem. "This is the responsibility of the high command," he told me. He said that after democracy returned, "they were in a position to give over the lists." But he said it would be unbecoming for him to talk about the disappearances now: "There's no Spaniard who can't tell you they knew of someone who was executed [during the Spanish Civil

War], but you don't talk about the horrors of war." I asked if he would say more if he were offered a reduced sentence. He said in theory he might, "but with these people [the current government], no. You can't believe these people." He told me that the "chance is lost. The climate that has been created over thirty-five years doesn't provide an opportunity. Someone is making money out of all of this; nothing is serious."

As the hour moved by, we addressed a number of topics—the current government ("authoritarian"); his former commander, Adm. Emilio Eduardo Massera ("not a clean person"); his training to do "intelligence work" ("I learned it on the job"); and about how much money the ESMA recovered from the Montoneros ("$2 or $3 million, but I only know about that secondhand"). Without my asking, he brought up the issue of stolen babies. "There was no systematic plan to take children. I don't want to say there weren't kidnappers. But in the majority of the cases, it was an easy way to make money," he said but did not clarify at all. He stated that if he had ever found a child in a house, he would have taken the child to the hospital. But he also told me that many grandparents did not know that they had grandkids and did not want to take care of them once they discovered them. I asked whether there were births in the ESMA. He replied, "I never saw one, but it did happen." I asked him what he thought about the women with children in the ESMA at the time. He told me that Silvia Labayrú, one of two women who were kidnapped by the ESMA to give birth to a child and survive, told him about her situation: "It's become so sinful now. We didn't think of it that way back then."

I also asked about the relationship he had with the prisoners. Did he ever feel any sympathy for them? The way some of the victims spoke about it, the barriers between prisoner and imprisoned broke down over meals, conversations, and other excursions. But he told me, "I wasn't interested in it. I didn't like them. Maybe, as a Christian, I could pardon them, but they brought so much pain." This I knew to be false, as several victims recalled this man approaching them and asking for sexual favors and accompanying them home and to meals. He insisted that the victims "transformed [our relationship] into something like a crime against women." The only reason he ever went out with women is because he "had to do it," because Acosta ordered the officers to take women around the city and back to their homes. He admitted that he once ate a meal in one of the victims' homes, but he had accompanied her there "for her protection," and it was the victim's mother who invited him in to dine.

A constant lie in the 1980s had been that the survivors were all voluntary collaborators. But he put that to rest. He told me some people collaborated, but only after time. And nobody showed up at the doorstep of the ESMA to turn themselves in.

It was impossible, given our short time frame, to ask about all the prisoners, all the victims, all the people he must have seen come and go through the ESMA on their way to freedom, or death, or recuperation. So I asked about the Mothers of the Plaza de Mayo, the iconic case that has always been an enigma: If they were going after the Montoneros and after terrorists, why the mothers? "There's no question that it happened. I can't understand it," he told me, skillfully and cynically removing himself from the equation. Though he had been convicted of his involvement in the disappearance of the Grupo Santa Cruz, he insisted he had nothing to do with it. I asked him if he could tell me who ordered it, but he said he doesn't like to name names. "The mothers weren't the enemy," he told me. Then after a contemplative pause, he added, "One of the objectives of the ERP and Montoneros was to find bonds with solidarity groups, to bring together artists and others. This obviously included victims' families. The Mothers of the Plaza de Mayo? The ERP and Montoneros saw them as very important." He told me that he found out that the Montoneros were financing solidarity groups in Europe and that they had helped raise money for the mothers to send them to Puebla, Mexico. Then he told me that not all the members of the Mothers of the Plaza de Mayo are "real mothers." He said, "Go ask them if they are really the mothers of the disappeared. The real feeling of pain has been commercialized."

As noon approaches, visitors are called to leave. We shake hands as I stand up, and I ask if I can come visit in a few days, when there is another visitation opportunity. "I think we are probably done talking," he tells me politely, keeping with him the answers to so many questions.

NOTES

Acknowledgments

1. Elias, "Constitutional Changes," 587.

2. Sam Ferguson, "The Unending War: Argentina's Quest for Justice," *Boston Review*, May 1, 2008.

Introduction

1. Reato, *Disposición final*, 54.

2. Comisión Nacional sobre la Desaparición de Personas, *Nunca más*, 83, 205, 230–31. Carlos Beltrán describes forcing a prisoner to dig a pit where fellow officers shot the prisoner and three others and burned their corpses. Brennan, *Argentina's Missing Bones*, 2, details recent searches by the Equipo Argentino de Antropología Forense (EAAF) for remains in Córdoba and the La Perla base. Despite extensive searching the EAAF has not located mass graves on the La Perla grounds. In 2014 and 2015, it did discover the remains of several young activists in a crude crematorium on the grounds of the base. In 2002, the EAAF exhumed hundreds of bodies at the San Vicente Cemetery that were transferred from the Córdoba Judicial Morgue in 1976 and 1977. The bodies arrived at the morgue after mass exhumations; morgue workers later wrote to de facto president Jorge Rafael Videla complaining of unsanitary working conditions because of the large number of bodies suddenly brought to the morgue, many of which showed gunshot wounds, signs of torture, and inked fingerprints. See also EAAF, *2006 Annual Report*, 44–45.

3. See, e.g., *Nunca más*, 232–35; "Argentine Police Get Life Term in 'Dirty War' Case," Reuters, July 11, 2008; and Sam Ferguson, "The Fatima Massacre," *Truthout* (Sacramento CA), July 30, 2008.

4. "Le Corbusier en Argentina y . . . la isla que no fue," *El Diario* (Buenos Aires), April 3, 2019.

5. See, e.g., Testimony of Martín Gras, Federal Oral Tribunal Number 5, *ESMA II*, case no. 1.270, August 18, 2010; Testimony of Graciela Daleo, Federal Oral Tribunal Number 5, *ESMA II*, case no. 1.270, April 29, 2010; Testimony of Silvia Labayrú, Federal Oral Tribunal Number 5, *ESMA II*, case no. 1.270, June 9, 2010; and *Nunca más*, 238.

6. See, e.g., Testimony of Martín Gras; Testimony of Graciela Daleo; Testimony of Silvia Labayrú; and *Nunca más*, 238.

7. Verbitsky, *Flight*, 49.

8. Testimony of Luis Fondebrider, Federal Oral Tribunal Number 5, ESMA *II*, case no. 1.270, December 10, 2012.

9. Lewin, *Skyvan*, 99–110.

10. Verbitsky, *Flight*, 18. In 2017 ESMA survivor and Argentine investigative journalist Miriam Lewin tracked down two of the planes used in the death flights. See generally Lewin, *Skyvan*.

11. *Nunca más*, 12–13, 395–419.

12. Graciela Fernández Meijide, interview with the author, September 23, 2009.

13. *Nunca más*, 14.

14. "A 45 años del golpe de Estado, suman 1025 las personas condenadas por crímenes de lesa humanidad en 254 sentencias," Procuradoría de Crímenes contra Humanidad, Ministerio Público Fiscal, March 24, 2021, https://www.fiscales.gob.ar/lesa-humanidad/a-45-anos-del-golpe-de-estado-suman-1025-las-personas-condenadas-por-crimenes-de-lesa-humanidad-en-254-sentencias/.

15. See generally Nino, *Radical Evil on Trial*, 59–106; Verbitsky, *Civiles y militares*; Romero, *History of Argentina*, 255–84; Andersen, *Dossier Secreto*, 295–314; Malamud Goti, *Game without End*, 59–70; Feitlowitz, *Lexicon of Terror*, 13–15; Robben, *Political Violence and Trauma*, 318–39; Alfonsín and Giussani, *¿Por qué, Doctor Alfonsín?*, 200–278; and Guest, *Behind the Disappearances*, 381–91.

16. *Nunca más*, 15.

17. Teitel, *Transitional Justice*.

18. See note 15.

19. National Decree 1.002/89, "Indultos," Boletín Oficial 26736 at 4, October 10, 1989; National Decree 2.741/90, Boletín Oficial 27044, January 3, 1991; "200 Military Officers Are Pardoned in Argentina," Associated Press, October 8, 1989; Shirley Christian, "Argentina Frees Ex-Junta Leaders," *New York Times*, December 30, 1990.

20. National Decree 1.002/89, "Indultos," Boletín Oficial 26736 at 4.

21. Ferguson, "Unending War."

22. The full text of the speech is available at "El texto completo del discurso presidencial," *La Nación* (Buenos Aires), May 25, 2003, https://www.lanacion.com.ar/politica/el-texto-completo-del-discurso-presidencial-nid498849/.

23. *Nunca más*, 8–9.

24. Jaime Rosemberg, "Mauricio Macri: 'Conmigo se acaban los curros en derechos humanos,'" *La Nación* (Buenos Aires), December 8, 2014, https://www.lanacion.com.ar/politica/mauricio-macri-conmigo-se-acaban-los-curros-en-derechos-humanos-nid1750419/.

25. Lucía Salinas, "Sospechas de corrupción: Piden elevar a juicio oral a los hermanos Schoklender por la causa Sueños Compartidos," *Clarín* (Buenos Aires), October 2, 2018, https://www.clarin.com/politica/piden-elevar-juicio-oral-hermanos-schoklender-causa-suenos-compartidos_0_YYZIGxG-d.html.

26. "La Corte Suprema applica el beneficio del 2x1 para la prisión en un caso de delito de lesa humanidad," *La Nación* (Buenos Aires), May 3, 2017, https://www.lanacion.com.ar/politica/la-corte-suprema-declaro-aplicable-el-beneficio-del-2x1-para-la-prision-en-un-caso-de-delito-de-lesa-humanidad-nid2020021/.

27. Daniel Santoro, "La Corte votará un nuevo fallo sobre el 2x1, a la luz de la ley que se publica hoy," *Clarín* (Buenos Aires), May 2, 2017.

28. Office of the Press Secretary, "Remarks by President Obama and President Macri of Argentina at Parque de la Memoria," White House, March 24, 2016, accessed October 7, 2022, https://obamawhitehouse.archives.gov/the-press-office/2016/03/24/remarks-president-obama-and-president-macri-argentina-parque-de-la.

29. "El Presidente rompió el silencio por el 2x1: 'Estoy en contra de cualquier herramienta que facilite la impunidad,'" *Ámbito Financiero* (Buenos Aires), May 10, 2017.

30. See generally Osiel, *Making Sense of Mass Atrocity*.

31. For a comprehensive discussion of these tensions, see Teitel, *Transitional Justice*, 3–26.

1. A Beginning of Sorts

1. "Recorrida en la ESMA," *Página/12* (Buenos Aires), November 15, 2009.

2. Claudio Savoia, "Pieza clave de la repression que se convirtió en símbolo de la dictadura," *Clarín* (Buenos Aires), December 12, 2009.

3. Argentina secretary of media communications, "Saludó Francia la voluntad política de realizar el juicio por causa ESMA," press release, December 11, 2009.

4. Diego Martinez, "Astiz, Cavallo y el Tigre Acosta, sin mascaras," *Página/12* (Buenos Aires), December 12, 2009.

5. Diego Martinez, "Ahora viene un año major que el anterior," *Página/12* (Buenos Aires), December 27, 2009.

6. Sam Ferguson, "Two Sentenced, Three Absolved in Argentine 'Dirty War' Trial, Angering Activists," *Truthout* (Sacramento CA), November 3, 2009.

7. Adriana Meyer, "La jueza no se baja del caballo," *Página/12* (Buenos Aires), March 21, 2008. See also Uki Goñi, "How Argentina 'Suicides' the Truth," *New York Times*, February 10, 2015.

8. See, e.g., Alejandra Dandan, "La ESMA era una verdadera maternidad," *Página/12* (Buenos Aires), August 3, 2011; Washington Uranga, "Los bautismos en la ESMA," *Página/12* (Buenos Aires), March 7, 2018; and "La justicia investigará 55 bautismos en la ESMA," *Página/12* (Buenos Aires), March 15, 2018.

9. Testimony of Víctor Basterra, Federal Oral Tribunal Number 5, *ESMA II*, case no. 1.270, April 30, 2010. All translations from testimonies are the author's.

10. "Simón, Julio Héctor y otros s/ privación ilegítima de la libertad," case no. 17.768, Corte Suprema de Justicia de la Nación, June 15, 2005.

11. Alfredo Solari, open letter of March 14, 2007 (on file with the author).

12. For the two most thorough investigations of the Astiz affair prior to the trial, see Rosenberg, *Children of Cain*, 77–142; and Goñi, *Judas*. For a treatment of Astiz and command responsibility, see Osiel, *Mass Atrocity, Ordinary Evil*.

13. Victoria Ginzberg, "Cuando la verdad resiste a la impunidad," *Página/12* (Buenos Aires), August 30, 2005.

14. Rosenberg, *Children of Cain*, 77–142; Goñi, *Judas*.

15. See, e.g., Calvin Sims, "Retired Torturer Now Lives a Tortured Existence," *New York Times*, August 12, 1997, A4.

16. Testimony of Marta Remedios Álvarez, Federal Oral Tribunal Number 5, ESMA *II*, case no. 1.270, August 6, 2010.

17. As quoted in Closing Statement of the Prosecution, Federal Oral Tribunal Number 5, ESMA *II*, case no. 1.270, July 4, 2011.

2. The Argentine Enigma

1. "Acentúase el aumento de precios de alimentos y arículos varios," *La Prensa* (Buenos Aires), March 5, 1976.

2. "Argentines Learn to Live, Unhappily, with Inflation of 335%," *New York Times*, January 8, 1976.

3. "Mrs. Peron Is Overthrown by Military in Argentina and Reported Arrested," *New York Times*, March 24, 1976.

4. "Argentines Learn to Live."

5. "Gestiona hoy la Argentina otro prestamo al FMI," *La Prensa* (Buenos Aires), March 8, 1976. See also "Intesificarán el control de precios en Buenos Aires," *La Prensa* (Buenos Aires), March 16, 1976.

6. "Mrs. Peron Is Overthrown."

7. "Argentina Military Takeover Threatens as Wrangling over the Regime Mounts," *New York Times*, February 15, 1976.

8. "At an Argentine Party after the Coup," *New York Times*, March 28, 1976.

9. "Iniciáronse a medianoche paros en los ferrocarriles," *La Prensa* (Buenos Aires), March 10, 1976; "Nuevos paros por mejoras salariales en el interior," *La Prensa* (Buenos Aires), March 12, 1976.

10. "Mrs. Peron Is Overthrown."

11. Rock, *Argentina, 1516–1987*; "Argentina Gives Civil Workers a 40% Pay Increase," *New York Times*, January 28, 1976; "Auméntanse los saldos un 20% desde el 1 de este mes," *La Prensa* (Buenos Aires), March 10, 1976; "Mrs. Peron Is Overthrown."

12. Rock, *Argentina, 1516–1987*, 354.

13. "Mrs. Peron Ousts 4 Cabinet Ministers," *New York Times*, January 16, 1975.

14. "2 Key Argentine Aides Replaced as Economic Troubles Worsen," *New York Times*, February 4, 1976.

15. "High Peron Aide Reported to Quit," *New York Times*, February 25, 1976.

16. "Argentina Orders a New Constitution," *Reuters* (Canary Wharf UK), February 14, 1976.

17. "Deputies Back Mrs. Peron, 120–70—a New Ouster Bid May Charge Incompetence," Associated Press, February 26, 1976.

18. "Argentina Military Takeover."

19. "New Threat to Mrs. Peron," *New York Times*, February 17, 1976.

20. "Mrs. Perón Says She Won't Accept a New Term in '77," *New York Times*, February 19, 1976.

21. "Mrs. Peron Moves to Block Challenge to Her by Congress," *New York Times*, February 17, 1976.

22. "Produjeronse ayer y anteayer en Córdoba nuevos secuestros," *La Prensa* (Buenos Aires), March 10, 1976. See also "11 Are Abducted in Argentine City," *New York Times*, March 11, 1976.

23. "Secuestraron a un ex gobernador de salta," *La Prensa* (Buenos Aires), March 12, 1976.

24. "En Córdoba hubo atentados anoche," *La Prensa* (Buenos Aires), March 14, 1976.

25. "Ataque a una delegación naval en Mendoza," *La Prensa* (Buenos Aires), March 15, 1976.

26. "Detención de un correo terrorista," *La Prensa* (Buenos Aires), March 15, 1976.

27. "Se atentó contra el commando del ejército," *La Prensa* (Buenos Aires), March 16, 1976.

28. "Asesinaron anoche a un policía federal." *La Prensa* (Buenos Aires), March 16, 1976.

29. "El cadáver de un hombre fue hallado en Pergamino," *La Prensa* (Buenos Aires), March 17, 1976.

30. "Hubo anoche varios atentados con bombas en esta capital," *La Prensa* (Buenos Aires), March 17, 1976.

31. "En atentados terroristas murieron cuatro policies," *La Prensa* (Buenos Aires), March 17, 1976.

32. "Victima de una acción terrorista murío un policía en Rosario," *La Prensa* (Buenos Aires), March 17, 1976.

33. "Incendio de ocho colectivos y cierre del comercio en La Plata," *La Prensa* (Buenos Aires), March 20, 1976.

34. "Los cadáveres de 4 mujeres halláronse en Santa Fe," *La Prensa* (Buenos Aires), March 21, 1976.

35. "Tres obreros y un estudiante fueron asesinados en La Plata," *La Prensa* (Buenos Aires), March 21, 1976.

36. "Fue muerto de un balazo un sindicalista tucumano," *La Prensa* (Buenos Aires), March 23, 1976.

37. "Seizure of Leftist Guerrilla Chief in Argentina Remains a Mystery amid Wave of Kidnappings and Murders," *New York Times*, January 11, 1976.

38. Lewis, *Guerrillas and Generals*, 127.

39. "Operativo militar en todo el país," *La Prensa* (Buenos Aires), March 24, 1976.

40. "Burden of Office Was Too Great," *New York Times*, March 25, 1976.

41. "In Argentina's 2d City, Coup Was No Surprise," *New York Times* March 25, 1976.

42. "Operativo militar."

43. "Mrs. Peron Is Overthrown."

44. Donald C. Hodges previously articulated many similar questions in Hodges, *Argentina's "Dirty War,"* 1–19. Similar questions have inspired many works, including Rock, *Argentina, 1516–1987*; and Shumway, *Invention of Argentina*.

45. Rock, *Argentina, 1516–1987*, 5–6.

46. Rock, *Argentina, 1516–1987*, 5–6.

47. Romero, *History of Argentina*, 3–11.

48. Nino, *Radical Evil on Trial*, 47.

49. Romero, *History of Argentina*, 3–11. This genocidal "conquest of the desert" was until recently still memorialized in Argentina. Roca was featured on Argentina's 100 peso note until 2012, when he was replaced by Evita. The Argentine Central Bank explains Roca's historical significance as "Preparing and managing the Conquest of the Desert (1875–1870) which significantly contributed to the development of the agricultural economy." See "El BCRA y vos: $100," Banco Central de la República Argentina, accessed January 2, 2023, http://www.bcra.gov.ar/MediosPago/100_Pesos.asp.

50. Romero, *History of Argentina*, 3–11.

51. Nino, *Radical Evil on Trial*, 42, says that in 1928, "Argentina [was] the seventh-largest economic power in the world."

52. Romero, *History of Argentina*, 12–18.

53. Helen Brady, "The Palacio Barolo: Architecture Inspired by Dante's *Divine Comedy*," *Culture Trip* (London), December 12, 2015, https://theculturetrip.com/south-america/argentina/articles/the-palacio-barolo-architecture-inspired-by-dante-s-divine-comedy/.

54. Romero, *History of Argentina*, 16–25. See also Finchelstein, *Ideological Origins*, 16–21.

55. Romero, *History of Argentina*, 4.

56. Finchelstein, *Ideological Origins*, 20.

57. Finchelstein, *Ideological Origins*, 23.

58. Finchelstein, *Ideological Origins*, 21. For an extended discussion on the origins of the two dominant strains of early Argentine political thought—elitist liberalism and nationalism—see Shumway, *Invention of Argentina*, 214–96. See also Gillespie, *Soldiers of Perón*, 4–5.

59. See generally Romero, *History of Argentina*, 59–64; Finchelstein, *Ideological Origins*, 26–32; Nino, *Radical Evil on Trial*, 42; and Rock, *Argentina, 1516–1987*, 213–17.

60. See generally Luna, *Golpes militares*.

61. Lewis, *Guerrillas and Generals*, 3.

62. See Sentencia (Acordada del 30), September 10, 1930, Supreme Court of Argentina, 158 Fallos 290 (1930), http://www.saij.gob.ar/corte-suprema-justicia-nacion-federal-ciudad-autonoma-buenos-aires-acordada-sobre-reconocimiento-gobierno-provincial-nacion-fa30996876-1930-09-10/123456789-678-6990-3ots-eupmocsollaf.

63. Nino, *Radical Evil on Trial*, 47–48. See also Natalia Volosin, "Detrás de la acordada del 30," *Palabras del Derecho* (blog), September 10, 2016, http://palabrasdelderecho.blogspot.com/2016/09/detras-de-la-acordada-del-30_10.html.

64. On Perón's rise, see generally Gillespie, *Soldiers of Perón*, 6–29; Lewis, *Guerrillas and Generals*, 5–8; Finchelstein, *Ideological Origins*, 65–92; and Page, *Perón, a Biography*, 41–330. On harboring Nazi exiles, see Goñi, *Real Odessa*. On Perón's complicated relationship with Argentina's Jews, see Diego Curubeto, "Una original mirada sobre Perón y el judaísmo," *Ámbito Financiero* (Buenos Aires), September 25, 2020.

65. Romero, *History of Argentina*, 93–96; Gillespie, *Soldiers of Perón*, 17–19.

66. For an articulation of Perón's philosophy, see Perón, *Una comunidad organizada*.

67. Romero, *History of Argentina*, 93–96.

68. Romero, *History of Argentina*, 95–97.

69. Romero, *History of Argentina*, 104–8.

70. Gillespie, *Soldiers of Perón*, 72–73.

71. Gillespie, *Soldiers of Perón*, 6–29.

72. Romero, *History of Argentina*, 108.

73. Romero, *History of Argentina*, 109–10.

74. Romero, *History of Argentina*, 110.

75. Romero, *History of Argentina*, 124–30.

76. Poder Ejectuvio Nacional, Decreto-Ley 4161, "Partidos Politicos Prohibidos," Boletín Oficial number 18107, March 5, 1956.

77. As quoted in Hodges, *Argentina's "Dirty War,"* 73.

78. Cooke, *Correspondencia Perón-Cooke*, 663.

79. Romero, *History of Argentina*, 139–41.

80. "Argentina: Killing the Sacred Cow," *Time*, August 4, 1958.

81. Romero, *History of Argentina*, 142–46.

82. Rock, *Argentina, 1516–1987*, 344–46; Romero, *History of Argentina*, 170–71.

83. O'Donnell, *Modernization and Bureaucratic-Authoritarianism*.

84. Riz, *La política en suspenso*, 13–65; Romero, *History of Argentina*, 173–74.

85. Gillespie, *Soldiers of Perón*, 43.

86. Gillespie, *Soldiers of Perón*, 60–70.

87. Page, *Perón, a Biography*, 161, 354.

88. Perón, *América Latina*.

89. Lewis, *Guerrillas and Generals*, 135–43; Hodges, *Argentina's "Dirty War,"* 124–43.

90. Lewis, *Guerrillas and Generals*, 135–43.

91. Trinquier, *Modern Warfare*, 3.

92. Trinquier, *Modern Warfare*, 6.

93. Trinquier, *Modern Warfare*, 21.

94. Testimony of Lisandro Raúl Cubas, Federal Oral Tribunal Number 5, ESMA *II*, case no. 1.270, July 30, 2010.

95. Ejército Argentina, Publication RC 8-1 "Publico (Provisional)," "Operaciones no convencionales (fuerzas especialies)," Instituto Geográfico Militar, 1968.

96. Ejército Argentina, Publication RC 5-2 "Reservado," "Operaciones Sicologicas," Instituto Geográfico Militar, 1968.

97. Ejército Argentina, Publication RV 150-10 "Publico," "Instrucción de lucha contra las guerrillas," Instituto Geográfico Militar, 1969.

98. Ejército Argentina, Publication RC 8-3 "Reservado," "Operaciones contra la subversion urbana," Instituto Geográfico Militar, 1969.

99. Ejército Argentina, Publication RC 8-2 "Publico," "Operaciones contra fuerzas irregulares," Instituto Geográfico Militar, 1970.

100. Ejército Argentina, Publication RC 17-3 "Publico," "Contrainteligencia—Censura Militar," Instituto Geográfico Militar, 1972.

101. Ejército Argentina, Publication RE 9-51 "Reservado," "Instrucción de Lucha Contra Elementos Subversivos," Instituto Geográfico Militar, 1976.

102. Anderson, *Che Guevara*, 512–28.

103. Gillespie, *Soldiers of Perón*, 60–82, 275–76; Romero, *History of Argentina*, 189.

104. Riz, *La política en suspenso*, 69–75; Romero, *History of Argentina*, 180–83. Romero cites a figure of twenty to thirty people who died.

105. Romero, *History of Argentina*, 189; Gillespie, *Soldiers of Perón*, 89–106.

106. Lewis, *Guerrillas and Generals*, 71.

107. Lewis, *Guerrillas and Generals*, 57.

108. Rock, *Argentina, 1516–1987*, 346–66.

109. Romero, *History of Argentina*, 194; Lewis, *Guerrillas and Generals*, 71–72.

110. Lewis, *Guerrillas and Generals*, 73. Lewis also notes the government's version of events, in which one of the prisoners allegedly reached for one of the guards' weapons and a melee ensued, resulting in the deaths of sixteen prisoners.

111. Lewis, *Guerrillas and Generals*, 74.

112. Lewis, *Guerrillas and Generals*, 81–84.

113. Lewis, *Guerrillas and Generals*, 88–89.

114. Gillespie, *Soldiers of Perón*, 42.

115. Romero, *History of Argentina*, 208–14; Lewis, *Guerrillas and Generals*, 94–95; Gillespie, *Soldiers of Perón*, 136–59.

116. "Burden of Office."

117. Poder Ejecutivo Nacional, "Decretos Secretos y Reservados, Operaciones Militares," Decreto 261/75 of February 5, 1975, published in Boletín Oficial number 32614 at 5, April 9, 2013, https://www.argentina.gob.ar/normativa/nacional/decreto-261-1975-210287/texto; Poder Ejecutivo Nacional, "Consejo de Seguridad Interna—Constitución—Competencia," Decreto 2770/75 of October 6, 1975, published in Boletín Oficial of November 4, 1975; Poder Ejecutivo Nacional, "Consejo de Defensa—Convenios con las provincias para colocar bajo su control operacional al personal policial y penitenciario para la lucha contra la subversion," Decreto 2771/75 of October 6, 1975, published in Boletín Oficial of November 4, 1975; Poder Ejecutivo Nacional, "Fuerzas Armadas—Ejecución de las operaciones militares y de seguridad necesarias para eliminar la subversion," Decreto 2772/75 of October 6, 1975, published in Boletín Oficial of November 4, 1975.

118. Feitlowitz, *Lexicon of Terror*, 6.

119. Carlos Osorio and Kathleen Costar, "Kissinger to the Argentine Generals in 1976: 'If There Are Things to Be Done, You Should Do Them Quickly,'" National Security Archive, August 27, 2004, https://nsarchive2.gwu.edu/NSAEBB/NSAEBB133/index.htm.

120. "So Far So Good," *Buenos Aires Herald*, March 25, 1976, 8.

121. "Los embarques de carnes," *La Prensa* (Buenos Aires), March 26, 1976.

122. "Juramento y acta de reorganizacíon nacional," *La Prensa* (Buenos Aires), March 25, 1976.

123. For brief profile of each commander, see "The Three Who Will Govern Argentina," *New York Times*, March 25, 1976.

124. "Juramento y acta de reorganizacíon nacional."

125. "Argentina's New Start," *New York Times*, April 4, 1976.

126. "Videla Reassures Argentines on Human Rights," *New York Times*, April 1, 1976.

127. "Juramento y acta de reorganizacíon nacional." See also "Videla Reassures Argentines."

128. "Reconocimiento de paises extranjeros," *La Prensa* (Buenos Aires), March 26, 1976.

129. "Justifican en europa el pronunciamiento militar," *La Prensa* (Buenos Aires), March 28, 1976.

130. "La Junta Militar assumió el Poder Ejecutivo Nacional," *La Prensa* (Buenos Aires), March 25, 1976.

131. "Argentine Junta under Army Chief Assumes Control," *New York Times*, March 25, 1976.

132. "Argentine Junta Makes Basic Changes," *New York Times*, April 3, 1976.

3. The Prosecution's Case

1. Argentine Criminal Procedural Code, Article 374.

2. See, e.g., February 12, 2007, Trial Elevation of Prosecutor Eduardo Taiano, Juzgado Nacional en lo Criminal y Correccional Federal Numero 12 [National Federal Criminal and Correctional Court number 12], *Megacausa* ESMA, case no. 14.217/03, pp. 14437–502.

3. Testimony of Martín Gras, Federal Oral Tribunal Number 5, ESMA *II*, case no. 1.270, August 18, 2010.

4. Juzgado Nacional en lo Criminal y Correccional Federal Numero 12 [National Federal Criminal and Correctional Court number 12], *Megacausa* ESMA, case no. 14.217/03, pp. 32163–71.

4. Opening Silence

1. Federal Oral Tribunal Number 5, ESMA *II*, case no. 1.270/09, 3085 (Report of the Forensic Medical Examiner of the Supreme Court of the Nation, November 13, 2009).

2. Testimony of Oscar Montes, December 11, 1986, National Chamber of Criminal and Correctional Appeals, "E.S.M.A.," case no. 761, p. 2903.

3. Testimony of Adolfo Donda, March 12, 2010, Federal Oral Tribunal Number 5, ESMA *II*, case no. 1.270.

4. Testimony of Jorge Eduardo Acosta, March 17, 2010, Federal Oral Tribunal Number 5, ESMA *II*, case no. 1.270.

5. Acosta letters to public defenders, dated October 12, 2008, November 12, 2009, and December 14, 2009, reprinted at Juzgado Nacional en lo Criminal y Correccional Federal Numero 12 [National Federal Criminal and Correctional Court number 12], *Megacausa* ESMA, case no. 14.217/03, pp. 40696, and 43269; and Federal Oral Tribunal Number 5, ESMA *II*, case no. 1.270, p. 3012.

6. Testimony of Alfredo Astiz, March 17, 2010, Federal Oral Tribunal Number 5, ESMA *II*, case no. 1.270.

7. Testimony of Antonio Pernías, May 6, 2010, Federal Oral Tribunal Number 5, ESMA *II*, case no. 1.270.

8. Testimony of Raúl Enrique Scheller, March 19, 2010, Federal Oral Tribunal Number 5, ESMA *II*, case no. 1.270/09.

9. Testimony of Raúl Enrique Scheller, March 19, 2010, Federal Oral Tribunal Number 5, ESMA *II*, case no. 1.270/09.

10. As quoted in McCaughan, *True Crimes*, 248.

11. Adm. Ramón Arosa, Navy Day speech, May 17, 1987, as quoted in Arosa, *De constitución a retiro*, 236.

12. As quoted in Moreno Ocampo, *Cuando el poder*, 10.

13. National Chamber of Criminal and Correctional Appeals, case no. 13/84, 1393.

5. Trials before the Trial

1. As quoted in Prosecutor's February 12, 2007, Request for Elevation to Trial, Juzgado Nacional en lo Criminal y Correccional Federal Numero 12 [National Federal Criminal and Correctional Court number 12], *Megacausa* ESMA, case no. 14.217/03, p. 14476.

2. Testimony of Lila Pastoriza, Federal Oral Tribunal Number 5, *ESMA II*, case no. 1.270, July 8, 2010; Testimony of Miriam Lewin, Federal Oral Tribunal Number 5, *ESMA II*, case no. 1.270, July 15, 2010; Declaration of Daniel Tarnopolosky, Juzgado Nacional en lo Criminal y Correccional Federal Numero 12 [National Federal Criminal and Correctional Court number 12], *Megacausa* ESMA, case no. 14.217/03, 12000–12002; Lila Pastroiza, "Su memoria se fue agigantando," *Página/12* (Buenos Aires), March 25, 2013. On the saga of the Tarnopolsky family, see Tarnopolsky, *Betina sin aparecer*.

3. As reprinted in Baschetti, *Documentos, 1976–1977*, 2:121–26.

4. CONADEP File 4450, pp. 5–19, containing Maggio's testimony of March 17, 1978, and April 10, 1978.

5. "Testimonio de Jaime Feliciano Dri, Prisionero de la Escuela de Mecánica de la Armada y del II Cuerpo de Ejército (Rosario, Santa Fe) Fugado el 19 de Julio 1978," correspondence dated September 18, 1978, from Paris, National Chamber of Criminal and Correctional Appeals, "E.S.M.A.," case no. 761, File [Legajo] 122. See also Testimony of Jaime Dri, Federal Oral Tribunal Number 5, *ESMA II*, case no. 1.270, December 16, 2010.

6. Testimonio de los sobrevivientes del genocidio en la Argentina, CADHU, National Chamber of Criminal and Correctional Appeals, "E.S.M.A.," case no. 761, File [Legajo] 23, pp. 28–61.

7. In a cover letter submitted from the Sixth Criminal Chamber in Buenos Aires to the CONSUFA on August 21, 1984, Judge Roberto Hornos transferred certified copies of 121 cases that had been filed in those chambers during and immediately before the dictatorship of kidnappings and disappearances. The scope and quantity of similar crimes should have left no doubt among the judges of the systematic nature of the repression, but most preferred to adhere to empty formalism and did not investigate the widespread kidnappings. National Chamber of Criminal and Correctional Appeals, case no. 13/84, pp. 1061–63.

8. Navy Expediente DJN, ADA no. 015"S"/80, September 10, 1981.

9. National Chamber of Criminal and Correctional Appeals, case no. 13/84, p. 180.

10. See Victoria Ginzberg, "Preparados para la impunidad," *Página/12* (Buenos Aires), March 23, 2014.

11. National Criminal and Correctional Court of the First Instance of the Federal Capital, "Antokoletz, y otros," case no. 6.511, p. 127, August 9, 1983.

12. "Forces State Their 'Dirty War' Case," *Buenos Aires Herald*, April 29, 1983, 1, reproduced at https://nsarchive2.gwu.edu/NSAEBB/NSAEBB85/830428%200000B044.pdf.

13. Carlos Acuña and Catalina Smulovitz, "Militares en la transición Argentina: Del gobierno a la subordinación constitutional," in Acuña et al., *Juicio, Castigos y Memorias*, 46–47.

14. James Neilson, "Forget, or Else . . . ," *Buenos Aires Herald*, September 29, 1983, 10.

15. Acuña and Smulovitz, "Militares en la transición Argentina," 48n64.

16. Acuña and Smulovitz, "Militares en la transición Argentina," 48n63. Novaro and Palermo give different figures: they say the Justicialist Party had 3,500,000 members versus the Radical Party's 1,400,000. Novaro and Palermo, *La dictadura militar*, 514.

17. Robert Powell, "Ítalo Lúder a Compromise Candidate," *Buenos Aires Herald*, September 8, 1983, 9.

18. "Artists Add Cultural Effervescence to Argentina's Political Renaissance," *Washington Post*, January 5, 1984; "It's Spring in Argentina and Freedom Is in the Air," *New York Times*, November 5, 1983.

19. Decreto 158/83, as reprinted in National Chamber of Criminal and Correctional Appeals, case no. 13/84, pp. 2–8.

20. Decreto 158/83, as reprinted in National Chamber of Criminal and Correctional Appeals, case no. 13/84, pp. 2–8.

21. Acuña and Smulovitz, "Militares en la transición Argentina," 50–53; Nino, *Radical Evil on Trial*, 73–75; Novaro, *Argentina en el fin*, 30–55.

22. Nino, *Radical Evil on Trial*, 79.

23. *Nunca más*.

24. "Las estrategias," *Diario del juicio*, May 25, 1985.

25. Nino, *Radical Evil on Trial*, 83; "Del 22 de abril al 26 de abril de 1985," *Diario del juicio*, May 27, 1985, 1–5, 14–15; "Del 29 de abril al 3 de mayo de 1985," *Diario del juicio*, June 4, 1985, 29–33, 44–48; "Del 6 al 10 de mayo de 1985," *Diario del juicio*, June 1, 1985, 62–66. On the trial testimony in general, see Camarasa, Felice, and González, *El juicio*, 105–81.

26. For a list of ESMA witnesses, see *Texto completo de la sentencia: Dictada el 9 de diciembre de 1985 por la excelentísima camara nacional de apelaciones en lo criminal y correccional federal de la capital federal* (Buenos Aires: Imprenta del Congreso de la Nación, 1987), 165–67. See also Camarasa, Felice, and González, *El juicio*, 170–78; "Massera sonrió y me dijo: ¿Sabe qué pasó con Poncio Pilatos . . . ," *Diario del juicio*, June 18, 1985, 2–3; "Quiero que se llegue a saber qué hicieron con mi hija," "Los documentos del gobierno," "Testimonio de Norma Burgos," and "El case Hidalgo Solá: Videla, Viola y Massera sabían todo," *Diario del juicio*, July 23, 1985, 2–4; "Las fotos de la ESMA," "El testimonio de la semana: Víctor Melchor Bastera," and "Un testigo ciego del horror," *Diario del juicio*, July 30, 1985, 1–4; "El caso de Elena Holmberg," *Diario del juicio*, August 13, 1985, 2; "Del 15 al 17 de julio de 1985," *Diario del juicio*, September 24, 1985, 389–408; "Día 18 de julio de 1985," *Diario del juicio*, October 15, 1985, 409–14; "Del 18 al 19 de julio de 1985," *Diario del juicio*, October 22, 1985, 421–31; "Día 22 de julio de 1985," *Diario del juicio*, October 29, 1985, 433–48; "Día 23 de julio de 1985," *Diario del juicio*, November 5, 1985, 452–64; "Día 24 de julio de 1985," *Diario del juicio*, November 12, 1985, 465–80; "Del 25 al 26 de juliio de 1985," *Diario del juicio*, November 19, 1985, 482–91; "Sara Solarz de Osatinsky y el horror de la ESMA," *Diario del juicio*, November 12, 1985, 2–3.

27. "El día que Borges asistió al Juicio a las Juntas y sintió que había descendido al peor de los infiernos," inbobae.com, July 22, 2020, https://www.infobae.com/sociedad/2020/07/22/el-dia-que-borges-asistio-al-juicio-a-las-juntas-y-sintio-que-habia-descendido-al-peor-de-los-infiernos/.

28. Camarasa, Felice, and González, *El juicio*, 110.

29. Camarasa, Felice, and González, *El juicio*, 178–79; see also "Del 22 de abril al 26 de abril de 1985," *Diario del juicio*, May 27, 1985, 6–10; "Del 9 al 13 de Agosto de 1985," *Diario del juicio*, December 24, 1985, 565–66.

30. "Se demostó qu optaron po la clandestinidad y la ilegalidad," *Diario del juicio*, December 11, 1985, 2.

31. "Se demostó qu optaron po la clandestinidad y la ilegalidad," *Diario del juicio*, December 11, 1985, 2.

32. *Texto completo de la sentencia*, 216.

33. Curiously, the ESMA case file bears a telling date stamp: August 23, 1983. See National Chamber of Criminal and Correctional Appeals, "E.S.M.A.," case no. 761, p. 9. The case was convened by military dictator Reynaldo Bignone months *before* Alfonsín's election. In retrospect, it might seem strange that the military would order a court-martial of the officers suspected of running the ESMA, but it was surely a show of "good faith" by Gen. Bignone to the incoming civilians that the military didn't intend to ignore the issue of the disappeared. The indictment against Adm. Emilio Eduardo Massera and his subordinates was proof. By 1983 Massera's position within the armed forces had been marginalized; his political ambitions had isolated him from many of his former colleagues in the navy and his associates in the army. In fact, the dictatorship threw him in jail on several occasions for speaking out against the economic policies of the regime, so there was little to be lost and much to be gained for Bignone by ordering the court-martial of Massera and other officers suspected of having run the ESMA. There was also an alternative motive: with dozens of court cases facing the ESMA officers in civilian courts, the court-martial would provide an opportunity for the military to consolidate all these cases in military courts, a more friendly and predictable jurisdiction. Indeed, the Supreme Council of the Armed Forces issued a dismissal of the charges against four naval officers, including Adm. Massera, on November 24, 1983, just two weeks before Alfonsín was slated to take office (case no. 761, p. 152). The decree was ultimately not effective, as Argentina's congress revoked the military's self-amnesty law.

34. National Chamber of Criminal and Correctional Appeals, "E.S.M.A.," case no. 761, p.1108.

35. National Chamber of Criminal and Correctional Appeals, "E.S.M.A.," case no. 761, pp. 1–600.

36. National Chamber of Criminal and Correctional Appeals, "E.S.M.A.," case no. 761, pp. 1113–17.

37. National Chamber of Criminal and Correctional Appeals, "E.S.M.A.," case no. 761, pp. 1113–17.

38. National Chamber of Criminal and Correctional Appeals, "E.S.M.A.," case no. 761, pp. 1143–44.

39. National Chamber of Criminal and Correctional Appeals, "E.S.M.A.," case no. 761, p. 1501.

40. National Chamber of Criminal and Correctional Appeals, "E.S.M.A.," case no. 761, p. 1688.

41. National Chamber of Criminal and Correctional Appeals, "E.S.M.A.," case no. 761, p. 1726.

42. National Chamber of Criminal and Correctional Appeals, "E.S.M.A.," case no. 761, pp. 1501–3.

43. National Chamber of Criminal and Correctional Appeals, "E.S.M.A.," case no. 761, pp. 2217–43.

44. National Chamber of Criminal and Correctional Appeals, "E.S.M.A.," case no. 761, Annex [Anexo] XX, 27.

45. National Chamber of Criminal and Correctional Appeals, "E.S.M.A.," case no. 761, p. 1579.

46. National Chamber of Criminal and Correctional Appeals, "E.S.M.A.," case no. 761, pp. 1588–96.

47. National Chamber of Criminal and Correctional Appeals, "E.S.M.A.," case no. 761, pp. 1597–603.

48. National Chamber of Criminal and Correctional Appeals, "E.S.M.A.," case no. 761, pp. 1655–67.

49. See National Chamber of Criminal and Correctional Appeals, "E.S.M.A.," case no. 761, pp. 1845–46, for the list of the declarations. See National Chamber of Criminal and Correctional Appeals, "E.S.M.A.," case no. 761, pp. 1588–738, for the transcript of the declarations.

50. National Chamber of Criminal and Correctional Appeals, "E.S.M.A.," case no. 761, pp. 1870–974.

51. National Chamber of Criminal and Correctional Appeals, "E.S.M.A.," case no. 761, pp. 1898–902.

52. National Chamber of Criminal and Correctional Appeals, "E.S.M.A.," case no. 761, pp. 1932–52.

53. National Chamber of Criminal and Correctional Appeals, "E.S.M.A.," case no. 761, pp. 1932–52.

54. National Chamber of Criminal and Correctional Appeals, "E.S.M.A.," case no. 761, pp. 1953–63.

55. National Chamber of Criminal and Correctional Appeals, "E.S.M.A.," case no. 761, pp. 2062–65.

56. National Chamber of Criminal and Correctional Appeals, "E.S.M.A.," case no. 761, pp. 2083–84. How were the answers so consistent? By accident, Néstor Savio disclosed that he had received a secret set of instructions issued by the navy high command for officers summoned to testify in court. These "Guidelines for Exposition for the Honorable Commanders"—marked "Confidential"—read like a script of the officers' testimonies in military court. (Years later, both Antonio Pernías and Adolfo Donda, two of the ESMA's most notorious officers, complained bitterly that they had been coached to deny what

happened in the ESMA on the promise that silence would help promote a "political solution" to the trials negotiated by the naval top brass.)

57. National Chamber of Criminal and Correctional Appeals, "E.S.M.A.," case no. 761, file [Legajo] 121, 82–85.

58. Testimony of Jorge Pinedo, Federal Oral Tribunal Number 5, *ESMA II*, case no. 1.270, January 27, 2011.

59. It was no accident that these two men decided to speak, as both had been sidelined from the navy, owing in large part to the fact that they spearheaded the navy's attempt (on behalf of Admiral Massera) to "recuperate" a series of prisoners, which in retrospect only guaranteed that there would be several dozen survivors who could pin responsibility on the naval officers responsible for the conduct of the GT 3.3/2.

60. National Chamber of Criminal and Correctional Appeals, "E.S.M.A.," case no. 761, pp. 2261–84.

61. National Chamber of Criminal and Correctional Appeals, "E.S.M.A.," case no. 761, pp. 2355–56.

62. National Chamber of Criminal and Correctional Appeals, "E.S.M.A.," case no. 761, pp. 2398–2415, 2461–2553.

63. National Chamber of Criminal and Correctional Appeals, "E.S.M.A.," case no. 761, pp. 2555–58.

64. National Chamber of Criminal and Correctional Appeals, "E.S.M.A.," case no. 761, p. 1560.

65. National Chamber of Criminal and Correctional Appeals, "E.S.M.A.," case no. 761, pp. 2686 et seq.

66. See Nino, *Radical Evil on Trial*, 87.

67. "Bid for a Coup Fails, Argentine Leader Says," *Los Angeles Times*, October 31, 1985.

68. "Argentina Ousts Commander of Restive Base," *Los Angeles Times*, May 28, 1986.

69. Méndez, *Truth and Partial Justice in Argentina*, 64–88.

70. National Chamber of Criminal and Correctional Appeals, "E.S.M.A.," case no. 761, pp. 2619–60.

71. "Rights Groups in Argentina File Charges," *Washington Post*, January 9, 1987. See also Nino, *Radical Evil on Trial*, 94–95.

72. National Chamber of Criminal and Correctional Appeals, "E.S.M.A.," case no. 761, pp. 2866–68.

73. National Chamber of Criminal and Correctional Appeals, "E.S.M.A.," case no. 761, pp. 3137–3237.

74. National Chamber of Criminal and Correctional Appeals, "E.S.M.A.," case no. 761, pp. 3415–16.

75. National Chamber of Criminal and Correctional Appeals, "E.S.M.A.," case no. 761, pp. 3447.

76. National Chamber of Criminal and Correctional Appeals, "E.S.M.A.," case no. 761, pp. 4574.

77. National Chamber of Criminal and Correctional Appeals, "E.S.M.A.," case no. 761, pp. 3656–93, 3705–6. Raúl Enrique Scheller, who was on vacation in Uruguay while the

court questioned other officers on February 27, 1987, was questioned and put in preventive detention upon his return (National Chamber of Criminal and Correctional Appeals, "E.S.M.A.," case no. 761, pp. 3765–66). Carlos Carela was also questioned and placed in preventive detention on March 11, 1987 (National Chamber of Criminal and Correctional Appeals, "E.S.M.A.," case no. 761, pp. 3789–91).

78. National Chamber of Criminal and Correctional Appeals, "E.S.M.A.," case no. 761, pp. 3696.

79. National Chamber of Criminal and Correctional Appeals, "E.S.M.A.," case no. 761, pp. 3996, 4020–21, 4090–4147.

80. Acuña and Smulovitz, "Militares en la transición Argentina," 62–63; Nino, *Radical Evil on Trial*, 95–98.

81. Nino, *Radical Evil on Trial*, 95–98.

82. Nino, *Radical Evil on Trial*, 98–99.

83. Nino, *Radical Evil on Trial*, 101–2. See also Andersen, *Dossier Secreto*, 312–14; and Romero, *History of Argentina*, 265–65.

84. *Truth and Partial Justice in Argentina*, 68–70.

85. National Chamber of Criminal and Correctional Appeals, "E.S.M.A.," case no. 761, pp. 4261.

86. *Truth and Partial Justice in Argentina*, 70.

87. National Chamber of Criminal and Correctional Appeals, "E.S.M.A.," case no. 761, pp. 4413–14, 4525–28.

88. National Chamber of Criminal and Correctional Appeals, "E.S.M.A.," case no. 761, pp. 4732–97.

89. Nino, *Radical Evil on Trial*, 102–3; Acuña and Smulovitz, "Militares en la transición Argentina," 65–76; Lewis, *Guerrillas and Generals*, 226–28.

90. Nino, *Radical Evil on Trial*, 103; Romero, *History of Argentina*, 273–83.

91. Nino, *Radical Evil on Trial*, 103; Romero, *History of Argentina*, 273–83.

92. Nino, *Radical Evil on Trial*, 103; Romero, *History of Argentina*, 273–83.

93. Nino, *Radical Evil on Trial*, 103–4; Romero, *History of Argentina*, 284–96; Lewis, *Guerrillas and Generals*, 232–37; Andersen, *Dossier Secreto*, 314–18; Novaro, *Argentina en el fin*, 251–321.

94. Nino, *Radical Evil on Trial*, 103–4; Romero, *History of Argentina*, 284–96; Lewis, *Guerrillas and Generals*, 232–37; Andersen, *Dossier Secreto*, 314–18; Novaro, *Argentina en el fin*, 251–321.

95. Inter-American Commission on Human Rights, *Report No. 28/92*, October 2, 1992, https://www.cidh.oas.org/annualrep/92eng/argentina10.147.htm.

96. Verbitsky, *Flight*. See also Feitlowitz, *Lexicon of Terror*, 193–256, on the "Scilingo effect."

97. Declaration of Jorge Radice, National Chamber of Criminal and Correctional Appeals, "E.S.M.A.," case no. 761, February 26, 1998.

98. Testimony of Jorge Radice, National Chamber of Criminal and Correctional Appeals, "E.S.M.A.," case no. 761 February 26, 1998.

99. Alejandra Dandan, "El Lavada de dinero que hizo la dictadura con su botín," *Página/12* (Buenos Aires), February 17, 2014.

100. "Detienen a Videla en un caso por robo de bebés," *Clarín* (Buenos Aires), June 10, 1998; Carlos Ares, "Detenido el ex almirante Massera, acusado del robo de recién nacidos," *El País* (Madrid), November 24, 1998.

101. Ferguson, "Unending War."

102. Ferguson, "Unending War."

103. Ferguson, "Unending War." See also Uki Goñi, "Menem Bows Out of Race for Top Job," *Guardian*, May 15, 2003.

104. "Néstor Kirchner: El hombre de la hora," *La Nación* (Buenos Aires), May 18, 2003.

105. José Claudio Escribano, "Treinta y seis horas de un carnaval decadente," *La Nación* (Buenos Aires), May 15, 2003.

106. "Néstor Kirchner: El hombre de la hora," *La Nación* (Buenos Aires), May 18, 2003.

107. See, e.g., Horacio Verbitsky, "Aberraciones," *Página/12* (Buenos Aires), May 12, 2003.

108. "El Texto completo del discurso presidencial," *La Nación* (Buenos Aires), May 25, 2003.

109. Adriana Meyer, "Estela Carlotto, con Beliz y Duhalde," *Página/12* (Buenos Aires), June 3, 2003.

110. Santiago Rodriguez, "No todos son lo mismo, como habíamos creído," *Página/12* (Buenos Aires), June 4, 2003.

111. Martín Granovsky, "No me interesa estar por estar," *Página/12* (Buenos Aires), June 5, 2003. See also "Confronting Argentina's Past," *New York Times*, June 22, 2003.

112. Fernando Cibeira and Irina Hauser, "Habría que juzgarlos a todos en Argentina," *Página/12* (Buenos Aires), July 31, 2003.

113. Eduardo Tagliaferro and Felipe Yapur, "Una votación con gusto a justiciar," *Página/12* (Buenos Aires), August 13, 2003; Eduardo Tagliaferro, "La noche de los aplausos," *Página/12* (Buenos Aires), August 22, 2003.

114. Daniel Gallo, "Sacaron los cuadros de Videla y Bignone," *La Nación* (Buenos Aires), March 25, 2004, http://www.lanacion.com.ar/585683-sacaron-los-cuadros-de-videla-y-bignone.

115. Casa Rosada, "Palabras del presidente de la nación, Doctor Néstor Kirchner, en el acto de firma del convenio de la creación del Museo de la Memoria y para la promoción y defensa de los derechos humanos," Casa Rosada, March 24, 2004, https://www.casarosada.gob.ar/informacion/archivo/24549-blank-79665064.

116. "Las Madres de la plaza lloran a Néstor Kirchner common uno de sus hijos," Redacción Rosario, October 27, 2010, https://redaccionrosario.com/2010/10/27/10095/.

117. Beatriz Sarlo, interview with the author, August 11, 2010.

118. Daniel Rafecas, interview with the author, August 2, 2007.

119. Daniel Rafecas, interview with the author, August 2, 2007.

120. Daniel Rafecas, interview with the author, August 2, 2007.

121. Gabriel Cavallo, interview with the author, August 12, 2007.

122. Federico Delgado, interview with the author, August 15, 2007.

123. Pablo Parenti, interview with the author, July 24, 2007.

124. Graciela Fernández Meijide, interview with the author, June 5, 2008.

6. The Brutality of the ESMA

1. Testimony of Martín Gras, Federal Oral Tribunal Number 5, *ESMA II*, case no. 1.270, August 18, 2010.

2. Testimony of Martín Gras, Federal Oral Tribunal Number 5, *ESMA II*, case no. 1.270, August 18, 2010.

3. Closing Statement of the Prosecution, Federal Oral Tribunal Number 5, *ESMA II*, case no. 1.270, June 15, 2011.

4. Testimony of Martín Gras, Federal Oral Tribunal Number 5, *ESMA II*, case no. 1.270, August 18, 2010.

5. Testimony of Silvia Labayrú, Federal Oral Tribunal Number 5, *ESMA II*, case no. 1.270, June 9, 2010.

6. Testimony of Martín Gras, Federal Oral Tribunal Number 5, *ESMA II*, case no. 1.270, August 18, 2010.

7. Testimony of Jaime Dri, Federal Oral Tribunal Number 5, *ESMA II*, case no. 1.270, December 16, 2010.

8. Testimony of Carlos Muñoz, Federal Oral Tribunal Number 5, *ESMA II*, case no. 1.270, April 28, 2010.

9. Testimony of Arturo Barros, Federal Oral Tribunal Number 5, *ESMA II*, case no. 1.270, November 4, 2010.

10. Testimony of Ana María Martí, Federal Oral Tribunal Number 5, *ESMA II*, case no. 1.270, June 25, 2010.

11. Testimony of Martín Gras, Federal Oral Tribunal Number 5, *ESMA II*, case no. 1.270, August 18, 2010.

12. Testimony of Ana María Martí, Federal Oral Tribunal Number 5, *ESMA II*, case no. 1.270, June 25, 2010.

13. Testimony of Silvia Labayrú, Federal Oral Tribunal Number 5, *ESMA II*, case no. 1.270, June 9, 2010.

14. Testimony of Fernando Kron, Federal Oral Tribunal Number 5, *ESMA II*, case no. 1.270, August 27, 2010.

15. Testimony of Mario Villani, Federal Oral Tribunal Number 5, *ESMA II*, case no. 1.270, June 22, 2010.

16. Testimony of Miguel Lauletta, Federal Oral Tribunal Number 5, *ESMA II*, case no. 1.270, November 5, 2010.

17. Testimony of Lisandro Raúl Cubas, Federal Oral Tribunal Number 5, *ESMA II*, case no. 1.270, July 30, 2010.

18. Testimony of Marta Álvarez, Federal Oral Tribunal Number 5, *ESMA II*, case no. 1.270, August 6, 2010.

19. Testimony of Martín Gras, Federal Oral Tribunal Number 5, *ESMA II*, case no. 1.270, August 18, 2010.

20. Testimony of Martín Gras, Federal Oral Tribunal Number 5, *ESMA II*, case no. 1.270, August 18, 2010.

21. Verbitsky, *Flight*, 49.

22. Plan de Capacidades, COAR no. 1"S"/75, 8 ("Misión").

23. Testimony of Martín Gras, Federal Oral Tribunal Number 5, ESMA *II*, case no. 1.270, August 18, 2010.

24. Massera, *El camino*, 17–18.

25. Testimony of Andrés Castillo, Federal Oral Tribunal Number 5, ESMA *II*, case no. 1.270, July 8, 2010.

26. Testimony of Jorge Eduardo Acosta, National Chamber of Criminal and Correctional Appeals, "E.S.M.A.," case no. 761, pp. 1905–10.

27. Testimony of Jorge Eduardo Acosta, National Chamber of Criminal and Correctional Appeals, "E.S.M.A.," case no. 761, pp. 1905–10.

28. Testimony of Jorge Eduardo Acosta, National Chamber of Criminal and Correctional Appeals, "E.S.M.A.," case no. 761, p. 1908.

29. Testimony of Marta Álvarez, Federal Oral Tribunal Number 5, ESMA *II*, case no. 1.270, August 6, 2010.

30. Testimony of Marta Álvarez, Federal Oral Tribunal Number 5, ESMA *II*, case no. 1.270, August 6, 2010.

31. Testimony of Jorge Eduardo Acosta, National Chamber of Criminal and Correctional Appeals, "E.S.M.A.," case no. 761, p. 1908.

32. Testimony of Jorge Eduardo Acosta, National Chamber of Criminal and Correctional Appeals, "E.S.M.A.," case no. 761, p. 1908.

33. Testimony of Juan Gasparini, Federal Oral Tribunal Number 5, ESMA *II*, case no. 1.270, September 20, 2010.

34. Testimony of Juan Gasparini, Federal Oral Tribunal Number 5, ESMA *II*, case no. 1.270, September 20, 2010.

35. Testimony of Jaime Dri, Federal Oral Tribunal Number 5, ESMA *II*, case no. 1.270, December 16, 2010.

36. Testimony of Jorge Eduardo Acosta, National Chamber of Criminal and Correctional Appeals, "E.S.M.A.," case no. 761, pp. 1905–12.

37. Testimony of Graciela García, Federal Oral Tribunal Number 5, ESMA *II*, case no. 1.270, August 6, 2010.

38. Testimony of Martín Gras, Federal Oral Tribunal Number 5, ESMA *II*, case no. 1.270, August 18, 2010.

39. Testimony of Miguel Lauletta, Federal Oral Tribunal Number 5, ESMA *II*, case no. 1.270, November 5, 2010.

40. Testimony of Lisandro Raúl Cubas, Federal Oral Tribunal Number 5, ESMA *II*, case no. 1.270, July 30, 2010.

41. Testimony of Miguel Lauletta, Federal Oral Tribunal Number 5, ESMA *II*, case no. 1.270, November 5, 2010.

42. Testimony of Alberto Girondo, Federal Oral Tribunal Number 5, ESMA *II*, case no. 1.270, July 1, 2010.

43. Testimony of Graciela García, Federal Oral Tribunal Number 5, ESMA *II*, case no. 1.270, August 6, 2010.

44. Testimony of Miriam Lewin, Federal Oral Tribunal Number 5, ESMA *II*, case no. 1.270, July 15, 2010.

45. Testimony of Graciela Daleo, Federal Oral Tribunal Number 5, *ESMA II*, case no. 1.270, April 29, 2010.

46. Testimony of Nilda Noemí Actis Goretta, Federal Oral Tribunal Number 5, *ESMA II*, case no. 1.270, May 7, 2010.

47. Testimony of Miriam Lewin, Federal Oral Tribunal Number 5, *ESMA II*, case no. 1.270, July 15, 2010.

48. Testimony of Martín Gras, Federal Oral Tribunal Number 5, *ESMA II*, case no. 1.270, August 18, 2010.

49. Testimony of Martín Gras, Federal Oral Tribunal Number 5, *ESMA II*, case no. 1.270, August 18, 2010.

50. Testimony of Ana María Martí, Federal Oral Tribunal Number 5, *ESMA II*, case no. 1.270, June 25, 2010.

51. Testimony of Nilda Noemí Actis Goretta, Federal Oral Tribunal Number 5, *ESMA II*, case no. 1.270, May 7, 2010.

52. Testimony of Andrés Ramón Castillo, Federal Oral Tribunal Number 5, *ESMA II*, case no. 1.270, July 8, 2010.

53. Testimony of Martín Gras, Federal Oral Tribunal Number 5, *ESMA II*, case no. 1.270, August 18, 2010.

54. Testimony of María Eva Bernst de Hansen, Federal Oral Tribunal Number 5, *ESMA II*, case no. 1.270, May 13, 2010.

55. Testimony of María Eva Bernst de Hansen, Federal Oral Tribunal Number 5, *ESMA II*, case no. 1.270, May 13, 2010.

56. Testimony of Juan Gasparini, Federal Oral Tribunal Number 5, *ESMA II*, case no. 1.270, September 20, 2010.

57. Testimony of Lisandro Raúl Cubas, Federal Oral Tribunal Number 5, *ESMA II*, case no. 1.270, July 30, 2010.

58. Testimony of Victor Fatala, Federal Oral Tribunal Number 5, *ESMA II*, case no. 1.270, May 20, 2010.

59. Testimony of Ana María Martí, Federal Oral Tribunal Number 5, *ESMA II*, case no. 1.270, June 25, 2010.

7. Rodolfo Walsh

1. Testimony of Jorge Eduardo Acosta, Federal Oral Tribunal Number 5, *ESMA II*, case no. 1.270, March 17, 2010.

2. Testimony of Martín Gras, Federal Oral Tribunal Number 5, *ESMA II*, case no. 1.270, August 18, 2010.

3. Testimony of Lilia Ferreyra, Federal Oral Tribunal Number 5, *ESMA II*, case no. 1.270, June 4, 2010.

4. Testimony of Lilia Ferreyra, Federal Oral Tribunal Number 5, *ESMA II*, case no. 1.270, June 4, 2010. See also Testimony of Jorge Pinedo, Federal Oral Tribunal Number 5, *ESMA II*, case no. 1.270, January 27, 2011.

5. Testimony of Roberto Gonzalez, National Chamber of Criminal and Correctional Appeals, "E.S.M.A.," case no. 761, March 4, 1998.

6. Juzgado Nacional en lo Criminal y Correccional Federal Numero 12 [National Federal Criminal and Correctional Court number 12], *Megacausa* ESMA, case no. 14.217/03, 14445.

7. Testimony of Miguel Lauletta, Federal Oral Tribunal Number 5, *ESMA II*, case no. 1.270, November 5, 2010.

8. Testimony of Miguel Lauletta, Federal Oral Tribunal Number 5, *ESMA II*, case no. 1.270, November 5, 2010.

9. Testimony of Juan Gasparini, Federal Oral Tribunal Number 5, *ESMA II*, case no. 1.270, September 20, 2010.

10. Testimony of Lisandro Raúl Cubas, Federal Oral Tribunal Number 5, *ESMA II*, case no. 1.270, July 30, 2010.

11. Testimony of Ricardo Héctor Coquet, Federal Oral Tribunal Number 5, *ESMA II*, case no. 1.270, August 5, 2010; Testimony of Miguel Lauletta, Federal Oral Tribunal Number 5, *ESMA II*, case no. 1.270, November 5, 2010.

12. Testimony of Ricardo Héctor Coquet, Federal Oral Tribunal Number 5, *ESMA II*, case no. 1.270, August 5, 2010; Testimony of Miguel Lauletta, Federal Oral Tribunal Number 5, *ESMA II*, case no. 1.270, November 5, 2010.

8. The Santa Cruz Raid

1. See, e.g., Testimony of Aída Bogo de Sardi, Federal Oral Tribunal Number 5, *ESMA II*, case no. 1.270, November 12, 2010; Testimony of María del Rosario Carballeda de Cerruti, Federal Oral Tribunal Number 5, *ESMA II*, case no. 1.270, October 11, 2010; Testimony of Ana María Careaga, Federal Oral Tribunal Number 5, *ESMA II*, case no. 1.270, April 28, 2010; Testimony of Nélida Fiordeliza de Chidichimo, Federal Oral Tribunal Number 5, *ESMA II*, case no. 1.270, April 22, 2010; Testimony of Cecilia De Vicenti, Federal Oral Tribunal Number 5, *ESMA II*, case no. 1.270, November 25, 2010.

2. Testimony of María del Rosario Carballeda de Cerruti, Federal Oral Tribunal Number 5, *ESMA II*, case no. 1.270, October 11, 2010.

3. Testimony of Cecilia De Vicenti, Federal Oral Tribunal Number 5, *ESMA II*, case no. 1.270, November 25, 2010.

4. Testimony of María del Rosario Carballeda de Cerruti, Federal Oral Tribunal Number 5, *ESMA II*, case no. 1.270, October 11, 2010.

5. Testimony of Cecilia De Vicenti, Federal Oral Tribunal Number 5, *ESMA II*, case no. 1.270, November 25, 2010.

6. Testimony of Gabrielle Domon, Federal Oral Tribunal Number 5, *ESMA II*, case no. 1.270, April 15, 2010.

7. Testimony of Ruth Chonchol, Federal Oral Tribunal Number 5, *ESMA II*, case no. 1.270, June 24, 2010.

8. Testimony of Cecilia Vázquez de Lutsky, Federal Oral Tribunal Number 5, *ESMA II*, case no. 1.270, June 9, 2010.

9. Testimony of Uki Goñi, Federal Oral Tribunal Number 5, *ESMA II*, case no. 1.270, February 11, 2011; Testimony of María del Rosario Carballeda de Cerruti, Federal Oral Tribunal Number 5, *ESMA II*, case no. 1.270, October 11, 2010; Testimony of Ana María Careaga, Federal Oral Tribunal Number 5, *ESMA II*, case no. 1.270, April 28, 2010.

10. Testimony of Uki Goñi, Federal Oral Tribunal Number 5, *ESMA II*, case no. 1.270, February 11, 2011.

11. Testimony of Nélida Fiordeliza de Chidichimo, Federal Oral Tribunal Number 5, *ESMA II*, case no. 1.270, April 22, 2010; Testimony of Cecilia De Vicenti, Federal Oral Tribunal Number 5, *ESMA II*, case no. 1.270, November 25, 2010.

12. Testimony of Nélida Fiordeliza de Chidichimo, Federal Oral Tribunal Number 5, *ESMA II*, case no. 1.270, April 22, 2010.

13. Testimony of María del Rosario Carballeda de Cerruti, Federal Oral Tribunal Number 5, *ESMA II*, case no. 1.270, October 11, 2010.

14. Testimony of Cecilia Vázquez de Lutsky, Federal Oral Tribunal Number 5, *ESMA II*, case no. 1.270, June 9, 2010.

15. Testimony of Roxana Salomone, Federal Oral Tribunal Number 5, *ESMA II*, case no. 1.270, October 13, 2010.

16. Testimony of Eustaquio Galeano, Federal Oral Tribunal Number 5, *ESMA II*, case no. 1.270, September 17, 2010; Testimony of Silvia Labayrú, Federal Oral Tribunal Number 5, *ESMA II*, case no. 1.270, June 9, 2010; Testimony of Uki Goñi, Federal Oral Tribunal Number 5, *ESMA II*, case no. 1.270, February 11, 2011.

17. Testimony of Uki Goñi, Federal Oral Tribunal Number 5, *ESMA II*, case no. 1.270, February 11, 2011.

18. Testimony of María del Rosario Carballeda de Cerruti, Federal Oral Tribunal Number 5, *ESMA II*, case no. 1.270, October 11, 2010.

19. Testimony of Silvia Labayrú, Federal Oral Tribunal Number 5, *ESMA II*, case no. 1.270, June 9, 2010.

20. Testimony of Silvia Labayrú, Federal Oral Tribunal Number 5, *ESMA II*, case no. 1.270, June 9, 2010.

21. Testimony of Ana María Martí, Federal Oral Tribunal Number 5, *ESMA II*, case no. 1.270, June 25, 2010.

22. Testimony of Graciela Daleo, Federal Oral Tribunal Number 5, *ESMA II*, case no. 1.270, April 29, 2010.

23. Testimony of Silvia Labayrú, Federal Oral Tribunal Number 5, *ESMA II*, case no. 1.270, June 9, 2010.

24. Testimony of Andrés Ramón Castillo, Federal Oral Tribunal Number 5, *ESMA II*, case no. 1.270, July 8, 2010.

25. Testimony of Juan Gasparini, Federal Oral Tribunal Number 5, *ESMA II*, case no. 1.270, September 20, 2010.

26. Testimony of Ricardo Coquet, Federal Oral Tribunal Number 5, *ESMA II*, case no. 1.270, August 5, 2010.

27. Testimony of Silvia Labayrú, Federal Oral Tribunal Number 5, *ESMA II*, case no. 1.270, June 9, 2010.

28. Testimony of Ricardo Coquet, Federal Oral Tribunal Number 5, *ESMA II*, case no. 1.270, August 5, 2010.

29. Testimony of Luis Fondebrider, Federal Oral Tribunal Number 5, *ESMA II*, case no. 1.270, December 10, 2012.

30. Testimony of Silvia Labayrú, Federal Oral Tribunal Number 5, *ESMA II*, case no. 1.270, June 9, 2010.

31. Testimony of Roxana Salomone, Federal Oral Tribunal Number 5, *ESMA II*, case no. 1.270, October 13, 2010.

32. Testimony of Juan Gasparini, Federal Oral Tribunal Number 5, *ESMA II*, case no. 1.270, September 20, 2010.

33. Testimony of Carlos García, Federal Oral Tribunal Number 5, *ESMA II*, case no. 1.270, May 28, 2010; Testimony of Ricardo Coquet, Federal Oral Tribunal Number 5, *ESMA II*, case no. 1.270, August 5, 2010.

34. Testimony of Silvia Labayrú, Federal Oral Tribunal Number 5, *ESMA II*, case no. 1.270, June 9, 2010.

35. Testimony of Ana María Martí, Federal Oral Tribunal Number 5, *ESMA II*, case no. 1.270, June 25, 2010.

36. Testimony of Miguel Lauletta, Federal Oral Tribunal Number 5, *ESMA II*, case no. 1.270, November 5, 2010.

37. Testimony of Miguel Lauletta, Federal Oral Tribunal Number 5, *ESMA II*, case no. 1.270, November 5, 2010.

38. Testimony of Alberto Girondo, Federal Oral Tribunal Number 5, *ESMA II*, case no. 1.270, July 1, 2010.

9. Between Memory, Truth, and Justice

1. Levi, *Drowned and the Saved*, 13–24.

2. Anonymous, interview with the author, November 17, 2009.

3. Testimony of Ana María Martí, Federal Oral Tribunal Number 5, *ESMA II*, case no. 1.270, June 25, 2010.

4. Closing Statement of the Prosecution, Federal Oral Tribunal Number 5, *ESMA II*, case no. 1.270, June 15, 2011.

5. Closing Statement of the Prosecution, Federal Oral Tribunal Number 5, *ESMA II*, case no. 1.270, June 16, 2011.

6. Closing Statement of the Prosecution, Federal Oral Tribunal Number 5, *ESMA II*, case no. 1.270, June 15, 2011.

7. Anonymous, interview with the author, March 16, 2010.

8. Beatriz Sarlo, interview with the author, August 11, 2010.

9. Graciela Fernández Meijide, interview with the author, September 23, 2009.

10. Interview with the author, April 23, 2012.

11. Anonymous, interview with the author, April 23, 2012.

12. Horacio Verbitsky, interview with the author, July 28, 2010.

13. Hugo Vezzetti, interview with the author, May 7, 2012.

10. The Jesuits

1. Testimony of Orlando Yorio, Federal Court number 4, "Lorusso," case no. 4.333, June 14, 1984; CONADEP File 6328 (Orlando Yorio); Testimony of María Elena Funes, Federal Court number 4, "Lorusso," case no. 4.333, November 5, 1984.

2. Testimony of Orlando Yorio, Federal Court number 4, "Lorusso," case no. 4.333, June 14, 1984; Orlando Yorio, letter to Father Moura, November 24, 1977 (on file with author and available at https://www.academia.edu/7891150/Carta_del_Padre_Yorio_al_Padre_Maura_de_la_Compañ%C3%ADa_de_Jesús_sobre_sus_conflictos_con_el_superior_Jorge_Bergoglio_de_1977); Testimony of Jorge Mario Bergoglio, Federal Oral Tribunal Number 5, *ESMA II*, case no. 1.270, November 8, 2010.

3. Father Juan Carlos Scannone, interview with the author, April 25, 2013; Father Ignacio Pérez del Viso, interview with the author, April 10, 2013.

4. See, e.g., Yorio, "El acontecimiento argentino"; Yorio, "Dios y los valores humanos"; and Yorio, "Reflexión crítica."

5. Testimony of Orlando Yorio, Federal Court number 4, "Lorusso," case no. 4.333, June 14, 1984; CONADEP File 6328 (Orlando Yorio).

6. Testimony of Rodolfo Yorio, Federal Oral Tribunal Number 5, *ESMA II*, case no. 1.270, February 18, 2011.

7. CONADEP File 6328 (Orlando Yorio).

8. Father Enrique Rastellini, interview with the author, August 23, 2013.

9. See generally Marchak and Marchak, *God's Assassins*; Di Stefano and Zanatta, *Historia de la Iglesia Argentina*, 418–545; Morello, *Catholic Church*; Mallimaci, *El mito de la Argentina*; Burdick, *For God and the Fatherland*, 45–215; Klaiber, *Church, Dictatorship and Democracy*, 66–91; Verbitsky, *Vigilia de armas*; and Verbitsky, *La mano izquierda*.

10. Testimony of Orlando Yorio, Federal Court number 4, "Lorusso," case no. 4.333, June 14, 1984; CONADEP File 6328 (Orlando Yorio).

11. See, e.g., Horacio Verbitsky, "La llaga abierta," *Página/12* (Buenos Aires), May 8, 1999, 12–13; Horacio Verbitsky, "Con el mazo dando," *Página/12* (Buenos Aires), April 25, 1999; and Verbitsky, *El silencio*, 101–11.

12. Yorio, letter to Father Moura; Testimony of Jorge Mario Bergoglio, Federal Oral Tribunal Number 5, *ESMA II*, case no. 1.270, November 8, 2010.

13. Verbitsky, *El silencio*, 105.

14. Testimony of Jorge Mario Bergoglio, Federal Oral Tribunal Number 5, *ESMA II*, case no. 1.270, November 8, 2010; Jorge Mario Bergoglio, letter to Federal Oral Tribunal Number 5, *ESMA II*, case no. 1.270, November 26, 2010, p. 5204.

15. Verbitsky, *El silencio*, 102–4.

16. Testimony of Orlando Yorio, Federal Court number 4, "Lorusso," case no. 4.333, June 14, 1984.

17. Mignone, *Iglesia y dictadura*, 158.

18. Verbitsky, "La llaga abierta," 12–13; Verbitsky, "Con el mazo dando."

19. Jalics, *Ejercicios de contemplación*, 159–60.

20. Emilio Mignone, memorandum of November 7, 1990, "Minuta" (on file with author).

21. Daniel Wakin, "Vatican Rejects Claims of Pope's Ties to Dirty War," *New York Times*, March 15, 2013; Nick Miroff, "Pope's Role in Dirty War under Scrutiny," *Washington Post*, March 15, 2013.

22. Jonathan Watts, "Pope Francis Did Not Denounce Me to Argentinian Junta, Says Priest," *Guardian*, March 20, 2013.

23. Horacio Verbitsky, "Bergoglio tiene la última palabra," *Cohete a la luna* (Buenos Aires), February 14, 2021.

24. Verbitsky, “La llaga abierta,” 12–13; Verbitsky, “Con el mazo dando.”

25. Ambrogetti and Rubin, *El Jesuita*. It was later rereleased under the title *Pope Francis: His Life in His Own Words; Conversations with Jorge Bergoglio*.

26. Ambrogetti and Rubin, *Pope Francis*, 200.

27. Elisabetta Piqué, “‘Cuentan conmigo,’ dijo el Papa a Carlotto y Cabandié,” *La Nación* (Buenos Aires), April 24, 2013.

28. Testimony of Emilio Mignone, National Chamber of Criminal and Correctional Appeals, case no. 13/84, hearing transcript, p. 5411 et seq.

29. Bob Cox, interview with the author, March 14, 2013.

30. Verbitsky, *La mano izquierda*, 15–16; Mignone, *Iglesia y dictadura*, 24–25.

31. “Declaraciones del monseñor Tortolo,” *La Opinión* (Buenos Aires), March 26, 1976, 7. See also “Posicíon de la Iglesia ante el Nuevo Gobierno,” *La Nación* (Buenos Aires), March 25, 1976, 5.

32. “Ceremonia del juramento,” *La Prensa* (Buenos Aires), March 30, 1976, 1.

33. Reato, *Disposición final*, 254.

34. Marchak and Marchak, *God's Assassins*, 236.

35. Conferencia Episcopal Argentina, “Carta Pastoral de la Conferencia Episcopal Argentina,” May 15, 1976, https://episcopado.org/assetsweb/documentos/11/1976-CartaPastoral_116.doc.

36. Memorandum of a conversation among Pio Laghi, Charles Bray, and Wayne Smith, December 10, 1976, https://foia.state.gov/Search/Results.aspx?searchText=(*)%20AND%20(pio%20bray)&collection=ARGENTINA.

37. Memorandum of a conversation among Pio Laghi, Patricia Derian, Fernando Rondon, and Robert Steven, March 29, 1977, https://foia.state.gov/Search/Results.aspx?searchText=(*)%20AND%20(laghi)&collection=ARGENTINA.

38. Frontalini and Caiati, *El mito*, 24.

39. “Bussi explicó para que se combate en Tucumán,” *La Opinión* (Buenos Aires), May 12, 1976, 8.

40. Ferguson, “Unending War.”

41. Conferencia Episcopal Argentina, *Documentos del episcopado Argentino*, 310.

42. Reato, *Disposición final*, 252–53.

43. Dri, *La hegemonía*, 50.

44. “‘Los obispos salvaron vidas,’ dijo Juan Pablo II,” *La Nación* (Buenos Aires), April 13, 1987, 14.

45. Jorge Mario Bergoglio, “Homilía del Sr. Arzobispo en la Solemnidad de Corpus Christi,” Arzobispado de Buenos Aires, June 9, 2007, https://www.arzbaires.org.ar/inicio/homilias/homilias2007.htm#Corpus_Christi.

46. Loris Zanatta, interview with the author, March 22, 2013.

47. “Solemne apertura del Concilio Vaticano II,” Vatican.va, October 11, 1962, http://www.vatican.va/content/john-xxiii/es/speeches/1962/documents/hf_j-xxiii_spe_19621011_opening-council.html.

48. “II Conferencia General del Episcopado Latinoamericano: Documentos finales de Medellín” (September 1968), Consejo Episcopal Latinoamericano y Caribeño, accessed November 10, 2022, https://www.celam.org/documentos/Documento_Conclusivo_Medellin.pdf.

49. "II Conferencia General del Episcopado Latinoamericano: Documentos finales de Medellín" (September 1968), Consejo Episcopal Latinoamericano y Caribeño, accessed November 10, 2022, https://www.celam.org/documentos/Documento_Conclusivo_Medellin.pdf.

50. Conferencia Episcopal Argentina, *Documentos del episcopado Argentino*, 68.

51. Conferencia Episcopal Argentina, *Documentos del episcopado Argentino*, 80.

52. Conferencia Episcopal Argentina, *Documentos del episcopado Argentino*, 85.

53. Conferencia Episcopal Argentina, *Documentos del episcopado Argentino*, 76.

54. Bresci, *Movimiento de sacerdotes*, 35.

55. Bresci, *Movimiento de sacerdotes*, 71–74.

56. Conferencia Episcopal Argentina, *Documentos del episcopado Argentino*, 102.

57. Gillespie, *Soldiers of Perón*, 46–47, 52–60.

58. Sacheri, *La Iglesia clandestina*, 8.

59. Sacheri, *La Iglesia clandestina*, 12.

60. Sacheri, *La Iglesia clandestina*, 13.

61. Sacheri, *La Iglesia clandestina*, 33.

62. Bresci, *Movimiento de sacerdotes*, 175. ("European and North American imperialism brought a liberalism that impregnated our intellectual formation; as such when popular movements . . . that expressed the pueblo—which is profoundly antiliberal—wanted to express themselves intellectually they did so within the liberal scheme." The priests saw that a "charismatic union with the leader" protected the pueblo from the "tremendous enemies like imperialism and the oligarchy." The priests saw "two great realities: army and oligarchy on one side and the Peronist movement on the other; the latter with its two pressure points: union organizations and armed organizations. We also see one great fact: the presence of Perón and the expectant and attentive masses.")

63. Gera, *Teología de la liberación*, document 10-11, pp. 17 18.

64. Bresci, *Movimiento de sacerdotes*, 177.

65. Testimony of Emilio Mignone, Federal Court number 4, "Lorusso," case no. 4.333, March 31, 1977.

66. *Texto completo de la sentencia*, 701–4.

67. Testimony of Orlando Yorio, Federal Court number 4, "Lorusso," case no. 4.333, June 14, 1984; CONADEP File 6328 (Orlando Yorio).

68. July 8, 1985, Testimony of Francisco Jalics via Exhorto Diplomático, National Chamber of Criminal and Correctional Appeals, case no. 13/84, pp. 12411–28.

69. Testimony of María Elena Funes, Federal Court number 4, "Lorusso," case no. 4.333; Testimony of Silvia Guiard, Federal Oral Tribunal Number 5, *ESMA II*, case no. 1.270, February 18, 2011.

70. Testimony of Olga Villar, Federal Court number 4, "Lorusso," case no. 4.333, November 5, 1984; Testimony of Silvia Guiard, Federal Court number 4, "Lorusso," case no. 4.333, September 25, 1984; Testimony of Orlando Yorio, Federal Court number 4, "Lorusso," case no. 4.333, June 14, 1984; CONADEP File 6328 (Orlando Yorio); Testimony of María Elena Funes, Federal Oral Tribunal Number 5, *ESMA II*, case no. 1.270, September 23, 2010.

71. Testimony of María Elena Funes, Federal Oral Tribunal Number 5, *ESMA II*, case no. 1.270, September 23, 2010.

72. Testimony of Silvia Guiard, Federal Court number 4, "Lorusso," case no. 4.333, September 25, 1984; Testimony of María Elena Funes, Federal Court number 4, "Lorusso," case no. 4.333, November 5, 1984.

73. CONADEP File 6328 (Orlando Yorio).

74. Testimony of Orlando Yorio, Federal Court number 4, "Lorusso," case no. 4.333, June 14, 1984; CONADEP File 6328 (Orlando Yorio).

75. CONADEP File 6328 (Orlando Yorio).

76. July 8, 1985, Testimony of Francisco Jalics via Exhorto Diplomático, National Chamber of Criminal and Correctional Appeals, case no. 13/84, pp. 12411–28.

77. *Texto completo de la sentencia*, 701–4.

78. Testimony of Orlando Yorio, Federal Court number 4, "Lorusso," case no. 4.333, June 14, 1984; CONADEP File 6328 (Orlando Yorio).

79. Testimony of Orlando Yorio, Federal Court number 4, "Lorusso," case no. 4.333, August 23, 1983.

80. July 8, 1985, Testimony of Francisco Jalics via Exhorto Diplomático, National Chamber of Criminal and Correctional Appeals, case no. 13/84, pp. 12411–28.

81. CONADEP File 6328 (Orlando Yorio).

82. Testimony of Orlando Yorio, Federal Court number 4, "Lorusso," case no. 4.333, June 14, 1984; CONADEP File 6328 (Orlando Yorio); Testimony of Orlando Yorio, Federal Court number 4, "Lorusso," case no. 4.333, August 23, 1983.

83. CONADEP File 6328 (Orlando Yorio).

84. Testimony of Orlando Yorio, Federal Court number 4, "Lorusso," case no. 4.333, August 23, 1983.

85. Testimony of Orlando Yorio, Federal Court number 4, "Lorusso," case no. 4.333, August 23, 1983.

86. Testimony of Orlando Yorio, Federal Court number 4, "Lorusso," case no. 4.333, June 14, 1984.

87. CONADEP File 6328 (Orlando Yorio).

88. Testimony of Orlando Yorio, National Chamber of Criminal and Correctional Appeals, case no. 13/84, hearing transcript, p. 5445 et seq.

89. Testimony of Orlando Yorio, Federal Court number 4, "Lorusso," case no. 4.333, August 23, 1983.

90. CONADEP File 6328 (Orlando Yorio).

91. Testimony of Orlando Yorio, Federal Court number 4, "Lorusso," case no. 4.333, August 23, 1983.

92. Testimony of Orlando Yorio, National Chamber of Criminal and Correctional Appeals, case no. 13/84, hearing transcript, p. 5445 et seq.; Testimony of Orlando Yorio, Federal Court number 4, "Lorusso," case no. 4.333, August 23, 1983.

93. CONADEP File 6328 (Orlando Yorio).

94. CONADEP File 6328 (Orlando Yorio).

95. July 8, 1985, Testimony of Francisco Jalics via Exhorto Diplomático, National Chamber of Criminal and Correctional Appeals, case no. 13/84, pp. 12411–28.

96. Jalics, *Ejercicios de contemplación*, 159–60.

97. Testimony of Orlando Yorio, Federal Court number 4, "Lorusso," case no. 4.333, June 14, 1984.

98. CONADEP File 6328 (Orlando Yorio).

99. CONADEP File 6328 (Orlando Yorio).

100. Testimony of Orlando Yorio, National Chamber of Criminal and Correctional Appeals, case no. 13/84, hearing transcript, p. 5445 et seq.

101. Testimony of Orlando Yorio, National Chamber of Criminal and Correctional Appeals, case no. 13/84, hearing transcript, p. 5445 et seq.

102. Ambrogetti and Rubin, *Pope Francis*, 46.

103. Antonio Spadaro, "A Big Heart Open to God: An Interview with Pope Francis," *America Magazine*, September 30, 2013.

104. Father Juan Carlos Scannone, interview with the author, April 14, 2013; Father Ignacio Pérez del Viso, interviews with the author, April 10 and 16, 2013; Father Ignacio García Mata, interview with the author, April 24, 2013; José María Poirier, interview with the author, March 18, 2013; Father Miguel Petty, interview with the author, April 23, 2013. See also Ivereigh, *Great Reformer*, 83–124.

105. Father Ignacio García Mata, interview with the author, April 23, 2013.

106. Father Pérez del Viso, interview with the author, April 10, 2013.

107. Jorge Scuro, interview with the author, April 25, 2013.

108. Centro de Investigación y Acción Social, *Algunas orentaciones*, 18.

109. Centro de Investigación y Acción Social, *Algunas orentaciones*, 10–11.

110. Centro de Investigación y Acción Social, *Algunas orentaciones*, 7–10.

111. Centro de Investigación y Acción Social, *Algunas orentaciones*, 17–20.

112. See generally Ivereigh, *Great Reformer*, 155–210; and Tóibín, "Bergoglio Smile."

113. Yorio, "Reflexión crítica," 131–72.

114. Testimony of Jorge Mario Bergoglio, Federal Oral Tribunal Number 5, ESMA *II*, case no. 1.270, November 8, 2010.

115. Poirier, interview with the author, March 18, 2013.

116. Spadaro, "Big Heart Open to God."

117. Father Pérez del Viso, interview with the author, April 10, 2013.

118. Yorio, letter to Father Moura.

119. Testimony of Jorge Mario Bergoglio, Federal Oral Tribunal Number 5, ESMA *II*, case no. 1.270, November 8, 2010.

120. Yorio, letter to Father Moura.

121. Testimony of Jorge Mario Bergoglio, Federal Oral Tribunal Number 5, ESMA *II*, case no. 1.270, November 8, 2010.

122. Testimony of Jorge Mario Bergoglio, Federal Oral Tribunal Number 5, ESMA *II*, case no. 1.270, November 8, 2010.

123. Testimony of Jorge Mario Bergoglio, Federal Oral Tribunal Number 5, ESMA *II*, case no. 1.270, November 8, 2010.

124. Yorio, letter to Father Moura.

125. Yorio, letter to Father Moura.

126. Yorio, letter to Father Moura.

127. Testimony of Jorge Mario Bergoglio, Federal Oral Tribunal Number 5, *ESMA II*, case no. 1.270, November 8, 2010.

128. Testimony of Jorge Mario Bergoglio, Federal Oral Tribunal Number 5, *ESMA II*, case no. 1.270, November 8, 2010.

129. Yorio, letter to Father Moura.

130. Testimony of Jorge Mario Bergoglio, Federal Oral Tribunal Number 5, *ESMA II*, case no. 1.270, November 8, 2010.

131. Testimony of Jorge Mario Bergoglio, Federal Oral Tribunal Number 5, *ESMA II*, case no. 1.270, November 8, 2010.

132. Testimony of Jorge Mario Bergoglio, Federal Oral Tribunal Number 5, *ESMA II*, case no. 1.270, November 8, 2010.

133. Testimony of Jorge Mario Bergoglio, Federal Oral Tribunal Number 5, *ESMA II*, case no. 1.270, November 8, 2010.

134. Testimony of Jorge Mario Bergoglio, Federal Oral Tribunal Number 5, *ESMA II*, case no. 1.270, November 8, 2010; Jorge Mario Bergoglio, November 26, 2010, letter to Federal Oral Tribunal Number 5, Federal Oral Tribunal Number 5, *ESMA II*, case no. 1.270, p. 5204.

135. Yorio, letter to Father Moura.

136. Testimony of Jorge Mario Bergoglio, Federal Oral Tribunal Number 5, *ESMA II*, case no. 1.270, November 8, 2010.

137. Testimony of Jorge Mario Bergoglio, Federal Oral Tribunal Number 5, *ESMA II*, case no. 1.270, November 8, 2010.

138. Testimony of Jorge Vernazza, Federal Court number 4, "Lorusso," case no. 4.333, August 21, 1984; Testimony of Rodolfo Ricciardelli, Federal Court number 4, "Lorusso," case no. 4.333, August 24, 1984.

139. Testimony of Gabriel Bossini, Federal Oral Tribunal Number 5, *ESMA II*, case no. 1.270, October 14, 2010; Father Gabriel Bossini, interview with the author, April 23, 2013.

140. Testimony of Emilio Mignone, Federal Court number 4, "Lorusso," case no. 4.333, March 31, 1977.

141. Testimony of Jorge Mario Bergoglio, Federal Oral Tribunal Number 5, *ESMA II*, case no. 1.270, November 8, 2010.

142. Testimony of Jorge Mario Bergoglio, Federal Oral Tribunal Number 5, *ESMA II*, case no. 1.270, November 8, 2010.

143. Father Victor Zorzín, interview with the author, April 23, 2013.

144. Yorio, letter to Father Moura.

145. Testimony of Jorge Mario Bergoglio, Federal Oral Tribunal Number 5, *ESMA II*, case no. 1.270, November 8, 2010.

146. Graciela and Rodolfo Yorio, interview with the author, April 9, 2013.

147. Rodolfo Yorio, interview with the author, April 23, 2013.

148. Testimony of Rodolfo Yorio, Federal Oral Tribunal Number 5, *ESMA II*, case no. 1.270, February 18, 2011.

149. Silvia Guiard, interview with the author, April 29, 2013.

150. Verbitsky, *El silencio*, 101–11.

151. Testimony of Jorge Mario Bergoglio, Federal Oral Tribunal Number 5, *ESMA II*, case no. 1.270, November 8, 2010.

152. Father Pérez del Viso, interview with the author, April 16, 2013.

153. Father Pérez del Viso, interview with the author, April 16, 2013.

154. Father García Mata, interview with the author, April 23, 2013.

155. Scuro, interview with the author, April 25, 2013.

156. Father Petty, interview with the author, April 23, 2013.

157. Father Petty, interview with the author, April 23, 2013.

158. Father Petty, interview with the author, April 23, 2013.

159. Father Petty, interview with the author, April 23, 2013.

160. As reprinted by "J. L. Caravias SJ: Bergoglio fue noble conmigo y me ayudó a escaper de una muerte cierta," Religión Digital, April 17, 2013, https://www.religiondigital.org/amistad_europea_universitaria/JL-Caravias-SJ-Bergoglio-conmigo_7_1456424359.html.

161. Father J. L. Caravias, interview with the author, July 19, 2013.

162. Father Pérez del Viso, interview with the author, April 16, 2013.

163. Father Petty, interview with the author, April 23, 2013.

164. Federico Finchelstein, interview with the author, April 2, 2013.

165. Jorge Mario Bergoglio, "Homilía del Sr. Arzobispo en la Solemnidad de Corpus Christi," June 9, 2007, https://www.arzbaires.org.ar/inicio/homilias/homilias2007.htm#Corpus_Christi.

166. Bergoglio and Skorka, *Sobre el cielo*.

167. Ambrogetti and Rubin, *Pope Francis*, 186–91.

168. Marcos Novaro, interview with the author, April 24, 2013.

11. Closing Arguments and Verdict

1. Closing Argument of Myriam Bregman, Federal Oral Tribunal Number 5, *ESMA II*, case no. 1.270, May 19, 2011; Closing Argument of Luis Zamora, Federal Oral Tribunal Number 5, *ESMA II*, case no. 1.270, May 13, 2011.

2. Closing Argument of Guillermo Coronel, Federal Oral Tribunal Number 5, *ESMA II*, case no. 1.270, July 14, 2011.

3. Closing Argument of Alfredo Solari, Federal Oral Tribunal Number 5, *ESMA II*, case no. 1.270, September 9, 2011.

4. Final Sentence, Federal Oral Tribunal Number 5, *ESMA II*, case no. 1.270, December 30, 2011, pp. 359–67.

Epilogue

1. Letter from Ricardo Miguel Cavallo to the author, January 28, 2010.

2. Letter from Ricardo Miguel Cavallo to the author, February 2, 2010.

3. Ernesto Weber, author visit to house, May 1, 2012.

BIBLIOGRAPHY

Actis, Munú, Cristina Aldini, Liliana Gardella, Miriam Lewin, and Elisa Tokar. *That Inferno: Conversations of Five Women Survivors of an Argentine Torture Camp*. Translated by Gretta Siebentritt. Nashville TN: Vanderbilt University Press, 2006.

Acuña, Carlos H., Inés González Bombal, Elizabeth Jelin, Oscar Landi, Luis Alberto Quevedo, Catalina Smulovitz, and Adriana Vacchieri, eds. *Juicio, Castigos y Memorias: Derechos humanos y justicia en la política Argentina*. Buenos Aires: Nueva Visión, 1995.

Agosti, Héctor P. *Mirar hacía adelante: Proyecto político para la unidad*. Buenos Aires: Sudamericana/Planeta, 1983.

Alfonsín, Raúl. *Memoria política: Transición a la democracia y derechos humanos*. Buenos Aires: Fondo de Cultura Económica de Argentina, 2004.

Alfonsín, Raúl, and Pablo Giussani. *¿Por qué, Doctor Alfonsín?* Buenos Aires: Sudamericana/Planeta, 1987.

Altamirano, Carlos. *Peronismo y cultura de izquierda*. Buenos Aires: Siglo XXI Editores, 2011.

Ambrogetti, Francesca, and Sergio Rubin. *El Jesuita: Conversaciones con Jorge Mario Bergoglio*. Buenos Aires: Vergara, 2010.

———. *Pope Francis: His Life in His Own Words; Conversations with Jorge Bergoglio*. Translated by Laura Dial Literary Agency Inc. New York: G. P. Putnam's Sons, 2013.

Amorín, José. *Montoneros: La buena historia*. Buenos Aires: Catálogos, 2005.

Andersen, Martin E. *Dossier Secreto: Argentina's Desaparecidos and the Myth of the "Dirty War."* Boulder CO: Westview, 1993.

Anderson, Jon L. *Che Guevara: A Revolutionary Life*. London: Bantam, 2010.

Andreozzi, Gabriele, Horacio Verbitsky, Marcos Novaro, and Bruno Nápoli. *Juicios por crímenes de lesa humanidad en Argentina*. Buenos Aires: Atuel, 2011.

Anguita, Eduardo, and Martín Caparrós. *La voluntad: Una historia de la militancia revolucionaria en la Argentina*. Vol. 1, *1966–1969*. Buenos Aires: Booket, 2011.

———. *La voluntad: Una historia de la militancia revolucionaria en la Argentina*. Vol. 2, *1969–1973*. Buenos Aires: Booket, 2011.

———. *La voluntad: Una historia de la militancia revolucionaria en la Argentina*. Vol. 3, *1973–1974*. Buenos Aires: Booket, 2011.

———. *La voluntad: Una historia de la militancia revolucionaria en la Argentina*. Vol. 4, *1974–1976*. Buenos Aires: Booket, 2011.

———. *La voluntad: Una historia de la militancia revolucionaria en la Argentina*. Vol. 5, *1976–1978*. Buenos Aires: Booket, 2011.

Arendt, Hannah. *Eichmann in Jerusalem: A Report on the Banality of Evil*. London: Penguin, 2007.

Arosa, Ramón A. *De constitución a retiro: Reseña y reflexiones del jefe de la armada 1984–1989*. Buenos Aires: Instituto de Publicaciones Navales del Centro Naval, 2008.

Asociación Madres de Plaza de Mayo. *Historia de las madres de plaza de mayo*. Buenos Aires: Asociación Madres de Plaza de Mayo, 1995.

———. *Massera, el genocida*. Buenos Aires: Página/12, 1999.

Association of the Bar of the City of New York. *Report of the Mission of Lawyers to Argentina, April 1–7, 1979*. New York: Association of the Bar of the City of New York, 1979.

Balza, Martín A. *Dejo constancia: Memorias de un general Argentino*. Buenos Aires: Grupo Editorial Planeta, 2001.

Bárbaro, Julio. *Juicio a los 70: La historia que yo viví*. Buenos Aires: Editorial Sudamericana, 2009.

Barragán, Carlos. *Soy la mierda oficialista*. Buenos Aires: Grupo Editorial Norma, 2011.

Baschetti, Roberto. *Documentos, 1970–1973: De la guerrilla Peronista al gobierno popular*. La Plata, Buenos Aires: Editorial de la Campana, 1995.

———. *Documentos, 1973–1976*. Vol. 1, *De Cámpora a la ruptura*. La Plata, Buenos Aires: Editorial de la Campana, 1999.

———. *Documentos, 1973–1976*. Vol. 2, *De la ruptura al golpe*. La Plata, Buenos Aires: Editorial de la Campana, 1999.

———. *Documentos, 1976–1977*. Vol. 1, *Golpe militar y resistencia popular*. La Plata, Buenos Aires: Editorial de la Campana, 2001.

———. *Documentos, 1976–1977*. Vol. 2, *"Resistir es vencer."* La Plata, Buenos Aires: Editorial de la Campana, 2011.

———. *Documentos de la resistencia Peronista, 1955–1970*. Vol. 1. La Plata, Buenos Aires: Editorial de la Campana, 2012.

———. *Documentos de la resistencia Peronista, 1955–1970*. Vol. 2. La Plata, Buenos Aires: Editorial de la Campana, 2012.

Bass, Gary J. *Stay the Hand of Vengeance: The Politics of War Crimes Tribunals*. Princeton NJ: Princeton University Press, 2000.

Beaufre, André. *La guerra revolucionaria: Las nuevas formas de la guerra*. Buenos Aires: Editorial Almena, 1979.

Berçaitz, Miguel A. *La guerra sucia: La obediencia debida*. Buenos Aires: self-published, 1985.

Bergoglio, Jorge M. *Mente abierta, corazón creyente*. Buenos Aires: Editorial Claretiana, 2013.

Bergoglio, Jorge M., and Abraham Skorka. *Sobre el cielo y la tierra*. Buenos Aires: Sudamericana, 2011. Kindle.

Blaustein, Eduardo, and Martín Zubieta. *Decíamos ayer: La prensa Argentina bajo el proceso*. Buenos Aires: Colihue, 2006.

Bohoslavsky, Juan P., and Marcelo Alegre. *¿Usted también, doctor? Complicidad de jueces, fiscales y abogados durante la dictadura*. Buenos Aires: Siglo Veintiuno, 2015.

Bonasso, Miguel. *Lo que no dije en recuerdo de la muerte*. Buenos Aires: Sudamericana, 2014.

———. *Recuerdo de la muerte*. Buenos Aires: Bruguera, 1984.

Braslavsky, Guido. *Enemigos íntimos: Los militares y Kirchner; De la purga a los juicios, crónica de una confrontación (2003–2008)*. Buenos Aires: Editorial Sudamericana, 2009.

Brennan, James P. *Argentina's Missing Bones: Revisiting the History of the Dirty War*. Berkeley: University of California Press, 2018.

Bresci, Domingo A. *Movimiento de sacerdotes para el tercer mundo: Documentos para la memória histórica*. Buenos Aires: Centro Salesiano de Estudios San Juan Bosco, 1994.

Bufano, Sergio. *Harpías y Nereidas: Pasiones y muertes en los setenta*. Buenos Aires: Losada, 2007.

Bufano, Sergio, and Israel Lotersztain. *Evita Montonera: Edición completa de la revista oficial de Montoneros, 1974–1979*. Buenos Aires: Ejercitar la Memoria, 2010.

Burdick, Michael A. *For God and the Fatherland: Religion and Politics in Argentina*. Albany: State University of New York Press, 1995.

Cafiero, Antonio F. *Desde que grité ¡viva Perón!* Buenos Aires: Pequén Ediciones, 1983.

Cahill, Thomas. *Pope John XXIII*. New York: Viking, 2002.

Calveiro, Pilar. *Poder y desaparición: Los campos de concentración en Argentina*. Buenos Aires: Colihue, 2006.

Camarasa, Jorge A. *El verdugo: Astiz, un soldado del terrorismo de estado*. Buenos Aires: Planeta, 2009.

Camarasa, Jorge A., Rubén Felice, and Daniel González. *El juicio: Proceso al horror*. Buenos Aires: Sudamericana/Planeta, 1985.

Cámpora, Héctor J. *La revolución Peronista*. Buenos Aires: Editorial Universitaria de Buenos Aires, 1973.

Camps, Ramón J. A. *Caso Timerman: Punto final*. Buenos Aires: Tribuna Abierta, 1982.

Cárdenas, Emilio, Javier V. Leguizamón, and Carlos A. Manfroni. *El terrorismo como crimen de lesa humanidad: Reflexiones sobre la impunidad en la Argentina, compendio*. Buenos Aires: Edivern, 2009.

Cassese, Antonio. *International Criminal Law*. Oxford: Oxford University Press, 2008.

Centro de Estudios Legales y Sociales. *Dechos humanos en Argentina: Informe annual enero–diciembre 1998*. Buenos Aires: Centro de Estudios Legales y Sociales, 1999.

Centro de Investigación y Acción Social. *Algunas orentaciones de la compañia de Jesus*. Buenos Aires: CIAS, 1975.

Ciancaglini, Sergio, and Martín Granovsky. *Nada más que la verdad: El juicio a Las Juntas*. Buenos Aires: Planeta, 1995.

Comisión Nacional sobre la Desparición de Personas. *Nunca más: Informe de la comisión nacional sobre la desparación de personas*. 8th ed. Buenos Aires: Editorial Eudeba, 2006.

Conferencia Episcopal Argentina. *Documentos del episcopado Argentino, 1965–1981: Colección completa del magisterio postconciliar de la conferencia episcopal Argentina*. Buenos Aires: Clarentiana, 1982.

———. *La Iglesia y los derechos humanos*. Buenos Aires: Conferencia Episcopal Argentina, 1984.

Cooke, John W. *Correspondencia Perón-Cooke*. Vol. 2. Compiled by Eduardo L. Duhalde. Buenos Aires: Colihue, 2007.

———. *La lucha por la liberación nacional: El retorno de Perón*. Buenos Aires: Granica, 1973.

Crenzel, Emilio, Diego Born, Carla Guastamacchia, and Claudia Feld. *Los desaparecidos en la Argentina: Memorias, representaciones e ideas, 1983–2008*. Buenos Aires: Editorial Biblos, 2010.

Curia, Walter. *El último Peronista: La cara oculta de Kirchner*. Buenos Aires: Sudamericana, 2006.

del Carril, Mario. *La vida de Emilio Mignone: Justicia, Catolicismo y derechos humanos*. Buenos Aires: Emecé, 2011.

Díaz Bessone, Ramón Genaro. *Guerra revolucionaria en la Argentina, 1959–1978*. Argentina: Editorial Fraterna, 1986.

———. *Testimonio de una década*. Buenos Aires: Círculo Militar, 1996.

Di Marco, Laura. *La Cámpora: Historia secreta de los herederos de Néstor y Cristina Kirchner*. Buenos Aires: Sudamericana, 2012.

Di Stefano, Roberto, and Loris Zanatta. *Historia de la Iglesia Argentina: Desde la conquista hasta fines del siglo XX*. Buenos Aires: Editorial Sudamericana, 2009.

Di Tella, Guido. *Perón-Perón, 1973–1976*. Buenos Aires: Hyspamérica, 1986.

Donda, Victoria, and Magda Bogin. *My Name Is Victoria: The Extraordinary Story of One Woman's Struggle to Reclaim Her True Identity*. New York: Other Press, 2011.

Douglas, Lawrence. *The Memory of Judgment: Making Law and History in the Trials of the Holocaust*. New Haven CT: Yale University Press, 2001.

Dri, Rubén R. *La hegemonía de los cruzados: La Iglesia Católica y la dictadura militar*. Buenos Aires: Biblos, 2011.

Elias, Jose Sebastian. "Constitutional Changes, Transitional Justice, and Legitimacy: The Life and Death of Argentina's 'Amnesty' Laws." *Hastings International and Comparative Law Review* 31, no. 2 (2008): 587.

Eliaschev, Pepe. *Los hombres del juicio: Por primera vez los jueces y el fiscal que condenaron a los ex comandantes cuentan la historia íntima del acontecimiento que cambió a la Argentina para siempre*. Buenos Aires: Sudamericana, 2011.

Equipo Argentino de Antropología Forense. *Latin American Initiative for the Identification of the Disappeared: Genetics and Human Rights / Iniciativa Latinoamericano para la identificación de desaparecidos: Genética y derechos humanos*. Buenos Aires: EAAF, 2008.

———. *2006 Annual Report*. Buenos Aires: EAAF, 2006.

Escobar, Raúl T. *Estrategia contrarrevolucionaria*. Buenos Aires: Editorial F. I., 1984.

Feierstein, Daniel. *Juicios: Sobre la elaboración del genocidio II*. Buenos Aires: Fondo de Cultura Económica de Argentina, 2015.

Feinmann, José P. *Peronismo: Filosofía política de una persistencia Argentina*. Vol. 1. Buenos Aires: Planeta, 2011.

———. *Peronismo: Filosofía política de una persistencia Argentina*. Vol. 2. Buenos Aires: Planeta, 2011.

Feitlowitz, Marguerite. *A Lexicon of Terror: Argentina and the Legacies of Torture*. Rev. ed. Oxford: Oxford University Press, 2011.

Fernández Meijide, Graciela. *La historia íntima de los derechos humanos en la Argentina: (A Pablo)*. Buenos Aires: Editorial Sudamericana, 2009.

Fernández Meijide, Graciela, and Héctor Leis. *El diálogo: El encuentro que cambió nuestra visión sobre la década del 70*. Buenos Aires: Sudamericana, 2015.

Finchelstein, Federico. *The Ideological Origins of the Dirty War: Fascism, Populism, and Dictatorship in Twentieth Century Argentina*. Oxford: Oxford University Press, 2014.

Florit, Carlos A. *Las fuerzas armadas y la guerra psicológica*. Buenos Aires: Editorial Arayú, 1963.

Franco, Marina. *Un enemigo para la nación*. Buenos Aires: Fondo de Cultura Economica, 2013.

Frasch, Carlos A. *Espíritu militar*. Buenos Aires: Instituto de Publicaciones Navales del Centro Naval, 1999.

Frontalini, Daniel, and María C. Caiati. *El mito de la "guerra sucia."* Buenos Aires: Centro de Estudios Legales y Sociales, 1984.

Gasparini, Juan. *Manuscrito de un desaparecido en la ESMA, el libro de Jorge Caffatti: Del asalto al policlínico bancario por Tacuara, a las FAP y el secuestro del jefe de la fiat en París*. Buenos Aires: Grupo Editorial Norma, 2006.

———. *Montoneros: Final de cuentas*. Buenos Aires: Puntosur Editorial, 1988.

Gera, Lucio. *Teología de la liberación*. Lima: Servicio de Documentacion, Movimiento Internacional de Estudiantes Catolicos / Juventud Estudantil Catolica Internacional, 1972.

Gillespie, Richard. *Soldiers of Perón: Argentina's Montoneros*. Oxford: Clarendon Press, 1982.

Giussani, Pablo. *Los días de Alfonsín*. Buenos Aires: Editorial Legasa, 1986.

———. *Montoneros: La Soberbia Armada*. Buenos Aires: Editorial Sudamericana, 2011.

Goñi, Uki. *Judas: La verdadera historia de Alfredo Astiz, el infiltrado*. Buenos Aires: Editorial Sudamericana, 1996.

———. *The Real Odessa: How Perón Brought the Nazi War Criminals to Argentina*. London: Granta, 2009.

Gonzalez, Breard E. *La guerrilla en Tucumán: Una historia no escrita*. Buenos Aires: Círculo Militar, 2001.

Gorbato, Viviana. *Montoneros: Soldados de Menem, ¿soldados de Duhalde?* Buenos Aires: Sudamericana, 1999.

Graham-Yooll, Andrew. *A State of Fear: Memories of Argentina's Nightmare*. London: Eland, 2009.

Granillo, Fernández A. *La paz Comunista*. Buenos Aires: Círculo Militar, 1970.

Grecco, Jorge, and Gustavo González. *¡Felices Pascuas! Los hechos inéditos de la rebelión militar, la crisis de Semana Santa, el germen de Monte Caseros*. Buenos Aires: Grupo Editorial Planeta, 1988.

Guest, Iain. *Behind the Disappearances: Argentina's Dirty War against Human Rights and the United Nations*. Philadelphia: University of Pennsylvania Press, 1990.

Guevara, Ernesto. *Guerrilla Warfare*. Melbourne: Ocean, 2006.

Guillermoprieto, Alma. *The Heart That Bleeds: Latin America Now*. New York: Knopf, 1994.

Gunther, John. *Inside Latin America*. New York: Harper & Brothers, 1941.

Hilb, Claudia. *Usos del pasado: Qué hacemos hoy con los setenta*. Buenos Aires: Siglo Veintiuno, 2013.

Hilb, Claudia, and Daniel Lutzky. *La nueva izquierda Argentina, 1960–1980: Política y violencia*. Buenos Aires: Centro Editor de América Latina, 1984.

Hilb, Claudia, Lucas G. Martin, and Philippe-Joseph Salazar. *Lesa humanidad: Argentina y Sudáfrica; Reflexiones después del mal.* Madrid: Katz, 2015.

Himitian, Evangelina. *Francisco: El papa de la gente.* Doral FL: Aguilar, 2013.

Hodges, Donald C. *Argentina's "Dirty War": An Intellectual Biography.* Austin: University of Texas Press, 1991.

Ivereigh, Austen. *The Great Reformer: Francis and the Making of a Radical Pope.* New York: Henry Holt, 2014.

Jalics, Francisco. *Ejercicios de contemplación: Introducción a la vida contemplativa . . . a invocación de Jesús.* Buenos Aires: San Pablo, 1995.

Jassen, Raúl, Carlos Ruiz, and Eduardo Marsillach. *Seineldin: El ejército traicionado, la patria vencida.* Buenos Aires: Editorial Verum et Militia, 1990.

Jaunarena, Horacio. *La casa está en orden: Memoria de la transición.* Buenos Aires: Taeda, 2011.

Jordán, Alberto R. *El proceso: 1976/1983.* Buenos Aires: Emecé Editores, 1993.

Joyce, Christopher, and Eric Stover. *Witnesses from the Grave: The Stories Bones Tell.* Boston: Little, Brown, 1991.

Klaiber, Jeffrey L. *The Church, Dictatorships, and Democracy in Latin America.* Eugene OR: Wipf & Stock, 2009.

Kohl, James, and John Litt. *Urban Guerrilla Warfare in Latin America.* Cambridge MA: MIT Press, 1974.

Lanusse, Lucas. *Montoneros: El mito de sus 12 fundadores.* Buenos Aires: Zeta, 2010.

Larraquy, Marcelo. *De Perón a Montoneros: Historia de la violencia política en la Argentina: Marcados a fuego II (1945–1973).* Buenos Aires: Aguilar, Alfaguara, Altea, Taurus, 2010.

———. *Fuimos soldados: Historia secreta de la contraofensiva Montonera.* Buenos Aires: Aguilar, 2006.

Larraquy, Marcelo, and Roberto Caballero. *Galimberti: De Perón a Susana, de Montoneros a la CIA.* Buenos Aires: Grupo Editorial Norma, 2000.

Levenson, Gregorio. *De los Bolcheviques a la Gesta Montonera: Memorias De nuestro siglo.* Buenos Aires: Colihue, 2000.

Levi, Primo. *The Drowned and the Saved.* Translated by Raymond Rosenthal. New York: Simon & Schuster, 2017.

Lewin, Miriam. *Skyvan: Aviones, pilotos y archivos secretos.* Buenos Aires: Sudamericana, 2017.

Lewis, Paul H. *Guerrillas and Generals: The "Dirty War" in Argentina.* Westport CT: Praeger, 2002.

Lipstadt, Deborah E. *The Eichmann Trial.* New York: Schocken, 2011.

Longoni, Ana. *Traiciones: La figura del traidor en los relatos acerca de los sobrevivientes de la represión.* Buenos Aires: Grupo Editorial Norma, 2007.

Lorenzetti, Ricardo L., and Alfredo J. Kraut. *Derechos humanos: Justicia y reparación; la experiencia de los juicios en la Argentina; crímenes de lesa humanidad.* Buenos Aires: Sudamericana, 2011.

Lotersztain, Gabriela. *Los judíos bajo el terror: Argentina 1976–1983.* Buenos Aires: Ejercitar la Memoria Editores, 2008.

Lúder, Ítalo. *El proceso Argentino.* Buenos Aires: Corregidor, 1977.

Luna, Félix. *Golpes militares y salidas electorales.* Buenos Aires: Editorial Sudamericana, 1983.

MacAdam, Andrew, and Viktor Sukup. *Raúl Alfonsín: La democracia a pesar de todo.* Buenos Aires: Corregidor, 2009.

Malamud Goti, Jaime. *Game without End: State Terror and the Politics of Justice*. Norman: University of Oklahoma Press, 1996.

Mallimaci, Fortunato. *El mito de la Argentina laica: Catolicismo, política y estado*. Buenos Aires: Capital Intelectual, 2015.

Manfroni, Carlos A. *Montoneros: Soldados de Massera; La verdad sobre la contraofensiva Montonera y la logia que diseñó los 70*. Buenos Aires: Editorial Sudamericana, 2012.

Marchak, M. Patricia, and William Marchak. *God's Assassins: State Terrorism in Argentina in the 1970s*. Montreal: McGill-Queen's University Press, 1999.

Márquez, Nicolás. *La otra parte de la verdad: La respuesta a los que han ocultado y deformado la verdad histórica sobre la década del '70 y el terrorismo*. Buenos Aires: N. Márquez, 2004.

Martínez, Tomás E. *The Perón Novel*. Translated by Helen R. Lane. New York: Vintage International, 1998.

Masetti, Jorge R. *Los que luchan y los que lloran*. Montevideo: Puntosur, 1987.

Massera, Emilio E. *El camino a la democracia*. Caracas: El Cid Editor, 1979.

McCaughan, Michael. *True Crimes: Rodolfo Walsh, The Life and Times of a Radical Intellectual*. London: Latin America Bureau, 2002.

Méndez, Eugenio B. *Confesiones de un Montonero: La otra cara de la historia*. Buenos Aires: Sudamericana/Planeta, 1986.

Méndez, Juan. *Truth and Partial Justice in Argentina (An Americas Watch Report)*. New York: Americas Watch Committee, August 1987.

Menéndez, Luciano B. *Así piensa Luciano Benjamín Menéndez*. Buenos Aires: Nemont Ediciones, 1981.

Mignone, Emilio. *Iglesia y dictadura: El papel de la Iglesia a la luz de sus relaciones con el régimen militar*. Buenos Aires: Colihue, 2006.

Minow, Martha. *Between Vengeance and Forgiveness*. Boston: Beacon, 1998.

Mochkofsky, Graciela. *Pecado original: Clarín, los Kirchner y la lucha por el poder*. Buenos Aires: Planeta, 2011.

Montero, Hugo, and Ignacio Portela. *Rodolfo Walsh: Los años Montoneros*. Buenos Aires: Peña Lillo, 2010.

Morello, Gustavo. *The Catholic Church and Argentina's Dirty War*. Oxford: Oxford University Press, 2015.

Moreno Ocampo, Luis. *Cuando el poder perdió el juicio: Cómo explicar el "proceso" a nuestros hijos*. Buenos Aires: Editorial Planeta Argentina, 1996.

Naipaul, V. S. *The Return to Eva Peron, with the Killings in Trinidad*. New York: Knopf, 1980.

Nelída, Bossio S., María R. Martínez, and Cecilia Piñeiro. *Patrimonio: Centros clandestinos de detención, tortura y exterminio y sitios de memoria*. Buenos Aires: Instituto Espacio para la Memoria, 2008.

Nino, Carlos S. *Radical Evil on Trial*. New Haven CT: Yale University Press, 1996.

Novaro, Marcos. *Argentina en el fin de siglo: Democracia, mercado y nación (1983–2001)*. Buenos Aires: Paidós, 2009.

Novaro, Marcos, and Vicente Palermo. *La dictadura militar, 1976–1983: Del golpe de estado a la restauración democrática*. Buenos Aires: Paidós, 2011.

O'Donnell, Guillermo A. *Modernization and Bureaucratic-Authoritarianism: Studies in South American Politics*. Berkeley: University of California Press, 1979.

O'Donnell, Santiago, and Mariano Melamed. *Derechos humanos®: La historia del CELS: De Mignone a Verbitsky, de Videla a Cristina*. Buenos Aires: Sudamericana, 2015.

Osiel, Mark. *Making Sense of Mass Atrocity*. Cambridge: Cambridge University Press, 2011.

———. *Mass Atrocity, Collective Memory, and the Law*. New Brunswick NJ: Transaction, 2000.

———. *Mass Atrocity, Ordinary Evil, and Hannah Arendt: Criminal Consciousness in Argentina's Dirty War*. New Haven CT: Yale University Press, 2002.

———. *Obeying Orders: Atrocity, Military Discipline and the Law of War*. New Brunswick NJ: Transaction, 2005.

Page, Joseph A. *Perón, a Biography*. New York: Random House, 1983.

Perdía, Roberto C. *Montoneros: El Peronismo combatiente en primera persona*. Buenos Aires: Planeta, 2013.

Perón, Eva. *Evita: In My Own Words*. Translated by Laura Dail. New York: New Press, 2005.

Péron, Juan Domingo. *América Latina ahora o nunca*. Buenos Aires: CS Ediciones, 2005.

———. *Discursos y mensajes del Tte. Gral. Juan D. Perón: enero a marzo 1974*. Buenos Aires: Presidencia de la Nación, Secretaría de Prensa y Difusión, 1975.

———. *Discursos y mensajes del Tte. Gral. Juan D. Perón: octubre a diciembre 1973*. Buenos Aires: Presidencia de la Nación, Secretaría de Prensa y Difusión, 1974.

———. *Doctrina Peronista*. Buenos Aires: CS Ediciones, 1996.

———. *La hora de los pueblos*. Buenos Aires: CS Ediciones, 2005.

———. *Una comunidad organizada y otros discursos académicos*. Buenos Aires: Machacha Guemes, 1973.

Piccirilli, Ricardo, and Leoncio Gianello. *Biografias navales*. Buenos Aires: Secretaria de Estado de Marina, 1963.

Pierron, Yvonne. *Misionera durante la dictadura*. Buenos Aires: Planeta, 2009.

Pigna, Felipe. *Lo pasado pensado: Entrevistas con la historia Argentina (1955–1983)*. Buenos Aires: Planeta, 2012.

Piñero, María T., and Angela Boitano. *Testimonios de la solidaridad internacional: Publicación de las ponencias del seminario realizado como cierre del ciclo anual de reflexión "a 30 años del golpe."* Buenos Aires: Ministerio de Relaciones Exteriores, Comercio Internacional y Culto, 2007.

Poder Ejecutivo Nacional. *El terrorismo en la Argentina*. Buenos Aires: Poder Ejecutivo Nacional, 1979.

Potash, Robert A. *1928–1945: Yrigoyen to Perón*. Stanford CA: Stanford University Press, 1969.

———. *The Army & Politics in Argentina, 1945–1962: Perón to Frondizi*. London: Athlone Press, 1980.

———. *The Army & Politics in Argentina, 1962–1973: From Frondizi's Fall to the Peronist Restoration*. Stanford CA: Stanford University Press, 1996.

Rabossi, Eduardo. *La carta internacional de derechos humanos*. Buenos Aires: EUDEBA, 1987.

Ramus, Susana J. *Sueños sobrevivientes de una Montonera: A pesar de la ESMA*. Buenos Aires: Colihue, 2000.

Reato, Ceferino. *Disposición final: La confesión de Videla sobre los desaparecidos*. Buenos Aires: Sudamericana, 2012.

———. *Operación Traviata: ¿Quién mató a Rucci? La verdadera historia*. Buenos Aires: Sudamericana, 2008.

Riz, Liliana de. *La política en suspenso, 1966–1976*. Buenos Aires: Paidós, 2010.

Robben, Antonius C. G. M. *Political Violence and Trauma in Argentina*. Philadelphia: University of Pennsylvania Press, 2007.

Robles, Adriana. *Perejiles: Los otros Montoneros*. Buenos Aires: Colihue, 2004.

Rock, David. *Argentina, 1516–1987: From Spanish Colonization to Alfonsín*. Berkeley: University of California Press, 1987.

———. *Authoritarian Argentina: The Nationalist Movement, Its History, and Its Impact*. Berkeley: University of California Press, 1995.

Roht-Arriaza, Naomi. *The Pinochet Effect: Transnational Justice in the Age of Human Rights*. Philadelphia: University of Pennsylvania Press, 2005.

Romero, Luis A. *A History of Argentina in the Twentieth Century*. University Park: Pennsylvania State University Press, 2002.

Rosenberg, Tina. *Children of Cain: Violence and the Violent in Latin America*. New York: Penguin, 1992.

Rouquié, Alain. *A la sombra de las dictaduras: La democracia en América Latina*. Buenos Aires: Fondo de cultura económica, 2011.

———. *The Military and the State in Latin America*. Translated by Paul E. Sigmund. Berkeley: University of California Press, 1989.

———. *Poder militar y sociedad política en la Argentina*. Buenos Aires: Emecé Editores, 1982.

Sacheri, Carlos A. *La Iglesia clandestina*. Buenos Aires: Cruzamente, 1970.

Saidon, Gabriela. *La Montonera: Biografía de Norma Arrostito*. Buenos Aires: Editorial Sudamericana, 2011.

Sancinetti, Marcelo A. *Derechos humanos en la Argentina postdictatorial: Juicio a los ex comandantes, punto final, obedencia debida, apéndice documental*. Buenos Aires: Lerner Editores Asociados, 1988.

Santucho, Mario R. *Poder burgués y poder revolucionario*. Buenos Aires: Populibros, 2007.

Sarlo, Beatriz. *La audacia y el cálculo: Kirchner 2003–2010*. Buenos Aires: Sudamericana, 2011.

———. *Tiempo presente: Notas sobre el cambio de una cultura*. Buenos Aires: Siglo XXI Editores, 2010.

Schoklender, Sergio M. *"Esta es mi verdad."* Buenos Aires: Editorial Abril, 1983.

———. *Schoklender: Infierno y resurrección*. Buenos Aires: Colihue, 1995.

Seisdedos, Gabriel. *El honor de Dios: Mártires Palotinos, la historia silenciada de un crimen impune*. Buenos Aires: Ciudad Nueva, 2011.

Seoane, María. *Todo o nada: La historia secreta y pública de Mario Roberto Santucho, el jefe guerrillero de los años setenta*. Buenos Aires: Debosillo, 2011.

Seoane, María, and Vicente Muleiro. *El dictador: La historia secreta y pública de Jorge Rafael Videla*. Buenos Aires: Editorial Sudamericana, 2001.

Shklar, Judith N. *Legalism: Law, Morals, and Political Trials*. Cambridge MA: Harvard University Press, 1986.

Shumway, Nicolas. *The Invention of Argentina*. Berkeley: University of California Press, 1993.

Sigal, Silvia, and Eliseo Verón. *Perón o muerte: Los fundamentos discursivos del fenómeno Peronista*. Buenos Aires: Eudeba, 2004.

Tarcus, Horacio, and Laura Ehrlich. *Diccionario biográfico de la izquierda Argentina: De los anarquistas a la "nueva izquierda"; 1870–1976*. Buenos Aires: Emecé, 2007.

Tarnopolsky, Daniel. *Betina sin aparecer: Historia íntima del caso Tarnopolsky, una familia diezmada por la dictadura militar*. Buenos Aires: Grupo Editorial Norma, 2011.

Taylor, Diana. *Disappearing Acts: Spectacles of Gender and Nationalism in Argentina's "Dirty War."* Durham NC: Duke University Press, 1997.

Teitel, Ruti G. *Transitional Justice*. Oxford: Oxford University Press, 2000.

Timerman, Jacobo. *Prisoner without a Name, Cell without a Number*. Madison: University of Wisconsin Press, 2002.

Tóibín, Colm. "The Bergoglio Smile." *London Review of Books* 43, no. 2 (January 2021).

Touris, Claudia, and Mariela Ceva. *Los avatares de la "nación Católica": Cambios y permanencias en el campo religioso de la Argentina contemporánea*. Buenos Aires: Editorial Biblos, 2012.

Trinquier, Roger. *Modern Warfare: A French View of Counterinsurgency*. Translated by Daniel Lee. London: Pall Mall, 1985.

Uriarte, Claudio. *Almirante cero: Biografía no autorizada de Emilio Eduardo Massera*. Buenos Aires: Planeta, 2011.

Vales, José. *Ricardo Cavallo: Genocidio y corrupción en América Latina*. Buenos Aires: Grupo Editorial Norma, 2003.

Verbitsky, Horacio. *Civiles y militares: Memoria secreta de la transición*. Buenos Aires: Editorial Contrapunto, 1987.

———. *El silencio: De Paulo VI a Bergoglio, las relaciones secretas de la Iglesia con la ESMA*. Buenos Aires: Sudamericana, 2005.

———. *Ezeiza*. Buenos Aires: Contrapunto, 1985.

———. *The Flight: Confessions of an Argentine Dirty Warrior*. New York: New Press, 1996.

———. *Hacer la corte: La construcción de un poder absoluto sin justicia ni control*. Buenos Aires: Planeta, 1993.

———. *Historia política de la Iglesia Católica*. Vol. 3, *Del Cordobazo de 1969 al 23 de marzo 1976*. Buenos Aires: Sudamericana, 2009.

———. *La mano izquierda de Dios*. Vol. 4, *La última dictadura (1976–1983)*. Buenos Aires: Sudamericana, 2010.

———. *La posguerra sucia: Un análisis de la transición*. Buenos Aires: Legasa, 1985.

———. *Medio siglo de proclamas militares*. Buenos Aires: Sudamericana, 2006.

———. *Robo para la corona: Los frutos prohibidos del árbol de la corrupción*. Buenos Aires: Planeta, 1992.

———. *Rodolfo Walsh y la prensa clandestina, 1976–1978*. Buenos Aires: Ediciones de la Urraca, 1985.

———. *Vigilia de armas*. Vol. 3, *Del Cordobazo de 1969 al 23 de marzo 1976*. Buenos Aires: Sudamericana, 2010.

Vezzetti, Hugo. *Sobre la violencia revolucionaria: Memorias y olvidos*. Buenos Aires: Siglo Veintiuno, 2009.

Vilariño, Raúl D. *Yo secuestré, maté y ví torturar en la Escuela de Mecanica de la Armada*. Buenos Aires: Editorial Perfil, 1984.

Villani, Mario, and Fernando Reati. *Desaparecido: Memorias de un cautiverio; Club Atlético, el Banco, el Olimpo, Pozo de Quilmes y* ESMA. Buenos Aires: Biblos, 2011.

Villegas, Osiris G. *Guerra revolucionaria Comunista*. Buenos Aires: Círculo Militar, 1962.

Waisman, Carlos H. *Reversal of Development in Argentina: Postwar Counterrevolutionary Policies and Their Structural Consequences*. Princeton NJ: Princeton University Press, 1987.

Walsh, Rodolfo J. *Operación Masacre*. Buenos Aires: Ediciones de la Flor, 2011.

Weschler, Lawrence. *A Miracle, a Universe: Settling Accounts with Torturers*. Chicago: University of Chicago Press, 1998.

Yofre, Juan B. *El escarmiento: La ofensiva de Perón contra Cámpora y los Montoneros, 1973–1974*. Buenos Aires: Editorial Sudamericana, 2010.

———. *Fuimos todos: Cronología de un fracaso, 1976–1983*. Buenos Aires: DeBolsillo, 2010.

———. *Nadie fue: Crónica, documentos y testimonios de los últimos meses, días y horas de Isabel Perón en el poder*. Buenos Aires: Sudamericana, 2008.

———. *Volver a matar: Los archivos ocultos de la "cámara del terror" (1971–1973)*. Buenos Aires: Sudamericana, 2009.

Yorio, Orlando. "Dios y los valores humanos." *Teologia* 11, no. 19 (1971): 60–83.

———. "El acontecimiento argentino como signo teológico." *Revista Biblica* 37 (1975): 61–92.

———. "Reflexión crítica desde la teología." *Stromata* 29, nos. 1/2 (January–June 1973): 131–72.

Zapata, Edgar A. *Guerrilla y Montoneros: Ensayo sobre el origen y evolución*. Rosario, Argentina: Editorial Fundación Ross, 1996.

Zedong, Mao. *On Guerrilla Warfare*. Translated by Samuel B. Griffith II. Urbana: University of Illinois Press, 2000.

INDEX